Knowing, Naming and Negation

A Sourcebook on Tibetan Sautrāntika

Knowing, Naming and Negation

A Sourcebook on Tibetan Sautrāntika

Translated, Annotated and Introduced by

Anne Carolyn Klein

with oral commentary by

Geshe Belden Drakba, Denma Lochö Rinbochay,
Jambel Shenpen Rinbochay, Lati Rinbochay,
and Kensur Yeshay Tupden

Snow Lion Publications
Ithaca, New York USA

To Loling Kensur Yeshay Tupden
1916–1988

A warm and tireless teacher, and
a luminary among what was perhaps
the last generation of Tibetan scholars to
complete their monastic education in a free Tibet.

Snow Lion Publications
P.O. Box 6483
Ithaca, New York 14851
U.S.A.

Printed in the USA

ISBN 0-937938-21-1 (paper)
0-937938-22-X (cloth)
Translations in Indo-Tibetan Buddhism Series ISBN 0-937938-98-X

Library of Congress Cataloging-in-Publication Data

Knowing, naming, and negation : a sourcebook on Tibetan Sautrāntika / translated, annotated, and introduced by Anne Carolyn Klein : with oral commentary by Geshe Balden Drakba . . . [et al.].
p. cm. — (Translations in Indo-Tibetan Buddhism)
Bibliography: p.
Includes index.
ISBN 0-937938-22-X. — ISBN 0-937938-21-1 (pbk.)
1. Sautrāntikas—China—Tibet. 2. Buddhism—China—Tibet--Doctrines. I. Klein, Anne C., 1947- II. Dpal-Idan grags-pa, Blo-gliṅ Dge-bśes. III. Series.
BQ7255.S38K56 1991
181'.043—dc19 88-38912
CIP

Contents

Acknowledgements

To Jeffrey Hopkins for crucial suggestions, criticism, and encouragement,

To the University of Virginia's Center for South Asian Studies for inviting the Tibetan scholars whose commentaries appear here,

To the Fulbright Foundation for support in researching important background material to these translations,

To Skip Martin, whose curatorship at the University of Virginia ensured that the necessary Tibetan books were on hand,

To Masatoshi Nagatomi for generous suggestions and for his own work on issues central here,

To Joshua Cutler (Director) and Diana Marks Cutler (Administrative Secretary), and Elizabeth Napper (Library Consultant), for making available resources of the Tibetan Buddhist Learning Center, Washington, N.J., and for ongoing friendship and encouragement,

To the Department of Religious Studies, Stanford University, for released time given while I was revising this manuscript,

To Carl Bielefeldt, Steven Goodman, P. J. Ivanhoe, and Don Lopez, whose wit and intellectual probity on matters which had nothing to do with this book lightened the labors of revision,

To Jim Casilio for mindful last-minute proofing of the ms. and Mark Siebold for meticulous inspection of the galleys,

To Harvey Aronson love, support, and a creative approach to book knowing.

Notes on Transliteration

The system of Tibetan transliteration used here was devised by Professor Turrel Wylie; it is modified slightly to capitalize the first pronounced letter in the names of persons and texts. Wylie's system gives a letter-by-letter correspondence from Tibetan into English, including letters that are unpronounced, and appears in the text italicized and enclosed in parentheses. It is given on a word's first appearance and in the glossary. For a readable phonetic rendering that maximally approximates actual Tibetan pronunciation (Lhasa dialect), an adaptation of the system created by Professor Jeffrey Hopkins[1] is used throughout the book wherever Tibetan names occur. In Hopkins' own system the line over a consonant indicates high, short, sharp pronunciation. The table below gives both the transliteration and phonetic systems, Wylie's being on the left and Hopkins' on the right.

Table 1

ka: ḡa	kha: ka	ga: ga	nga: nga
ca: j̄a	cha: cha	ja: ja	nya: nya
ta: d̄a	tha: ta	da: da	na: na
pa: b̄a	pha: pa	ba: ba	ma: ma
tsa: d̄za	tsha: tsa	dza: dza	wa: wa

zha: sha	za: sa	'a: a	ya: ya
ra: ra	la: la	sha: s̄ha	sa: s̄a
ha:ha			

In the present adaptation of the Hopkins system, lines over consonants will not appear in the text. Thus, for example, when the phonetic *ga* replaces the first column *ka* it signifies a high pronunciation; when it replaces the third column *ga* it does not. A few examples will suffice to give the gist of the system:

Table 2

B̄el-den-chö-jay (dPal-ldan-chos-byed)
D̄ak-tsang (s̄Tag-tshang)
D̄en-dar-hla-ram-ba (bs̄Tan-dar-lha-ram-pa)
Ḡön-chok-jik-may-wang-bo (dKon-mchog-'jigs-med-dbang-po)
Gyel-tsap (rGyal-tshab)
J̄ang-ḡya (lCang-skya)
Nga-wang-b̄el-den (Ngag-dbang-dpal-ldan)
Nga-wang-d̄ra-shi (Ngag-dbang-bkra-shis)
Pur-bu-j̄ok (Phur-bu-lcog)
Ra-d̄ö (Rva stod)
S̄ö-nam-drak-ba (bSod-nams-grags-pa)

In addition, the phonetic system substitutes *k* and *p* for the Wylie *g* and *b* in the suffix position. For those wishing to train in the pronunciation, we note that when *ba* occurs as the final syllable it is *not* pronounced high due to its end position.

Regarding the pronunciation of Tibetan vowels, *a* in the phonetic system indicates the vowel sound in the English word 'opt'; *i* the vowel sound of 'it' or 'eat'; *u* the vowel sound of 'soon'; *ay* the vowel sound of 'bake'; *o* indicates the vowel sound of 'boat' and *ö* indicates the vowel sound of 'purr'.

In deference to common usage, a few exceptions to the system are permitted: the familiar Tsong-ka-ba, actually pronounced Dzong-ka-ba, is retained; also the title *Geshe*, which strictly in this system would be rendered Ge-shay. Personal names are hyphenated in phonetic transliteration except in cases where contemporary Tibetan scholars are themselves using unhyphenated renderings of their own names. However, in accordance with a growing trend and to make a visual distinction between these and other proper nouns, the names of the different religious orders of Tibet, such as Gelubka (*dGe-lugs-pa*), and monastery names such as Drebung (*'Bras spungs*) are not hyphenated.

Sanskrit equivalents for Tibetan terms are given wherever possible; an asterisk beside an entry indicates reconstruction of the Sanskrit from Tibetan. Full Sanskrit and Tibetan text titles are found in the bibliography which is arranged alphabetically according to English titles of sutras and according to the phonetic rendering of the authors of Sanskrit and Tibetan works. Original-language terms and titles are found in the index, referenced with their English translation. Authors' dates, when available, also appear in the bibliography.

Preface

The three texts translated here address some of the epistemological consequences of our being constituted, in significant measure, as creatures of conceptual thought and of direct experience. These two ways of knowing are fundamentally different, yet inextricably related. The primary objects of the conceptual and the directly knowing subjects are also different. As discussed in the first text, these four elements—thought, direct perception, and their respective objects—are all involved in the complex perceptual process of learning to name the world we experience.

Conceptual and verbal references to the known are here described as operating by way of exclusion, that is, through a negative route which mentally separates the intended object from all else. The second text explores the process of exclusion, or negation, and describes this in terms of the two-fold structure of perception just noted.

Building on this, the third text examines the relationship between thought, the mental images which represent objects of the world to thought, and the direct sensory experience which is the starting point of most mental imagery.

These three texts, together with the oral commentary that accompanies them, represent the system known in Gelukba scholarship as the Sautrāntikas Following Reasoning. This system contributes much to the theoretical basis on which rests the entire edifice of Gelukba philosophical reflection and religious endeavor.*

Anne Carolyn Klein
San Jose, California
September 17, 1987

*These three works, which remain part of contemporary studies in Gelukba monastic universities, also informed and helped frame the issues discussed in A. Klein, *Knowledge and Liberation* (Ithaca: Snow Lion Publications, 1986).

PART I
GENERAL INTRODUCTION

Dignāga

General Introduction

OVERVIEW

The Sautrāntika tenet system described in the texts translated here has for six centuries been an object of intense study in the Gelukba monastic universities of Tibet. There are two major reasons for such interest. The Sautrāntika system, as Gelukba formulates it, is valued for detailed descriptions of how thought (*rtog pa, kalpanā*) and direct perception (*mngon sum, pratyakṣa*) know their objects, and for relevant interpretations of Dignāga and Dharmakīrti. In addition, Gelukba curriculum emphasizes Sautrāntika because such study is considered helpful in preparing students for the philosophical subtleties of Mādhyamika, especially Prāsaṅgika-Mādhyamika. Indeed, this pedagogical concern arguably has been a significant factor in shaping Gelukba interpretations of Sautrāntika positions.[1]

The first and last phases of the twenty-year Geshe curriculum are devoted to the non-Mahāyāna tenet systems: Vaibhāṣika (which in many respects is similar to what Gelukbas call Sautrāntikas Following Scripture) and especially Sautrāntika, here meaning Sautrāntikas Following Reasoning (*Rigs pa'i rjes su 'brangs pa, Nyāyānusārin*). The initial period of study lasts from three to six years, depending on the college.[2]

A student becomes acquainted with the format and topics of logic and epistemology (*bsDus grva*) by memorizing and debating tenets and definitions derived primarily from Tibetan readings of Dharmakīrti's Seven Treatises, especially the *Commentary on (Dignāga's) "Compendium on Valid Cognition"* (*Tshad ma rnam 'grel, Pramāṇavārttika*), and only secondarily from Vasubandhu's *Treasury of Knowledge* (*mNgon pa'i mdzod, Abhidharmakośa*), which is studied in detail much later. (This latter text is considered to be of the Vaibhāṣika school although Vasubandhu's own commentary on it is said to be written from the viewpoint of Sautrāntikas Following Scripture.) Sautrāntika interpretations of Dharmakīrti's Seven Treatises (which in general are said to take the viewpoint of Cittamātra) are the basis for works by scholars such as Jam-yang-chok-hla-öd-ser, Pur-bu-jok, Den-dar-hla-ram-ba, and Jam-bel-drin-lay[3] who extrapolate from these Treatises a system named in other Gelukba genres as the Sautrāntikas Following Reasoning. However, from the earliest to the most modern, the Collected Topics texts as a rule do not identify their point of view as that of Sautrāntikas Following Reasoning.[4] There is no reference to any tenet system. That Gelukbas do so identify the assertions found in these texts can be clearly understood from presentations of tenet systems in works such as those by Jang-gya and Jam-yang-shay-ba, as well as earlier debate texts. Thus the system Gelukbas call Sautrāntikas Following Reasoning dominates the initial years of study and provides a basis for the Mahāyāna studies of the Perfection of Wisdom (*Phar phyin*) and Middle Way (*dbU ma*).

This tenet system also provides the context for the subsequent study of Awareness and Knowledge (*bLo rig*) and Signs and Reasoning (*rTags rigs*). Like the Collected Topics, these groups of texts do not espouse a tenet system by name, but they and the oral discourse that accompanies them focus on tenets unique to Sautrāntikas Following Reasoning, for example, the assertion that the categories of impermanent phenomena and ultimate truths are co-extensive, as are the categories of permanent phenomena and conventional truths. Largely because of the epistemology derived from these tenets, the Sautrāntika system undergirds Gelukba understanding of the relationship between intellectual and meditational religious endeavor.

TEXTS

Genres

Indigenous Tibetan works on Sautrāntika fall into three general types. The first are the debate texts mentioned above. These consist of topically arranged groups of debates, using the syllogistic style and language of Indo-Tibetan logic. They enumerate definitions, categories, and instances of important terms: in this format positions are presented and defended. Such debates cover a range of subject matter known as the "collected topics" (*bsDus grva*).[5] This genre has been an important feature of Gelukba scholarship since the fifteenth century.

Second are presentations of tenets (*grub mtha', siddhānta*) which systematically lay out the basic assertions of non-Buddhist and Buddhist tenet systems. Their emphasis is on giving a comprehensive picture of philosophical systems. Exploration of controversial points, though often of considerable interest, are secondary to the broader presentation. Unlike the debate texts, these are written in an expository style, using syllogistic language only occasionally. The tenet genre, which has its precedents in Indian *siddhānta*, gained importance in Gelukba with the publication of the *Great Presentation of Tenets* (*Grub mtha' chen mo*) by Jam-yang-shay-ba (*'Jam-dbyangs-bzhad-pa*, 1648–1721). Texts of this type frame the tenets featured in the Collected Topics literature as the system of Sautrāntikas Following Reasoning (*Rigs pa'i rje su 'brangs pa'i mdo sde pa*).[6]

The third category of texts on Sautrāntika offers neither the syllogistic inquiry of the debate genre nor the systematic overview of works on tenets. These are more focused works, written in an expository style, whose purpose is to investigate particular issues relevant to Sautrāntika. Certain of Gyel-tsap and Kay-drup's fifteenth-century commentaries on Dharmakīrti can be considered early examples of this genre.[7] Unlike these, however, Den-dar-hla-ram-ba's nineteenth-century work translated here is not a commentary and thus its author arguably has a freer hand in his selection of issues. Of the three texts included in this volume, this is the most accessible, being closest in form to the style of contemporary Western scholarship (and for this reason it appears first in the translation section).

An example of each of the three types of Tibetan materials on Sautrāntika is translated and annotated here. In chronological order, these are: (1) the presentation of negative and positive phenomena from a Gomang College debate text, *The Collected Topics by a Spiritual Son of Jam-yang-shay-ba* (*Sras bsdus rva*), (2) the Sautrāntika chapter from Jang-gya's *Presentation of Tenets* (*Grub mtha'i rnam bzhag*), and (3) selections from Den-dar-hla-ram-ba's *Presentation of Generally and Specifically Characterized Phenomena* (*Rang mtshan spyi mtshan gyi rnam gzhag*).

Missing from these genres is the type of text most crucial to other major philosophical foci of Gelukba studies, especially Mādhyamika. That is, there are no Tibetan commentaries on Indian texts which themselves espoused Sautrāntika. As Jang-gya (*lCang-skya*, 1717–1786) observes, this is because works by Indian Sautrāntikas such as Kumarata, Shirata, and Dzun-ba-ra-ta (*bTsun-pa-ra-ta*) were never translated into Tibetan. Thus, there is nothing in Sautrāntika studies comparable, for example, to Tsong-ka-pa's *Clarification of (Candrakīrti's) "Entrance to [Nāgārjuna's] 'Treatise on the Middle Way'"* (*dbU ma dgongs pa rab gsal*) which is pivotal to Tibetan Mādhyamika studies.[8] Instead, we have commentary and interpretation based on texts such as Vasubandhu's *Treasury* and on works by Dignāga and Dharmakīrti (see below), which are not themselves Sautrāntika but which, from various vantage points, offer windows onto what Gelukbas came to know as Sautrāntika. It is partly this absence of a *fait accompli* system which allowed the broad interpretive moves by which Gelukba forged two distinct systems of Sautrāntika, the Followers of Scripture and of Reasoning (*mDo sde'i rjes su 'brangs pa/rLung gi rje su drangs pa, Āgamānusārin*, and *Rigs pa'i rjes su 'brangs pa, Nyāyānusārin*).[9]

Jang-gya gives the major Indian sources for Sautrāntika as Vasubandhu's *Explanation of the "Treasury of Knowledge"* (*mNgon pa'i mdzod, Abhidharmakośabhāṣya*) and Dharmakīrti's Seven Treatises on Valid Cognition (see Bibliography), as well as Dignāga's *Compendium on Valid Cognition* (*Tshad ma kun las btus pa, Pramāṇasamuccaya*). He does not distinguish, in his introduction, the sources for the Sautrāntikas Following Scripture from those for the Followers of Reasoning. However, according to Gön-chok-jik-may-wang-bo (*dKon mchog-'jigs-med-dbang-po*, 1728–1791) Sautrāntikas Following Scripture rely mainly on Vasubandhu's *Treasury* whereas the Followers of Reasoning rely mainly on the Seven Treatises.[10] Jang-gya appears implicitly to hold the same position insofar as he takes the former's definitions of the two truths from Vasubandhu, and the latter's from Dharmakīrti.

According to Jang-gya, the most frequently quoted sources for tenets held by Sautrāntikas Following Reasoning are Dignāga's *Compendium on Valid Cognition* (*Tshad ma kun las btus pa, Pramāṇasamuccaya*) and Dharmakīrti's *Commentary on (Dignāga's) "Compendium on Valid Cognition"* (*Tshad ma rnam 'grel, Pramāṇavārttikakārikā*), which, as mentioned above, are held to be primarily Cittamātrin treatises. Additional important sources are (1) Asanga's *Compendium of Knowledge* (*mNgon pa kun btus, Abhidharmasamuccaya*) which mainly sets forth Cittamātra, (2) Bhāvaviveka's *Blaze of Reasoning, Commentary on the "Heart of the Middle Way"* (*sbU ma snying po'i 'grel pa rtog ge 'bar ba, Madhyamakahṛdayavṛttitarkajvālā*) which primarily presents Svātantrika, and (3) Śāntarakṣita's *Compendium of Suchness* (*De kho na nyid bsdus pa'i tshing le'ur byas pa, Tattvasaṃgraha*) and the commentary on this by his main student, Kamalaśīla, *Commentary on the Difficult Points of (Śāntarakṣita's) "Compendium of Suchness"* (*De kho na nyid bsdus pa'i dka' 'grel, Tattvasaṃgrahapañjikā*), both of which are also mainly Svātantrika.

1. Debate Texts

The earliest Gelukba enumeration of definitions and categories which was to form the core of the Collected Topics literature was written by the founder of that order, Tsong-ka-ba (*Tsong-kha-ba*, 1357–1419) in a short text that was his only work entirely devoted to Dharmakīrti, *Door of Entry to the Seven Treatises* (*sDe bdun la 'jug pa'i sgo*). His chief students, Gyeltsap and Kay-drup, together wrote a number of texts on the work of Dignāga and Dharmakīrti. The first work to describe itself, not as a commentary but as a series of "collected topics" culled primarily from Dharmakīrti's *Commentary on (Dignāga's) "Compendium"* (*Tshad ma rnam 'grel, Pramāṇavārttika*), was written by Jam-yang-cho-hla-ö-ser (*'Jam-dbyangs-phyogs-lha-'od zer*, fifteenth century). He compiled what remains to this day the largest and most important work on the Collected Topics, still used as a reference in all three major Gelukba monastic universities, the *Collected Topics of Ra-dö* (*Rva stod bsdus grva*). The subtitle of this work describes it, in part, as "opening the door to the collected central issues of Dharmakīrti's *Commentary on (Dignāga's) 'Compendium on Valid Cognition.'* " This work of 453 folios retains Tsong-ka-ba's manner of listing definitions and categories; it also incorporates much of Tsong-ka-ba's material and offers hundreds of debates on related matters of taxonomy and logic, opening each "topic" with several quotations from Dharmakīrti. All subsequent works in the Collected Topics genre owe an immense debt to it. Eventually, the colleges within the three major Gelukba monastic universities—Drebung, Sera, and Ganden—developed their own introductory debate textbooks. Even in the most recent of these, written several hundred years after Ra-dö's work, the major definitions and categories remain virtually identical with his. Such texts include Pur-bu-jok's (*Phur-bu-lcog Byams-pa-rgya-mtsho*, 1825–1901) *Magic Key to the Path of Reasoning* (*Rig lam 'phrul gyi sde mig*), still used by Sera Jay College, the *Compendium on the Meaning of the Collected Topics* by Jam-bel-drin-lay (*'Jam-dpal 'Phrin-las*, twentieth century) used in Loseling and the *Spiritual Son's Collected Topics of Logic and Epistemology* by Nga-wang-dra-shi (*Ngag-dbang-bkra-shis*, 1648–1721) currently included in the curriculum of Gomang College, Drebung. The two-part discussion of positive and negative phenomena from the latter text is here translated with the interlinear oral commentary of Jambel Shenpen Rinbochay, preceptor of Ganden.

2. Studies of Tenet Systems

Texts whose primary focus was the systematic exploration of Buddhist and non-Buddhist schools of tenets became an important part of Gelukba scholarship in the seventeenth century. Until that time sutra-vehicle study focused on elaborations of Indian texts on Valid Cognition (*tshad ma, pramāṇa*) and Mādhyamika by Tsong-ka-ba, Kay-drup, and Gyel-tsap. The non-Mahāyāna systems, Vaibhāṣika and Sautrāntika, were studied mainly through Collected Topics manuals, as well as through Tibetan commentaries on the work of Dignāga and Dharmakīrti, most notably Kay-drup's *Clearing Away Mental Darkness with Respect to the Seven Treatises* (*sDe bdun yid kyi mun sel*) and Gyel-tsap's *Commentary on (Dharmakīrti's) "Ascertainment of Valid Cognition"* (*rNam nges ṭik chen*); *Explanation of Dharmakīrti's "Commentary on (Dignāga's) 'Compendium on Valid Cognition' "* (*rNam 'grel gyi thar lam gsal byed*); *Eradication of Forgetfulness Regarding the Chapter on Direct Perception in (Dharmakīrti's) "Commentary on (Dignāga's) 'Compendium on Valid Cognition' "* (*mNgon sum le'u'i brjed byang*); *Great Eradication of Forgetfulness Regarding Valid Cognition* (*Tshad ma'i brjed byang chen mo*) and *Clarification of the Thought, An Extensive Commentary on (Dharmakīrti's) "Ascertainment of Valid Cognition"* (*bsTan bcos tshad ma rnam nges kyi ṭik chen dgongs pa rab gsal*).

Tenet texts typically organize their presentations of Buddhist systems around the three main headings of bases, paths and fruits (*gzhi, lam, 'bras bu*). These discuss, respectively, 1) objects (*yul, viṣaya*), 2) subjects (*yul can, dharmin*), that is, consciousnesses which know objects—especially those minds significant in religious practice—and 3) the effects or fruits of such practice. The model of a graduated series of practices which characterizes Gelukba religious life is reflected in this structure. Jang-gya, whose chapter on Sautrāntika is translated here, also embeds his treatment in this structure.

a. Jam-yang-shay-ba. Gelukba literature offers several smaller and two major works on non-Buddhist and Buddhist tenets.[11] The first full-length presentation of tenets within Gelukba is Jam-yang-shay-ba's *Great Exposition of Tenets* (*Grub mtha' chen mo*), a prose commentary of 530 folios on the author's own 60-folio *Presentation of Tenets* (*Grub mtha'i rnam bzhag*). This text, written in verse that, like virtually all Tibetan verse, is unrhymed, explicitly discusses tenets of the Sautrāntikas Following Reasoning. The copious commentary on Jam-yang-shay-ba's work given by Bel-den-chö-jay (*dPal-ldan-chos-rje*, b. 1797) in *Annotations for the "Great Exposition of Tenets"* (*Grub mtha' chen mo*), a text slightly longer than the *Great Exposition* itself, also uses and appears to take for granted the school of Sautrāntikas Following Reasoning. Yet both writers were certainly aware of interpretations at odds with their own.

In his *Great Exposition of Tenets*, Jam-yang-shay-ba drew from and refuted an earlier important and lengthy work on tenets by the Sa-gya-ba scholar Dak-tsang (*sTag-tshang*, b. 1405), *Ocean of Good Explanations* (*Legs bhsad kyi rgya mtsho*), a commentary on his own brief, versified exposition of tenets known as *Freedom from Extremes Through Understanding All Tenets* (*Grub mtha' kun shes nas mtha' bral grub pa*). (See Bibliography for full entry.) Dak-tsang's exposition of tenets makes no mention of the Followers of Reasoning in its discussion of Sautrāntika and, moreover, interprets that system's discussion of the two truths so as to make such a subdivision unlikely.[12] Nevertheless, neither Jam-yang-shay-ba nor his annotator, nor any other Gelukba tenet text of this period, indicates that the extensive use of this category is controversial.

A special feature of Jam-yang-shay-ba's work is his use of Indian materials to highlight differences of opinion on issues of interest to him; yet he neither gives an extended discussion of these nor elaborates their context in this text.[13] For example, he enumerates descriptions of how aspected direct perception functions and Sautrāntika views on this, referring to Śāntarakṣita's *Ornament to the Middle Way* (*dbU ma rgyan, Madhyamakālaṇkāra*) and Kamalaśīla's commentary on it, but he does not elaborate the merits and flaws in each position.[14]

b. Jang-gya. The next major Gelukba text in the tenet genre was the *Presentation of Tenets* (*Grub mtha'i rnam bzhag*) written by Jang-gya. He too follows the threefold structure of bases, paths, and effects. His chapter on Sautrāntika is notable for its introduction to difficult topics important in Sautrāntika, sometimes in considerable detail. The wider context of his interesting problematics however is not considered. For example, Jang-gya highlights issues concerning the nature of mental images and the relationship between objects and mental designations of objects, but he does not explain the relevance this has for the use of correct inference to gain direct insight, an important Gelukba concern. He apparently assumes the reader is sufficiently well read or, given the importance of oral scholarship, well-heard, to know that this issue is crucial to Gelukba soteriology. His concise exposition and wide range, however, require considerable commentary to make it accessible, and even then it is only in juxtaposition with other texts, such as the Den-dar-hla-ram-ba work included here, that the issues which sustained Gelukbas' interest in Sautrāntika begin to crystallize.

In order to provide such background, Jang-gya's chapter on Sautrāntika is translated here in conjunction with oral commentary from three contemporary Tibetan scholars, Lati Rinbochay, abbot emeritus of Ganden Shardzay College, Denma Lochö Rinbochay, a senior scholar of Loseling College, and Geshe Belden Drakba, also of Loseling, and presently Head Librarian and Professor of Tibet House, New Delhi.

3. Topical Expositions

From the third category of Tibetan literature on Sautrāntika, that which focuses on specific topics without giving an overview of any system, I have selected Den-dar-hla-ram-ba's *Presentation of Generally and Specifically Characterized Phenomena* (*Rang mtshan dang spyi mtshan gyi rnam gzhag*). The sections translated here elaborate one of the most crucial and controversial points in the Gelukba systemization of Sautrāntika. Taking as a given the equivalence of specifically characterized phenomena with impermanent, functioning things,[15] the text explores how terms and conceptual thought, which in many respects are limited in their access to impermanent things, nonetheless can "undeniably get at," "explicitly realize," and "explicitly express" such objects.[16] This point will gain our attention again below.

CENTRAL ISSUES FOR THE SYSTEM OF SAUTRĀNTIKAS FOLLOWING REASONING

Gelukba takes its study of Sautrāntikas Following Reasoning to be significant for understanding Mādhyamika in three important ways: (1) its description of ultimate truths as specifically characterized phenomena helps identify that which is negated in the Prāsaṅgika-Mādhyamika theory of emptiness, (2) its discussion of the relationship between thought and direct perception provides a rationale for the *modus operandi* of analytical reflection, and (3) its presentation of negative phenomena, especially non-affirming negatives, gives an important context for Prāsaṅgika discussions of emptiness, a non-affirming negative which is described as the mere absence of inherent existence.

1. Sautrāntikas Following Reasoning consider impermanent phenomena to be substantially established and inherently existent.[17] By contrast, Prāsaṅgika theories of selflessness deny that any existent things have such status. In studying Sautrāntika, therefore, one becomes familiar with aspects of the conception of self which Prāsaṅgika theory seeks to undermine. This is of no small consequence. In Prāsaṅgika analysis, an identification of that which will be negated (*dgag bya*, *pratiṣedhya*) is the first and most difficult step leading to an understand-

standing of emptiness or selflessness. Only after identifying the experienced sense of self, namely, that which is imputed to exist by an innate conception of inherent existence (*bden 'dzin hlan skyes, *sahajātmagrāha*), can analysis proceed satisfactorily.

2. The process of analysis itself depends on words and conceptual thought. Thus, the main Prāsaṅgika method for realizing subtle impermanence or emptiness, for example, features the use of reason. Reasoned analysis is meant to clarify conceptual understanding of the hypothetical inherent existence and the lack of this in actuality. "Inherently existent phenomena," which do not exist, are thereby distinguished from conventional or imputedly existent phenomena, which exist. Therefore, a vital issue for Gelukba is how thought or words do and do not express that which must be realized in order to attain liberation. This topic receives greatest attention, in Gelukba writings, in the system of Sautrāntikas Following Reasoning. In this volume we will see Jang-gya and Den-dar-hla-ram-ba consider the relationship between words and impermanent objects. They, like other Gelukba scholars, find in Sautrāntika a basis for asserting the usefulness of words and thought.[18] In fact, it may well have been the need to make such a case which shaped Gelukbas' systemization of Sautrāntikas Following Reasoning.

3. The emptiness which Prāsaṅgika-Mādhyamika describes as a lack of inherent existence, that is, the mere absence of the type of self negated in its theory of selflessness, is not nothing, but is a negative phenomenon. That a mere absence can be cognized, and thus be a valid object of knowledge (*shes bya, jñeya*), is for Tsong-ka-ba an important tenet by which Gelukba distinguishes itself from other interpretations of Mādhyamika.[19] The groundwork for this tenet is found in the Sautrāntika presentation of negative phenomena.[20]

Epistemological Issues

We have seen that Gelukbas consider Dharmakīrti's work, especially his *Commentary on (Dignāga's) "Compendium on Valid*

Cognition" (*Tshad ma rnam 'grel, Pramāṇavārttika*), to be a major source on Indian Sautrāntika, and more specifically on the system they call Sautrāntikas Following Reasoning. Therefore, in systemizing Sautrāntika and developing from it an epistemological theory that emphasizes the liberative possibilities of words, Gelukbas do not want to set forth a theory in contradiction to Dharmakīrti. Indeed, their presentation of Sautrāntika gains much of its authority by claiming to interpret and clarify Dharmakīrti's texts. Yet, there are numerous statements in Dharmakīrti and elsewhere which seem to indicate that words do not express, and conceptual thought does not realize, actual functioning impermanent phenomena. If thought is in fact limited in this way, verbal articulation or conceptual reflection regarding impermanence or emptiness would be little help in gaining direct, experiential realization of impermanence, a soteriologically salient quality of all produced things.

The need to expand on the significance of conceptual thought for religious endeavor may have been part of the impetus, as I have already suggested, for the interpretive maneuvers by which Gelukbas divided Sautrāntika into two sub-systems.[21]

Gelukba scholars maintain that the system of Sautrāntikas Following Reasoning is faithful to Dignāga in that impermanent objects are appearing objects of direct perception, and because such impermanent objects, seen as co-extensive with the categories of specifically characterized phenomena (*rang mtshan, svalakṣaṇa*) and appearing objects of direct perception (*mngon sum gyi snang yul, *pratyakṣa-pratibhāsaviṣaya*) are characterized in accordance with Dignāga's statement that direct perception is caused by many substances—that is, by aggregated atoms—and that the objects of direct perception have multiple specific characteristics.[22]

In the Gelukba systemization of Sautrāntikas Following Reasoning, impermanent thing (*mi rtag pa'i chos, anitya-dharma*) functioning thing (*dngos po, bhāva*), appearing object of direct perception (*mngon sum gyi snang yul, pratyakṣa-pratibhāsaviṣaya*) and specifically characterized phenomenon (*rang mtshan, svalakṣaṇa*) are equivalent.[23] Hence, in their view, Dharmakīrti is referring to all of these when he, following Dignāga, states that such phenomena appear fully only to direct perception and not to conceptual thought.

This principle is effectively an epistemological caveat to those who would contend that thought and words can be used to cultivate direct experience of specifically characterized or impermanent functioning phenomena. The premise underlying such possibility is that conceptual thought, which in Gelukba includes anything from abstruse intellectual verbiage to rarified and all-but-nondualistic mental images, can under the proper circumstances lead to a valid and direct non-verbal, non-conceptual experience of actual functioning phenomena. Thus, the question analyzed by Gelukba scholars such as Den-dar-hla-ram-ba and Jang-gya is this: If only direct perception can cognize impermanent phenomena in all their richness of detail, in what sense can words or thought be said to realize them, if at all? It is a crucial issue because direct perception will not necessarily *ascertain* (*nges pa, niścaya*) all that appears to it, a deficit which has considerable soteriological significance. Subtle impermanence, for example, is not ascertainable by direct perception unless conceptual thought, more specifically inference (*rjes dpag, anumāna*), ascertains it first. Thus, Gelukba had to have their epistemological cake and eat it as well.

The cake they must have is adherence to Dharmakīrti's statement that specifically characterized or impermanent phenomena do not fully appear to conceptual thought. They must also, given the religious use Gelukbas make of textual study and intellectual analysis, "dine" on the assertion that words and thought significantly attend to actual impermanent phenomena, and not only to mental images. This is an important principle of praxis for Gelukbas; namely, that before attaining a direct cognition of subtle impermanence or, in Mādhyamika, selflessness, it is necessary to develop a mental image of them. Such an image is based on analytical understanding and built up through the use of words. If, however, the explicit object of an expression such as "A table is impermanent because of being a product" were an image irrevocably removed form actual tables, it would be difficult to demonstrate the soteriological necessity for conceptual thought or analysis. If words did not relate to actual phenomena in some significant manner, verbal analysis and conceptual thought could never precipitate experience of actual impermanence, which in Gelukba Mādhyamika is a necessary precursor to realization of emptiness.

In the *Presentation of Specifically and Generally Characterized Phenomena* translated in this volume, Den-dar-hla-ram-ba devotes three sections to a discussion of how specifically characterized or impermanent phenomena are indicated through words or perceived by conceptual thought. Taking for granted the equivalence of impermanent phenomenon and ultimate truth, which is a tenet unique to Sautrāntikas Following Reasoning, Den-dar-hla-ram-ba states that specifically characterized phenomena are so named "because when they appear to the direct perceiver which directly perceives them, they have characteristics that appear without depending on the appearance of any other phenomenon."[24] Moreover, because direct perceivers are ultimate minds in the system of Sautrāntikas Following Reasoning, specifically characterized phenomena "which are true in the face of these [ultimate minds] are also ultimate truths."[25] They are also ultimately established; a direct perceiver such as an eye consciousness comprehends the mode of subsistence (*sdod lugs*), or manner of residing (*gnas lugs*), of its object.[26] None of these descriptions is true of permanent, or generally characterized phenomena, which fully appear only to thought, not to direct perception.

Only specifically characterized phenomena can be "appearing objects" (*snang yul*) of direct perception (*mngon sum, pratyakṣa*). Only they can appear "distinctly" (*thun mong ma yin par*) to such a mind. Moreover, impermanent, or specifically characterized, phenomena are incapable of *fully* appearing merely through the causal condition of expressional terms. Naming or describing a specifically characterized phenomenon will never cause it to appear *fully* to a conceptual mind which arises in dependence on such terms. The question is, of what relevance is thought to the realization of actual, specifically characterized, impermanent, and ultimately established phenomena? In the context of Gelukba's systemization of Sautrāntikas Following Reasoning, this question arises with more urgency than in virtually any other Indo-Tibetan Buddhist philosophical context. This system is unique in (1) maintaining that all impermanent phenomena are ultimate truths and ultimately established—thus granting them a status Buddhist systems usually reserve for emptiness, suchness, and the like, and (2) asserting that such phenomena can fully appear only to direct perception. This leaves a considerable hiatus between the processes of conceptual thought and the realization of ultimate truths. For a scholarly tradition like Gelukba, it naturally raises the question of how conceptual thought relates to direct perception of such important Buddhist truths as impermanence and so forth; it also raises important questions regarding the interpretation of key statements by Dignāga and Dharmakīrti.

In accordance with Dharmakīrti, Den-dar-hla-ram-ba maintains that there is a sense in which impermanent functioning things are *not* realized by conceptual thought. For example, a thought consciousness reflecting on an object conceives of that object by way of an image. "In terms of what is to be understood from this," he writes, "the thought consciousness apprehending pot does not *explicitly* (*dngos su*) apprehend pot. . . ."[27] This is the "cake" of the adherence to Dharmakīrti's position. Throughout the Gelukba presentation of Sautrāntika, assertions such as this are used to indicate the capacities which direct perception alone possesses. In this vein, Den-dar-hla-ram-ba continues:

> . . . the term expressing pot does not explicitly express pot; it explicitly expresses pot's term-generality (i.e., a mental image of a pot).[28]

Having made this point with sufficient strength, Den-dar-hla-ram-ba goes on to refine it by describing a way in which thought *does* explicitly realize and terms *do* explicitly express impermanent phenomena. He maintains that although impermanent phenomena cannot be the explicit object of expression (*dngos gyi rjod bya*) of terms and thought,

> . . . in dependence on these [terms and thought, one can] undeniably get at the specifically characterized pot, due to which it is necessary to assert that the thought consciousness apprehending pot explicitly realizes pot and that the term "pot" expressing pot explicitly expresses pot.[29]

In other words, even though a pot is not an explicit object of expression (*dngos gyi brod bya*) of the term "pot," it is explicitly expressed (*dngos su brjod*) by that term. Even though thought does not explicitly apprehend it (*dngos su ma 'dzin*), thought does explicitly realize (*dngos su rtogs*) it. Through making these distinctions between an explicit object of expression and an explicitly expressed object on the one hand, and between explicit apprehension and explicit realization on the other, Den-dar-hla-ram-ba holds both sides of the point regarding the relationship between direct perception and impermanent things.

Thus, Den-dar-hla-ram-ba's clarification of the relationship between thought and impermanent objects pertains to a viewpoint that Gelukba in general considers unique to Dharmakīrti's Seven Treatises. He finds justification in Dharmakīrti's work for the possibility of an impermanent phenomenon such as a pot being explicitly expressed—though not the explicit object of expression—of the term "pot."

Both Jang-gya and Den-dar-hla-ram-ba retain an emphasis on the special properties of direct perception while refining their theories so as to maintain that thought and words signify actual impermanent things. Jang-gya contends that impermanent phenomena can be explicit objects of thought because thought is able to get at such objects. He then makes a distinction between explicit objects of thought and the self-isolates (*rang ldog, vivartana*) of such objects. A "self-isolate" is a conceptually isolable entity. For example, although a pot never exists separately from its specific color, shape, and so forth, it is possible mentally to isolate "pot" without considering any of its characteristics. Thought isolates "pot" by functionally eliminating all that is not one with pot. Although pot itself is the self-isolate of "pot," the self-isolate of an explicit object of thought is necessarily only a mental image, considered a permanent phenomenon.[30] But Jang-gya holds that an impermanent phenomenon such as a pot is also an explicit object of thought. Jang-gya's use of the term "self-isolate" here implies that this is somehow "more" of a conceptual object than a merely explicit object of thought. Because thought arrives at mental images through a process of exclusion (*gzhan gsal, anyāpoha*), the issue of isolates is a sub-topic of the discussion of negatives. Jang-gya himself gives a summary presentation of this topic; the subtle parameters of what is and is not a negative phenomenon are analyzed in considerable detail in the Gomang Debate Manual's section on "Positive and Negative Phenomena" which has for that reason been included in this volume. There too, the underlying issue remains the efficacy and limits of thought's ability to know actual objects.

Jang-gya, having presented the "cake" of a clear distinction between the self-isolates of an explicit object of thought and explicit objects of thought, then finds a way to "dine" on the efficacy of verbalization by explaining how impermanent phenomena are knowable through words: "Because the two appearing factors [the image of a pot and an actual pot] are undifferentiable from the viewpoint of appearance, this is said to be the mixing of appearance [the actual pot] and imputation [its image] as one." Because image and object are intimately related in this way, it is considered that the actual object appears, mixed with its image, to thought. This is held despite the obvious difficulty that an object such as a pot is impermanent but its image is "permanent" in the sense of not materially disintegrating from one moment to the next.[31] In this way, both Den-dar-hla-ram-ba and Jang-gya maintain that thought and words do significantly relate to actual impermanent phenomena. Both say that these objects actually *appear* to thought (*rtog pa la snang*). Objects and concepts of objects remain intimately related; however, the problem of how names are learned, and the manner of their relationship to objects named, concerns both Jang-gya and Den-dar-hla-ramba and is an implicit issue in the discussion of the *via negativa* of words in general.[32]

In developing their interpretations, Den-dar-hla-ram-ba and Jang-gya, like Gelukba scholars as a whole, adhered to the Dignāga-Dharmakīrti principle of a twofold division of valid cognizers and their objects. That is, directly perceiving consciousnesses (*mngon sum, pratyakṣa*) take only specifically characterized phenomena as their appearing objects whereas inferential valid cognizers (*rjes dbag, anumāna*) or any other type of conceptual thought take only generally characterized phenomena as their appearing objects. This has been an essential epistemological classification within Buddhism since at least the fifth century B.C.E. when Dignāga stated in the *Compendium on Valid Cognition* (*Tshad ma kun las btus pa, Pramāṇasamuccaya*):

> The valid cognizers are direct perception and inference.[33]

Dharmakīrti reiterated this classification, distinguishing the two types of valid cognition on the basis of the types of objects [fully] comprehended by them. One of the most famous lines of his *Commentary on (Dignāga's) "Compendium on Valid Cognition"* (*Tshad ma rnam 'grel, Pramāṇvārttika*), states:

> Because there are two objects of comprehension there are two [types of] valid cognition [direct and inferential].[34]

In brief, the clearly stated pairing of specifically characterized or impermanent phenomena with direct perception, and of generally characterized phenomena with conceptual thought, meant that Gelukba scholars were required to find skillful means of interpretation in order to develop a theory which incorporates thought as an integral part of the religious path.

THE ORAL TRADITION

The works in all three categories represented here are terse, dense, and presume considerable scholarly background. Even the most accessible among them are meant to be read (1) in conjunction with an oral explanation, at which time the text serves as lecture notes to the instructor who expands on and questions points in the text, and (2) as a complement to other rigorous textual study and debate.

The tradition "lives" in the connection between its texts and the oral interpretation of them. Such oral scholarship takes place in two distinct contexts. One is the discourse of the master-scholar through whose comments and person the tradition's use of a text is conveyed to the next generation; the other is through formal debate among members of the same generation. In both cases, the language exhibits rigorous philosophical diction, sometimes as turgid as the texts themselves, laced with colloquialisms.[35] The oral philosophical tradition is where probing questions are asked, and where connections to other texts and other scholars' thinking are made.

The proportion of a master-scholar's oral comment to the text he is teaching varies widely; often the commentary represents considerably greater compass—in terms of time, subject matter, detail, and analysis—than the text which forms its point of departure. As a step toward an exploration of the wider dimensions of the oral tradition, and in order to indicate some of its breadth, our three texts are translated here in conjunction with a distillation of oral comments made upon them by several major scholars within the Gelukba circle. Even with this sampling it is significant that, in terms of style and rigor, the oral commentary from these scholars is remarkably similar, and its form does not vary noticeably with the differences in textual styles. Moreover, in the case of the two longer texts, on which I obtained oral comment from more than one scholar, I found considerable consanguinity of content. This uniformity is itself evidence of a genuine oral tradition of scholarship. Certainly individual questions are entertained, and details vary from scholar to scholar; nevertheless, there is also a general body of knowledge available orally, and only in that form. The vitality with which this large body of oral material has been maintained can be seen as an outgrowth of the oral debates into which Gelukba scholars have poured their energies. Indeed, in the last two centuries, it is arguable that the debating courtyard has absorbed the energy that in other cultural circumstances would have taken the shape of written argumentation.[36] The texts translated here represent a portion of what may be the last strata of written scholarship in Tibet on the crucial topics of knowing, naming, and negation.

PART II
TRANSLATIONS

Selections from

Presentation of Specifically and Generally Characterized Phenomena

by Den-dar-hla-ram-ba

TRANSLATOR'S PREFACE

Since the time of the third Dalai Lama, So-nam Gya-tso (*bSod-nams-rGya-mtsho*, 1543–1588), Tibet as a whole and the Gelukba order[1] in particular has had a close relationship with Mongolia, both politically and religiously. Mongolian Buddhists who came to Tibet for their religious education usually entered the Gomang College of Drebung Monastic University.[2] Den-dar-hla-ram-ba (*bsTan-dar-lha-ram-pa*, b. 1758), from the Alashan-Ölöts in Southern Mongolia, was one of these.

Perhaps because of his foreign origins, Den-dar-hla-ram-ba's written style is particularly clear and his interests broad. His *Collected Works*,[3] containing thirty-six titles, include several works on Dignāga and Dharmakīrti: a commentary on Dignāga's *Examination of Objects of Observation* (*dMigs pa brtag pa, Ālambanaparīkṣā*), another on Dharmakīrti's *Proof of Other Continuums* (*rGyud bzhan grub pa zhes bya ba'i rab tu byed pa, Saṃtānāntarasiddhināmaprakaraṇa*), and an unfinished work on selected points in Dharmakīrti's *Commentary on (Dignāga's) "Compendium on Valid Cognition"* (*Tshad ma rnam 'grel, Pramāṇavārttikakārikā*).

Two other works, unrelated to the present one, give further indication of Den-dar-hla-ram-ba's scholarly breadth. At the age of eighty he published a widely acclaimed Tibetan-Mongolian dictionary.[4] Moreover, he appears to be the same Den-dar-hla-ram-ba who authored a commentary to the *Treasury of Good Qualities* (*Yon tan mdzod*) by the Nyingma scholar-yogi Jig-may-ling-ba (*'Jigs-med-gling-pa*, 1729/30–1787).[5]

The present translation is from Den-dar-hla-ram-ba's *Presentation of Generally and Specifically Characterized Phenomena* (*Rang mtshan spyi mtshan gyi rnam gzhag*). In it the author focuses on an issue central to the Gelukba formulation of Sautrāntikas Following Reasoning, a system already well established in his day; he analyzes the characteristics of conventional and ultimate truths. Earlier Gelukba texts, well known both to Dendar and his readers, had described generally characterized phenomena (*spyi mtshan, sāmānyalakṣaṇa*), permanent phenomena and conventional truths as mutually inclusive, and specifically characterized phenomena (*rang mtshan, svalakṣaṇa*), impermanent phenomena, and ultimate truths as likewise mutually inclusive in the system of Sautrāntikas Following Reasoning.[6] In order to delineate the characteristics for which these types are named, Den-dar examines the sense in which they have specific and general characteristics respectively. In doing so, he discusses how such objects are known by direct perception (*mngon sum, pratyakṣa*) and conceptual thought (*rtog pa, kalpanā*). Directly perceiving consciousnesses are, in general, correct observers of impermanent objects.[7] Such perceivers do not confuse aspects or factors of one object with those of another, as does conceptual thought. Thought, however, is limited in the specificity with which it can know its referent object. For example, a thought consciousness apprehending a flower—that is, taking to mind flowers in general—cannot distinguish between (1) the factor of being a flower which pertains to a rose and (2) the factor of being a flower which pertains to a gardenia. These factors do however appear distinctly to an eye consciousness. Yet thought's *range* surpasses that of ordinary sense perception: thought can apprehend its flower in the midst of an empty ocean, the eye sense cannot.

The unrestricted range of thought and its inability to mimic the detail of direct perception derive from its function of isolating or abstracting qualities that, for example, distinguish flowers from non-flowers. Thought, like words, thus is said to operate by way of exclusion or negation (see following translation section). Den-dar himself touches on this issue in order to consider the relationship of thought to actual objects and the process by which names are learned.

Having acknowledged that thought consciousnesses do not realize actual, impermanent objects in all their specificity, Dendar seeks to clarify how, or the extent to which, thought does realize external objects. In this context it is useful to remember that Gelukba soteriology privileges the cultivation of increasingly forceful and precise forms of conceptual understanding. The most forceful, in the sense of being incontrovertible, is inferential cognition (*rjes dpag, anumāna*), said to be invincible because of its grounding in correct reasoning. The most precise, in that its appearing object is a mental image which most closely approximates the actual or referent object, is the inferential consciousness on the highest level of the path of preparation (*spyor lam, prayoga mārga*), known as the level of supreme mundane qualities (*'jig rten pa'i chos kyi mchog, laukikāgryadharma*). Through such cultivation, Gelukba maintains, one can gain a potentially liberating direct perception of impermanence or, in the Mādhyamika tenet system, emptiness.[8] Thus thought, despite its limitations regarding actual phenomena, must be shown to have some genuine purchase on them.

In discussing the mode of perception by thought and the mode of expression by terms, Den-dar-hla-ram-ba makes the point that both thought and words, in a qualified but crucial sense, do actually realize, or get at, their referent objects. In using reasoning to develop an increasingly accurate mental image of subtle impermanence, for example, one is said to understand something about *actual* subtle impermanence, even though neither words nor thought can gain full access to subtle impermanence as it appears to direct perception. Den-dar-hla-ram-ba's particular contribution is to come at this issue by way of a fairly elaborate etymological analysis which also leads him to consider the significance of characterizing thought and direct perception as complete engagers (*sgrub 'jug gi blo, *viddhipravṛttibuddhi*) and partial engagers (*sel 'jug gi blo, *apohapravṛttibuddhi*).

To further develop this issue, Den-dar-hla-ram-ba, like Jang-gya, considers how names are learned. This leads him to consider the process of negation or exclusion (*gzhan sel, anyāpoha*) by which thought operates, the way such exclusion permits identification of the typologies by which the naming process procedes, and the relationship between general types, or generalities, and their instances. To develop this relationship, he briefly explores how Sāṃkhyas and Buddhists attempt to resolve this difficult issue.[9]

Between 1978 and 1981 I collected oral commentary on this text from Denma Lochö Rinbochay (Loseling) and Jambel Shenpen Rinbochay (Ganden Jang-dzay and the Tantric College of Lower Lhasa). Unless otherwise noted, the oral commentary interpolated in this translation represents a consensus of their views. Here, as in the following translations, the oral commentary is indented and set in smaller type so that it can be easily distinguished from the translated text.

TRANSLATION

With Oral Commentary from
Dema Lochö Rinbochay and Jambel Shenpen Rinbochay

SPECIFICALLY CHARACTERIZED PHENOMENA (*158.2*)

The definition of a specifically characterized phenomenon (*rang mtshan, svalakṣana*) is: a functioning thing which is established as its own uncommon mode of subsistence without being merely imputed by thought. An illustration is, for example, a pot which is an appearing object of valid direct cognition (*mngon sum tshad ma, pratyakṣa-pramāṇa*).

According to Sautrāntika, specifically characterized phenomena—impermanent phenomena—are their own mode of subsistence. In other words, the mode of subsistence of a pot is a pot.

Such are called specifically characterized phenomena because when they appear to the direct perceiver which directly perceives them they have characteristics which appear without depending on the appearance of any other phenomenon.[10]

This means that a specifically characterized phenomenon's own characteristics appear to direct perception. There is no need for the direct perception of such phenomena to depend on the appearance of some other thing. In Sautrāntika, impermanent or specifically characterized phenomena are said to appear from their own side without being imputed by thought. This is very different from the Prāsaṅgika-Mādhyamika system which asserts that all phenomena are just imputed by thought. According to Sautrāntika, only permanent phenomena—not impermanent (i.e. specifically characterized) phenomena—are considered to be merely imputed by thought.

This etymology of a specifically characterized phenomenon as one that appears to direct perception without depending on the appearance of some other phenomenon does not apply to all specifically characterized phenomena. For, persons are specifically characterized phenomena but appear to direct perception in dependence on the living body appearing. When you see someone's hand or face, this functions as seeing the person; this is what it means to see the person. (If you see a corpse, however, this does not function as seeing the person, for the corpse is not a living body.)[11]

However, if the phrase "appears without depending on the appearance of any other phenomena" is understood to mean "appears without depending on the appearance of any other phenomenon *which is a generally characterized phenomenon*," then persons would also be included in this etymology.

The person is an imputedly existent (*btags yod, prajñapti-sat*) specifically characterized phenomenon which must be known in dependence on knowing some phenomenon other than itself. Strictly speaking, this etymology applies only to instances of specifically characterized phenomena which are substantially existent, but not to persons which are imputedly existent.

There is no difference between a specifically characterized phenomenon (*rang mtshan*) and an objective specifically characterized phenomenon (*don rang mtshan*). The term "objective specifically characterized phenomenon" signifies an actual object or a genuine object [that is, an object which exists by way of its own nature].

However, generally characterized phenomena can be considered genuine in a broader sense, for it would be inappropriate to hold that uncaused space, for example, is an artificial or non-genuine phenomenon. It is not false; it just does not exist by way of its own nature.

A direct perceiver which explicitly comprehends such [specifically characterized phenomena] is asserted in Sautrāntika to be an unmistaken consciousness which is not contaminated by any of the four causes of error.[12] Furthermore, specifically characterized phenomena are established in the face of an unmistaken direct perceiver which is an ultimate mind; therefore they are ultimately established (*don dam par grub pa, paramārthasiddhi*). Because [specifically characterized phenomena] are true in the face of these [ultimate minds], they are also ultimate truths. In this system, the mode of subsistence of a specifically characterized phenomenon is established as its own mode of abiding. Therefore, when a direct perceiver comprehends [a specifically characterized phenomenon], it also comprehends the mode of abiding of that object. Tsong-ka-ba's *Clarification of (Candrakīrti's) "Supplement to (Nāgārjuna's) 'Treatise on the Middle Way'* " says:

> In Sautrāntika, to posit [something] as an object of comprehension through the force of valid cognition [i.e., through the force of its being validly cognized] means that the object's mode of abiding or mode of subsistence is realized by valid cognition.

Therefore this is [the meaning of] the statement that what the Proponents of True Existence [Vaibhāṣika, Sautrāntika, and Cittamātra] assert as the meaning-isolate (*don ldog*) [the mere definition or meaning] of [being] specifically characterized, the Prāsaṅgikas assert to be the object refuted by a reasoning consciousness analyzing the ultimate.

> In other words, that which the Sautrāntikas posit as the very meaning of being specifically characterized is targeted as the principal thing to be refuted in Prāsaṅgika.

Therefore, the meaning-isolate of [being] a specifically characterized phenomenon signifies a [functioning] thing which is true in the face of a non-mistaken direct perceiver—an ultimate mind. An illustration-isolate [i.e., an instance of] a specifically characterized phenomenon is a [functioning] thing which is unmixed in place, time, and nature.

> Non-mixture of place means that a pot in a certain location is only in that location and not in another. Or, to put it another way, that my house and your house are not each other. Non-mixture of time means that the table of yesterday does not exist today. Non-mixture of nature means that the factor of being a tree which is related with a specific tree is not the factor of being a tree which is related with another tree.
>
> In the Prāsaṅgika system, whatever is a meaning-isolate of [being] a specifically characterized phenomenon necessarily does not exist. For, these are phenomena that are untrue in the face of a Buddha's exalted knower. Prāsaṅgika-Mādhyamika is unique in asserting that functioning things do not have their own nature and thus are not specifically characterized. Svātantrika-Mādhyamikas and the other schools of thought disagree, saying

that something merely imputed by thought cannot perform functions.

In the Prāsaṅgika system, the very meaning of being a specifically characterized phenomenon is unacceptable, for according to that system everything is just imputed by thought.

Question: What is the meaning of being unmixed in place, time, and nature?
Answer: First it is important to understand [how conceptual thought operates] because [the way in which direct perception apprehends objects] is opposite to the manner of apprehension by thought, which apprehends [phenomena] as *mixed* in place, time, and nature. Therefore, this will be discussed here briefly. For example, a person who does not know the convention "pot" would, on seeing a golden bulbous thing to the east, ask, "What is this?" whereupon someone tells him, "This is a pot." At this time, there develops in the continuum of the one who hears this a thought consciousness which thinks, "That golden bulbous thing is a pot." [This thought is] induced by the expression "pot." Because the golden bulbous thing appears as a pot in the perspective, or way of apprehension of this conceptual consciousness, it also appears as opposite from non-pot [to that consciousness].[13] This very appearance as opposite from non-pot is the meaning of the term pot. However, because that thought consciousness perceives[it] within mistaking [the meaning-of-the-term] to *be* a specifically characterized pot, it is said that "for this thought consciousness the appearance [i.e., the actual pot] and the imputation [the appearance as opposite from non-pot] appear to be mixed as one."

Here, "appearance" refers to the specifically characterized object [the actual pot], and "imputation" refers to the meaning of the term pot [the image of pot—an appearance as opposite from non-pot]. That thought consciousness thus perceives the meaning-of-the-term itself which is an appearance of golden pot as opposite from non-pot, and for this reason a specifically characterized pot does not actually appear—only a meaning-of-the-term, which is the appearing object.

Therefore when this person sees a copper bulbous thing in the west a thought consciousness thinking, "This is a pot," develops without any [further need] for relying on an appellation [supplied by an informant]. In terms of the appearance to this thought consciousness, all the factors of being a pot which were earlier perceived in the golden pot in the east also appear to exist in the copper pot in the west. This is the way in which place appears mixed to thought.

It is not that for thought *all* the factors of a particular pot are mixed with *all* the factors of another pot. If this were so it would absurdly follow that the golden appeared red like the copper one. Thus, the "mixture of place" is that the pots in the east and west are mixed together in that they both appear as pot. This single appearance as pot seems to exist equally in the east and west.

The eye consciousness does not see pots this way. For when, after seeing a gold pot the eye consciousness sees a copper pot, the gold pot has already ceased; thus, even though both copper and golden pots *appear as pots* to the eye consciousness they are not mixed in place, time, and nature.

Similarly, when one who has seen a golden pot in the morning sees a copper pot in the afternoon, all the factors [of being a pot] associated with the golden pot seen in the morning appear [to a thought consciousness apprehending pot] also to exist in the copper pot seen in the afternoon. This is how time appears to be mixed [to thought].

The innate apprehension of permanence is the misconception of earlier and later appearing to be mixed. Thus, it seems that the person you saw yesterday is the same as the one that appears today. In this way one conceives of phenomena as permanent or non-disintegrating. Direct perception does not see specifically characterized phenomena this way, it sees them as momentarily disintegrating. However, unless one has already cognized impermanence directly, one cannot ascertain this correct direct perception.

Moreover, these two—the golden pot's factor of being a pot and the copper pot's factor of being a pot—appear to be one [to a thought consciousness apprehending pot]. This is how nature appears to be mixed [to thought].

> Thought cannot distinguish between the factor of a copper pot appearing as a pot and the factor of a golden pot appearing as a pot. These are in fact different, however, and they appear so to direct perception.

This thought consciousness [apprehending a pot in which place, time, and nature appear as mixed] also perceives as unitary all the factors of being a pot in all manifestations of pot. "Manifestations of pot" is to be understood as "instances of pot."

> Although both copper and golden pots are one entity with pot, golden and copper pots themselves are different substantial entities. Therefore, thought is mistaken in seeing these as one, for the pot *which is* a copper pot and the pot *which is* a golden pot are different substantial entities.

In brief, an example of how thought apprehends former and later as one is this: recognizing that "This is the Devadatta [whom I saw] earlier" is a sign of apprehending earlier and later as mixed.

The factors which are the minute particles and moments of a pot do not actually appear to the thought consciousness apprehending pot. Rather, the meaning-of-the-term [which is the mental image of] the gross object—a collection of the particles of pot and of the continuum of former and later moments of pot—appears as pot. For example, when crossing a river, a man's shoe is carried away by water. Then, even though a long time has passed, that man points a finger at the river and says, "This is the water which carried away my shoe." In fact, the continuum of water that carried away the shoe has passed, but such is said due to thought's adhering to the appearance of the meaning-of-the-term (*sgra don, śabdhārtha*) or generic [image] of the former and latter [parts] of the water's continuum as one.[14]

Such a meaning-of-the-term does not appear to a sense consciousness. However, the minute particles, which are factors not to be differentiated as separate substantial entities from that specifically characterized phenomenon [e.g. a pot], as well

as the object's impermanence, momentariness, and so forth appear as they are [to that sense-consciousness, i.e., they appear correctly]. This is because when the eye consciousness views the river, except for the presently appearing minute water particles [together with] their momentariness and impermanence appearing as they are [to the eye consciousness], the minute water particles which flowed earlier and those which will flow later do not at all appear. [Thus, unlike conceptual thought, direct perception does not perceive time as mixed.]
Objection: Are the particles of a pot not minute and thus beyond the notice of an ordinary being? Is the impermanence of a pot not a subtle impermanence [and thus realizable only by a Superior]?
Answer: Although they [particles and impermanence] are very subtle, by reason of their being a single substantial entity, undifferentiable from pot in establishment and abiding, they [like a pot] do appear [to the sense consciousness of an ordinary being].

It is explained that because the sense consciousness apprehending a pot is a complete engager (*sgrub 'jug gi blo, vidhi-pravṛti-buddhi*), when the pot appears everything that is one substantial entity of establishment and abiding (*grub bde rdzas gcig*) with the pot must appear. Furthermore, although the individual minute particles of a pot do not appear [as isolated particles] to that sense consciousness, it is not contradictory for numerous particles, which are many particles collected as a cohesive unit, to appear. For example, in order for a fist to appear it is necessary for a collection of five fingers to appear. . . .

That the two, a pot and the impermanence of a pot, are one substantial entity in the sense of an undifferentiability of establishment and abiding means the following. [The impermanence of the pot] is produced, abides, and ceases simultaneously with pot; further, that which is pot's substantiality is also the substantiality of pot's impermanence, and that which is the substantiality of pot's impermanence is pot's substantiality. From that point of view, it cannot happen that one appears to a direct perceiver and the other does not. For this reason, pot also appears as impermanent to the sense consciousness apprehending it.

> The table and the impermanence of the table are not different substantial factors, they are indivisible. Similarly, the legs of the table are one substantiality with the table. You cannot separate out the parts of a table or the impermanence of a table from the table. When you see one you see the other. Subtle impermanence *appears* to the ordinary eye consciousness, although it is not *ascertained*. Nevertheless, when you look at the coarse table you *see* its subtle impermanence [though without noticing this]. Pot and golden pot are one substantiality of establishment and abiding, but are not one substantiality of establishment and abiding in terms of place, time, and nature. If they were, then there would have to be an appearance of golden pot whenever a pot appeared. But this does not occur because a silver or clay pot can appear without a golden pot appearing.

Objection: Insofar as a sense direct perceiver apprehending a sound realizes [that] sound directly, it would [also absurdly] induce ascertainment of the impermanence of sound [because it is a complete engager, meaning that it perceives all aspects of its object]. If this were so, signs [i.e., logical reasons] which prove sound to be impermanent and inferences [of such] would be pointless.

Response: There is no fallacy. Although a sense direct perceiver apprehending a sound directly perceives those features [including impermanence] which are undifferentiable as separate substantial factors from sound, in terms of inducing ascertainment consonant with what it perceives, it is unable to induce ascertainment of some factors. This is due to internal conditions, thick predispositions for adhering to permanence, and external conditions, perceiving the apparent [continuity of the object]. Also, when such unfavorable conditions do not exist, the sense consciousness apprehending a pot can induce ascertainment with respect to the impermanence of some of its appearing objects. . . .[15]

GENERALLY CHARACTERIZED PHENOMENA (177.2)

With respect to the second, the explanation of generally characterized phenomena (*spyi mtshan, sāmānyalakṣaṇa*), the definition of a generally characterized phenomenon is: that which is merely imputed by thought without being an entity whose mode of subsistence is established from its own side.

> Here, to be established from an object's own side means that the object is capable of performing a function. Therefore, only those phenomena which are not imputed by thought—specifically characterized phenomena—are said by the author to have a mode of subsistence that exists from its own side.

An illustration is an object that appears to a thought consciousness apprehending places, times, and natures as mixed, such as the appearance as opposite from not being a pot to the thought consciousness apprehending pot.

The subject [an appearance as opposite from not being a pot] is called a generally characterized phenomenon because it has a character which is realized by way of a generality, it being impossible [for a thought consciousness apprehending pot] to realize pot by way of its own entity. Here, "generality" refers, for instance, to the meaning-of-the-term of a gold pot.

Question: To what does meaning-of-the-term refer?

Answer: It refers to the appearance of a gold pot as opposite from not being a pot to the thought consciousness apprehending pot.

The subject [the appearance as opposite from not being a pot] is called a "generality" (1) because of being a generality [which applies to] all manifestations of pot, (2) because gold pot, copper pot, and so forth are also instances of it, and (3) because gold and copper pots and so forth also appear as pots to a thought consciousness apprehending pot.

With respect to this, it is necessary to know how a thought consciousness perceives and how a term expresses [its objects]; therefore, these will be explained.

Gyel-tsap's *Explanation of (Dharmakīrti's) "Commentary on (Dignāga's) 'Compendium on Valid Cognition'"* says that there are two ways in which a silver and a gold pot can appear to thought in relation to pot: either like the stars and the sky—that is, as different—or like milk and water—that is, as undifferentiable. To the thought which thinks "gold and silver pots" these pots seem to be instances of the generality pot; here the generality and instances seem different for thought, just as the stars and sky are different. This is a mistaken appearance because a generality and its instances are not different [entities]. [Instances of pot such as] a gold pot or a silver pot are one entity with the self-isolate of pot (*bum pa'i rang ldog*). A thought consciousness is mistaken in its perception that a gold or a silver pot is different in entity [from pot], as if the instance—silver pot—were not one entity with the generality. The thought consciousness to which there is an appearance of gold and silver pots as a single entity, like milk and water, is also mistaken. They appear as one in the sense that their natures appear mixed for the thought consciousnesses apprehending just pot, whereas their natures are not mixed in fact.

1. *The mode of perception by thought* (177.6)

For example, one sees with one's eye consciousness a gold pot inside a temple; then, when one proceeds to another location, the shape, color, and so forth of that former gold pot appear distinctly to the mind. The mind to which such appears is a thought consciousness not a direct perceiver. The appearance which appears to that thought consciousness is the meaning-generality of the gold pot, not the actual golden pot. If it were the actual gold pot, then even if that gold pot [in the temple] were smashed with a hammer and changed into another form, it would have to appear [to thought] just as it is i.e., in its new [broken] form and not as a gold pot; however, it does not appear so.

To [put this] another way, if that appearance to thought were the actual pot, the appearance would be able to perform functions such as holding water. If this were the case, then since wherever a thought consciousness apprehending pot exists a pot would have to exist, no one would be bereft of a pot. Therefore, this thought consciousness is mistaken with respect to [its] appearing object because this appearance of gold pot as a pot appears to it as a pot whereas it is not a pot.

> The meaning-generality which is an appearance as opposite from non-pot to the thought consciousness apprehending pot is both a generality (*spyi, sāmanyā*) and a generally characterized phenomenon (*spyi mtshan, sāmānya lakṣaṇa*). All generalities are not necessarily generally characterized phenomena; for example, pot is a generality that is concomitant with all instances of pot, but pot is a specifically characterized phenomenon. The appearance as opposite from non-pot, however, is a generally characterized phenomenon because it is permanent, and it is a generality because it has the nature (*rang bzhin*) of the external pot and the nature of the internal consciousness—the thought apprehending that meaning-generality or generic image.

[However, a correct conceptual thought] is not mistaken with regard to its referent object because in the mode of apprehension of that thought consciousness there exists a conception [rightly] thinking, "A golden pot is a pot," but there does not exist a conception [wrongly] thinking, "That appearance is a pot." For example, when one looks in the mirror wanting to discover whether or not there is grime on one's face, just that image in the mirror appears as the face and in dependence on this fact [the condition of] the face is understood, but there is [usually] no conception [wrongly] thinking, "That image itself is my face." In just the same way, the thought consciousness apprehending pot conceives of pot by way of the appearance of an image of pot, but does not conceive the image of pot to be a pot.

Thus, in terms of what is to be understood from this, the thought consciousness apprehending pot does not explicitly apprehend pot but explicitly apprehends a pot's meaning-generality. Also, the term expressing pot does not *explicitly* express pot; it explicitly expresses a pot's term-generality. However, in dependence on these [one can] undeniably get at the specifically characterized pot; because of this it must be asserted that the thought consciousness apprehending pot explicitly realizes pot and that the term expressing pot explicitly expresses pot. If it were not so, one would have to assert that whatever is a specifically characterized phenomenon is only an implicit object of a thought consciousness and is only something implicitly indicated by a treatise.

According to Jangdzay College of Ganden Monastic University, once the term "pot" explicitly expresses the meaning-generality which is an appearance as opposite from non-pot, then it must also express pot because it expresses these as mixed together. Thus, both pot and the meaning-generality of pot are explicit objects of expression (*dngos gyi brjod bya*) of the term "pot." The thought consciousness apprehending pot, therefore, explicitly understands or realizes pot. However, even though pot is an explicit object of expression of "pot," the word "pot" does not explicitly express the specifically characterized pot.

If, on hearing the words "impermanent sound" one did not explicitly understand impermanent sound, then the inference, (*rjes dpag, anumāna*) realizing impermanent sound would also not understand this explicitly. For, in that case the inferential consciousness would explicitly understand the meaning-generality but not impermanent sound itself. The *specifically characterized* impermanent sound, however, is not an explicit object of expression of the term "impermanent sound" because in order to express a specifically characterized sound the words would have to express a sound which was not mixed with the meaning-generality of impermanent sound. It is only the isolate of impermanent sound, and not the meaning-generality mixed with it, that is the explicit object of expression the term "impermanent sound."

The final reason why a thought consciousness apprehending pot explicitly realizes pot is this: when a direct perceiver apprehending pot is first produced, it establishes a predisposition for conceiving pot, and when that predisposition is later activated, it produces a thought consciousness apprehending gold pot and so forth as pot. Because that thought consciousness—in dependence on the appearance of gold pot as opposite from not being a pot—has the effect of getting at a specifically characterized pot, factually concordant (*don mthun, anvartha*) thought consciousnesses for the most part ultimately derive from direct perception. For, even a thought consciousness which apprehends space derives from a direct perceiver which apprehends an obstructive tangible object.

Objection: It follows that whatever is a thought consciousness is not necessarily mistaken with respect to its appearing object because (1) the thought consciousness apprehending object of knowledge perceives the meaning-generality of object of knowledge *as* an object of knowledge and (2) the meaning-generality of object of knowledge *is* an object of knowledge.
Answer: There is no entailment because merely by this it cannot be proven that such a thought consciousness is non-mistaken with respect to its appearing object. This is because when the meaning-generality of an object appears to a thought consciousness, the [following] appearances occur:

1) just that meaning-generality appears as if it were the entity of that object,

2) the meaning-generality appears as if it were one with that object,

3) the meaning-generality appears as if it were opposite from not being that object.

> These are really three ways of describing the same appearance. The meaning-generality which is the appearing object of a thought consciousness that apprehends object of knowledge is itself an object of knowledge; therefore, this thought consciousness, unlike most conceptual consciousnesses, is not mistaken with respect to its appearing object in all three ways mentioned above. That is, the first type of error listed above does not apply to the meaning-generality which is an appearance as opposite from not being an object of knowledge, for it both appears to be and is the entity of an object of knowledge; it is an illustration-isolate or an instance of object of knowledge. Therefore, the thought consciousness which apprehends this meaning-generality as if it were one with object of knowledge is mistaken.

Also, since the meaning-generality of object of knowledge appears to be one with object of knowledge, that thought consciousness is mistaken with respect to the appearing object. . . .Therefore, whatever is a thought consciousness does not necessarily mistake a meaning-generality as that actual object [though most do], but does necessarily mistake the meaning-generality as one with that object.

To take it this way is very good.

Objection: With regard to both an inferential consciousness which realizes sound as impermanent and a superimposing consciousness which apprehends sound as permanent, it follows that a difference of incontrovertibility and controvertibility does not exist because they do not differ with respect to being mistaken consciousnesses.

Answer: These two are similar in being mistaken consciousnesses; however, through an inferential consciousness one is able to get at the object of engagement (*'jug yul*) whereas through a superimposing consciousness one cannot get at the object of engagement. For example, the apprehension of a jewel's light as a jewel and the apprehension of a butter lamp's light as a jewel are similar in being mistaken; however, through the jewel's light one can get at a jewel but through the butter lamp's light one cannot. . . .

> A thought consciousness realizing pot, for example, does realize the specifically characterized pot. If it did not, it would not realize pot. However, thought does not realize pot ultimately, nor do terms express it ultimately. To realize pot or any other specifically characterized phenomenon ultimately means to realize it unmixed with any meaning-generality. Thus, although a pot is an object of thought and expression, it is not so ultimately. Both direct perception and thought realize specifically characterized phenomena such as pots, but direct perception realizes them ultimately—unmixed with a meaning-generality—whereas thought does not.

The way in which terms and thought consciousnesses operate by means of elimination should be understood well because Kay-drup's *Great Commentary on (Dharmakīrti's) "Commentary on (Dignāga's) 'Compendium on Valid Cognition'"* says:

> The explicit object of expression of the term expressing pot is not substantially established, but it is not necessary that whatever is explicitly expressed by that not be substantially established. [Pot is explicitly expressed but is not the explicit object of expression.] This mode is to be understood as an uncommon feature of the Seven Treatises on Valid Cognition.

"Uncommon feature" means that it does not appear in any other text except the Seven Treatises.

A direct perceiver apprehending a pot is a complete engager. Hence, it comprehends [a pot] not from the viewpoint of merely eliminating non-pot, but by way of a pot's aspect being cast just as it is. Because a thought consciousness apprehending pot is a partial [or eliminative] engager, it does not comprehend [pot] by way of pot's aspect being cast just as it is; rather, it comprehends a mere mental imputation, which is an elimination of non-pot, through the mere appearance as opposite from non-pot.

> When direct perception sees a pot, the entire collection of factors that are one substantiality of establishment and abiding with that pot appear: its productness, impermanence, and so forth. Because the complete collection appears to it, a direct perceiver is known as a mind of complete engagement (*sgrub 'jug gi blo, viddhipravṛttibuddhi*).
>
> By contrast, the thought consciousness apprehending pot is a mind of eliminative or partial engagement (*sel 'jug gi blo, apohapravṛtti-buddhi*). It is eliminative because it eliminates some qualities or factors related with the pot and engages with others. It does not realize all the factors—being a product, impermanence, and so forth—which are one substantiality of establishment and abiding with the pot.

For that thought consciousness, pot has become an object of explicit ascertainment, but has not become the appearing object, and a meaning-generality of pot has become the appearing object but not the object of ascertainment. Thus thought, having mixed the two—the appearance [the actual pot] and the imputation [a mental image of pot] as one—takes an imputed phenomenon as an appearing object....

2. *The mode of expression by terms* (182.2)

The term expressing pot has these three functions: as the name, convention, and appellation of pot. Therefore, these three are not mutually exclusive. However, there is a special purpose in explaining these as separate from the viewpoint of their isolates. What is the purpose? The subject, the term expressing "pot," is called a "name" (*ming, nāma*) because of directing or leading the mind to the meaning, the bulbous thing.

The term expressing "pot" is called a "convention" (*tha snyad, vyavahāra*) because of being for the purpose of knowing that the bulbous thing, through being able to perform the function of holding water, is needed for pouring water and is not needed in holding up rafters. [The term pot thus not *only* directs the mind to the object but also conveys usages of the object.]

The subject [the term expressing "pot"] is called an appellation (*brda, saṃketa*) because of being affixed by [the original namer's] wish for the sake of [another person] knowing to use the convention that a bulbous thing is a pot.

Thus, based on [the original] connection of the appellation "pot" to the bulbous thing, there arises the knowledge of how to use the convention, thinking, "This bulbous thing is a pot," and that is called ascertainment of the relationship between pot's name and meaning. Therefore, whatever is a thought consciousness connecting a name [with a meaning] must have the nature of mixing the two as one—the *name* previously affixed at the time of [the original] terminological connection and the *meaning* subsequently seen at the time of [using] the convention.

In general, understanding the meaning depends on appellations and any appellation is suitable to be applied to any object. For example, when "*kāli*" is expressed, those of Central India [Magadha] understood it as expressing "time," but those of South India understood it as expressing "insanity." However, later, when those [from the South] perceived the Maghadis using it to express time, the former understanding disappeared, and they [also] understood it as expressing time. Therefore, expressive terms are used merely through acceptance [and not through having an intrinsic relationship with the object they express].

Thus, the term "pot" is known as a term of the prevailing preference. For, the initial affixer of the appellation fixed the appellation "pot" to the bulbous thing arbitrarily through the power of his preference, and, in dependence on that, "pot" prevails as the actual name of the bulbous thing.

> One's own wish or intention has great power with respect to words and is thus like a king (*rgyal po*) of words. Hence the name "pot" arises due to the force of someone's own thought or preference (*'dod pa*). Just as a king is powerful, so whatever conversation one makes is under the power of the mind; the choice of words is arbitrary.

Later, although others designate names [in connection with a bulbous thing], these cannot become renowned as its actual name. Thus, the term "pot" is renowned as the actual name of these bulbous things on account of being the appellation originally affixed through [someone's] wish to express it. On account of its incapacity to be renowned as the actual name of something else, the term "pot" becomes definite as the actual name of these bulbous things, and not the actual name of something else.

However, the term "pot" is not unsuitable to be affixed to other than bulbous things because even if one affixes the name "pot" to woolen cloth, due to the power of conditioning after some time even the meaning-generality of pot could appear for woolen cloth. Therefore, "pot" is not objectively established as related with bulbous things.

In brief, any appearing object of thought is suitable to be expressed by any expressive term. Therefore, correct signs of renown are established effortlessly.

In general, appellation (*brda, saṃketa*) and convention (*tha snyad, vyavahāra*) are synonymous. Conventions are of three types—mental conventions such as thinking "pot," verbal conventions such as expressing "pot," and physical conventions such as making a sign with the hand, etc. [to indicate] a pot.

With respect to how the conventions of generality and common locus are affixed: the Sāmkhyas assert a general principal (*spyi gtso bo, sāmānya-pradhāna*) which is said to be a partless permanent thing, as the generality of the manifestations [or instances of pot]. Although the manifestations are states different [from each other] they are one nature within the general principal. Therefore, the two, generality and manifestation, are asserted to be one substantial entity. However, the Vaiśeṣikas assert these two as different substantial entities.

Sāṃkhyas assert that even though the various instances or manifestations themselves are different entities, the generality is one entity with each of these. Moreover, the instances are only different entities adventitiously or temporarily; they are capable of dissolving back into the generality. The Vaiśesikas, on the other hand, consider instance and generality to be different substantial entities. (In their view, whatever can appear to the mind as a distinct feature is a different substantial entity.)

In the Buddhist view, generality and instance are neither one substantial entity nor different substantial entities because they are not substantially established. A phenomenon's being a generality or instance is merely imputed by thought.

In our own system, these two—generality and instance—are neither one substantial entity nor different substantial entities, because of not being [functioning] things.

Although a generality which is a [functioning] thing, such as opposite-from-not-being-a-pot, exists, the generality through which all [its] manifestations are understood—the generality to which the term is [initially] affixed—is mainly an appearing object of a thought consciousness. Furthermore, when the appellation is [initially] connected [to the object for someone else, as when an instructor states] "This golden bulbous thing is a pot," one is affixing the appellation "pot" to the appearance-as-opposite-from-not-being-a-pot of the thought consciousness apprehending pot. At that time there can thus be produced in the continuum of the hearer an appearance which characterizes the golden bulbous thing as a pot.

Because that appearance is called pot's mark [i.e., the mark of being a pot], from the viewpoint of taking to mind—in dependence on that mark—the connection of the name and that which has the name, "This golden bulbous thing is a pot," there arises the knowledge of how to use the convention that the golden bulbous thing is a pot. This is said to be a realization of [what] pot [is].

> You can apply the name "pot" in a general way, without meaning any specific type of pot such as golden, silver, or clay. For example, you can say "hand" without meaning either the left or right one.
>
> The referent object of the name "pot" (*sgra'i zhen yul*) is not the meaning-generality but the actual impermanent pot. The explicit object of expression of the term (*dngos kyi brjod bya*) is the meaning-generality which is an appearance as opposite from non-pot.

Therefore, this is the meaning of the Vaibhāṣika assertion that the term operates with respect to the name, the name operates with respect to the mark, and from the mark one understands the meaning.

In brief, the term "pot" explicitly expresses the term-generality of pot without being able to explicitly express the specifically characterized pot. Through this expression of the term-generality, the name of pot is expressed; therefore, in dependence on this name, the thing is characterized as being pot, whereby one realizes [what a] pot [is].

Why is it that the term expressing "pot" is unable to express explicitly the specifically characterized pot? "The specifically characterized pot" is the present color, shape, and so forth of the pot as these appear to a direct perceiver apprehending a pot. Because the color and shape which existed previously [during direct perception] have ceased when the term is later expressed, how could [terms] express them just as they are? If they did have this capacity, a pot's [impermanence] would also be expressed by that [term "pot"] because, when a pot appears to a direct perceiver apprehending a pot, the impermanence of the pot also appears. If this were so, then the term "pot" would be a complete engager.

The Sāṃkhyas consider expressive terms to be complete engagers; therefore, [according to them], the term "pot" also expresses impermanent pot. Similarly, because product and impermanent thing are one substantial entity, the term "product" also expresses impermanent thing.

In general, impermanent thing is not positable separate from the substantial entity of product, and product is not positable separate from the substantial entity of impermanent thing. Therefore, both we [Buddhists] and others maintain that those two are one substantial entity. About this a Sāṃkhya says: When you prove to me that sound is impermanent [via the syllogism: The subject, sound, is impermanent because of being a product], is the "product" which is stated as the reason the product which is of the [same] substantiality as impermanence? Or is product merely imputed by thought? If it is the latter, that reason would be a reason which is not established. The former [is likewise unsuitable]. For, when [you] state, "The subject, sound, is impermanent because of being a product," the phrase "because of being a product" also expresses impermanence. In that case, one segment of the thesis [the thesis being, "A product is impermanent"] would be stated as the reason [and this is unsuitable because a reason must have three different elements, subject, predictate, and reason or sign].

The Sāṃkhyas hold sound to be permanent. For the Buddhists sound, like all products, is impermanent. Why is being a product a sign of, or reason for, being impermanent? Because products are made by causes and conditions and nothing produced in dependence on causes and conditions can be permanent.

To be impermanent means to disintegrate from one moment to the next. How do products disintegrate from one moment to another? Why do they lack the power to sustain themselves for a second moment? Consider a house, for example. It has no power to sustain itself; it did not even come into existence under its own power but was made by causes and conditions. From its very first moment, it is entirely dependent on causes and conditions. Thus, it cannot abide permanently. Being powerless in this way, it has no capacity to prevent its own disintegration. However long a house may last—a year, five years, a hundred years—this comes about through the power of causes and conditions, not through its own power. Therefore, as the power of these causes is [gradually] extinguished, the house itself disintegrates from one moment to the next.

An example of a permanent phenomenon is uncaused space. It was not made by causes and conditions. It is a mere absence of obstructive contact; it does not disintegrate or change, it never becomes hot or cold. The atmosphere changes temperature, but not the mere absence of obstructive contact. [A particular uncaused space, though permanent, is not eternal. For example, the space inside a cup comes into existence when the cup is produced and goes out of existence when the cup is destroyed.]

The Buddhist position does not accept either of the two consequences offered by the Sāṃkhyas. The thesis here is, "sound is impermanent." There are two names involved here, "sound" and "impermanent." Once there are two names, there should be two objects. However, the Sāṃkhyas here argue that if the Buddhists consider product and impermanent thing to be the same substantial entity, then when one realizes sound to be a product, one must also realize the product which is of the substantial entity of impermanent thing.

When one realizes the product which is of the substantial entity of impermanent thing, one realizes the substantial entity of impermanent thing and thus the nature of impermanence. This is the Sāṃkhya position, but the Buddhists do not agree.

[Buddhist:] Your qualm comes about due to your [Sāṃkhya] assertion that permanent sound is a complete engager. Therefore, in our own system, because terms and thoughts are partial engagers, [your doubt] must be answered from the viewpoint of establishing well how one posits a presentation of [impermanence and product as] one entity but different isolates (*ldog pa, vivartana*) by reason of terms and thought consciousnesses being eliminative [or partial] engagers. Therefore, this is the mode of that [presentation]: the term "product," for example, expresses a product by way of excluding non-product. The thought consciousness that apprehends this perceives [it] in the manner of opposite-from-non-product, therefore, having excluded opposite-from-non-product, it perceives product. Thus, both terms and thoughts are said to engage [their objects] through exclusion [i.e., to be eliminative or partial engagers].

The reason which proves sound to be impermanent, does *not* also establish that sound is able to perform a function, that it is a cause, or an effect, or anything else. Only the fact of its being impermanent is established by the syllogism, "The subject, sound, is impermanent because of being a product." Thus, the thought consciousness that realizes sound to be impermanent is a mind of eliminative or partial engagement; it engages only the factor of sound being a product, not any of the other factors of function and so forth. Although sound, impermanence, and product are one entity, they are different isolates. Thus, the term that expresses sound and the thought that realizes it are eliminative engagers.

Product and impermanent thing are different isolates because the manner of their appearance to thought is different. Product is realized through excluding non-product and impermanence is realized through excluding permanence. But there are not two different entities of which it can be said, "This is the product, that the impermanence."

A thought consciousness is a partial engager because it separates out, or isolates, factors contained within the same substantial entity and focuses on only one of them. Impermanence is not realized by a thought consciousness realizing product, and product is not realized by a thought consciousness realizing impermanence.

Product and impermanent thing appear differently to thought, but not to direct perception. For example, both product and impermanent thing appear to the ear consciousness that hears a sound. Direct perceivers are complete engagers that operate with respect to all the factors which are one substantiality of production and abiding with their appearing object. However, direct perceivers are also involved in exclusion; for example, the direct perceiver realizing product does eliminate non-product. However, it is not sufficient merely to exclude "non-product" for a consciousness to be considered a partial engager. A consciousness which is a partial engager excludes all that is one substantiality of establishment and abiding with its appearing object except for the factor being realized.

Therefore, although the term "product" expresses opposite-from-non-product, it does not express opposite-from-non-impermanent-thing. Also, although the term "impermanent thing" expresses opposite-from-non-impermanent-thing, it does not express opposite-from-non-product. For this reason, on the basis of how they are expressed, opposite-from-non-product and opposite-from-non-impermanent-thing are established as different. This, therefore, is the significance of saying that the two, product and impermanent thing, are different isolates.

Thus, product and impermanent thing are said to be different isolates on the basis of how they are expressed or perceived by

> thought, not on the basis of how they are observed in direct perception. However, although there is no difference in the way these *appear* to direct perception, the way in which direct perception *realizes* them is slightly different. Our own direct perception can realize that things are products, but subtle impermanence is difficult to realize. We can see with our own eyes that sprouts, for example, are produced in dependence on certain causes and conditions, but we do not directly ascertain the subtle impermanence of sprouts. Thus, the ways of realizing these are different.

However, that which is the entity of product is also the entity of impermanent thing, and that which is the entity of impermanent thing is also the entity of product. For this reason, the two—product and impermanent thing—are a single entity. Yet, the term "product" does not explicitly express impermanence and the term "impermanence" also does not explicitly express product.

> When we study, it is necessary to explain separately impermanence, product, the ability to perform a function and so forth. This is a sign that [the terms expressing them] are partial engagers. For, they are all one entity, and if the term were a complete engager it would be necessary to explain only one of them and all would be understood.

Also, the thought consciousness which is induced by such a term [as "product" or "impermanence"] takes one as its object and does not explicitly apprehend the other. Therefore, when expressing "product" others understand only product, they do not understand impermanence. For this reason, the two—product and impermanent thing—are one entity but different isolates. It is difficult for the Sāṃkhyas to posit in such a way.

Therefore, at the time of stating, "The subject, sound, is an impermanent thing because of being a product," the product which comes to be the reason and the impermanent thing which comes to be the predictate of the probandum are one entity, but the term which expresses the reason—product—does not express the predicate of the probandum—impermanent thing. Hence, there is no fault of the [unwanted] consequence that one portion of the thesis is stated as the sign [of a sound being an impermanent thing].

Similarly, the positing of [something as] a common locus [of two or more things] is in the eliminative perspective of terms and thought. The reason is as follows: when, for example, a person wishing to speak of a flower as being both an *utpala* and blue, says, "This flower is a blue *utpala*," then, even though in this one flower there are not two different substantial entities—the blue which is not *utpala* and *utpala* which is not blue—with respect to the manner of expression of the term "blue *utpala*," the blue and the *utpala* emerge serially. In the same way, a thought consciousness to which the two, *utpala* and blue, appear to be different, develops in the continuum of the hearer. In dependence on this appearance, the single flower itself is understood to be a common locus of *utpala* and blue.

> In the same way a table, for example, is a common locus of product and impermanent thing, but this does not mean that a term expressing the one expresses the other, or that a thought consciousness realizing one realizes the other, because terms and thoughts are partial engagers, expressing or realizing only some of the factors in a single entity or common locus. By contrast, when direct perception sees a table, all the factors of impermanence, product, and so forth appear. Thus, direct perceivers are complete engagers.

When one just says "*utpala*" no appearance of blue develops in the mind of the listener. The reason for understanding such is that at the time [of hearing the words "blue *utpala*"] a composite of the two—opposite-from-non-*utpala* and opposite-from-non-blue—appear to the thought consciousness in the continuum of the listener. Therefore, except for [our] positing a common locus in dependence on the appearance of a composite of two isolates to thought, the *utpala* and the blue do not exist as different substantial entities with that single flower.

In brief, all the conventions of [a syllogism such as the] probandum [thesis], probans [reason], predicate, and subject, are used based on their appearance to thought. Otherwise, if they were taken as specifically characterized phenomena, [it would be absurd]. For, when impermanent thing is established with respect to sound, then when sound is first ascertained, there is an appearance for thought of sound as if it did not exist previously and is newly established. Following that, when the two, product and impermanent thing, are serially ascertained in relation to sound, product and impermanent thing are like a [potted] juniper depending on a metal trough, or a white woolen cloth becoming red [in that] there is first an appearance of [sound as a] product and, following that, [as an] impermanent thing—as if [this were] a new establishment of what did not exist previously. [However], this seriality of former and later [appearances of the establishment of sound as a product and an impermanent thing] is not feasible with respect to specifically characterized phenomena. For, at the mere production of a sound, it is already simultaneously produced as an entity which is a product and an impermanent thing.

In brief, the meaning of direct perceivers being complete engagers and conceptual consciousnesses partial engagers is this: When, for example, blue is perceived by a direct perceiver apprehending blue, the features which are one entity with blue appear in the manner of being included in, or established as, objects of that [direct perceiver]; from this point of view, the specifically characterized blue appears. [By contrast], when blue is perceived by a thought consciousness apprehending blue, those features do not appear insofar as those features are eliminated or excluded as its object, and there is an appearance of a phenomenon that is a superimposition by the thought which is an elimination of non-blue.

Furthermore, because terms have no referent objects (*zhen yul, *adhyavasayaviṣayạ*), it is indeed said that there are no referent objects of expression.[16] [However], the thought consciousness which wishes to express a term expresses it upon thinking, [I] will speak of "pot," putting pot as the referent object. The reason why the listener unmistakenly understands pot derives from this. Thus [since in this context] terms do have referent objects of expression, there is something [meaningful] to be understood [about expressive terms].

Also, opposite-from-non-pot is pot's objective specifically characterized exclusion; for this reason, opposite-from-non-pot is a functioning thing.

Opponent: [With regard to this], it follows that such is not correct, because opposite-from-not-being-a-pot is permanent.

Response: The reason—that opposite-from-not-being-a-pot is permanent—is not established.

Opponent: It follows with respect to the subject, a pot, that opposite-from-not-being-it is permanent because being it is permanent.

Response: The reason—that being a pot is permanent—is not established.

Opponent: It follows with respect to the subject, a pot, that being it is permanent, because being it exists.

Although this is an off-shoot of a reasoning in the Seven Treatises [on Valid Cognition], if one takes opposite-from-non-pot as being a functioning thing, I think it accords with the great texts.

Someone [else] says: Your saying that the term which expresses "product" expresses it as [or in the manner of] opposite from non-product is incorrect because if this were correct, it would [absurdly] follow that the subject, the term expressing "product," explicitly expresses opposite-from-non-product because of explicitly expressing [product] as opposite from non-product. If you accept this, it [absurdly] follows that the subject, the thought consciousness which explicitly apprehends product, explicitly apprehends opposite-from-non-product because (1) such is expressed by the term which expresses product and (2) both terms and thought consciousnesses have the same [style of] operation.

Answer: It is true that such is expressed by the term which expresses product and that both terms and thought consciousnesses have the same [mode of] operation, but this does not entail that the thought consciousness which explicitly apprehends product explicitly apprehends opposite from non-product.

Jangdzay College has a different assertion here: Once the term "product" *explicitly* expresses product, it *implicitly* expresses opposite-from-non-product. Similarly, the thought consciousness realizing product explicitly realizes product and implicitly realizes opposite-from-non-product.

For example, if I say "I am a human" you explicitly understand that I am a human being, and implicitly understand that I am opposite from not being a human. It is not necessary to explain this latter separately.

If one accepted that the thought consciousness which explicitly apprehends product explicitly apprehends opposite-from-non-product, it would [absurdly] follow that the subject, opposite-from-non-product, is one with product because of being the explicit object of the thought consciousness which explicitly apprehends product.

According to Jangdzay College, it does not follow that whatever is an explicit object of the thought consciousness apprehending product is necessarily one with product. For example, the thought consciousness apprehending product explicitly apprehends the meaning-generality of product; this meaning-generality is an explicit object of the thought apprehending product because it is the *appearing object* of that thought. For, whatever is an appearing object of a thought consciousness is necessarily an *explicit object* of that thought consciousness, but is not necessarily an explicit object of comprehension.

However, though it is indeed renowned that terms and thought operate in the same way, this is subject to analysis. For, it would [absurdly] follow that whatever is explicitly expressed by some term would necessarily be explicitly apprehended in the same way by a thought consciousness because [according to you] those two, terms and thought consciousness, operate in the same way.

Jangdzay College would accept this.

If it is accepted that whatever is explicitly expressed by some term is necessarily explicitly apprehended in the same way by a thought consciousness, [such is contradicted by the following]. For, Pan-chen Sö-nam-drak-ba says, "It is established that valid cognition's manner of operation is different from the operation of the expression of terms because, although the phrase stating that 'whatever is permanent is not a product' expresses product's absence in the permanent, the valid cognizer which comprehends that whatever is permanent is not a product does not realize that product's absence in the permanent."[17] In the same vein, the omniscient Jam-yang-shay-ba also says: "Although the two, terms and thoughts, are similar in that they are partial engagers of their own objects, the inferential consciousness (*rjes dbag, anumāna*) which realizes permanent phenomena as empty of [being] products does not realize product's absence in the permanent. However, the term which indicates that among the permanent there are no products indicates product's absence in the permanent. Such very subtle and intricate reasons should be cherished."

If this is expressed in a way that is easily understood; it means that the term expressing that "whatever is permanent is necessarily not a product" does express that products are empty of being permanent, but the thought consciousness which comprehends that "whatever is permanent is necessarily not a product" does not comprehend that products are empty of being permanent. Therefore, it should be understood how, although both terms and thought consciousnesses are the same merely in that they operate by way of exclusions with respect to their own object, there is no definiteness that everything which is expressed by a term is apprehended in the same way by a thought consciousness.

When I say that I am not a non-person, I also express that a non-person is not me. However, the valid cognizer which realizes that I am not a non-person does not realize that a non-person is not me.

In stating that permanent phenomena are not products, one also expresses that products are not permanent. However, the thought consciousness which realizes that permanent phenomena are not products does not realize that products are not permanent. This is a very subtle distinction.

According to Jay-dzun-ba, the term expressing "product" expresses "opposite-from-non-product" implicitly; it does not express this explicitly. The thought consciousness apprehending product also implicitly realizes opposite-from-non-product. However, Jam-yang-shay-ba says that thought and terms are not similar in what they realize and express.

APPLICATION OF NAMES

The initial connecting of an appellation (*brda, saṃketa*) or name (*ming, nāma*) to an object occurs when a person who knows, for example, the convention "ox," tells a person who does not know it, "This is an ox." Thus, "connecting an appellation" (*brda sbyar ba*) in this context refers to initially connecting a term with an object; "convention" (*tha snyad, vyavahāra*) refers to later usage of a term that has been learned.[18]

In terms of connecting an appellation [or name] to an ox, the opposite-from-non-ox is called the generality, and white, black, and so forth oxen are its instances. The two—generality and instances—are one substantiality, and, furthermore, the generality itself pervades all its instances.

A generality and its instances must be one substantial entity or one entity. All instances of oxen are pervaded by the generality, that is, by being opposite from non-ox.

With respect to this, although both the insiders, Buddhists, and the outsiders, Sāṃkhyas, concur in asserting the mere expression "generality," they have incongruent identifications of this generality.

Both agree that generalities exist, but they have different explanations of what a generality is and how it relates to its instances.

For generalities are known to be of two sorts, type generalities (*rigs spyi, *gotra-sāmānya*) and collection generalities (*tshogs spyi*), and there the Buddhists assert that a type generality—an exclusion which is the opposite from non-ox, an elimination of what is not ox—is the generality [concomitant with] the instances of ox. The Sāṃkhyas, however, say that there is a permanent generality, a "principal" (*gtso bo, pradhāna*) that pervades all instances [whatsoever] and that this is the generality of the instances of ox.

Unlike opposite-from-non-ox, which is an impermanent phenomenon and an objective specifically characterized exclusion, and which does not exist apart from its instances, the Sāṃkhya generality is permanent and does exist apart from its instances.

Furthermore, the Buddhists and Sāṃkhyas concur in asserting that due to having connected the appellation ["ox"] to a white ox, for instance, all the remaining types of oxen [black, spotted, and so forth] are understood to be oxen. They also concur in asserting that the purpose of affixing appellations is to understand a convention [that is, facilitate later usage], but they disagree on the reasons for [how affixing the name leads to] understanding such.

The Buddhists say that when the appellation "This is an ox" is affixed through one's having initially taken a white ox, for instance, as the basis, that appellation is affixed to the opposite-from-non-ox [that is, to the generality] by reason of the fact that this bulky thing has the nature of being an aggregation of a hump, dewlap, and so forth.

One can distinguish between ox and non-ox by way of the presence or absence of the distinguishing mark or sign of an ox, the aggregation of a hump and dewlap. According to the Buddhists, the name is initially affixed to the opposite-from-non-ox. The white ox is only taken as the *basis* of affixing or connecting the name; the name is not actually *applied* to it. Because opposite-from-non-ox is an aggregation of a hump and dewlap, it is suitable to receive the name "ox." Such a name can only properly be applied to what is opposite-from-non-ox, that is, only to what is ox—not to horse, tiger, or anything else. This opposite-from-non-ox to which the name is affixed itself pervades, or is concomitant with, all instances of ox. Therefore, once the name has been affixed to this, one can use the convention "ox" for oxen of other colors.

If the name "ox" were initially affixed to the specific white ox, one would not recognize a black animal with a hump and dewlap as suitable to be called an ox.

[Thus, affixing the name to the generality, opposite-from-non-ox, allows one to recognize all instances of oxen because] (1) it is applied to opposite-from-non-ox and (2) opposite-from-non-ox is concomitant with all instances of oxen.

According to the Sāṃkhyas, the term "ox" is a complete engager [evoking an understanding of everything that is of one substantial entity with ox] and therefore must express everything that is one entity with ox. For this reason it also expresses the generality which is a permanent functioning thing.

According to Sāṃkhya, the name "ox" is not an eliminative or partial engager operating through the exclusion of non-ox because it is not established merely through the power of terminology but through the power of the thing—here, the ox—itself; therefore, it is a complete engager. A term of complete engagement must express everything that is of one entity with the object expressed. Since the generality ox is one entity with the individual ox, the term "ox" must express both the general and the specific ox.

Therefore when someone initially takes a white ox as a basis and affixes the appellation saying, "This is an ox," the appellation is also affixed to the generality which is a permanent functioning thing. Due to the fact that [according to Sāṃkhya] the general principal pervades all instances of oxen, later when one sees a black ox, one understands [what it is] and thinks "ox" without needing to consider any other reasons.

The Sāṃkhyas assert that the general principal is partless and that it is a permanent functioning thing. On the basis of this they posit ox and tree generalities and so forth that are permanent functioning things, but due to their not knowing how to posit [generality and instance] as different isolates in connection with how these are expressed by terms, they have to say that since the generality which is a permanent functioning thing is concomitant with its instances, the nature of a mottled ox itself is the nature of a pale yellow ox and the nature of a pale yellow ox is the nature of a mottled one.

They are forced to take this position because of their assertion that the ox generality which equally pervades yellow and mottled oxen is itself partless. Thus, argue the Buddhists, its entire indivisible nature must be present in each of its instances; consequently, the nature of all instances must be the same. Therefore, although the Sāṃkhyas do distinguish between generalities of different types—between an ox generality and a tree generality, for example—they are forced to say that the entire partless ox generality resides in or applies to all instances of ox. This ox generality itself is a permanent functioning thing; the oxen which it pervades are impermanent.

In the Buddhist view, the Sāṃkhyas are credited with understanding how to assert that a generality and its instances are one entity but not with understanding that they are different for thought or, more technically, different isolates. Sāṃkhyas do not see that terms such as "generality" and "instance" are posited by the force of terminology but consider these as posited by the force of the thing.

Dharmakīrti's *Commentary on (Dignāga's) "Compendium on Valid Cognition"* in many places throughout the text demonstrates damage to this assertion.

Further, the Hearer schools [Vaibhāṣika and Sautrāntika] assert partless particles and the Sāṃkhyas assert a partless general principal; although the name is the same, the meanings [of "partless"] differ. For, the [Vaibhāṣika and Sautrāntika] assertion that minute particles are partless means that [such a particle] does not have many parts which are itself and which are of its own essential nature. The [Sāṃkhya's] meaning of the principal's being partless is that it does not have many isolate-factors that are concomitant with its many instances.

In the Hearer (*nyan thos, śrāvaka*) schools it is not contradictory for a minute particle, even though partless, to be a generality. For [such a partless particle] is the generality of minute particles in the east, west, and so forth.

Question: Although these three—a sandalwood tree, an aloewood tree, and a pot—are equally different entities, an awareness of [their being the] same type is generated with respect to sandalwood and aloewood, but an awareness of [being the] same type does not develop with respect to sandalwood and a pot? Why is this?

Answer: The Sāṃkhyas say that this [awareness that sandalwood tree and aloewood tree are the same type in the sense of both being trees] occurs due to the tree general principal, the reason being that the tree general principal is concomitant with these two—sandalwood and aloewood—but is not concomitant with a pot.

Question: Since this demonstrates a reasoning proving the existence of a [partless] principal, what is such [a principal]?

Answer: With respect to the subjects, the manifestations of tree such as sandalwood and aloewood, and the manifestations of pot such as gold pot and copper pot, there must be some cause for understanding these individually as a single type [that is, the former as trees and the latter as pots] without confusing them for, if there were not, such an understanding would not occur. Thereby it is proven that a cause exists which is the agent of various individual effects; and it would not be suitable for this cause to be other than the general principal.

Question: What is the nature of this general principal?

Answer: It is a non-manifest functioning thing [that cannot appear to anyone's awareness] which includes the natures of all instances into one. Because the [formerly non-manifest] instances are made manifest by it, they are called manifestations.

For example, the Sāṃkhyas say that when the seed of an oak tree exists, a non-manifest oak exists right with that seed. As the seedling grows, the oak tree becomes manifest. Because this tree is said to be pervaded by the oak tree general principal, it is a manifestation or instance of that generality.

Our own [Buddhist system], having refuted this [Sāṃkhya assertion] of a general principal, says that opposite-from-non-tree, an exclusion [or negative phenomenon] itself is common to sandalwood and aloewood but not to oxen. However, sameness of type cannot be posited merely due to that. If it could, then it would follow that the two, a human and an ox, would be one type because the exclusion opposite-from-non-sentient-being is concomitant with both.

Persons and oxen are not one type even though both are instances of opposite-from-non-sentient-being. However, from one point of view it can be said that all impermanent phenomena are of the same type in that they are all products. Similarly, all existing phenomena are one type in the sense that the exclusion, opposite-

from-non-object-of-knowledge, is common to all. However, this does not prove that they are one type in general.

Therefore, the final reason for positing [certain phenomena as] the same type is: two phenomena are posited as one type [if] those trained in terminology naturally develop a mental conception of them as similar through merely seeing them up on turning the mind [to them]. Therefore, it follows that the subjects, a white ox and a black one, are the same type because they appear to be similar to the innate minds of those trained in terminology upon [such persons] merely seeing them. It follows that the subjects—the two, a white ox and a pot—are not the same type because they do not appear to be similar to the innate minds of such persons.

There is a reason for the appearance of such similarity and dissimilarity. It is due to the internal conditions of a predominant familiarization [or conditioning] with predispositions from beginningless time for calling both white and black oxen a single type, "ox," and there are no predominant predispositions of expression for conceiving that the two, a white ox and a pot, are a single type of this sort.

[The appearance of similarity of type also occurs] because of external conditions. Both white and black oxen equally possess a hump, dewlap, and so forth whereas the two, a white ox and a pot, do not equally possess such features. Beyond that, from the viewpoint that both the white and black oxen are equal in being the opposite of non-ox, these two are also one type of isolate. Therefore, an awareness of sameness of type develops with respect to the two of them. For example, although the colors of human beings are many [white, black, yellow, and so forth] the black color of their shadows appear to be a single type.

Therefore, between the two kinds of sameness of type: (1) being the same type of isolate [that is, being the same opposite from non-] and (2) being the same substantial type, the two—gold pot and copper pot—are an example of the first. Because these two are the same in being opposite from non-pot, they are said to be one type of isolate. [An example] of the second kind [sameness of type] is two different kernels of barley that are produced from a single barley kernel. Because these two are the same in having been produced from the single barley kernel which is their substantial cause, they are one substantial type (*rdzas rigs gcig*), but they are not one substantiality (*rdzas gcig*), for if one has ceased, the other has not necessarily ceased.

With that as an illustration, if one wishes to analyze [the term] "substance" (*rdzas, dravya*) it undoubtedly is understood differently by (1) the Vaiśeṣikas, when they speak of a substance that acts as a basis for qualities which are factually different [from itself]; (2) the Sāṃkhyas, and so forth when they speak of the non-manifest general principal as substantially existent in the sense of being self-sufficient; (3) the poets, when they speak of an epithet which expresses the nature of a substance; (4) followers of the Collected Topics on Valid Cognition, when they speak of substantial phenomena and reverse phenomena; (5) the Vaibhāṣikas, when they speak of the three uncaused [phenomena] as substantial and of the sameness of substance of the vows of male and female clergy; (6) the Sautrāntikas, when they speak of that which is able to perform the function of holding up rafters as having all three qualities and being substantially existent; (7) the Cittamātrins, when they speak of the single substantial entity of the two—the blue and the eye consciousness perceiving blue; and (8) the Mādhyamikas, when they speak of not asserting substantial establishment. Being of dull faculties, I am not competent to state these just as they are. However, you who have great wisdom, please decide it.

Thus when, having taken a white ox as the basis, the appellation "This bulky thing is an ox" is affixed due to the essential of the appellation "ox" being affixed by virtue of this bulky thing being an aggregation of a hump and so forth; then, because black oxen also are aggregations of a hump and so forth, all oxen are of one type.

All oxen, regardless of color, can be designated "ox" because they

> are all aggregations of hump, dewlap, and so forth. They are the same type. Thus, a person who knows terminology, without needing to rely on any other reason, develops a similar type of mind with respect to oxen of any color.

Question: When, taking a white ox as the base, the appellation "ox" is applied, what is the object of engagement (*'jug yul, pravṛttiviṣaya*) of that appellation?
Answer: At that time the white ox itself is the base of affixing the appellation "ox," but it is not the object of engagement. For, if it were the object of engagement of the term "ox," it would have to be the object of the mode of apprehension (*'dzin stangs kyi yul*) of the thought consciousness which apprehends ox, in which case it would also be the referent object (*zhen yul, *adhyavasaya-viṣaya*) of that term.

> The questioner is wondering whether the white ox present at the time of initially learning the name is the object of engagement of the term "ox." It is not. The white ox is just the basis of affixing the term, the place of apprehending (*'dzin sa*) the actual referent object of expression of the term "ox"—the opposite from non-ox, or ox itself. However, the *white ox* is not the referent object of the expression; it is merely the base which serves as a specific example of what is referred to by the term "ox." When one initially learns the name ox, one thinks, "This is an ox," not "This is a white ox."
>
> It would be unsuitable if, at the time of learning the name, the instructor said, "This is a white ox." For, later when one saw a black ox, one would incorrectly call it a "white ox." In fact, the name is affixed by reason of the object's being a bulky thing which is an aggregation of hump and dewlap, and not due to the feature of its having the color white. Therefore, later when one sees an ox of a different color, one can recognize it as suitable to be called an ox because of its shape.

Therefore, the actual objects of engagement of the appellation "ox" are the two, ox and opposite-from-non-ox. For, Kay-drup's *Clearing Away Mental Darkness with Respect to the Seven Treatises* (*sDe bdun yid kyi mun sel*) says:

> When the appellation "ox" is [initially] connected [to an object] with a white ox taken as the basis, there

> are two main objects of that appellation: ox [a positive phenomenon] and opposite-from-non-ox, an exclusion (*sel ba, apoha*) [or negative phenomenon]. The meaning-of-the-term ["ox"]—the appearance of white ox as opposite from non-ox—is also a mere object of the appellation.

You cannot make a terminological connection without having some base. The base in this case is the white ox, but the name is not intended to express merely a white ox. Rather, opposite-from-non-ox is the main object, and it appears in dependence on the specific white ox. The white ox is part of the process of connecting the name, but the purpose of this process is not to cause ascertainment of only that particular white ox. For, the white ox is an object of lesser pervasion than the main object—the opposite-from-non-ox—which is concomitant with, or applies to, all instances of oxen.

This is so; it is like the fact that when the expression "impermanent sound," for example, is stated, sound is the basis of affixing the term "impermanent," but it is not the object of engagement of the term "impermanent" [that is, it is not the referent of the term "impermanent"].

Sound is just the basis of which impermanence is a quality. Thus, when impermanence is expressed in relation to a sound, the impermanence is a quality of sound and shares the same locus with it, but what appears to the mind is impermanence, not sound. This point is addressed in the following debate.

Opponent: When, having taken a white ox as a basis, the terminological connection "This is an ox" is made in the continuum of the hearer, does there or does there not develop a thought consciousness apprehending that the white ox is an ox? If you say that such is developed, then it follows that the subject, the thought consciousness apprehending a white ox as an ox, apprehends a composite meaning of white ox and ox because (1) the thought consciousness apprehending sound as impermanent apprehends an object that is a composite of sound and impermanence and (2) terms and thought consciousnesses operate similarly.

Our own scholars respond: There is no fault here. For, the purpose of proving sound to be impermanent is to prove impermanence in relation to sound; therefore, when the thing being proven by that proof [i.e., that sound is impermanent] is realized, [the realizing consciousness] must engage a composite meaning of the quality [impermanence] and the qualified [sound]. [However], the purpose of connecting the appellation "ox" [is different], for the appellation is [initially] connected for the sake of [later] understanding black oxen and so forth as oxen when one uses the convention [in the future]. Since the terminological connection is not made for the sake of understanding the composite meaning of white ox and opposite-from-non-ox, there is no fault.

> Even though thought consciousnesses and terms are similar in being partial engagers, they are not similar in all respects. For example, the purpose of stating or proving that "sound is impermanent" is to realize sound as qualified by impermanence; thus, the expression refers to both the base—the sound—and its quality of impermanence. The initial connection of the name "ox," however, is for the sake of understanding what oxen are, not for the sake of understanding a composite of basis and quality, for its main object of engagement is just opposite-from-non-ox, not white ox.

In brief, it is unsuitable that only specifically characterized phenomena and not other-exclusions be explicit objects of terms and thoughts. Therefore if, at the time of a terminological connection, the appellation were applied only to the specifically characterized phenomenon and not to the exclusion [such as opposite-from-non-ox], then when the appellation for "ox" is initially connected to a white ox, the terminological connection would be made to just the substantial entity of a white ox. In that case, later when one saw a black ox, it would [absurdly] follow that there would be no way to use the convention, "This is an ox." For, the white ox at the time of previously connecting the appellation is not concomitant with the black ox at the time of [later using] the convention. This reason follows because the white ox of the time of previously connecting the appellation has ceased and does not exist at the time of [later using] the convention.

The time of connecting the appellation refers to the occasion of initially hearing or identifying, "This is an ox." The time of using the convention refers to when one has understood the name and is using it with respect to various instances of, for example, oxen. In general, "appellation" and "convention" mean the same thing, but the time of connecting the appellation is different from the time of making a terminological connection using the convention.

Question: Does this fault not apply to you too?
Answer: The fault does not apply [to us] because [we consider] the terminological connection is made to opposite-from-non-ox—an exclusion which is a mere elimination of non-ox—which itself does not cease but exists at the time [of later using the convention].

This is another way of emphasizing that the appellation is connected to a mere elimination, opposite-from-non-ox, not to the white ox in particular. This mere elimination is common to all manifestations or instances of oxen.

Or, [it could be said that the reason why the above fault does not apply to us is that] at the time [of later using the convention], the meaning-of-the-term—the appearance to thought of white ox as opposite from non-ox—has not ceased but exists. In this vein, Sagya Paṇḍiṭa's *Treasury of Reasoning* says:

> Because individual specifically characterized phenomena
> Are limitless, an appellation cannot be [connected to each].
> Also, at the time of using the convention
> It is difficult to find the initial specifically characterized phenomenon.

This means that if the appellation "ox" did explicitly express specifically characterized oxen, then since oxen are limitless, the connection of an appellation to such [a limitless number of objects] would be impossible. Even if one allowed that it was possible, then since the oxen at the time of connecting the appellation would be different in place, time, and nature when [later using] the convention, it would be difficult to find the original oxen just as they were.

Furthermore, an opponent says: When the appellation "ox" is initially connected to a white ox, is the appellation [also] applied to black ones or not? If the appellation is [also connected to black oxen and so forth], then it follows that the subject, the term "ox" is a complete engager [as the Sāṃkhyas propound] because it expresses that all manifestations of oxen—black ones and so forth—are oxen. If, however, the appellation is not connected [to black oxen] how is a black ox understood as an ox at the time of [later using] the convention?

Response: Even though the appellation is not explicitly connected to black oxen at the time of initially connecting the appellation, there is no fault of not being able to understand [a black ox] as an ox at the time of [later using] the convention. For, when the appellation for ox is initially connected, that terminological connection is made to opposite-from-non-ox—that is, to the elimination of non-ox. At that time, therefore, a thought consciousness develops in the continuum of the hearer which apprehends the white ox as being an ox, within thinking, "the convention 'ox' is designated to this sort of bulky thing which is an aggregation of hump, dewlap, and so forth." [As long as] the functioning [i.e., impact] of this thought does not deteriorate, when [the person] sees a black ox he understands [that it is an ox], thinking, "Because this bulky thing is also an aggregation of a hump, dewlap, and so forth, it is an ox."

About this an opponent says: In that case, when it is stated that "This pot is impermanent," it [absurdly] follows that the appellation also refers to opposite-from-non-impermanent, because you asserted [the above].

It was presented above that when the appellation "ox" is initially

> connected to a white ox, the terminological connection is made to opposite-from-non-ox. This, it was also mentioned, is present in all types of oxen.

If you accept this, when the hearer later hears a sound, he would understand that this sound also is impermanent; and that being the case, there would be no point in reasonings and inferences proving that sound is impermanent.

Response: There is no fault of such a consequence. Saying that "by connecting the appellation to a generality all its instances can be understood" is just a loose explanation; it is not held that it is necessarily so [in all circumstances]. If there were such binding necessity, even in our own system [there would be the fault of contradicting] that it does indeed happen that even though the appellation "ox" had been earlier connected with respect to a small ox, there are cases, when a large ox is seen later on, of being mistaken due to the difference in size such that one does not understand [the larger ox] to be an ox.

> Thus, there is no definiteness or pervasion that a person for whom a small ox has been designated as an ox will later develop a mind that thinks "ox" with respect to a large ox.

There is no denying that such [error] can occur; nevertheless, such a person sees with direct perception a bulky thing which is an aggregation of hump, dewlap, and so forth in connection with the large ox, due to which he has realized the complete meaning-isolate [the mere actual meaning] of ox. Yet, merely due to not knowing how to use the convention "ox" with respect to this [large one], there is a purpose in setting out a reason establishing the mere convention ["ox"] for the sake of his understanding [that this bulky thing is called an ox].

> The person already knows the aggregation of hump, dewlap, and so forth; what remains is just to learn that this is called an ox. For this, it is necessary to set out a reasoning establishing the name or convention.

Also, a means of establishing the mere [verbal] convention exists. This is stated [as follows]: "The subject, this large bulky thing which has a lump of flesh directly above its two shoulders, is an ox because of having the nature of [being] an aggregation of hump, dewlap, and so forth." When [this is stated], in dependence on the functioning of that syllogism, the person is not caused to realize newly a meaning in addition to the object that he has already seen directly. However, the purpose of stating this [reasoning], called a "proof of *mere* convention" [and not a combination of convention and meaning] through this syllogism is established when there occurs (1) the mere understanding of how to use the term "ox" in relation to this [large bulky thing] and (2) the mere understanding of how conceptually to use newly the convention in thought, thinking "ox" [in relation to the large bulky thing]. Therefore, this syllogism is stated for the sake of establishing the mere convention "ox" for one who does not understand that a bulky thing which is an aggregation of hump, dewlap, and so forth, is the sign of the meaning of an ox.

Through this illustration, the meaning of all reasonings proving mere conventions is to be understood in the same way. Further, there is another reason why once one has ascertained a pot as impermanent one does not later, on hearing a sound, understand sound as impermanent. For, in general, the continuum of a pot exists for years and months due to the prolongation of a continuum of similar type, but with regard to a sound, direct perception establishes that there is no continuum lasting that long; therefore, compared to sound it is not easier to realize pot as impermanent. Nevertheless, due to the power of mistaken conceptions that pollute the continuum through [mistaken] tenets, there are persons who have previously ascertained pot as impermanent and for whom it is necessary to later ascertain sound as impermanent.

"Positive and Negative Phenomena"

from

The Collected Topics by
A Spiritual Son of Jam-yang-shay-ba

by Nga-wang-dra-shi

TRANSLATOR'S PREFACE

The Gelukba scholar-monks who maintain the oral traditions of their order are mainly those who attain the rank of Geshe. From beginning to end of the approximately twenty-year Geshe curriculum, the student hones his understanding of philosophical points through exchanging syllogistic probes and barbs with fellow students.[1] The syllogistic language of debate gives the enterprise its formal structure but, beyond the beginning stages, the mental agility required to analyze complex philosophical issues makes this endeavor both creative and educational. It demands intense concentration, speedy and precise repartee. Nor is all the action mental. The standing challenger maintains an almost constant motion of swirling arms, stamping feet, and clapping hands, the latter often startlingly close to the face of the seated defender. Fellow students and, at public debates, members of the audience, relate to this spectacle with vociferous enthusiasm; indeed the annual performances in Lhasa of Geshe candidates from the major Gelukba colleges, an important part of traditional New Year celebrations, was as galvanizing in Tibet as our own New Year's gridiron events are in contemporary North America.

The defender must keep his wits about him in the face of all such distractions. He must respond to the challenger, either by accepting statements given, questioning the reason stated, or denying a logically significant relationship between reason and predicate. Both he and the challenger have trained in the same major texts; as advanced students, they have mapped out complex taxonomies and memorized hundreds of definitions as well as thousands of lines from sutra and commentarial literature. Buddha's famous injunction to "Examine my teaching as a goldsmith examines gold" is here executed with vigor. In the debating courtyard students learn to challenge their material, at the same time becoming steeped in its particular horizons of inquiry. Embedded as it is in monastic life and commitment, this is not the activity of a skeptic. The intellectual agility required in such debate thus serves to preserve, not to undermine, the tradition itself.

The *Collected Topics by a Spiritual Son of Jam-yang-shay-ba* by Nga-wang-dra-shi (*Ngag-dbang-bkra-shis*, 1648–1721) was written as a debate text for Gomang College. The section on negative and positive phenomena translated here offers relatively simple debates exploring the meaning and parameters of these categories. This topic has two sub-sections, a refutation of erroneous views and a presentation of the text's own system (*rang lugs*).[2]

The first sub-section consists of a series of debates, each of which opens with an opponent, or defender, making a statement pertinent to negative or positive phenomena.[3] The respondent challenges this statement by pointing out the absurdities it entails or inconsistencies derived from it. The defender is thus caused to participate, step by step, in a logical argument that may undermine his initial assertion. The sanctioned purpose is neither to embarrass the defender nor exalt the challenger—though this does happen—but to refine and extend the understanding of both.

The second sub-section is a presentation of Gomang College's own position on negative phenomena. Readers may find the topic more comprehensible if they turn to this section first. Debaters memorize the definitions and explanations in this section for use in their own debates; they also study other texts to garner different opinions and approaches to the topic—the better to outwit their next opponent. It is said that a good debater can defend any side of a position; can, for example, refute Prāsaṅgika on the basis of Cittamātrin tenets and then refute Cittamātra through Prāsaṅgika assertions. One argues a position, not necessarily out of conviction, but to pit one textual perspective against another so as to aid conceptual grasp of material that, in the Gelukba system, is essential to meditation praxis.[4] The various colleges within the Gelukba monastic university system have developed their own texts which, until recently, were often jealously guarded from students at rival colleges.

The points raised in the debates translated here are vital to the Gelukba understanding of negative and positive phenomena. This topic, in turn forms an integral part of their presentation of a path to liberation. In accordance with their interpretation of Prāsaṅgika-Mādhyamika, Gelukbas maintain that a direct cognition of emptiness, the lack of inherent existence, is indispensable to liberation. This emptiness is a negative phenomenon. To study the characteristics of negative phenomena in general is therefore to approach an understanding of emptiness. It is also to understand the possibility of cognizing that which is a *mere absence* of something else. In this context, it is important to note that according to Gelukba interpretations, negatives, and thus emptinesses, are objects to be known, not verbal descriptions of such objects, and that some negative phenomena can be realized directly.

Enthusiasm for scholastic debate continues vigorously among the Tibetan refugee monastic communities in India. The country of Buddhism's birth has offered land in Karnataka and Mysore states for the resettlement of Tibetan monasteries, which were destroyed or emptied as the Cultural Revolution took its toll in Tibet. In South India the traditional style of Tibetan education continues, slowly intermingling with new educational agendas such as the learning of English. The zest displayed during long hours of debate is impressive. Going down to the courtyard, the students can be heard rehearsing questions and issues; returning several hours later they walk slowly in twos and threes, still engrossed in their debates of the day. It is unclear how long such matters will continue to attract the best minds of Tibet's next generation. It will be a study unto itself to observe how the traditional agenda of perpetuating textual authority may change in the face of modern western alliances with the hermeneutics of suspicion, with all the problems this raises about issues of authority, methods of inquiry, and the nature of truth.

TRANSLATION

with oral commentary from Jambel Shenpen Rinbochay

REFUTATION OF ERRORS AND ELIMINATION OF OBJECTIONS

REFUTATION # 1 (451.18)

Opponent: Whatever is a functioning thing[5] is necessarily a positive phenomenon.[6]
Response: It [absurdly] follows that the subject, impermanent sound, is a positive phenomenon because of being a functioning thing. You have already accepted the entailment that whatever is a functioning thing is necessarily a positive phenomenon.[7]

> Most other Gelukba texts say that impermanent sound is a positive phenomenon. According to this text, however, impermanence itself as well as impermanent sound are negative phenomena.

Opponent: I accept that impermanent sound is a positive phenomenon.
Response: It follows that the subject, impermanent sound, is not a positive phenomenon because of being a negative phenomenon.
Opponent: The reason—that impermanent sound is a negative phenomenon—is not established.
Response: It follows that the subject, impermanent sound, is a negative phenomenon because (1) it is a phenomenon which must be realized through an explicit elimination of its own object of negation by the mind that explicitly realizes it and (2) it is a phenomenon that must be expressed through an explicit elimination of its own object of negation by the term which expresses it.
Opponent: The second reason—that impermanent sound is a phenomenon which must be expressed through an explicit elimination of its own object of negation by the term which expresses it—is not established.
Response: The subject, impermanent sound, is a phenomenon which must be expressed through an explicit elimination of

its object of negation by the term which expresses it because it [impermanent sound] is that which is expressed *as* impermanent sound upon the verbally explicit elimination that sound is permanent by the term expressing impermanent sound. The case is similar also with respect to a mind apprehending impermanent sound.

> The monastic colleges other than Gomang maintain that even though the literal phrase "impermanent sound" does explicitly eliminate permanent sound, when impermanent sound is realized, permanent sound is not explicitly eliminated. Momentarily disintegrating sound is explicitly established but permanent sound is not explicitly eliminated by a mind realizing impermanent sound. Rather, momentary disintegration is mainly what appears. Thus, for these colleges impermanent sound is a positive phenomenon. According to all colleges, whether something is positive or negative does not depend on the literal words expressing or naming that thing, but on how the phenomenon appears to the mind. Even if the term expressing a phenomenon does not contain negative words or syllables such as "not," "less," "im," and so forth, if the way that object appears to the mind is through the explicit elimination of an object of negation, it is a negative phenomenon. All colleges, including Gomang, agree on this. Therefore, although whatever has a negative particle according to Gomang, necessarily expresses a negative phenomenon, all negative phenomena are not necessarily expressed by terms having negative particles.

REFUTATION # 2 (452.14)

[This debate revolves around the way negatives are expressed in Tibetan.]

Opponent: Whatever is a phenomenon whose own actual name ends in the [Tibetan] syllable "*med*" [analogous with "less" in the English words "selfless" or "hatless"] is necessarily a non-affirming negative.

Response: It [absurdly] follows that the subject, the Buddha-Whose-Life-Is-Limitless (*Tshe-dpag-med*, *Amitāyus*) is a non-affirming negative (*med dgag*, *prasajyapratiṣedha*) because it is a phenomenon whose own actual name ends in the syllable "less." You have asserted the entailment that whatever is a phenomenon whose own actual name ends in the syllable "less" is necessarily a non-affirming negative.

Opponent: The reason—that the Buddha-Whose-Life-Is-Limitless is a phenomenon whose own actual name ends in the syllable "less"—is not established.

Response: It follows that the subject, the Buddha-Whose-Life-Is-Limitless, is a phenomenon whose own actual name ends in the syllable "less" because (1) the term "Buddha-Whose-Life-Is-Limitless" is his actual name and (2) it is manifestly established that the syllable "less" is at the end of that term.

Opponent: [I concede these points but] I accept [the original consequence] that the Buddha-Whose-Life-Is-Limitless is a non-affirming negative.

Response: It follows that the subject, the Buddha-Whose-Life-Is-Limitless, is not a non-affirming negative because of being a functioning thing.

Opponent: There is no entailment that whatever is a functioning thing is necessarily not a non-affirming negative.

Response: There is such entailment because whatever is a non-affirming negative is necessarily permanent.

The Buddha-Whose-Life-Is-Limitless is an affirming negative (*ma yin dgag, paryudāsapratiṣedha*) not a non-affirming negative. Even though in general Buddhas, like other persons, are positive phenomena, the Buddha-Whose-Life-Is-Limitless is a negative phenomenon because when one understands Buddha-Whose-Life-Is-Limitless one understands a person qualified by a lifetime that has no limit—not a hundred years, six hundred, or a million years. [In other words], that his life-span has a limit is explicitly negated; by way of this negation one understands a person whose life is measureless. Thus, this person of limitless life appears by way of a negation of limited life and a suggestion of a person of limitless life in its place. Because a positive phenomenon—a Buddha—is implied in place of the object negated, this is an affirming negative, not a non-affirming negative which would not suggest any positive in place of what is negated.

Similarly, an empty wallet is an affirming negative because the statement "empty wallet" suggests the wallet—a positive phenomenon—which is qualified by being empty. However, "There is no money in an empty wallet" expresses a non-affirming negative because nothing is suggested in place of the money which is negated.

REFUTAION # 3 (453.10)

Opponent: Whatever is a negative phenomenon necessarily has a negative syllable as part of its actual name.
Response: It [absurdly] follows that the subject, space (*nam mkha', ākāśa*) is a phenomenon having a negative syllable as part of its actual name because it is a negative phenomenon. You have already asserted the entailment that whatever is a negative phenomenon has a negative syllable as part of its actual name.
Opponent: The reason—that space is a negative phenomenon—is not established.
Response: It follows that the subject, space, is a non-affirming negative that is a mere lack of obstructive contact because it is uncaused space.
Opponent: [I concede these points but] I accept [the original consequence] that space is a phenomenon having a negative syllable as part of its actual name.
Response: It follows that the subject, space, is not a phenomenon having a negative syllable as part of its actual name because there is no negative syllable that is part of its actual name.
Opponent: The reason—that there is no negative syllable that is part of the actual name "space"—is not established.
Response: It follows with respect to the subject, space, that there is no negative syllable which is part of its actual name because (1) the term "space" is its actual name and (2) this is not a negative syllable.[8]

Furthermore, [if you assert that whatever is a negative phenomenon necessarily has a negative syllable as part of its actual name] it would [absurdly] follow that the subject, reality (*chos nyid, dharmatā*) is a phenomenon which has a negative syllable as part of its actual name[9] because it is a negative phenomenon. You have asserted the entailment that whatever is a negative phenomenon necessarily has a negative syllable as part of its actual name.
Opponent: The reason—that reality is a negative phenomenon—is not established.

Response: It follows that the subject, reality, is a negative phenomenon because it is a non-affirming negative. You cannot assert the converse of the first consequence[10]—that reality is not a negative—because although there is no negative syllable that is part of its actual name, it is a phenomenon which must be realized through an explicit elimination of its object of negation by the mind that explicitly realizes it.
Opponent: There is no entailment that whatever is a phenomenon which must be realized through an explicit elimination of its own object of negation by the mind that realizes it is necessarily a negative phenomenon even though there is no negative syllable that is part of its actual name.
Response: There is entailment that whatever is realized in this way is necessarily a negative phenomenon because any phenomenon which must be realized by way of the explicit elimination of its object of negation by the mind that explicitly realizes it is necessarily a negative phenomenon.

REFUTATION # 4 (455.5)

Opponent: It follows that the subject, form, is a negative phenomenon because it is a phenomenon which must be realized by way of an explicit elimination of its own object of negation by the mind that explicitly realizes it.
Response: The reason—that form is a phenomenon which must be realized by way of an explicit elimination of its own object of negation by the mind that explicitly realizes it—is not established.
Opponent: The subject, form, is a phenomenon which must be realized by way of an explicit elimination of its own object of negation by the mind that explicitly realizes it because it is a phenomenon that must be realized by way of an explicit elimination of its own object of negation by the thought consciousness that explicitly realizes it.
Response: The reason—that form is a phenomenon which must be realized by way of an explicit elimination of its own object of negation by the thought that explicitly realizes it—is not

established.
Opponent: It follows that the subject, form, is a phenomenon which must be realized through an explicit elimination of its own object of negation by the thought that explicitly realizes it because it is a phenomenon which must be realized by way of the elimination of what is not itself by the thought that apprehends it.
Response: There is no entailment that whatever is a phenomenon which must be realized through an elimination of what is not itself by the thought that apprehends it is necessarily a phenomenon which must be realized by way of an explicit elimination of its own object of negation by the thought consciousness that apprehends it.
Opponent: The reason—that form is a phenomenon which must be realized through an elimination of what is not itself by the thought that apprehends it—is not established.
Response: It follows that the subject, form, is a phenomenon which must be realized through an elimination of what is not itself by the thought that realizes it because it is an established base.

All established bases—all phenomena that exist—are realized through the elimination of what is *not* that established base by the thought consciousness realizing them. Although what is not that thing is eliminated, it is not necessarily *explicitly* eliminated. For example, the thought consciousness explicitly realizing the presence of money implicitly realizes the non-existence of a lack of money and implicitly eliminates a lack of money, but this implicit elimination does not mean that money is a negative phenomenon. For although there is no thought consciousness which is an *ex*plicit realizer of something without also being an *im*plicit realizer of something else, this does not mean that whatever is cognized by thought is a negative phenomenon.

REFUTATION # 5 (456.1)

Opponent: It follows that the subject, a pot, is not a positive phenomenon because it is a negative phenomenon.
Response: The reason—that a pot is a negative phenomenon—is

not established.
Opponent: It follows that the subject, a pot, is a negative phenomenon because it is a phenomenon which must be realized by way of the explicit elimination of what is not it by the thought consciousness that explicitly realizes it.
Response: There is no entailment that whatever is a phenomenon which must be realized by way of the explicit elimination of what is not it by the thought consciousness that explicitly realizes it is necessarily a negative phenomenon.

The reason—that a pot is a phenomenon which must be realized through an elimination of non-pot by the thought consciousness that explicitly realizes it—is established because it is an established base.[11]

Opponent: [I concede these points but] I accept the initial consequence that a pot is a negative phenomenon.
Response: It follows that the subject, a pot, is not a negative phenomenon because it is a positive phenomenon.
Opponent: The reason—that a pot is a positive phenomenon—is not established.
Response: It follows that the subject, a pot, is a positive phenomenon because it is one with pot.

> A thought consciousness explicitly realizing pot realizes it by way of eliminating that which is not a pot, but does not realize it by way of *explicitly* eliminating such. Therefore, it does not follow from this reason that a pot is a negative phenomenon. For example, if one has a thought consciousness realizing "I have money" this thought consciousness realizes its object by way of eliminating the lack of money but does not do so explicitly.

REFUTATION # 6 (456.16)

Opponent: Whatever is an affirming negative is necessarily a phenomenon expressed by a term that explicitly suggests another phenomenon—either an affirming negative or a positive phenomenon—in place of its own negated object of negation.
Response: It [absurdly] follows that the corpulent Devadatta's not eating during the day is expressed by a term that explicitly suggests another phenomenon which is either an affirming

negative or a positive phenomenon in place of its own negated object of negation because it is an affirming negative. You have accepted the entailment.
Opponent: The reason—that the corpulent Devadatta's not eating during the day is an affirming negative—is not established.
Response: It follows that the subject, the corpulent Devadatta's not eating during the day, is an affirming negative because the term that expresses it suggests another phenomenon—either an affirming negative or a positive phenomenon—through an explicit and literal negation of its own object of negation. That the reason is so follows because (1) the term expressing it [the above subject], having explicitly negated eating during the day, implicitly suggests eating at night and (2) eating at night is a positive phenomenon.
Opponent: [I concede this but] I accept the initial consequence that the corpulent Devadatta who does not eat during the day is expressed by a term that explicitly suggests either a non-affirming negative or a positive phenomenon in place of its own negated object of negation.
Response: This cannot be accepted because even though the phrase "The corpulent Devadatta does not eat during the day" does not explicitly suggest another phenomenon that is either an affirming negative or a positive phenomenon upon the verbally explicit negation of its object of negation, it does *implicitly* suggest such [i.e., it implicitly suggests a positive phenomenon].

It follows that the phrase ["The corpulent Devadatta does not eat during the day"] does implicitly suggest a positive phenomenon because the phrase "The corpulent Devadatta does not eat during the day," having explicitly negated eating during the day, implicitly suggests eating at night.

An affirming negative or a positive phenomenon is suggested *in place of* what is negated, like a person's getting up from a chair and someone else's sitting down on the same chair. Here, the object of negation is Devadatta's eating during the day. The locus of this non-eating during the day is Devadatta. For example, if someone says, "I have no money," the locus of the lack of money is that person. In the same way, Devadatta here is the base of the negation. In place of the eating during the day that is negated, it is suggested that Devadatta eats at night. The implication arises because Devadatta is described as fat. If it were not specified that Devadatta is fat, his eating at night would not be implied. For example, if Diana is very busy and declines to eat when invited by others, and if a friend of hers reports that "Diana didn't eat during the day," only non-eating is suggested. There is no implication that she will eat at night. Thus, this latter statement expresses a non-affirming negative.

Context can alter whether a phrase expresses an affirming or a non-affirming negative. For example, if someone says "I have no money," one way to understand this is as a non-affirming negative but in certain contexts it could also be understood to mean, "Do *you* have any money?" Or even, "Do you have any money to loan me?" How much a given phrase suggests depends to some extent on circumstances. Therefore, under certain conditions, the phrase "Devadatta does not eat during the day" could suggest that he eats at night. When it does so suggest, the phrase expresses an affirming negative. In general, however, "Devadatta does not eat during the day" expresses a non-affirming negative.

REFUTATION # 7 (458.5)

Opponent: It follows that the term "The corpulent Devadatta does not eat during the day" does not implicitly suggest another phenomenon—either an affirming negative or a positive phenomenon—upon the verbally explicit negation of its own object of negation because the term "Brahmins do not drink beer" does not implicitly suggest another phenomenon that is either an affirming negative or a positive phenomenon upon the verbally explicit negation of its own object of negation.
Response: There is no entailment that if the term "Brahmins do not drink beer" does not implicitly suggest another phenomenon—either an affirming negative or a positive phenomenon—upon the verbally explicit negation of its own object of negation, then the term "The corpulent Devadatta does not eat during the day" does not implicitly suggest another phenomenon that is either an affirming negative or a positive phenomenon upon the verbally explicit negation of its own object of negation.

The reason—that [the statement] "Brahmins do not drink beer" does not implicitly suggest another affirming negative or a positive phenomenon upon the verbally explicit negation of its own object of negation—is established because the phrase "Brahmins do not drink beer" neither explicitly nor implicitly suggests another phenomenon upon the verbally explicit negation of its own object of negation.

The reason follows because the phrase "Brahmins do not drink beer" does not suggest another phenomenon that is either an affirming negative or a positive phenomenon upon the verbally explicit negation of its own object of negation. This follows because Brahmins' non-drinking of beer must be posited as a non-affirming negative.

The statement, "Brahmins do not drink beer," merely negates that they drink beer; it does not suggest that they drink anything else. [This example is a carryover from Mimāṃsā where it merely prohibits Brahmins from drinking alcohol without suggesting any other activity in place of what is prohibited.][12] However, if you say "The wet-throated Brahmin does not drink beer" this does suggest that he drinks something else. Moreover, although the phrase "Brahmins do not drink beer" does implicitly suggest Brahmins—positive phenomenon—Brahmins are not suggested *in place of* the object of negation. Therefore, a positive phenomenon [drinking something else] is not suggested in place of the negated object. Thus, Brahmins' not drinking beer is a non-affirming negative.

A term that expresses an affirming negative must suggest a positive phenomenon *in place of the object negated*. Here, Brahmins are the locus or basis of the negation of drinking beer; the statement simply posits a positive phenomenon that is the *locus* of the negation—Brahmins. The statement about Devadatta, on the other hand, suggests a positive phenomenon—eating at night—*in place of* what is being negated, mainly, eating during the day.

REFUTATION # 8 (459.7)

Opponent: Whatever is an affirming negative is necessarily expressed by a term that suggests another phenomenon—either an affirming negative or a positive phenomenon—upon the verbally explicit negation of its own object of negation.[13]

Response: It [absurdly] follows that the subject, a permanent phenomenon,[14] is expressed by a term that suggests another phenomenon–either an affirming negative or a positive phenomenon–upon the verbally explicit negation of its object of negation because it is a permanent phenomenon. You have asserted the entailment–that whatever is expressed by a term that indicates another phenomenon which is either an affirming negative or a positive phenomenon upon the verbally explicit negation of its own object of negation is necessarily an affirming negative.
Opponent: The reason–that a permanent phenomenon is an affirming negative–is not established.
Response: It follows that the subject, a permanent phenomenon, is an affirming negative because (1) it is a negative and (2) it is not a non-affirming negative.
Opponent: The first reason–that a permanent phenomenon is a negative–is not established.
Response: It follows that the subject, a permanent phenomenon, is a negative because it is permanent.
Opponent: There is no entailment that whatever is a permanent phenomenon is necessarily a negative phenomenon.
Response: The entailment–that whatever is a permanent phenomenon is necessarily a negative phenomenon–follows because there is no permanent positive phenomenon which is under its own power.[15]
Opponent: The reason–that there is no permanent positive phenomenon which is under its own power–is not established.
Response: It follows that there is no permanent positive phenomenon which is under its own power because whatever is a positive phenomenon which is under its own power is necessarily an [impermanent] functioning thing.
Opponent: [I concede these points but] I accept the original consequence that a permanent phenomenon is expressed by a term that suggests another phenomenon–either an affirming negative or a positive phenomenon–upon the verbally explicit negation of its object of negation.
Response: This cannot be asserted because although the term

which expresses [a permanent phenomenon] does suggest either an affirming negative or a positive phenomenon, it does not verbally negate its own object of negation because the term expressing "a permanent phenomenon" does not contain a negative word.

All the Gelukba colleges agree that the term "a permanent phenomenon" expresses an affirming negative insofar as when you understand the meaning of "a permanent phenomenon" you understand a common locus of being a phenomenon and being non-momentary (which is the definition or meaning of "permanent"). Even though there is no negative term in the phrase "a permanent phenomenon," when you understand its meaning you do so by way of explicitly eliminating the object of negation—momentary disintegration. Therefore, a permanent phenomenon is necessarily a negative phenomenon. However, Gomang goes further and asserts that *whatever* is a permanent phenomenon is necessarily a negative phenomenon. Therefore, unlike other colleges, Gomang asserts that object of knowledge (*shes bya, jñeya*), object of comprehension (*gzhal bya, prameya*) and so forth are negative phenomena. Gomang asserts this because object of knowledge and so forth are not positive phenomena which are under their own power. This is due to the fact that such phenomena are merely imputed by thought. According to Gomang, once they are not positive phenomena under their own power, they cannot be positive phenomena at all. The other colleges disagree on this point, saying that there are positive phenomena which are merely imputed by thought.

REFUTATION # 9 (460.9)

Opponent: Whatever is expressed by a term that suggests another phenomenon—either an affirming negative or a positive phenomenon—is necessarily a negative phenomenon.
Response: It [absurdly] follows that the subject, product (*byas pa, kṛta*), is a negative phenomenon because the term expressing it suggests another phenomenon which is either an affirming negative or a positive phenomenon. [It suggests the latter.]
Opponent: The reason—that product is expressed by a term that suggests another phenomenon which is either an affirming negative or a positive phenomenon—is not established.

Response: It follows that the term expressing the subject, product, suggests another phenomenon which is either an affirming negative or a positive phenomenon because this expressive term [implicitly] suggests the causes and conditions [of that product].

Opponent: [I concede these points but] I accept the original consequence that product is a negative phenomenon.

Response: It follows that the subject, product, is not a negative phenomenon because it is a positive phenomenon.

Opponent: The reason—that product is a positive phenomenon—is not established.

Response: It follows that the subject, product, is a positive phenomenon because (1) it is a functioning thing and (2) those two [product and functioning thing] are both similar [in being positive phenomena].

> The main point here is that product is not realized through an explicit elimination of its object of negation by the thought consciousness that realizes it even though the term "product" implicitly suggests the causes and conditions that produced the effect or product. However, these are not being suggested in place of an explicit object of negation.

REFUTATION #10 (461.8)

Opponent: The subject, product, is not a positive phenomenon because it is a negative phenomenon.

Response: The reason—that product is a negative phenomenon—is not established.

Opponent: It follows that product is a negative phenomenon because the product, sound, [literally: sound which is a product] is a negative phenomenon.

Response: The reason—that the product, sound, is a negative phenomenon—is not established.

Opponent: It follows that the product, sound, is a negative phenomenon because it is a phenomenon which must be expressed by the term [i.e., phrase] expressing "Sound is a product" by way of eliminating that sound is not a product.

Response: There is no entailment that if the product, sound, is a phenomenon which must be expressed by the term expressing "Sound is a product" by way of eliminating that sound is not a product, it is a negative phenomenon. For, it would [absurdly] follow for you that form is a negative phenomenon, because form is a phenomenon which must be expressed by way of the elimination of non-form by the term expressing "form".

Opponent: I accept the consequence that form is a negative phenomenon.

Response: It [absurdly] follows that positive phenomena do not exist because form is not a positive phenomenon.

Opponent: I accept the consequence that positive phenomena do not exist.

Response: It [absurdly] follows that whatever is an established base is necessarily a negative phenomenon because it is [not][16] a positive phenomenon. You have accepted the reason—that whatever is an established base is not a positive phenomenon. You cannot accept the consequence that whatever is an established base is necessarily a negative phenomenon.

> Once it has been explicitly understood that I have a hundred dollars, it is *implicitly* understood that I do not lack a hundred dollars. Nevertheless, the statement, "I have a hundred dollars" expresses a positive phenomenon. Similarly, if one says "form" it is *implicitly* understood that there is not non-form or that there is not an absence of form. Nevertheless, the term "form" expresses a positive phenomenon.

REFUTATION #11 (462.5)

Opponent: Form is not a phenomenon which must be expressed by way of the elimination of non-form by the term that expresses "form."

Response: It follows that form is a phenomenon which must be expressed through an elimination of non-form by the term that expresses "form" because [form] is a phenomenon which must be expressed by way of the exclusion of non-form by the term that expresses "form." It follows that [form] is a phenomenon which must be expressed through an exclusion of non-form by the term that expresses "form" because the term expressing "form" is a partial engager with respect to form.

There is the entailment that if form is expressed by a term which is a partial engager, it must be expressed through an exclusion of non-form by the term that expresses "form." This is because the meaning of being a partial engager must refer to excluding what is not that phenomenon.

PRESENTATION OF THE TEXT'S OWN POSITION (462.16)

The definition of a negative phenomenon is: a phenomenon which must be realized upon the explicit elimination of its own object of negation by the mind that explicitly realizes it.

Instead of saying that negative phenomena are realized by the *mind* perceiving them, most texts say that such phenomena are realized by the *thought consciousness* perceiving them. This is done in order to exclude direct perception because the direct perception in a Buddha's continuum realizes that Brahmins do not drink beer without explicitly eliminating that they do not drink beer. Buddhas never cognize through an explicit elimination; everything is known to them directly.

These four—negative [phenomenon] (*dgag pa, pratiṣedha*), exclusion (*sel ba, apoha*), other-exclusion (*gzhan sel, anyāpoha*), and reverse (*vyatireka ldog pa*)—are synonymous.

Negatives are divided into two [types]: affirming negatives and non-affirming negatives.[17]

The definition of an affirming negative is: A negative that is expressed by a phrase indicating another phenomenon—either an affirming negative or a positive phenomenon—in place of its own object of negation. An illustration of this is impermanent sound.

Impermanent sound is an affirming negative because the term expressing it—"impermanent sound"—indicates a positive phenomenon *in place of* the object of negation—permanent sound.

Conversely, the statement "Brahmins do not drink beer" refutes that they drink beer and also implies Brahmins, which are positive phenomena, but does not imply them in place of the object of negation. Therefore, the term "Brahmins do not drink beer" expresses a non-affirming negative.

The definition of a non-affirming negative is: A negative which is expressed by a phrase that does not indicate another phenomenon—either an affirming negative or a positive phenomenon—in place of its own object of negation. An illustration of this is the selflessness of persons.

If someone says "The self (*bdag, ātman*) of a person exists because the I (*nga, āham*) of a person exists," there is no entailment. The word "I" is a factually concordant word. Everyone uses it as in "I am reading," "I am tired," and so forth. Someone might think that if there is no self there is no I because in general self and I are synonymous, but here, however, the term "self" has a different meaning from the term "I" or "person." These latter two are factually concordant, corresponding to something that actually exists. The self of persons, however, refers to a self which is not merely imputed in dependence on the aggregates. Because no such self exists, the term "self" here is not factually concordant. Therefore, Buddhism teaches that the conception that such a self does exist must be abandoned.

Ordinary activities in the world are done for the sake of abandoning things that harm—such as fatigue and poverty—and taking up things that help. Thus, if one asks what is the thing to be abandoned by studying the Buddhist teaching, it is this: the powerless travelling in cyclic existence, the sufferings of birth, sickness, aging, and death. You cannot just throw these away like old clothing. Because the sufferings of birth and so forth are established in dependence on the body, one will definitely continue to cycle in these sufferings.

On what do the sufferings of birth and sickness depend? On beginningless actions and afflictions. And the root of these is the conception of a self of persons. If you come to realize selflessness thoroughly, then the actions and afflictions of cyclic existence become non-existent. Thereby, cyclic existence itself becomes non-existent [for you].

Thus, all established bases—everything that exists—as well as what does not exist are without a self of persons. The enemies that an Arhat [which the Tibetan etymologizes as "Foe Destroyer"] overcomes are birth, aging, sickness, and death. In order to abandon these, it is necessary to abandon the afflictions (*nyon mongs, kleśa*), the three poisons of desire, hatred, and ignorance. If one can abandon these, one is an Arhat.

The five divisions [of negatives] are those expressed by phrases: (1) explicitly suggesting, (2) implicitly suggesting, (3) both explicitly and implicitly suggesting, (4) contextually suggesting, and (5) not suggesting another phenomenon—either an affirming negative or a positive phenomenon—upon the verbally explicit negation of its own object of negation.

1. Affirming Negatives of Explicit Suggestion

A negative expressed by a phrase that explicitly suggests another phenomenon—either an affirming negative or a positive phenomenon—upon the verbally explicit negation of its own object of negation exists because the existence of a pot's lack of self of persons is such.

Opponent: It is not established [that the existence of a pot's lack of a self of persons is expressed by a phrase that explicitly suggests another phenomenon which is either an affirming negative or a positive phenomenon upon the verbally explicit negation of its own object of negation].

Response: It follows that the subject, the existence of a pot's lack of a self of persons, is a negative phenomenon expressed by a phrase that suggests another phenomenon—either an affirming negative or a positive phenomenon—upon the verbally explicit negation of its own object of negation because (1) the phrase expressing it is a verbally explicit elimination of its own object of negation and (2) [that phrase] explicitly suggests another phenomenon which is either an affirming negative or a positive phenomenon.

The selflessness of persons or lack of a substantially existent person exists. For, the lack of such a self is realized by valid cognition.

The first reason—that the phrase "the existence of a pot's lack of a self of persons" is a verbally explicit negation of its own object of negation—is established because the statement "the existence of a pot's lack of a self of persons" is a verbally explicit negation of the self of persons of a pot.

The second reason—that this phrase explicitly suggests another phenomenon which is either an affirming negative or a positive phenomenon—is established because the term "the existence of a pot's lack of a self of persons" (1) explicitly suggests the existence of a pot's lack of a self of persons and (2) the existence of a pot's lack of a self of persons is an affirming negative.

The first reason—that the phrase "the existence of a pot's lack of a self of persons" explicitly suggests the existence of a pot's lack of a self of persons—is easy [to establish, i.e, it is obvious and requires no further proof].

If it is objected that the second reason—that the existence of a pot's lack of a self of persons is an affirming negative—is not established, [we respond that] it follows with respect to the subject, the lack of a pot's self of persons, that its existence is an affirming negative because it is an established base.

According to Gomang, the existence of any phenomenon is an affirming negative because that existence is permanent. A positive or impermanent phenomenon has its own power; it is not just imputed by thought. For example, form is a positive phenomenon, but the existence of form is a negative phenomenon.

2. *Affirming Negatives of Implicit Suggestion*

A negative expressed by a phrase that implicitly suggests another phenomenon which is either an affirming negative or a positive phenomenon upon a verbally explicit negation of its own object of negation can be posited because the corpulent Devadatta who does not eat during the day is such. The reason follows because (1) the phrase "The corpulent Devadatta does not eat during the day" upon explicitly negating its own object of negation—that Devadatta eats during the day—implicitly suggests that he eats at night, and (2) eating at night is a positive phenomenon. The [last] reason follows because eating is a positive phenomenon.

To say "something exists" explicitly suggests that the thing exists but does not *explicitly* eliminate the non-existence of that thing.

If it did, then the thought consciousness which realizes that pot exists would also explicitly realize opposite-from-the-non-existence of pot (*bum pa yod pa ma yin pa las log pa*) whereas it actually realizes this implicitly. If the non-existence of pot were explicitly eliminated, there would have to be an explicit realization of the lack of non-existence of pot. Moreover, if the thought consciousness realizing that pot is a product realizes it by explicitly eliminating that pot is a non-product, then pot would be a negative phenomenon. More significantly, the inferential consciousness explicitly realizing impermanent sound would also have to realize non-permanent sound explicitly.

3. *Implicit and Explicit Suggestion*

A negative expressed by a phrase that both explicitly and implicitly suggests another phenomenon—either an affirming negative or a positive phenomenon—upon the verbally explicit negation of its own object of negation can be posited. For, the existence of a non-emaciated corpulent Devadatta who does not eat during the day is such.[18] This reason follows because the phrase "the existence of a non-emaciated corpulent Devadatta who does not eat during the day" (1) implicitly suggests that he eats at night upon explicitly negating that he eats during the day, and (2) explicitly suggests the existence of his not being emaciated, and (3) eating at night is a positive phenomenon and (4) the existence of a non-emaciated body is an affirming negative.

These two modes of suggestion, implicit and explicit, are not simultaneous but serial. They are suggested by sub-phrases that occur serially in the statement. It can be said that as each part of the phrase is spoken, the corresponding mental image appears to thought. Another explanation is that the words together add up to a single meaning-generality. The two explanations are not contradictory because it is possible to build up to a complex mental image gradually, adding on qualities serially.

4. *Contextual Negative*

A negative expressed by a phrase that contextually suggests another phenomenon—either an affirming negative or a positive phenomenon—upon the verbally explicit negation of its own object of negation is positable because at a time when one has ascertained that a certain person is either of royal or Brahmin lineage but has not ascertained the particular one, the phrase, "He is not of the Brahmin lineage," suggests that he is of the royal lineage through a verbally explicit negation that he is of the Brahmin lineage.

> In general the statement "He is not a Brahmin" does not indicate that someone is of the royal lineage, but in this particular context it does.

5. Non-affirming Negatives

A negative expressed by a phrase that does not implicitly suggest another phenomenon which is either an affirming negative or a positive phenomenon upon a verbally explicit negation of its own object of negation can be posited because Brahmins' not drinking beer is such. This reason follows because the term "Brahmins do not drink beer" neither explicitly, implicitly, nor contextually suggests another phenomenon—neither an affirming negative nor a positive phenomenon—upon a verbally explicit negation of its own object of negation.

> The statement, "Brahmins do not drink beer," does suggest Brahmins which are positive phenomenon but does not suggest them in place of the explicit negation of an object of negation.

All these [five types of negatives] can be condensed into two: (1) affirming negatives and (2) non-affirming negatives because the first four must be posited as affirming negatives and the last one as a non-affirming negative.

Whatever is a negative is not necessarily expressed by a term that verbally negates its own object of negation because (1) this is not necessarily the case with respect to affirming negatives and (2) this is not necessarily the case with respect to non-affirming negatives.

The first reason—that affirming negatives are not necessarily expressed by a phrase which verbally negates its own object of negation—is established because although both permanent phenomenon and object of knowledge are affirming negatives, the phrases which express these do not verbally negate their own objects of negation.

> This assertion is unique to Gomang. According to other colleges both permanent phenomenon and object of knowledge are positive phenomena. When object of knowledge appears to the mind, only something positive appears—it is not necessary to get at it by eliminating the object of negation.

The second reason—that non-affirming negatives are not necessarily expressed by a phrase that verbally negates its object of negation—is established because both uncaused space (*nam mkha, ākāśa*), and reality (*chos nyid, dharmatā*) are non-affirming negatives, but the terms which express them do not verbally negate their own objects of negation.

"The Sautrāntika Tenet System"

from the

Presentation of Tenets

by Jang-gya-rol-bay-dor-jay

TRANSLATOR'S PREFACE

The author of this text, Jang-gya-rol-bay-dor jay (*lCang-skya-rol-pa'i-rdo-rje*, 1717–1786) had a broad education, apparently the fortunate result of innate ability and good family connections. Born in Lang-dru (*Lang gru'u*) in the Ba-ri (*dPa'ri*) region of Amdo, now in Xinghai province, in an area known as the "Western Lotus District" (*Nub padmo'i sde*), he is reported to have been a "miracle child with an illustrious pedigree."[1]

In 1724, at the age of nine, he was sent to Beijing where he studied Chinese, Mongolian, and Manchu. He formed close ties with the future Chinese emperor, Kao-tsung, and the twelfth Manchu prince. In later years, appointed by his friend the Emperor, he headed a group of scholars in revising the Mongolian translation of the *Tanjur*, "the pearl of Mongolian literature," completed in 1749. Jang-gya was a prolific and widely respected scholar; his works—including the books on tenets of which a chapter is here translated—were studied in the monastic colleges of Tibet, Mongolia, and Huang-chung.

The present text is one of two full-length expositions of tenets renowned in Gelukba monastic colleges. The work is particularly interesting for the way it threads together a variety of topics that are crucial both to the system of Sautrāntikas Following Reasoning and to Gelukba understanding of Prāsaṅgika.

After a brief introduction which indicates the main sources of Sautrāntika, Jang-gya's chapter opens with a discussion of the two truths, ultimate and conventional.[2] This is for him, as for Den-dar-hla-ram-ba and the Gelukbas in general, the main axis around which the Sautrāntika system is constructed. It is in this context that Jang-gya will enter into the most difficult, and for this translator the most interesting, sections of his text—the discussion of how thought is to be defined and how the image, or meaning-generality (*don spyi, artha-sāmānya*), that appears to thought is etymologized and understood.

In this context Jang-gya, like other Gelukba writers, takes

impermanent phenomena such as tables to be ultimate truths. This is asserted on the grounds that they are objects of an ultimate mind: the eye consciousness perceiving a table is such a mind because, unlike thought, it is not obscured regarding the specific characteristics of its object. For example, an eye consciousness is called ultimate because all the factors related with its objects, such as their subtle impermanence, individual qualities of color and shape, and so forth, clearly appear to it, even though it may not be able to ascertain all that appears.[3] As Den-dar-hla-ram-ba and others also state, the appearing objects (*snang yul, pratibhāsaviṣaya*) of such consciousnesses are necessarily impermanent and specifically characterized phenomena, because only these possess the plurality of aspect that makes them known to direct perception. To be an appearing object means that an object appears in all its particularity; thus although a specifically characterized phenomenon such as a table can be an *object* of thought, it cannot be an *appearing object* of thought.

Permanent phenomena such as uncaused space and emptiness are said to be conventional truths because, lacking a multiplicity of characteristics; they are appearing objects only with respect to thought, never of direct perception (except in the case of a Buddha). Thought deals primarily with images, and these are necessarily less vivid and detailed than objects seen directly. Thus, the topic of the two truths, for Jang-gya as for Den-dar-hla-ram-ba, has to do with the distinction between thought and direct perception.

To clarify this further, Jang-gya focuses on how thought associates names and objects. The mental images to which names are affixed are only nominally imputed; they do not exist substantially in the manner of impermanent phenomena. Because the primary reference points of names and thought are internal mental images, which are negative phenomena, the topic of exclusions (*sel ba, apoha*), is also introduced here. It is largely because of this system's capacity for analyzing negative phenomena, especially non-affirming negatives, that Sautrāntika is considered a more subtle system than Vaibhāṣika.

Jang-gya also turns his attention to the impermanent

phenomena which are objects of direct perception. His emphasis here is that, from the first moment of its production, a thing has a nature of disintegration. The factors of aging and deterioration which appear to beset it subsequently are with it from the first; they are not imposed from outside but come into existence with it, for they are produced by the very causes on which the object itself depends. This understanding of impermanence is a vital sub-topic of the first noble truth, as Jang-gya will briefly explain toward the end of his chapter.

From the discussion of external phenomena, Jang-gya turns to a presentation of the minds, or awarenesses, which apprehend them. The basic divisions of the topic of Awareness and Knowledge (*bLo rig*) are mentioned, along with an introduction to the syllogistic format which grounds the study of Signs and Reasoning (*rTags rigs*). This syllogistic format, also seen in the Collected Topics literature, is an important tool of debate and pedagogy, and, just as importantly, is a prime meditation technique. Reasoning is a crucial element in what Jang-gya calls "The main path," that is, "the wisdom understanding selflessness." This latter point is subtly underscored by Jang-gya's discussion here.

To say, as Jang-gya does, that a syllogism can have a non-existent subject means it is possible to make syllogistic statements about soteriologically important non-existent subjects such as a self-sufficient self. More technically, this means that even in such a syllogism, the reason (*rtags, liṅga*) is a quality of that subject, as when one states: The subject, an independent self-sufficient person, does not exist *because it is a dependent arising.* The crucial oral commentary from Geshe Belden Drakba on this point explains that although "being a dependent arising" could not, of course, qualify a non-existent phenomenon, there is a distinction to be made between the stated subject (*smra ba'i chos can*), which is the hypothetical self-sufficient person, and the basal subject (*rang rten gyi chos can*), which is the mental image of such. The basal subject serves as a base to be qualified by the reason. In the case of an existent subject, stated and basal subjects are identical; in the case of a non-existent subject, as here, they are not. Nevertheless, Jang-gya emphasizes that in an important sense the self-sufficient person *is* the subject. If it were not, it could not be refuted, and the "main path" of the wisdom cognizing selflessness—the recognition of the absence of that very subject—could not result from logical analysis. All Gelukba scholars agree that analysis is a cause of such insight; however, as Geshe Belden Drakba points out, scholars disagree as to whether the subject of a syllogism must necessarily be an established base, which is to say it must exist.

This question relates to an issue which is an important theme in each of the works translated here, the question of how thought operates, and how and what it knows. Here Jang-gya quotes Gyel-tsap's description of the error which is undone through reasoned analysis into the status of the self-sufficient self: "The opponent, having mistaken the self-sufficient person and the appearance as such as one, wishes to know [whether or not it exists]." The error natural to thought, that of mixing the actual object with its image, is thus broadly analogous to an important aspect of another fundamental error, the misconception of self. This mistake is said to shape the entire course of cyclic existence. How can reason, the tool of thought, undo such a knot? Ultimately, of course, it will have to lead to direct cognition of the lack of such a mistakenly construed self, but it will do so by undermining the mistaken image which is mistakenly construed as that self. Den-dar-hla-ram-ba and, earlier in this chapter, Jang-gya himself, laid the ground for the assertion that thought is able to get at, or reference, actual objects by way of the images which alone are thought's appearing objects. Here however Jang-gya speaks to the importance of undermining images which *mistakenly* seem to refer to actual objects. This suggests (1) that mistaken images are an important factor governing experience, (2) that these can be undermined through reasoning, and (3) that doing so will result in a previously inaccessible valid cognition of the conventionally existent self.

Thus, the tenets of Sautrāntika are important for Gelukba

in that they establish thought's access to actual objects, as well as the ability of analytical thought to undermine its own inappropriate, but deeply entrenched, images. This model is directly applicable to Prāsaṅgika-Mādhyamika analysis, where it is the inherently existent self, rather than the self-sufficient one, which is disproved. Gelukba Prāsaṅgika fuses this Sautrāntika-based epistemology, on which it premises its Nāgārjunian-style analysis, with its closely related discussion of negative phenomena. However Prāsaṅgika, unlike Sautrāntika, maintains that a non-affirming negative phenomenon such as the lack of an inherently existent person, *can be* an appearing object of direct perception, even though it is permanent.[4]

Having thus provided a basis for understanding the central issues of the higher systems—specifically, of how the more subtle selflessness of phenomena taught in Prāsaṅgika can be understood--Jang-gya's chapter closes with a brief presentation of the four noble truths and the fruits, or effects, of a practice founded on the principles articulated in his discussion.

TRANSLATION

with oral commentary from Lati Rinbochay, Denma Lochö Rinbochay, and Geshe Belden Drakba

INTRODUCTION (97.7)

The explanation of Sautrāntika tenets has three parts: etymology, divisions, and assertion of tenets.

Etymology (97.8)

Bodhibhadra[5] and so forth explain that Sautrāntikas [literally, Followers of the sets of sutras] are so called because they posit tenets in accordance with the sets of sutras (*mdo sde, sutrānta*). They explain that Sautrāntikas are renowned as Exemplifiers (*dPe ston pa, Dārṣṭāntika*) because they are skilled in teaching through examples.

Divisions (97.10)

There are two divisions of Sautrāntikas: Followers of Scripture and of Reasoning. The former propound tenets from the viewpoint of only asserting literally what appears in the sets of sutras. The latter are Sautrāntikas who follow reasoning in accordance with the explanations in Dharmakīrti's Seven Treatises on Valid Cognition.

> The Followers of Reasoning also accept Buddha's sutras; however, because they follow both sutra and reasoning they are known as followers of reasoning. Their thought is more subtle than that of the Followers of Scripture.[6]

From the viewpoint of assertions on aspects (*rnam ba, ākāra*) there are three types of followers of reasoning: [Non-Pluralists, Half-Eggists, and Proponents of an Equal Number of Subjects and Objects]. These will be discussed below [p. 160].

Assertion of Tenets (97.15)

This section has two parts: the texts Sautrāntikas follow and their mode of positing tenets according to these texts [described in following chapter].

Texts Sautrāntikas Follow (97.16)
Actual texts [by Sautrāntikas] which set forth Sautrāntika tenets from their own viewpoint were not translated into Tibetan, but the bulk of their assertions appear frequently in Vasubhandu's *Explanation of the "Treasury of Knowledge"* (*Chos mngon pa'i mdzod kyi bshad pa, Abhidharmakośabhāṣya*) and other commentaries on this [such as those by Yaśomitra and Purnavardhana], as well as the root text of Asaṅga's *Compendium of Knowledge* (*mNgon pa kun btus, Abhidharmasamuccaya*) with Rājaputra's [Yaśomitra's] commentary, and Dharmakīrti's Seven Treatises on Valid Cognition (see Bibliography), as well as Dignāga's *Compendium on Valid Cognition* (*Tshad ma kun las btus pa, Pramāṇasamuccaya*). [Their assertions] are also explained here and there in texts by Bhāvaviveka [specifically, the *Heart of the Middle Way* (*dbU ma'i snying po, Madhyamakahṛdayakārikā*), and his commentary on it, *Blaze of Reasoning* (*dbU ma'i snying po'i 'grel pa rtog ge 'bar ba, Madhyamakahṛdayavṛttitarkajvālā*,)] and by the spiritual father Śāntarakṣita [in his *Compendium on Suchness* (*De kho na nyid bsdus pa'i tshig le'ur byas pa, Tattvasaṃgrahakārikā*)] and the commentary on this by his spiritual son [Kamalaśīla's *Commentary on the Difficult Points of (Śāntarakṣita's) "Compendium on Suchness"* (*De kho na nyid pa'i dka' 'grel, Tattvasaṃgrahapañjikā*)].

[All Sautrāntikas] assert that the Seven Treatises of Knowledge are not Buddha's word. [Some] hold that these were composed by Arhats, but most maintain that these were not composed even by Arhats since they contain many incorrect explanations such as that space (*nam mkha', ākāśa*) is a permanent substantial entity (*rtag rdzas, *nitya-dravya*). Therefore, they assert that the Treatises were composed by common beings having the same names as Arhats.

For example, a common person named Śāriputra who wrote the *Aggregate of Phenomenon* (*Chos kyi phung po, Dharmaskhanda*),[7] is not to be confused with the Arhat Śāriputra.

The Sautrāntika masters renowned among earlier [scholars] are Kumarata, Śirata, Dzunparata (*bTsun-pa-ra-ta*), and so forth.

CHAPTER ONE
THE TWO TRUTHS (98.6)

The presentation of the Sautrāntikas' way of positing tenets following those texts has three parts: assertions regarding the three—bases, paths [see chapter seven], and fruits [see chapter nine].

Bases (98.7)

Their assertion of bases has two parts: a general explanation of bases and a detailed explanation of the manner in which consciousnesses apprehend objects [discussed in chapter five].

General Explanation of Bases (98.8)

This section has two parts: assertions regarding (1) the two truths and (2) permanent and impermanent phenomena [discussed in chapter two], and external phenomena [discussed in chapter four].

The Two Truths (98.9)

The Sautrāntikas Following Scripture assert the two truths (*bden pa gnyis, satyadvaya*) in accordance with the Vaibhāṣika system [explained] earlier [in Jang-gya's chapter on that system through citing Vasubandhu's *Treasury of Knowledge*, VI.4]: "A conventional truth (*kun rdzob bden pa, saṃvṛtisatya*) is any phenomenon which, when broken or mentally subdivided [is not longer understood as that object]."

For example, if a pot is shattered by a hammer, the mind that perceives the pieces does not think, "This is a pot." [Therefore, pots and all other gross phenomena are conventional truths for Sautrāntikas Following Scripture.] Ultimate truths are for example, uncaused space—because no matter how minutely divided, it will always be perceived as space—or a partless particle of matter because it cannot be further subdivided.

With respect to the assertions on the two truths by the Followers of Reasoning, Dharmakīrti's *Commentary on (Dignāga's) "Compendium on Valid Cognition"* (*Tshad ma rnam 'grel gyi tshig le'ur byas pa, Pramāṇavārttika*) says:

> Whatever ultimately is able to perform a function exists ultimately here [in this system]; other [phenomena, unable to do so] exist conventionally. These set forth specifically and generally characterized [phenomena].

Thus, specifically characterized phenomenon (*rang mtshan, svalakṣaṇa*), that which is able to perform a function (*don byed nus pa, artha-kriyā-śakti*), and ultimate truth (*don dam bden pa, paramārtha-satya*) are synonymous. Phenomenon which is a non-thing (*dngos med kyi chos, abhāva-dharma*), phenomenon unable to perform a function, (*don byed mi nus pa'i chos, nārtha-kriyā-kāri-dharma*), and conventional truth (*kun rdzob bden pa, saṃvṛti-satya*) are synonymous.

Therefore, the entity [or definition] of an ultimate truth is: that which is able to bear reasoned analysis due to its own mode of subsistence without depending on imputation by terminology or thought.

The entity [or definition] of a conventional truth is: that which is established as merely posited by terms (*sgra, śabda*) and thoughts (*rtog pa, kalpanā*)—such as mental application (*yid la byed pa, manaskāra*) and so forth which are other than it.

In the Sautrāntika system, the ability to "bear reasoned analysis" means that an object can withstand analysis as to whether it appears to direct perception by casting its aspect toward the perceiving consciousness. The perception of such an object does not have to depend on hearing the name of that object or on thinking about it; the mere presence of the object is sufficient. Phenomena which can be perceived in this way—all impermanent phenomena—are known as ultimate truths. Permanent phenomena such as uncaused space or selflessness do not cast their aspect toward a directly perceiving consciousness and thus are not established from their own side and are not able to bear analysis by reasoning. Such phenomena are therefore conventional truths. They are appearing objects of thought. They come to be such either through the power of being posited by terms or through the power of conceptualization. For example, one may state or hear the name or term "uncaused space" and thereby take space as an appearing object of thought, or one may make the effort or mental application (*yid la byed pa, manaskāra*) to mentally eliminate obstructive contact, whereby space becomes an appearing object of thought.

This way of positing the definitions [of ultimate and conventional truths] accords with what is clearly stated by Tsong-kaba's two main spiritual sons [Gyel-tsap and Kay-drup]. Dharmakīrti's statement that "Whatever ultimately is able to perform a function exists ultimately here [in this system]; other [phenomena] exist conventionally" indicates *illustrations* of the two truths but not their definitions.

Therefore, in the Sautrāntika system that which is ultimately existent (*don dam par yod pa, paramārtha-sat*) and ultimate truth (*don dam bden pa, paramārtha-satya*) are co-extensive, and that which is merely conventionally existent (*kun rdzob du yod pa, saṃvṛti-sat*) and conventional truth (*kun rdzob bden pa, saṃvṛti-satya*) are co-extensive.[8]

A phenomenon which is only posited by terms and thought is conventionally existent. It is a conventional truth because it only appears to a thought consciousness—to a conventional mind—and is true only from the viewpoint of such a consciousness. It is not true from the viewpoint of an ultimate mind—a non-conceptual consciousness.

These definitions of the two truths are also asserted by Cittamātrins, but their way of positing illustrations of these is not the same.

Specifically characterized phenomena (*rang mtshan kyi chos, svalakṣana-dharma*) which in the system of the Sautrāntikas Following Reasoning are synonymous with ultimate truths, exist by way of their own nature without being posited by terms or thought. According to these Sautrāntikas, *only* products can be so defined, but Cittamātrins also define the non-product selflessness or emptiness—which they consider an ultimate truth--in this way.[9] Therefore, according to the Sautrāntikas only products can be posited as illustrations of ultimate truths. The Cittamātrins, however assert that the non-product selflessness—which in Sautrāntika is considered an example of a conventional truth—is also an illustration of an ultimate truth. Thus, although the Sautrāntikas and Cittamātrins agree on the definitions of the two truths, they differ in the illustrations or examples they posit for these.

[The way the Sautrāntikas Following Reasoning] assert the two truths is not the same as that explained in Vasubandhu's *Treasury of Knowledge*. This is because [as asserted by the Vaibhāṣikas and the Sautrāntikas Following Scripture] the *Treasury* posits pots and so forth as conventional truths whereas [the Sautrāntikas Following Reasoning] posit pots as specifically characterized phenomena and as ultimate truths.

Etymologies of the Two Truths. (99.10) Generally characterized phenomena (*spyi mtshan, sāmānyalakṣaṇa*) are called conventional truths because of being true for a conventional [or obscured] mind. Here, an obscured mind refers to a conceptual consciousness, called obscured (*kun rdzob, saṃvṛti*) because of being obstructed with respect to actually taking a specifically characterized phenomenon as its apprehended object [that is, its appearing object].

Though a specifically characterized phenomenon such as a pot does appear to a thought consciousness apprehending pot, it is not an appearing object of that thought. The image or meaning-generality (*don spyi, arthasāmānya*) of pot is the appearing object of a thought consciousness apprehending pot. That image prevents thought from perceiving the appearance of an actual pot which is unmixed with the image of pot.[10]

Specifically characterized phenomena are called ultimate truths because of being true for an ultimate mind. Here, an "ultimate mind" is a consciousness which is not mistaken with respect to its appearing object.

An ultimate mind or direct perceiver is unmistaken especially in the sense that it perceives distinctly all the specific characteristics of its appearing object without in any way confusing the actual object and its characteristics with a generic image or with similar characteristics possessed by other phenomena of similar or dissimilar type.

Merely the way that the Sautrāntikas Following Scripture posit definitions and illustrations of the two truths is similar to that of the Vaibhāṣikas, but their [further] presentations of these differ greatly. For, whatever the Vaibhāṣikas assert as existing (*yod pa, sat*), they also assert as substantially established (*rdzas su grub pa, dravya-siddha*) [and therefore, for them, uncaused or permanent phenomena are substantially established] whereas no Sautrāntika asserts such.

In the system of the Sautrāntikas [Following Reasoning] generally characterized phenomena are [permanent] uncaused phenomena such as space. Phenomena imputed by thought such as generality, common locus, particular, illustration, one, many, relation, the thesis being proven, proof, and so forth, are also generally characterized phenomena. However, whatever *is* [a specific instance of any of] these need not be a generally characterized phenomenon.

Even though generality, for example, is a generally characterized phenomenon, something can be a generality but not be a generally characterized phenomenon. For example, a pot is a generality because it is concomitant with the various instances of silver, gold, and clay pots, but a pot is not a generally characterized phenomenon. It is an impermanent thing and, therefore, a specifically characterized phenomenon.

A pot is also a common locus of being both a product and an impermanent thing; it is a particular because it is a specific type of existent; it is an illustration of the general class of objects of knowledge, and it is one because it is a single. Despite being all these things—which, like generality, are generally characterized phenomena—a pot itself is a specifically characterized phenomenon. Thus, whatever *is* a generality and so forth is not necessarily a permanent or generally characterized phenomenon.

This is because although the self-isolate (*rang ldog*) of the explicit object of a thought consciousness [the image which is that thought's appearing object] is not a specifically characterized phenomenon [since it is a mental image and thus permanent and imputed by terms and thought], it is not contradictory for a specifically characterized phenomenon [such as a pot] to be an explicit object of thought [because thought is capable of actually getting at impermanent phenomena].

> An impermanent phenomenon such as a pot can be the explicit object of the thought consciousness apprehending pot because it realizes pot explicitly. Although only the image of pot—which is the self-isolate of the explicit object of thought—and not pot itself is the appearing object of the thought apprehending pot;[11] pot does appear to that consciousness mixed with the image of the meaning-generality of pot.[12]

Therefore, a golden pot appears as a pot to the thought consciousness apprehending golden pot as pot, and [the image of pot which is that thought consciousness's] explicit object of apprehension also appears as a pot. The two factors that appear [the impermanent golden pot and the permanent generic image of pot] appear mixed as one. The two appearing factors are undifferentiable from the viewpoint of appearance; therefore, this is said to be the mixing of appearance and imputation as one. The "appearance" is a specifically characterized phenomenon [pot], and the "imputation" is the meaning-of-the term (*sgra don*, *śabdārtha*), [a generic image of pot. Thus, the actual object appears, mixed with its image, even to thought.]

To what does "meaning-of-the-term" refer? It refers to both (1) the appearance, [which is an image] of a golden pot as a pot that appears as if right in front of oneself to the thought consciousness apprehending pot and (2) that appearance's appearing as opposite from non-pot [that is, the image's appearing to be a pot].

The appearance of golden pot as opposite from non-pot and that very appearance [the image itself] appearing as opposite from non-pot appear mixed. Although these two are not distinguished from the viewpoint of appearance, the thought consciousness does not apprehend them thinking, "These two are one."

> Even factually concordant thought is mistaken in two ways with

respect to its appearing object:
1) appearance (the actual object) and imputation (the mental image) appear undifferentiably mixed, and
2) the image of pot appears to *be* a pot but is not. Although an image and a pot *appear* to be one, thought does not actively *conceive* them to be one. Thus, it is not a wrong consciousness (*log shes*) even though it is a mistaken consciousness (*'khrul shes*).

Therefore, whereas the appearance itself of golden pot as pot to a thought consciousness is not opposite-from-non-pot [for opposite-from-non-pot is pot itself and the image is not a pot], it appears to be, and thus [the thought consciousness] is mistaken with respect to its appearing object. However, a [factually concordant] mind's mode of apprehension is to *apprehend* the golden pot within thinking that it is a pot; however, the mind] does not *conceive* that the meaning-of-the-term [the image] is a pot or that the appearance [or image] of golden pot itself is a pot. Therefore, it is not mistaken with respect to its referent object, [the golden pot, and thus is not a wrong consciousness].[13]

"Meaning-of-the-term" is as explained above [with *śabdārtha* being interpreted as a genitive *tat puruṣa: śabdasya artha*]. The foremost lama Tsong-ka-ba and his spiritual sons explain many times that "*śabdārtha*" is not to be interpreted [as a *dvandva* compound] and divided into "term generality and meaning generality" (*śabdasāmānya arthasāmānya cha*) [because the sense that an internal image is what is expressed or referred to by a term would be lost].

Those propounding as the definition of a thought consciousness "a conceptual knower which apprehends a meaning-of-a-term" are [unnecessarily] faulted by most of our latter day scholars who say that there is the uncertainty of [how to categorize] thought conciousnesses in the continuum of children untrained in terminology.

A child untrained in language does not associate the term "pot," for example, with its meaning but does have a thought consciousness apprehending a pot.

In setting up their own system[these scholars] define a thought consciousness as "a conceptual knower which apprehends term and meaning generalities as *suitable* to be mixed or associated."[14] In my opinion, making such a fine distinction is of little import.

> Jang-gya, like the first group mentioned above, supports the shorter definition.

The presentations of definitions, illustrations, and so forth in the great texts [such as Dharmakīrti's Seven Treatises on Valid Cognition, Asaṅga's *Compendium of Knowledge*, and Vasubandhu's *Treasury of Knowledge*][15] are stated for the sake of understanding the meaning itself of the entities and attributes of objects. All uncommon modes of apprehension by all the varieties of people that exist need not be included among the components of a definition [even though the definition applies to them].

> Jang-gya's point is that the shorter definition of a thought consciousness is sufficient to produce understanding of what a thought consciousness is. That this definition does not account for all possible types of thought—namely, that it does not account for the thought of untrained children—is not a fault because it is not the purpose of a definition to take into account all possible variations of the thing being defined.

Moreover, your propounding "a conceptual knower which apprehends the term [generality] and meaning [generality] of pot as suitable to be mixed" to be the definition of a thought consciousness is also incorrect since there is no certainty [that every instance of such thought conforms to this]. For, the convention "pot" is not renowned [in all languages as a name] for bulbous containers, and [thus] there are the thought consciousnesses in the continuums of people of [other] times and places who express these by other verbal conventions [that is, using other languages].

Furthermore, there is no doubt that [the Sautrāntika system] holds that even to children untrained in terminology a pot appears as the basis of verbal conventions which are imputations of its entity and attributes, and that such children have conceptions [of a pot] as a basis of such verbal conventions.

This does not mean that the child consciously thinks, "This is a basis of a verbal convention." The point is that if language were available to the child, his perception of things is such that those things seem *capable* of being named. In this sense, even children who do not know the names of things perceive objects as suitable to receive a name such as a pot, as do their attributes of shape, color, function and so forth.

Animals can also recognize their own offspring, discriminate what is and is not food and so forth. This is done conceptually but without words. Recognition is based on certain visual signs, smells, and the like. This type of conceptual discrimination would be classified as correct assumption (*yid dpyod*) among the seven types of awarenesses.[16]

That is because this mode of appearance—in which pot appears as naturally being the basis of such verbal conventions—in the continuum of those untrained in terminology is correct according to the proponents of truly existent [external] objects [Vaibhāṣikas and Sautrāntikas] whereas according to the Cittamātrins it is mistaken. This is explained more than once in [Tsong-ka-ba's] *Essence of the Good Explanations* (*Legs bshad snying po*) and in textbooks analyzing this topic.

All three, Vaibhāṣika, Sautrāntika, and Cittamātra, agree that things appear to be naturally established as the bases of names. The Cittamātrins and Mādhyamikas consider this appearance to be mistaken. According to them, things do not, by way of their own nature, exist as bases of names; the realization that things do not exist this way is, in Cittamātra, the realization of a subtle selflessness of phenomena.

[The following is a debate as to whether or not objects can appear as the bases of names to persons who have not yet learned language.]

Objection: [The appearance and conception of objects as naturally being the bases of the verbal conventions of their entity and attributes] applies only to people trained in terminology. *Response:* If that were the case, how could the Cittamātrin system posit the conception of a self of phenomena (*chos kyi bdag 'dzin, dharmātmagrāha)* which is an imputation of entities and attributes as descriptive of children untrained in terminology?

Imputation of an entity means to think of a pot, for example, as naturally established as the basis of a name. Imputation of attributes or features means to think that the impermanence of a pot is naturally established as the basis of a name. [The Cittamātra system posits phenomena's *lack* of being naturally established as the bases of names or verbal conventions as a subtle selflessness of phenomena. They also assert that all beings—not just those trained in terminology—make the mistake of perceiving phenomena to be naturally established as the bases of names.]

Objection: Although indeed [such a child] has no apprehension [that a bulbous container] is a basis of affixing the term "pot," [his conception of pot as naturally being the basis of the verbal convention of its entity] occurs in the context of [conceiving it to be] the basis of conception by the thought consciousness *thinking* "pot."

The opponent wishes to make a distinction between saying "pot" and thinking it, but the difficulty remains of how the untrained child would even think "pot."

Response: [Do you hold that] the thought consciousness in this person's continuum is independent of any verbal convention [because you feel one can think "pot" without saying the name "pot"]? If so, you must explain just how that thought consciousness conceives its object and how the object appears to that thought consciousness. Or [do you hold that] this is a thought consciousness which depends on a verbal convention such as the name "pot" or [in the case of imputing attributes] a qualifying phrase [such as] "the form of pot"? If so, you have given up your position that this is a person untrained in terminology.

Or do you consider that this thought consciousness depends on names and phrases which are verbal conventions other [than "pot"]? If so, explain just what kind of other verbal conventions of entity and attributes it depends upon.

Objection: In the continuum of a child untrained in terminology, there is no conception of a bulbous container as the basis of affixing the specific terms "pot" and so forth; nevertheless, it is not contradictory for the child to determine [that a bulbous container] is a basis for affixing a verbal convention which in general exists for thought.

The child would see the bulbous container as the basis of *some* expression such as any nonsense syllables that might appear to his mind. [Jang-gya does not dispute this position, for his point all along has been that all the possibilities of specific verbal conventions and so forth cannot be included in a definition.]

Response: In that case it would be appropriate for part of the definition to express just what [nonsense syllables] exist for the thought consciousnesses of [untrained children].

Objection: Since the varieties of people are endless, it is impossible to express [particulars applying to each in a single definition].

Response: That indeed is very true [and has been Jang-gya's point all along]. Therefore, I think it would be better to leave as they are most of the terms in the great commentaries that are effectively able to bestow understanding. Give up making fine distinctions that would necessitate a full detailing of characteristics equal to the number of objects of knowledge (*shes bya, jñeya*); give up finding the fault of indefiniteness due to the divisions of varieties of persons in time and place in the presentation of definitions, divisions, definite enumerations, and so forth of the great texts in general and the writings of the foremost [Tsong-ka-ba] and his spiritual sons.

[In contrast to Jang-gya] the omniscient Gyel-tsap's *Explanation of (Dignāga's) "Compendium on Valid Cognition"* [seems to support the view that *śabdārtha* should be interpreted as "term-generality and meaning-generality" rather than as "meaning-of-the-term' when] commenting on the lines:

> A direct perceiver (*mngon sum, pratyakṣa*) is that which is free from a thought consciousness that applies names, types, and so forth.

Gyel-tsap says that the [reference to "thought consciousness"] includes the thought consciousnesses in the continuum of a child untrained in terminology, these being such that the object of expression and the expression are *suitable* to be mixed [though not actually associated. His specifying "object of expression" and "expression"] does not signify that the "meaning-of-the-term (*śabdārtha*) which is the actual object of a thought consciousness should be interpreted as [a *dvandva* compound] "term-generality and meaning-generality."

> Scholars who say that the definition of thought is "that which apprehends a meaning-generality and a term-generality as suitable to be mixed" might cite Gyel-tsap's statement above. They would be correct to understand "object of expression" and "expression" as referring to meaning-generality and term-generality respectively, but mistaken in inferring that *śabdārtha* therefore always must be interpreted as referring to those two and never as "meaning-of-the-term." Jang-gya's point is that the appearing object of thought is simply the image of an object and that there is no need here to specify the two types—term-generalities and meaning-generalities. For, the emphasis that the actual object of a term is an internal image will be lost.

Therefore, the Lord of Reasoning [Dharmakīrti] says [in his *Commentary on (Dignāga's) "Compendium on Valid Cognition,"* III.2]:

> Any consciousness that apprehends a "meaning-of-a-term" is a thought consciousness with respect to that [image].

In commentaries and subcommentaries on this and in many writings of the great foremost father [Tsong-ka-ba] and his spiritual sons on this passage, it is explained that just the self-isolate[17] of the actual object of a thought consciousness, or just the self-isolate of a term's object of expression, is the meaning-of-a-term [depending on whether one is thinking or speaking]. They say that *śabdārtha* is not to be explained through separating out [*śabda*] as term-generality (*śabdasāmānya*) and [*artha*] as meaning-generality (*arthasāmānya*).

The actual objects of thought can be divided into term-generalities and meaning-generalities, but in referring to thought's actual object in general as "a meaning-of-a-term" this division does not apply.

The reason for calling [the self-isolate] of the explicit object of a thought consciousness or the self-isolate of a term's object of expression a meaning-of-the-term is the following.

In general, both Buddhists and non-Buddhists agree that:
(1) a base such as a spotted ox is a basis for [initially] affixing an appellation [that is, connecting the name "ox" with that type of animal for the first time]
(2) having taken one basis as an illustration and having affixed the appellation, all [instances of, for example, ox] are recognized [as oxen]
(3) the affixing of an appellation is for the sake of [later] conventional [usage].

However, Buddhists and non-Buddhists do not agree on the reasons why [naming one ox can cause all oxen] to be understood.

Affixing an appellation means to connect an object with a name for the first time. Usually parents first connect terms to objects for children; they point out a cow saying, "This is a cow," and on the basis of this the child afterwards understands white, black, and spotted cows as cows. It is not necessary for parents to apply the term "cow" to each animal individually.

Non-Buddhists say that because the single, partless generality to which the appellation is affixed exists in all its instances, once the appellation has been affixed to one [instance], other instances are also understood as "ox" when that generality is perceived in them. This is why it is not necessary to have the appellation [newly] affixed with each instance individually.

According to the non-Buddhists, in connecting the name "ox" with the animal for the first time, the instructor is pointing out the ox-generality existing in one of its instances. Once he has caused the listener to notice the ox-generality in one ox, that person can recognize it in others without any further instruction.

Buddhists assert that an appellation is [initially] affixed to an other-exclusion (*gzhan sel, anyāpoha*) which is the opposite of non-ox; since this [other-exclusion] applies equally to all instances of ox, it is not necessary to affix the appellation [newly] with each instance individually.

> When the name is initially given on the basis of a particular ox, the instructor also causes one to connect this name with a mental image that is an appearance in the manner of an elimination of everything except ox. This image or other-exclusion applies to all oxen, because whatever is an ox is necessarily opposite from, or an other-exclusion of, non-ox. Therefore, since all oxen, tan, white, and so forth are also opposite from non-ox, on the basis of this image one can understand them as oxen. This is why it is not necessary to make a new appellation/object connection for each individual ox.[18]

Therefore, [in the Buddhist interpretation] when the appellation is affixed, it is not affixed to the composite of the spotted ox and the opposite of non-ox; rather, when a spotted ox is taken as the basis in affixing the appellation, the appellation ["ox"] is affixed to [a negative phenomenon], the other-exclusion which is the opposite from non-ox, taking the possession of a hump, dewlap, and so forth as the [distinguishing] characteristics. That is the reason why [the image which is the explicit object of thought] is called a meaning-of-the term [since the term directly refers to it].

> The base in dependence on which the name is affixed is the actual spotted ox, and the reason for applying this name is that the ox possesses a hump and dewlap. What appears to the mind at the time of learning this name—that is to say, the actual object to which the name is affixed and what allows one to relate this name to other instances of ox—is the mental image of the exclusion of non-ox.[19]

Similarly, the teacher Kamalaśīla writes:

> The view of those who [mistakenly] propound the meaning-of-a-term to be a positive phenomenon (*sgrub ba, vidhi*) is that: "Terms explicitly establish and negate; terms establish the nature of a thing. Therefore,

a positive phenomenon itself is the meaning-of-the-term." [However, Buddhists], who are proponents of exclusion, maintain that ultimately terms do not in the least express a thing's own entity. For, all consciousnesses [arisen from] terms are mistaken; they engage in disparate objects as if they were not different.

For example, there are many different types of trees, and there is no generic tree that exists apart from its individual instances.

That [terminological consciousness] which is indirectly related with a thing is mistaken, but is to be viewed as incontrovertible (*mi slu ba, avisaṃvādin*) with respect to the meaning (*don, artha*).

It is mistaken with respect to or in terms of its appearing object, the meaning-generality or image of the object, in that the disparate appear to be non-disparate; however, it is incontrovertibly correct in getting at its referent object, for example, a tree.

This is because any mind that is an imputing thought consciousness comes [to know its referent object] through the power of experiencing a thing [which is the appearance of] the opposite-from-what-is-other-than-that-entity, which is not different from that object. [Such a consciousness] is mistaken because [the image] appears to be opposite from what is other [than the object; that is, it appears to be the actual thing itself, just as a mirror image of a face appears to be a face]. However, [this consciousness is incontrovertible] because [the image] is definitely conjoined with [the object's] meaning as [depicting] the reverse of what is other than it [the object]. Also, since the effect [of the thought consciousness' apprehension by way of an image] is a realization of a thing which is an other-exclusion, it is called "that which has an other-exclusion."

The effect or result of a valid cognizer is a realization of the meaning. Therefore, through producing a terminological imputing consciousness of tree, for instance, one can correctly realize or identify the actuality of tree. Therefore, when Kamalaśīla speaks of thought as "realizing" an other-exclusion he probably is referring to the fact that the appearing object is an other-exclusion.

Thus, it is established that the meaning-of-a-term is an exclusion.

Non-Buddhist schools assert that the mere elimination of the object of negation [non-pot][20] does not appear to the mind thinking "pot"; [they say that] a positive phenomenon [the actual pot-generality] appears by way of its own power. With this as their reason, they assert that because all terms and thought consciousnesses engage [their objects] by the power of the thing, they are complete engagers [in that all the qualities of the object collectively appear with it to the mind as in direct perception].

The text just quoted states that "*śabdārtha*" is to be understood as "meaning-of-a-term" (*śabdasya artha*). Because the sixth [genitive] case is used, there is not much need for the merely tiresome activity of separating [*śabdārtha*] into "term-generality" (*śabdasāmānya*) and "meaning-generality" (*artha-sāmānya*) and then calling the ability of one mind to take both as its object "mixing" and using the term "suitable to be mixed" in order to include those untrained in terminology who take either of these [the term-generality or the meaning-generality] as their object.

Furthermore, [although] Dharmakīrti's *Ascertainment of Valid Cognition* (*Tshad ma rnam par nges pa, Pramāṇaviniścaya*) says that "a thought consciousness is a consciousness which perceives [a meaning-of-a-term] as suitable to be mixed with an expression," this means, as was explained in Kay-drup's *Clearing Away Mental Darkness [With Regard to the Seven Treatises]* that:

> A meaning-of-the-term appears to thought and that meaning-of-a-term is also the object to which the appellation is actually connected; therefore, it is said to be suitable to be mixed [or associated] with an expression. [The passage is] not [saying] that the verbal designation of a mixture of these two is used to refer to the

existence of both a term-generality and a meaning-generality for a thought consciousness [in the sense of both simultaneously being objects of one consciousness].

Jang-gya may be disputing the notion that the two are associated as in a mixture of two things, for he may hold that they do not exist for thought simultaneously.

Therefore, the self-isolate of the basis to which the mental convention, which is the thought "This is an ox," or the verbal convention, which is such an expression [as "ox"], is affixed is merely imputed by thought; it is a [permanent] generally characterized phenomenon.

The self-isolate of the basis to which a convention is affixed is just a meaning-of-a-term, an internal image. It explicitly appears to thought; it does not exist except for being imputed by thought, and it is permanent in the sense of not disintegrating from one moment to the next.

Ox and so forth, which are the illustration-isolates [or specific referents] of [the basis to which a convention is affixed], are [impermanent] specifically characterized phenomenon. That is why generalities which encompass [or pervade] their instances can be [either impermanent] things or [permanent] non-things: the objective exclusion [impermanent negative phenomenon] opposite-from-non-ox which encompasses both spotted and black oxen and the mental exclusion [permanent negative phenomenon] which is the appearance to thought as opposite from non-ox [and which encompasses both spotted and black oxen]. [The appearance to thought as opposite from non-ox is] an illustration of a meaning-of-a-term.

The import of this is explained in detail by the king of scholars, Kamalaśīla, in the chapter on investigating meaning-of-a-term in his *Commentary on the Difficult Points of (Śāntarakṣita's) "Compendium on the Suchness of Valid Cognition"* (*De kho na nyid bsdus pa'i dka' 'grel, Tattvasaṃgrahapañjikā*). [It was also explained] in the master Śākyabuddhi's *Explanation of (Dharmakīrti's) "Compendium on Valid Cognition"* (*Tshad ma rnam 'grel gyi 'grel bshad, Pramāṇavārttikaṭīkā*) and [Gyel-tsap's] *Eradication of Forgetfulness Regarding (Dharmakīrti's) "Chapter on Valid Cognition"* (*mNgon sum le'ur brjed byang*) and so forth by the two main spiritual sons [Gyel-tsap and Kay-drup] of the foremost omniscient Tsong-ka-ba and in their great commentaries on Dharmakīrti's *Commentary on (Dignāga's) "Compendium on Valid Cognition* and *Ascertainment of Valid Cognition."*

Although [these writers] acted kindly in clarifying [this subject] through analyzing the final points in detail, present day logicians, not valuing the great texts highly, take refuge in mere deceptive verbal entanglements. They take a garland of foam—dry consequences which do away with the essential meaning—as the best of essences. Such people see only a portion [of the meaning of the great texts by Dharmakīrti and so forth]; the actual thought is beyond their ken. Therefore, for them those scriptures have become like diamond words [impossible to penetrate].

CHAPTER TWO
PERMANENT AND IMPERMENENT PHENOMENA (105.17)

With respect to the [Sautrāntikas'] assertions on (1) permanent and impermanent phenomena and (2) external objects, the former has two parts: their actual assertions on permanent and impermanent phenomena and their presentation of exclusions [presented in chapter three].

Assertions on Permanent and Impermanent Phenomenon (105.20)
In accordance with the explanation above,[21] non-Buddhist schools and the Buddhist Vaibhāṣikas assert that with regard to whatever is permanent, whatever existed formerly also exists at a later time [because for them the permanent is what exists forever].

With regard to impermanent phenomena, the Vaibhāṣikas assert that things (*dngos po, bhāva*) can be either permanent or impermanent [because according to them all existents are able to perform functions, this being the definition of *bhāva*].

The Vaibhāṣikas [also assert that] when the characteristics of products—production, abiding, and disintegration—characterize the form aggregate (*gzugs gyi phung po, rūpa-skandha*), for instance, as a product, these three factors do not characterize it by way of the form aggregate's being produced, [abiding, and disintegrating]; rather they characterize it as a product through the existence of producers, [abiders, and disintegrators] which are other than it [i.e. than the form aggregate].

Whereas Sautrāntikas posit the factors or activities of production and so forth to be simultaneous, Vaibhāṣikas do not. According to Vaibhāṣika, production consists of the causes that produce a phenomenon, the activity of which causes occurs prior to the time of the object. During the time of the object, only its activity of abiding is posited. Its disintegration occurs when the object ceases. The three *factors* exist simultaneously but their *activities* occur serially. Thus for them, unlike for the Sautrāntikas, production, abiding, and disintegration are external to and different from the phenomena that they qualify and act upon.[22] The three characteristics are the agents of these activities.

Therefore, [the Vaibhāṣikas] do not assert the characteristics to be the *activities* of production and so forth; instead, they assert these as the separate substantial entities of the agent of production, agent of abiding, and agent of disintegration. [According to Vaibhāṣika] things which are bases that are characterized [as products], such as forms and so forth, do possess the four characteristics[23] simultaneously but the [four] are asserted as operating [that is, generating their respective activities] successively: first the activity of production, then the activity of abiding, then the activity of aging, and then the activity of disintegration.

The characteristics of any object must exist simultaneously with the object; for example, a pot exists at the same time as bulbous, flat-based, and capable of holding water. If the Vaibhāṣikas did not posit the four as in some sense simultaneous, they could not

> claim to call them characteristics of products. Thus, they say the four exist together but perform their respective activities serially.

The Sautrāntikas find fault with this [position], saying that if it were [as the Vaibhāṣikas maintain] products would not be momentary [but would exist over the four moments of the four activities] The Vaibhāṣikas say, "Our 'momentariness' refers to however long it takes the four activities to be completed." Since Vasubandhu's own commentary to his *Treasury* [describes their assertion this way], the Vaibhāṣikas indeed do not assert that impermanent things are not momentary; however, their mode of positing momentariness is not like that of the Sautrāntikas and above, [i.e., the Cittamātrins and Mādhyamikas].

Sautrāntikas assert the characteristics of products—production and so forth—as the *activity* of production, the *activity* of abiding, and the *activity* of disintegration. Just as, despite the fact that the definition of ox is "A composite including a hump and dewlap," [that composite] is not a different substantial entity from ox, so production and so forth are imputedly existent (*btags yod, prajñaptisat*) phenomena which are not separate substantial entities from forms and so forth.

> The activities of production, abiding, and disintegration here in Sautrāntika are imputedly established (*btags du sgrub pa, prajñaptisiddha*) because their appearance to a mind depends on the appearance of the form which is their basis. The form itself is substantially established (*dzas su grub pa, dravyasiddha*) because its appearance does not depend on some other thing appearing to the mind.[24]

Production is the arising newly of something such as a sprout which did not exist previously; abiding is an ongoing of that which is similar in type to what was previous; disintegration is [the object's] not staying for a second moment after the time of its establishment, aging is the later moment's being dissimilar in nature from the former one. These [four] characteristics are asserted to be established [or to occur] simultaneously.

Furthermore, things which are composed through an aggregation of causes and conditions are only the mere moment of [their] production. Moreover, since it cannot be said that the two—[a thing's] entity of production and its entity of disintegration—are different, [a thing] is only momentary. Thereby, one should understand that things are produced by their own causes as having a nature of disintegration and that they are not produced as stable things. Thus [one can understand that] they are just disintegrative in the sense that they do not abide for a second moment after the time of their own establishment.

A [two-branched] syllogistic statement on this is:
1. [Pervasion:] That which at any time has a nature of disintegration will not abide immediately thereafter, as in the case, for example, of an entity abiding in its final moment;
2 [Presence of the reason in the subject:] Forms and so forth have the nature of disintegration from the time of their production.
This is a sign of sameness of entity (*rang bzhin gyi rtags, svabhāvaliṅga*).

The proof that [forms and so forth] have the nature of disintegration is: anything which, without depending on other subsequent causes to become a certain type of entity, is established as such an entity, is necessarily definite as such an entity. This is the case, for example, with the production of a barley stalk by the final causal collection of a barley stalk. Products also are established as entities of disintegration without depending on other subsequent causes for them to become entities of disintegration.

This pervasion is established by direct perception. The establishment of the property of the subject (*phyogs chos, pakṣadharma*) is to be known through an undermining sign. Concerned that it would be too much, I will not write [more about this] here.[25]

The property of the subject is the factor of the reason's being a quality of the subject. In this case, the reason—being produced as having a nature of disintegration—is the quality of the subject, forms and so forth. The syllogism in an easier rendering is: The subject, forms and so forth, do not abide for a second moment after their production because they are produced by their own causes as having a nature of disintegration. In other words, there is no hiatus between the time a form is produced and its disintegration is produced, for the causes of the form are themselves the causes of its characteristic of disintegration.

Because disintegration (*'jig pa, vināśa*)—the not staying for a second moment after the time of establishment—is produced from the causes [of the object it characterizes], it is a [functioning, impermanent] thing.

The disintegration of, for example, a table, arises only from the causes of that table, it does not have any causes other than these.

However, the state of [an object's] having disintegrated (*zhig pa*) in its second moment is not a thing; therefore, [this state of having disintegrated] is asserted to be causeless.

There is a difference between disintegration (*'jig pa*) and the state of having disintegrated (*zhig pa*). The former is both an impermanent thing that arises in dependence on causes and a positive phenomenon whereas the latter is a non-product and a non-affirming negative.

Therefore, with respect to how permanence is posited, the king of reasoning [Dharmakīrti] says:

> That whose nature does not disintegrate
> The scholars say is permanent.

Accordingly, a phenomenon which has no nature of disintegration is asserted [as permanent]; this is unlike the non-Buddhist and Vaibhāṣika assertion [that the permanent is what exists continuously in the past, present, and future]. Therefore, although a clay pot's state of having disintegrated did not exist earlier, when the pot had not disintegrated, and does exist later [when the pot has ceased], it must be posited as permanent [since it does not disintegrate moment by moment]. Thus, it need not be a permanent phenomenon which exists at all times. For example, the analytical cessation (*so sor brtags 'gog, prati-*

saṃkyānirodha) which is a state of having abandoned the objects to be abandoned by the path of seeing (*mthong lam, darśanamārga*) does not exist until those objects to be abandoned are removed, but does exist when they are removed. Still, [this abandonment] is posited as permanent [because the continuous and unchanging state of cessation is the factor that prevents the afflictions from recurring]. Although the Prāsaṅgikas do indeed assert that the state of having disintegrated (*zhig pa*) is an [impermanent] thing, [the presentation] here is made from the viewpoint of Sautrāntika, Cittamātra, and Svātantrika-Mādhyamika.

In the same way, even the reality (*chos nyid, dharmatā*) which is the very pure nature [of a phenomenon] disappears when the subject [which is its basis, such as a pot] disappears. Therefore, [the emptiness or reality of a pot] exists [only] temporarily; still, it is not impermanent because it is a non-affirming negative (*med dgag, prasajyapratiṣedha*) which is the mere elimination of its object of negation. Also, when the substratum [such as a pot] disappears, its attribute [emptiness] disappears; however, it is not that [the emptiness] has disintegrated due to having a nature of disintegration.

The reality which is related with former and future times is suitable as an illustration of [something that is] singular but does have many parts [or instances].

Suchness or reality always exists and we can speak of suchness in general as a single phenomenon. However, there is no contradiction in referring to the many suchnesses—the emptiness of a table, of a chair, and so forth—as multiple, just as table is one or singular but there are many tables.

The non-existence of, for example, pot is posited as existing in place of its own object of negation [pot] and a sprout is posited as existing when it has been produced by its own causes. However, except for the similarity of being posited as existent, the modes of existence of these [two] are not the same. For, the former [the non-existence of pot] is posited [as existing] not from the viewpoint of the entity of [that non-existence] itself, but by way of the mere elimination of the object of negation. [Such elimination is] due to the fact that such a thing as the object of negation—pot—does not exist [in a certain place]. In the latter case [of the existence of a sprout], the sprout need not be posited from the viewpoint of eliminating what is other [than it]; it can be posited from the viewpoint of eliminating what is its own entity.

Thus, even mere absences are existent phenomena in Sautrāntika. [The ability to posit such is one important reason why Sautrāntika is considered more subtle than the Vaibhāṣika system which asserts that whatever exists is substantially established and which, therefore, cannot assert the existence of mere absences at all.]

Other [non-Buddhist] schools assert that the disintegration of things necessarily depends on other subsequent causes. [Thus they do not assert that a thing is an entity of disintegration at the time of its own production.] Also, because the Vaibhāṣikas assert a period of abiding which occurs between the two—production and disintegration—and which is other than these, their assertions on impermanence are utterly unlike [those of the Sautrāntikas and above]. Because [the Vaibhāṣikas] posit even permanent phenomena as existing by way of their own entity, they have to assert that uncaused space and so forth are functioning things (*dngos po, bhāva*) thus, their assertions on permanent [phenomena] are totally unlike those [of the Sautrāntikas and above].

Here the terms *dngos po* (*bhāva*) and *dngos med pa* (*abhāva*) are taken to mean functioning and non-functioning thing, the latter category including both permanent phenomena and non-existents. In other contexts, these terms may simply mean existent and non-existent.

The Sautrāntikas distinguish permanent from impermanent phenomena on the basis of the ability to perform a function. An impermanent phenomenon can perform the function of acting as a causal condition for the production of an ultimate consciousness —a direct perceiver—as well as producing its own continuation, and so forth. Permanent phenomena cannot. [The Sautrāntikas, Cittamātrins, and Mādhyamikas further assert that permanent phenomena do not exist by way of their entity, which is to say they do not exist by way of their own power but are imputed by thought.]

Impermanent things are momentary because they are produced by their causes as having a nature of disintegration, and non-functioning things (*dngos med, abhāva*) [such as encased space] must be posited as non-momentary because they are not so produced. It appears that, due to not understanding this essential, some in the past who claimed to be scholars and those who nowadays claim that [merely] reciting the words of a text is essential develop many [wrong views, such as] holding that momentariness signified only the non-existence at a later time of something which existed formerly. If one makes a detailed analysis without being misled by pleasant non-analytical words, it is apparent that now also just this appears [as the meaning of momentariness] in the deepest [thoughts] of most of those claiming skill in [the topics of] the Middle Way (*mādhyamika*) and Valid Cognition (*pramāṇa*). Thus, they even have difficulty understanding the meaning-isolate (*don ldog*) of impermanent sprout.

[It is possible for thought to isolate or zero in on impermanence in many ways. To zero in on the meaning of impermanence entails isolating only its meaning-isolate—that is, its definition: that which is momentary. To zero in on illustrations of impermanence is to isolate just illustrations of it, such as pot or sprout, which are thus illustration-isolates (*gzhi ldog*) of impermanence. To zero in on impermanence itself is to isolate just that generality alone, without considering its meaning or illustrations—just impermanence itself—which is called the self-isolate (*rang ldog*) or generality-isolate (*spyi ldog*). Thus, the term "isolate" (*ldog pa*) is used to indicate a conceptual zeroing in on one aspect of a multifaceted object. Here, Jang-gya is bemoaning his contemporaries' inability to comprehend the meaning of impermanence—momentariness—and all that it suggests such as the fact that the disintegration of products is built into them, not requiring further causes and making it such that things cannot stay for a second moment.]

Past, Present, and Future (109.13)

What is this system's presentation of the three times [past, present, and future]? I will explain. The Sautrāntika, Cittamātra, and Svātantrika-Mādhyamika systems have similar ways of presenting the three times. They maintain that any functioning thing is necessarily a present object and any past or future object is necessarily a non-functioning thing. Moreover, when a thing such as a sprout has disintegrated, all the entities which are its parts cease without [that cessation's] becoming any other thing. There is not even the slightest entity of a past or future object which is not a mere elimination of its object of negation; for this reason, it is thought that any past or future object cannot be an impermanent thing [but must be a non-affirming negative].[26]

Further, to use a sprout as an illustration, the past of a sprout is the state of its [i.e., the sprout of the first moment] having disintegrated (*zhig pa*) in the moment right after the sprout has been produced by causes and conditions. The sprout's future [occurs when], in general, the causes which are producers of the sprout exist but, due to the incompleteness of causes and conditions in some place or time such as an eastern field in wintertime, the sprout is for the time being not produced. The present [time] of the sprout is the time of the sprout's own establishment when the sprout has been produced and has not ceased.

Thus, the positing of a phenomenon's past and future times in relation to its present time accords with the texts of the great charioteers [Nāgārjuna and Asaṅga].

> The past and future times of a product are not posited on their own strength or due to their own power, but only in relation to the present time of that object.

Accordingly, the definition of a past object is: The state of having passed beyond a thing's own [present] time in relation to which [the past] must be posited.

The definition of a future object is: A phenomenon which is a state of a thing's not having arrived at its own [present] time, in relation to which [the future] must be posited.

The definition of a present object is: A phenomenon which has been produced in the present and has not ceased.

A functioning thing is a present object, but that present exists for only one moment; in the second moment it has ceased.

These definitions also, like what is found in the great texts, are made from the viewpoint of understanding; they are not constructed primarily to eliminate verbal entanglements [such as are incurred when] the general entities [of the three times] and so forth [are considered].

For example, there is the problem of whether the past and future are *times*. If so, they must be impermanent things. However, according to Sautrāntika all impermanent phenomena are presently existing phenomena.[27]

I have intended this as a discussion for those who advocate reasoning, not as something to be discussed by raving childish expostulators intent merely on passing time in essenceless debate by [flinging consequences that] undermine [the opponent's view].

After [wrongly] propounding that neither past nor future [objects] are established bases [and are thus non-existent], some people posit definitions for these. [Positing definitions for the non-existent] is not the system of any of the four schools of tenets, and [these people] are merely taking as their basis the rote words of proud fools of the past. For no scholar would tire himself out positing a definition for the horns of a rabbit!

CHAPTER THREE
EXCLUSIONS (111.2)

Here "exclusion" (*sel ba, apoha*) and "negative phenomenon" (*dgag pa, pratiṣedha*) are synonymous. Therefore, if exclusions are divided, there are two types: exclusions which are non-affirming negatives (*med dgag gi sel ba, *prasajya-pratiṣeda-apoha*) and exclusions which are affirming negatives (*ma yin* *dgag gi sel ba, *paryudāsa-pratiṣedha-apoha*). The first of these consist of objective phenomena and mental phenomena. These are mentioned by the master Śāntarakṣita [in his *Ornament to the Middle Way*]:

> Here, exclusions are of two types
> Affirming and non-affirming.
> Non-affirming [negatives] are of two types
> Because they are divided [into] mental and objective [phenomena].

Regarding this, exclusions which are affirming negatives as well as objective phenomena are, for example, opposite-from-non-pot, opposite-from-non-impermanent sound and so forth.

Non-pot (which itself is a negative phenomenon) is opposite from everything that is not pot; the opposite of this is pot. When opposite-from-non-pot appears to the mind, it is by way of negating or eliminating non-pot. Thus, it is a negative phenomenon. Specifically, it is an affirming negative because something positive, pot, is suggested in place of its object of negation, non-pot.

Dharmakīrti's *Commentary on (Dignāga's) "Compendium on Valid Cognition"* states:

> By the former proofs
> An affirming [negative] is established.

For example, if one says, "The subject, sound, is opposite from non-impermanent because of being a product" the reason—a product—proves the existence of an affirming negative.[28]

Definitions (111.12)

The definition of a mere exclusion is: An object realized by way of actually excluding [its] object of negation.

The definition of an affirming negative exclusion is: An exclusion which suggests another phenomenon which is positive.

The definition of a non-affirming negative exclusion is: An exclusion which does not suggest another phenomenon which is positive.

Suggesting or not suggesting another phenomenon signifies

suggesting or not suggesting [some other positive object or affirming negative] in place of [the exclusion's] own object of negation.

The definition of a mental exclusion is: An affirming-negative exclusion with the status of a mere imputation by thought.

The definition of an objective exclusion is: An exclusion that is an affirming negative established by way of its own nature and is not a mere mental imputation.

Objection: In that case, one would have to assert that even the specifically characterized phenomenon which is a pot is an exclusion because it excludes [phenomena of] dissimilar type that are its objects of exclusion [since any phenomenon excludes, or is not, everything but itself].

Answer: Then according to you, [pot] would be a negative phenomenon because it negates [phenomenon of] dissimilar type which are its objects of negation.

An exclusion does eliminate phenomena of dissimilar type which are its object of exclusion, but whatever eliminates or negates phenomena dissimilar from itself is not necessarily an exclusion or a negative phenomenon. In order to be a negative phenomenon an object must be *conceptually realized by way of an explicit elimination* of its object of negation. Otherwise, all phenomena would be negatives because any object excludes everything of a type dissimilar to itself.

There are four ways in which an affirming negative may suggest another phenomenon in place of the object negated. (1) For example, [the fact that] "the fat Yajñadatta does not eat during the day" suggests another positive phenomenon implicitly [because it suggests that Yajñadatta eats at night]. (2) "The existence of non-production from self" both explicitly suggests another phenomenon [existence] and eliminates the object of negation [production from self] with a single phrase.

If the statement did not stipulate the *existence* of non-production from self, no other positive object would be suggested, and the phrase would express a non-affirming negative.

(3) "A non-emaciated fat Yajñadatta who does not eat during

the day exists" suggests another phenomenon both explicitly and implicitly.

It explicitly suggests that Yajñadatta exists and implicitly suggests that he eats at night.

(4) The statement "He is not a Brahmin" [when said] after one has ascertained that a person is either of royal or Brahmin lineage and has not yet ascertained his particular lineage makes its suggestion [that he is of the royal lineage] by way of context.

Further, Avalokitavrata's *Commentary on (Bhāvaviveka's) "Lamp for (Nāgārjuna's)* 'Wisdom' " quotes [a stanza which describes the four modes by which affirming negatives can indicate positive phenomena or other affirming negatives].

> Negative [phenomena] (1) which indicate [a positive phenomenon] implicitly,
> (2) Which with one phrase [explicitly] establish [a positive phenomenon and eliminate an object of negation],
> (3) Which involve [both of] those [implicit and explicit indication],
> And (4) the words of which do not indicate [a positive phenomenon except through context] are affirming [negatives].[29]

A negative [expressed by a term] which does not make a suggestion [or implication] in any of these four ways is a non-affirming negative; "What is other [than these four] is other [that is, a non-affirming negative]."

Therefore, [in answer to the objection (p.151) that pot would be an exclusion because of excluding dissimilar types] it is in fact not sufficient that [a phenomenon] eliminate an object of negation; either the term expressing it must eliminate [an object of negation] or the aspect of explicitly eliminating an object of negation must appear to the mind which realizes it.

A negative phenomenon is posited from the viewpoint of either (1) the term which expresses it or (2) the appearance to the thought consciousness that realizes it. In the former case, the term that expresses it does so *by way of* explicitly eliminating an object of negation as in the case of non-pot; in the latter, the appearance to the thought consciousness realizing it is *by way of* explicitly eliminating the object of negation as is the case with reality (*chos nyid, dharmatā*)[30] which even though it contains no negative term such as "non" or "less" is merely an elimination of an object of negation, a substantially existent self.

A phenomenon suggested [by an affirming negative] must be either an [other] affirming negative or a positive object. Suggesting another phenomenon which is a non-affirming negative does not make something an affirming negative.

A non-affirming negative can imply another non-affirming negative. For instance, that Brahmins do not drink beer suggests that they do not drink malt beer.

All things [permanent and impermanent] naturally abide without being mixed with other entities; therefore, they abide as opposite from all [phenomena of] similar and dissimilar types.

For example, pot is opposite or different from things of similar type—such as pillar, wall, and even golden pot—and also from objects of dissimilar type such as uncaused space.

Therefore, with respect to a basis [or phenomenon] such as sound, it is suitable to make many divisions of reverses [or isolates] consisting of opposite from [phenomena of] similar type [such as other products] and opposite from dissimilar types [such as the non-product space]. For, the Lord of Reasoning [Dharmakīrti] said:

> Because all things naturally abide in their own entity they possess dependence on reversal from other things.[31]

The fact that a thing abides in its own entity means that it is not mixed with the entities of other phenomena. It is reversed or isolated from them. Pot's self-isolate and pot have the relationship of basis and depender respectively; still, they are one entity.

Many reverses from dissimilar types can be posited with respect

> to pot. It is reversed from the non-produced and thus is produced; similarly, it is reversed from the permanent, the non-existent, and things.[32]

Even though the actual basis of refutation and proof [which is a mental image of the subject being debated] does not ultimately exist [since it is merely imputed by thought],[33] in dependence on it one realizes well the ultimate mode of subsistence [of impermanent sound, for example,] by thoroughly realizing the specific characteristic of impermanent sound from the viewpoint of [its] many reverses. This is how conventional valid cognizers become causes of realizing the ultimate mode of subsistence.

With respect to understanding these [systems'] divisions of the two truths, it is indispensable [to understand how conventional valid cognition causes realization of the ultimate truth] and so forth. Although it is indeed necessary to settle this in greater detail, fearing it would run to too much, I will not write on it further.

CHAPTER FOUR
EXTERNAL OBJECTS (113.8)

This section has two parts, the actual assertions on external objects and assertions on non-revelatory forms (*rnam par rig byed ma yin pa'i gzugs, avijñaptirūpa*).

Actual Assertions on External Objects (113.10)

[Like the Vaibhāṣikas] this system also asserts partless particles, which are said to be the final of minute particles and incapable of being further broken down [even by thought].[34] Asaṅga's *Compendium of Knowledge* (*mNgon pa kun btus, Abhidharmasamuccaya*) says:

> It is stated that a composite of minute particles is known as an aggregation of forms. With respect to that, a minute particle is known as without corporeality [because a single such particle is non-obstructive].[35] A

minute particle is posited through making the finest possible mental division.

Although minute particles have the nature of the four elements [earth, water, fire, and wind] and the four elemental transformations [visible form, odor, taste, and tangibility], unlike the Vaibhāṣikas, the Sautrāntikas do not assert [a minute particle] to be a collection of eight separate atomic substances.

There is a difference between minute (*rdul phra rab, paramāṇu*) and small particles (*rdul phran*) because a composite of seven minute particles is asserted as a single small particle. For Vasubandhu's *Treasury of Knowledge* says (3.85-86.a):

> [The final divisions of form, name, and time]
> Are [respectively] minute particle, [letter, and] moment
> Just as a minute particle [consists of seven subtle particles]....

Matter is achieved through a conglomeration of minute particles. As was explained before in the Vaibhāṣika section, there are three [ways in which the minute particles are arranged]: touching, encircling, and without interstice. The explanation of this in Śāntarakṣita's *Ornament to the Middle Way* (*dbU ma'i rgyan gyi 'grel ba, Madhyamakālaṃkāravṛtti*) and Kamalaśīla's *Commentary on the Difficult Points of Śāntarakṣita's "Ornament"* (*De kho na nyid bsdus pa'i dka' 'grel, Tattvasaṃgrahapañjikā*) can be applied to both Vaibhāṣika and Sautrāntika.

Some scholars [Jam-yang-shay-ba is one] mistakenly think that there are Sautrāntikas Following Reasoning who assert minute particles as having parts. They say this because Dignāga's *Examination of Objects of Observation* (*dMigs pa brtags pa, Ālambanaparīkṣāvṛtti*) and commentary explain that in debates between Sautrāntikas and Cittamātrins, the Sautrāntikas maintain that when minute particles having parts aggregate, they individually cast an aspect similar to themselves [to the consciousness perceiving them]. However, those texts are merely explaining that when the Sautrāntikas are forced by the Cittamātrins' reasoning, they must propound that once many minute particles have aggregated and formed a gross object, that gross object has parts and casts its image [to the perceiving consciousness], in which case it would not be contradictory for even the minute particles which serve as the building blocks of that gross object to cast their images. Dignāga's text then describes how to refute the position [which the Sautrāntikas are forced to accept]. Nevertheless, in the Sautrāntikas' own basic tenets I do not think there is any explanation that minute particles are asserted to have parts.[36] Although there are many reasons for this, I will not write about them here; the intelligent should examine this in detail.

Non-Revelatory Forms (114.12)

This system asserts that although non-revelatory forms exist, they are not fully qualified forms. [In this vein] Jetāri's *Work on the Texts of the Sugata* (*bDer gshegs gzhung gi rab byed, Sugatamatavibhāṅgakārika*) says, "Non-obstructive form does not exist."[37] Also the *Ṭik chen de nyid snang ba*[38] says: "Non-obstructive non-revelatory form does not exist as fully qualified form."

With respect to proof by reasoning [that non-revelatory form is not fully qualified form], Vasubandhu's *Explanation of the "Treasury of Knowledge"* says:

> Some Sautrāntikas state that [non-revelatory forms which are vows] do not substantially exist (1) because [a vow which] has been taken is merely the non-doing [of an infraction of that vow, such as not killing], (2) because [the vow] is imputed in dependence on great elements in the past [the ritual and recitation at the time of taking the vow], (3) because even those [great elements] are not the entity [of the vow], and (4) because it does not have the characteristics of form.

According to the Sautrāntikas, a vow is not an actual form, but a mind of abandonment.[39] However, since the sound which acts as a cause of the vow is form, the name of the cause is applied to the effect, and the vow itself is called a form.[40]

Question: What are non-revelatory forms asserted to be?
Answer: They are asserted to be imaginary forms which are phenomena-sources (*Chos kyi skye mched, dharmāyatana*).[41]

[The five sense objects—forms, sounds, odors, tastes, and tangible objects—act as causes for or sources (*skye mched, āyatana*) of the sense-consciousnesses which observe them. Thus, for example, forms are causes for, or sources of, the eye consciousness; in recognition of this fact they are called form-sources; sounds, as causes or sources of the ear consciousness, are sound-sources and so forth. In the same way, those phenomena which are objects of and, therefore, sources of the mental consciousness are known as phenomena-sources.]

Vasubandhu's Explanation of the "*Treasury*" says:

> That form which is undemonstrable [to the senses][42] and non-obstructive is included among phenomena-sources.

The Vaibhāṣika and Sautrāntika statements on this are explained at length in Vasubandhu's *Explanation of the "Treasury"* at the point of commenting on [the following line] from the *Treasury* [4.4]:

> . . . Because the three aspects and non-contaminated form are taught [in sutra]
> As are the increasers [of virtue, harmful deeds] not done [by oneself but ordered done by others], paths and so forth.

The three aspects of form are (1) demonstrable and obstructive forms, such as tables; (2) undemonstrable and obstructive forms, such as the eye sense power; and (3) undemonstrable and unobstructive forms such as a non-revelatory form. Because non-revelatory forms are unobstructive, they are not actual forms, but since they are the only phenomena posited for this category mentioned in sutra, they must exist.

"Non-contaminated form" refers to the body and speech of Superiors. When one has taken a vow, the merit of maintaining it increases even while one sleeps; this could not occur if there were no non-revelatory form. Similarly, if one causes someone else to perform a non-virtue such as murder, at the time of his actually carrying out the murder one's own continuum undergoes a subtle transformation, and one accumulates the non-virtue of the existence of non-revelatory form.[43]

If one wishes to know about this, those [texts] should be consulted.

CHAPTER FIVE
CONSCIOUSNESS (115.8)

The detailed explanation of how consciousnesses apprehend objects has three parts: the actual explanation, the presentation of valid cognizers which are comprehenders, and the presentation of reasoning, a branch of inferential cognition. [The latter is presented in chapter six.]

Actual Explanation (115.9)

When a consciousness apprehends an object, it does not do so without [being generated in the] aspect [of that object] but within having the aspect [of the object]. For if the object itself were known clearly without [any] aspect, that object would be an entity of illumination and in that case would be apprehended even without reliance on a consciousness.

If the object could be known without having to interact with the consciousness in any way, then the object itself would have the characteristics of being clear and knowing. Since being clear and knowing are the unique features of a consciousness, this would mean that the object could be known—or would know itself—without having to be realized by any consciousness external to itself.

As to [the way in which] an object is known by a consciousness, the master Bodhibhadra's *Explanation of (Āryadeva's) "Compendium of Wisdom"* (*Ye shes snying po kun las btus pa shes bya ba'i bshad sbyar, Jñānasārasamuccayanāmanibandhana*) gives this explanation:

> When a person observes a glass whose color is altered due to [reflecting] a hue, his eye apprehends both the

glass-crystal and the color. The person apprehends the glass through direct perception and the hue by means of a reflection, whereby he apprehends two objects.

When one looks in the mirror, one does not see one's face but an image of it. Similarly, in looking at a tree through a window one sees an image of the tree appearing in the glass. Both glass and tree are obstructive forms and both obstruct vision; the fact that glass is transparent means images can appear in it; it does not mean that one sees through the glass. If one looks "through" yellow glass, one will see a yellow mountain even though such does not exist; this is a sign that one is observing an image and not the actual object.[44]

Similarly, that which is perceived by a direct perceiver is an aspect of just consciousness. External objects which are collections of minute particles and which are a separate entity from [the perceiving] consciousness are the basis for the appearance of the consciousness [in the aspect] of color and shape.

[The Sautrāntikas] do not, like the Vaibhāṣikas, say that the physical eye sense power sees;[45] the agents of seeing and so forth [hearing, smelling, tasting, and touching] are only the consciousnesses. However, one does not see that which is intercepted by walls and so forth because such are blocked from appearing to a consciousness. It is not correct that, as the Vaibhāṣikas maintain, the physical sense sees [objects] but does not see anything which is blocked [by form], for even when there is *mching bu* [a yellow translucent stone], mica, glass, or water intervening, one sees [through it in the sense of perceiving the object's image there].

The statement [in sutra] that "the eye sees forms" [does not mean that the eye sense power (*dbang bo, indriya*) sees forms but] is a case of imputing the activity of the consciousness—the supported—to the physical sense power which is its support. The Blessed One used doctrinal terminology which accords with the conventions of the world; thus, one should rely on the meaning and not be attached to mere words. This is explained extensively in the first chapter of Vasubandhu's *Explanation of the "Treasury."*

[The Sautrāntika system] has three ways of asserting consciousnesses as having aspects.[46] The Non-Pluralists maintain that many aspects appear to a single consciousness; the Half-Eggists, that only a single aspect appears to a single consciousness; and the Proponents of an Equal Number of Subjects and Objects maintain that when many aspects appear, the consciousnesses are also multiple. The foremost [Tsong-ka-ba] and his spiritual sons explain that when Dharmakīrti's *Ascertainment of Valid Cognition* and *Commentary on (Dignāga's) "Compendium on Valid Cognition"* are asserted as [presenting] the Sautrāntika system, they should be interpreted in accordance with [the system of] the Non-Pluralists.

The Non-Pluralists (116.16)
Whatever number of aspects exist that are one substantiality of establishment and abiding with blue—its productness, impermanence and so forth—that many aspects of the object are cast [toward the perceiving consciousness]. Nevertheless, the subjective consciousness is generated into having the aspect just of mere blue. For example, although the many aspects of blue, yellow, and so forth of a mottled object are cast to the sense consciousness apprehending a mottle, the eye consciousness is generated into having not that number [of aspects] but just the aspect of a mottle.

The Half-Eggists (116.20)
Aspects such as productness which are one entity of establishment and abiding with the object blue are not cast individually [toward the consciousness]; only the aspect of blue is cast, and the consciousness also is generated into having the aspect of just blue. [For example] to an eye consciousness apprehending a mottle, the object merely casts an aspect of a mottle, and the subject [the consciousness] is also generated into having the aspect of just a mottle.

Proponents of an Equal Number of Subjects and Objects (117.4)
Whatever number of aspects exist that are one substantiality

of establishment and abiding with blue—such as the productness and impermanence related with blue—that many aspects are cast [toward the consciousness], and the consciousness is simultaneously generated into having that number of aspects.

The Non-Pluralists are the opponents [refuted] in Śāntarakṣita's *Commentary to the "Ornament to the Middle Way"* in the context of a debate between Sautrāntika Non-Pluralists and proponents of Cittamātra in which the former maintain that if, as the proponents of Cittamātra claim, subject and object were the same entity, it would be impossible for there to be many aspects and only one perceiving consciousness: "If the consciousness is just singular in nature and the aspects [it perceives] are many, then they abide as contradictory phenomena [of which nothing can exist that is both]. Therefore, that the consciousness and the aspects [it perceives] are not different [entities] is contradicted."

Regarding the Half-Eggists, Jetāri states:

> The internal perceiver is other [than the external object]
> And the external appearance is also other [than the consciousness]
> That which is illuminated [the object] and the illuminator [the subject]
> Are not the same, like a butter lamp [and what it illumines].

The Proponents of an Equal number of Subjects and Objects are mentioned in Śāntarakṣita's *Ornament to the Middle Way* where it says (*4a.2*):

> If one asserts that in seeing a displayed painting
> Many simultaneous minds similar [in number] arise with respect to it...

Although both the Sautrāntikas and Cittamātrins have these three ways of asserting aspects, they differ in that the Cittamātrins do not consider external objects to cast their image [toward the consciousness] whereas the Sautrāntikas do.

Śāntarakṣita's *Ornament to the Middle Way* says (*3b.2*):

> "Consciousnesses arise serially
> With respect to the white and so forth [of a mottle].
> [Because they arise very quickly
> Fools think they are simultaneous.]"

Later scholars explain that the sequential arising of various [consciousnesses] taught in this passage [is asserted by] only the Sautrāntikas Following Scripture. If one analyzes the order and the relationship of former and later passages in the explanations of *Ornament to the Middle Way* and its commentary, the presence of two ways of [propounding] an equal number of subjects and objects—simultaneous and serial arising of various consciousnesses—is not contradictory. [Thus, this can be considered a category with two subdivisions, rather than as two types of proponents as Jam-yang-shay-ba has it.]

The individual modes of debate and so forth can be understood from the root text and commentaries of Śāntarakṣita's *Ornament to the Middle Way*.

It does not appear that the foremost omniscient father [Tsong-ka-ba] and his spiritual sons [Gyel-tsap and Kay-drup] clearly explained whether or not Sautrāntika has a system of asserting aspects in the mode of the Half-Eggists. Only a small indication occurs in Kay-drup's *Clearing Away the Mental Darkness with respect to the Seven Treatises*, and Gung-ru Gyel-tsen-sang-bo (*Gung-ru-rgyal-mtshan-bzang-po*), an actual student of the foremost [Tsong-ka-ba], explains the Half-Eggists in accordance with the above in his *Thousand Dosages of the Middle Way*. The great lord of scholars and adepts, the foremost Jam-yang-shay-ba-dor-jay says:

> Though some say Jetāri's text indicates that [the Half-Egg theory] is common to both Sautrāntika and Cittamātra, it appears difficult to posit this second mode of assertion [that only a single aspect of blue or mottle is cast toward a single consciousness] in the Sautrāntika system.

It is just as he said.

Presentation of Valid Cognizers Which Are Comprehenders (118.11)

Due to objects of comprehension being definite as the two, specifically characterized phenomena (*rang mthsan, svalakṣāna*) and generally characterized phenomena (*spyi mtshan, sāmānya-lakṣaṇa*) or as the two, manifest (*mngon gyur, abhimukhī*) and hidden (*lkog gyur, parokṣa*) phenomena, valid cognizers (*tshad ma, pramāṇa*) are definite as the two, direct (*mngon sum, pratyakṣa*) and inferential (*rjes dpag, anumāna*). Furthermore, these are asserted as necessarily eliminating a third possibility both negatively and positively.

A third possibility—a valid cognizer that is neither direct nor inferential—is eliminated from both negative and positive viewpoints. For example, from the negative side, "It follows that there are definitely two valid cognizers because there is no third type of valid cognizer which is neither a direct valid cognizer nor an inferential cognizer."

On the positive side, "It follows that there are definitely two valid cognizers because whatever is a final illustration (*mtshan gzhi mthar thug pa*) of a valid cognizer is necessarily either direct or inferential."

The thesis itself can also be either negative or positive: (1) there is no third [valid cognizer] which is neither direct not inferential and (2) there is no third [valid cognizer] which is both [direct and inferential].[47]

All [tenet systems] from Sautrāntika through Svātantrika concur [in these assertions].

Prāsaṅgikas are not included here because they do not assert specifically characterized phenomena. Vaibhāṣikas are not included because they do not assert non-affirming negatives and thus have a different perspective on generally characterized phenomena.

The definition of a valid cognizer is: A new undeceived knower.

A direct valid cognizer is a non-conceptual and non-mistaken consciousness which is a prime cognizer. [Valid cognizers] are of two types, other-knowers and self-knowers.

The divisions of other-knowers by way of their empowering condition (*bdag rkyen, adhipatipratyaya*) are: sense, mental, and yogic direct perceivers. The first type depends on a physical sense power to be its empowering condition, the second on mere mind to be its empowering condition, and the third on a union of calm abiding and special insight to be its empowering condition.

A mental direct perceiver is produced for only one moment at the end of a continuum of sense direct perception. Furthermore, the omniscient Gyel-tsap follows Pan-chen Gyel-nga-dun-ba (*rGyal-rnga-bdun-pa*) in saying that for common beings [a mental direct perceiver] is a very hidden phenomenon. Even though this assertion is widely renowned nowadays, the omniscient Kay-drup explains it just a little differently, but I will not elaborate on this here.

A self-knower is: That which (1) solely has the aspect of the apprehender, (2) is directed inward, and (3) for which the dualistic appearance of subject and object has vanished.

The great scholar Dharmottara explains that the continuation of a direct perceiver is a subsequent cognizer (*bcad shes, *pariccinnajñāna*), and for the most part our own scholars assert subsequent cognizers similarly. However, there does not appear to be a clear explanation of a presentation of self-knowers by the Sautrāntikas Following Scripture.

An inference is: a consciousness which (1) arises in dependence on its own base, a sign having the three modes, and which (2) thoroughly infers the object being proved.[48]

A correct reason *has* the three modes in the sense of *being* them. For example, a syllogism proving that sound is impermanent because of being a product is analyzed as follows:

THE SUBJECT, SOUND, IS IMPERMANENT BECAUSE OF BEING A PRODUCT.

THE SUBJECT, SOUND,	IS IMPERMANENT	BECAUSE OF BEING A PRODUCT.
subject	predicate	reason
thesis or probandum		

Generally speaking, the three modes of the reason to be ascertained are:

1. Property of the subject (*phyogs chos, pakṣadharma*). One ascertains that the reason is a quality of the subject "sound."
2. Pervasion (*rjes khyab, anvayavyāpti*). One ascertains that the reason exists only among phenomena of the same class as the predicate. Roughly speaking, for example, whatever is a product is necessarily impermanent.
3. Counter-pervasion (*ldog khyab, vyatirekavyāpti*). One ascertains that whatever is not of the same class as the predicate is necessarily not the reason; for example, whatever is not impermanent is necessarily not a product.

There are three types of valid inferences: (1) inferential valid cognizer by the power of the fact, (2) inferential valid cognizer through renown, and (3) inferential valid cognizer through belief.

An inferential valid cognizer by the power of the fact is one that understands an object by the power of the thing itself. For example, an inference realizing sound to be impermanent comprehends this fact through the force of the sound's being established in its own actuality as impermanent.

An inferential valid cognizer through renown is one recognizing that any name is suitable to be applied to any object of knowledge. For example, the "rabbit possessor" (the lunar orb in which the shape of a rabbit is said to appear) is suitable to be called "the moon."

An inferential valid cognizer through belief is a consciousness which, on the basis of correct reasonings, ascertains a phenomenon that is very hidden and which, therefore, is inaccessible either to direct perception or to other types of inference. An example is the inferential consciousness which realizes the validity of the passage which indicates the causes and effects of actions by stating that "From giving (arise) resources, from ethics (arise) happiness."[49]

The Sautrāntika System's Explanation of the Three Empowering Conditions of Sense Direct Perceivers (119.12).

An empowering condition (*bdag rkyen, adhipatipratyaya*) [of a sense direct perceiver] is a sense power that empowers the uncommon feature of the sense consciousness which is its own effect. [For example, the empowering condition of an eye consciousness, the physical eye sense, gives its power with respect to colors and shapes, not with respect to sounds, odors, tastes, or objects of touch.]

An object-condition (*dmigs rkyen, ālaṃbanapratyaya*) is any object which directly generates the consciousness apprehending it into having its aspect. [For example, the object blue causes an eye consciousness to be generated into having the aspect of blue.]

An immediately preceding condition (*de ma thag rkyen, samanantarpratyaya*), is a consciousness (1) which precedes [a sense or mental consciousness] without any other consciousness intervening between them and (2) which produces [the sense or mental consciousness] into an experiencing entity. [For example, a consciousness which arises immediately prior to a sense direct perceiver apprehending form gives the latter its quality of being able to *experience* its object.]

In this system the two—object-condition and apprehended object (*gzung don*)—are co-extensive [i.e. synonymous].

CHAPTER SIX
REASONING (119.18)

Dharmakīrti's *Commentary on (Dignāga's) "Compendium on Valid Cognition"* says:

> [A correct reason] which is a quality of the subject
> And is pervaded by the predicate is of just three types.

Accordingly that which is the three modes (see p. 164) is the entity [or definition] of a correct sign.

If correct signs are divided, there are the three:

1. Correct effect sign (*bras rtags yang dag, samyak-kārya-liṅga*),
2. Correct nature sign (*rang bzhin kyi rtags yang dag, samkyak-svabhāva-liṅga*),
3. Correct non-observation sign (*ma dmigs pa'i rtags yang dag, samyak-anupalabdhi-liṅga*).

Correct effect signs [which prove the existence of a cause by the sign of an effect] have five divisions:

1. Proving an actual cause.
   Example: With respect to the subject, on a smokey pass, fire exists because smoke exists.[50]
2. Proving a preceding cause.
   Example: The subject, the bluish rising smoke in the intermediate space, is preceded by its own former cause, fire, because of being smoke.
3. Proving a general cause.
   Example: The subjects, the appropriated aggregates, have their own causes because of being occasionally produced things.
4. Proving a particular cause.
   Example: The subject, a sense consciousness perceiving blue, has its own object-condition because of being a thing which is not produced without the existence of its object-condition.
5. Effect sign which is a means of inferring causal attributes.[51]
   Example: With respect to the subject, possession of a lump of molasses in the mouth, there exists the capacity of the former taste of molasses to generate the later form of molasses because the present taste of molasses exists.

Nature signs [in which the reason and predicate are of one nature] are of two types:

1. Nature sign that is free of qualification.
   Example: The subject, a sound, is an impermanent phenomenon because of being a thing.
2. Nature sign involving a qualification.

The latter is of two types:

a) That which implies a qualification [or agent] which is another substantial entity [from the subject].
   Example: The subject, the sound of a conch, is an impermanent phenomenon because of being a created phenomenon.
b) That which implies [a qualification or agent which] is not another substantial entity [from the subject].

Example: The subject, sound, is an impermanent phenomenon because of being a product.[52]

Non-observation signs [which are synonymous with signs of negative phenomena] are of two types:

1. Sign which is a non-observation of the non-appearing [such as an invisible spirit].

   Example: With respect to the subject, here in this place in front, there does not exist a factually concordant subsequent cognizer—one that ascertains a flesh eater—in the continuum of a person for whom a flesh-eater is a supersensory object because there does not exist a valid cognizer—one that observes a flesh-eater—in the continuum of a person for whom a flesh-eater is a supersensory object.

2. Sign which is a non-observation of the suitable to appear. The latter is of two types:

   a) Non-observation of a related object.
   b) Observation of a contradictory object.

Signs which are a non-observation of a related object are of four types [depending on whether the related object is a]:

1. Cause.

   Example: With respect to the subject, on a lake at night, smoke does not exist because of the non-existence of fire.

2. Pervader.

   Example: With respect to the subject, on a craggy cliff where trees are not observed by valid cognition, an aśoka tree does not exist because of the non-existence of trees.

3. Nature [or definition].

   Example: With respect to the subject, on a place where a pot is not observed by valid cognition, a pot does not exist because of the non-observation of a pot by valid cognition.

4. Direct effect [of the predicate of the negandum i.e., that which is negated].

Example: With respect to the subject, the inside of a walled circle devoid of smoke, the direct cause of smoke does not exist because of the non-existence of the direct effect, smoke.

Non-observation signs which are an observation of a contradictory object are of six types, [signifying the] observation of what is:

1. Contradictory with the nature [of the designated predicate of the probandum].

   Example: With respect to the subject, on a place in the east covered by a large powerful fire, the continuous tangible object, cold, does not exist because of being a placed covered by a large powerful fire.
2. A contradictory effect [i.e., an effect contradictory with the nature of the designated predicate of the negandum].

   Example: With respect to the subject, on a place in the east covered by strongly billowing smoke, the continuous tangible object, cold, does not exist because of being a placed covered by strongly billowing smoke.
3. Contradictory with a cause [of the designated predicate of the probandum].

   Example: With respect to the subject, a place in the east covered by a large powerful fire, continuous goose bumps which are an effect of the cold do not exist because of being a place covered by a large powerful fire.
4. An effect of that which is contradictory with the cause [of the designated predicate of the probandum].

   Example: With respect to the subject, on a place in the east covered by strongly billowing smoke, continuous goose bumps which are an effect of cold do not exist because of being a place covered by strongly billowing smoke.
5. Contradictory with a pervader [of the designated predicate of the negandum].

   Example: With respect to the subject, on a place in the east covered by a large powerful fire, the continuous tangible object, snow, does not exist because of being a place covered by a large powerful fire.

6. An effect of an object which is contradictory [with the predicate of the probandum].[53]

   Example: The subject, a place in the east covered by strongly billowing smoke, does not abide harmlessly together with goose bumps which are an effect of cold because of there being strongly billowing smoke.

   These are contradictory in the sense of not abiding together with the predicate of the negandum. For example, heat cannot abide together with goose bumps, which are an effect of cold, without interference.

Gyel-tsap, Kay-drup, and the venerable Gen-dun-drup (*dGe-'dun-grub*) very extensively set forth and give a final analysis of the definite enumeration of signs [proving] that there are ten negative phenomena. [They interpret this] as the meaning of Dharmakīrti's *Ascertainment of Valid Cognition* which says, "Thus, this non-observation is of ten types by way of syllogistic differences." Therefore, other explanations of a greater number are simply pointless.

Furthermore, the ways of asserting the [five] aggregates, [eighteen] constituents, [twelve] sources, and five basic objects of knowledge (*shes bya, jñeya*) are for the most part similar to the [Vaibhāṣika assertions] explained earlier.

The five aggregates are: form, feelings, discriminations, compositional factors, and conciousnesses. The eighteen constituents are: the six objects—forms, sounds, odors, tastes, tangible objects, and phenomena—the six sense powers which are the empowering conditions for the six consciousnesses perceiving these objects—body and mental sense powers; and the six consciousnesses.

The six objects and six sense powers are the twelve sources.[54] The five basic objects of knowledge as presented in the Vaibhāṣika system are the appearing form base, main mind base, accompanying mental factor base, non-associated compositional factor base, and non-product base.[55]

The differences in the mode of asserting fifty-one mental factors and twenty-three non-associated compositional factors as well as the divisions of uncaused [phenomena] and so forth should be looked into elsewhere.[56]

CHAPTER SEVEN PATHS (120.19)

The presentations of the thirty-seven harmonies with enlightenment, the nine successive meditative absorptions, the six perfections, the eight Enterers and Abiders[57] and so forth are also asserted by this [Sautrāntika system]. With respect to the difference between the three paths of the Hearer, Solitary Realizer and Bodhisattva, it is asserted that although there is no difference in their mode of realizing selflessness, their paths can be differentiated by factors of method such as [the presence or absence of] great compassion and so forth.

Solitary Realizers spend more time accumulating merit on the path of accumulation than Hearers; only Bodhisattvas generate great compassion.[58]

An ascertainment of the sixteen aspects of the four noble truths—impermanence and so forth—which are the objects of the path is indispensably the very essence of the path; therefore, I will explain the mode [of this ascertainment] a little.[59]

How to Settle the Selflessness of Persons (121.5)

Whatever is neither one in nature with nor different in nature from its own aggregates is necessarily without inherent existence (*rang bzhin, svabhāva*). For example, the horns of a rabbit [are without inherent existence because they are neither one with nor different from their own aggregates]. A self-sufficient person which is not merely imputed to the collection or continuum [of the aggregates] is not established as either one in nature with or different in nature from its own aggregates. This is a sign of non-observation of a pervader.

The format here is that of a proof statement having two branches—the pervasion and the reason—as a property of the subject. The thesis or conclusion—that a self-sufficient person which is not merely imputed to the collection or continuum of its aggregates is without inherent existence—is not explicitly given.

A simpler example of this format is: "Whatever is a product is necessarily impermanent; for example, a pot. Sound is also a product." The person to whom this reason is stated understands that products are necessarily impermanent and can apply this understanding to pots, but has not yet applied it to sound. Hearing and reflecting on this proof statement, he would understand the conclusion, that sound is impermanent.

According to the syllogistic diagram on p. 164, this reasoning is as follows: "The subject, a self-sufficient person which is not merely imputed to the collection or continuum [of its aggregates], is without inherent existence because of being neither one in nature with, nor different in nature from, its own aggregates."

For example, wherever there is smoke there is fire, and if fire is not seen on, for example, a lake at night where it would be clearly visible, one can be certain that there is no smoke on the lake. Similarly, if an inherently existent person exists, it must be either the same as or different in nature from its aggregates, and, if neither of these conditions is fulfilled, it can be definitively concluded that a person does not inherently exist.

This reason is a sign of non-observation of a pervader because its thesis is established by the absence of a pervasive condition—being the same or different in nature from the aggregates—of that which is being negated—an inherently existent self-sufficient person. Further, this pervader is something that would be observed if it did exist. The fact that it is not found means that a self-sufficient person does not inherently exist, meaning here that it does not exist at all.

A self-sufficient person would be one that could appear to the mind without depending on the appearance of the mind and body. However, it can easily be established that there is no way for a person to appear without at least some of the mental and physical aggregates appearing.

A self-sufficient person would have to be either inherently one with or inherently different from its aggregates. The person, however, is not inherently one with the aggregates, for if it were, it would be one with them, and then just as there are five aggregates at any one time there would have to be five persons, or there could only be one aggregate since there is only one person. This is not the case. Moreover, the person is not naturally different from its aggregates, for this would entail their being entirely separate, like moon and stars.[60]

From among [reasons which establish] meanings and verbal conventions [usually definitions and definiendums, respectively] this reason is asserted as establishing a verbal convention [in that the reason itself is the meaning of non-inherent existence].

It is also possible for a reason to establish both a definition and a definiendum, that is, the object being defined. For example, "The subject, sound, is an impermanent thing because of being a product." "Impermanent thing" itself is a definiendum, but it is actually being proved both that sound is a momentary thing—this being the definition of impermanent thing—and that this momentary thing is called "impermanent thing." Sound is a subject which is an established base. It is also possible to have as a subject a non-established base such as a self-sufficient person.

Objection: This reason is not suitable as a correct one because the base [of the reason]—the subject—is negated by the sign [i.e., reason] whereby the composite of sign and subject is also negated and thus the thesis is eliminated by valid cognition. Furthermore, the reason would not be established as the property of the subject [for it could not be a quality of a subject negated by valid cognition].

Response: There is no fault. When both the reason and predicate are mere eliminations [non-affirming negatives], it is suitable to have a non-established base as the subject.

A correct sign of a negative phenomenon is possible with respect to a subject which is a non-established base; however, a correct sign of a positive phenomenon is possible only if the subject is an established base. The opponent thinks that because the subject—a self-sufficient person—does not exist, it would be impossible to have the first of the three modes of a reason which stipulates that the reason be a quality of the subject.

Also, with respect to why this is so, the master Dignāga says:

> Direct perception [only develops due to the appearance toward it of the aspects of its] object.
> Inference [by the power of the fact] as well as by way of belief or renown operates with respect to its own basis [the subject].

In explaining the meaning of these [lines], the glorious Dharmakīrti writes: "[Dignāga] said 'own basis' for the sake of indicating that a reason which eliminates a predicate, a basal subject, and the composite of those two, would be faulty; but eliminating the composite meaning of a merely [propounded] subject [such as a self-sufficient person, which does not exist] and the predicate is not faulty."

> The "composite" of the syllogism in question is: "The self-sufficient person which is not merely imputed to the collection or continuum of the aggregates is without inherent existence. Such a person does not in fact exist inherently, and therefore this composite or thesis is not eliminated as an object of valid cognition; in other words, it can be comprehended by a valid cognizer. The lack of inherent existence does exist, and therefore to eliminate this composite would be a fault, because it also exists.[61]
>
> There are two types of subjects: one is merely spoken but does not exist, the other is an object that actually serves as a basis for the reason—for example, sound. In the case of the former, when for example, the self-sufficient person appears to the mind, the meaning-generality or mental image of such serves as the basis which is qualified by the reason; thus, it is possible even with a non-existent subject to have the first mode of the reason, the qualification of the subject by the reason. The sign of non-inherent existence is established in dependence on that meaning-generality.[62]

Although a "merely [propounded] subject" is called a subject, it is not the basis of the predicate on this occasion [of stating as the subject "a self-sufficient person which is not merely imputed to the collection or continuum of the aggregates"]. Therefore, ["merely propounded subject" or "mere subject"] comes to mean a plain subject.

> Such a subject is merely spoken; it is not a basis upon which thought or valid cognition acts. A synonym of this is "stated subject" (*smra ba'i chos can*). In a syllogism which has this type of subject the reference is to the *appearance* or image of, for example, a person who is not merely imputed to its aggregates; since the image exists, it can serve as the basis upon which valid cognition acts. A self-sufficient person, however, does not exist and thus is a plain or mere subject in the sense that it cannot serve

as the base of the predicate.[63]

Every syllogism has both a stated and a basal subject. These may or may not be the same. For example, in the syllogism "Sound is impermanent because of being a product," sound is both the stated subject—because the object of expression of the term "sound" is sound itself—and the basal subject—because it is the base of the quality of impermanence. In a syllogism with a non-existent subject, however, the stated and basal subjects are different. If one states as the subject "a self-sufficient person which is not merely imputed to the collection or continuum of aggregates" the stated subject is this self-sufficient person but the basal subject is the meaning-generality of such a person because it is this meaning-generality that is qualified by the predicate and reason of the syllogism. Thus, there are four alternatives (*mu bzhi*) in the relationship between the two, stated subject and basal subject. The subject, "A self-sufficient person which is not merely imputed to the aggregates," in the above syllogism is a stated subject but not a basal subject. The meaning-generality of such a self-sufficient person is a basal subject but not a stated one. Sound, in the syllogism "the subject sound is impermanent because of being a product" is both the stated and basal subject. "Stated subject" and "non-existent subject" are not mutually inclusive, however, because, as in the example above, sound is the stated subject and does exist.[64]

In stating a syllogism with a non-existent subject such as a substantially existent self, or the general principal of the Sāṃkhyas, it is not necessary to say "The subject, the meaning-generality of the self-sufficient self. . . ." It is suitable just to say "the subject, the self-sufficient self. . . ." According to Gyel-tsap, but not for Kay-drup, it is not just the general principal or self-sufficient self that is the subject, it is the meaning-generality of these. The meaning-generality and its referent object appear undifferentiably to the mind of the opponent. Thus, for Gyel-tsap, the subject is an established base (*gzhi grub*), but whatever *is* a subject is not necessarily an established base. The subject is an established base because a meaning-generality is an established base; however, the self-sufficient self and the general principal are also the subjects even though they do not exist and thus are not established bases.

However, in the syllogism "The subject, a sound, is impermanent because of being a product" it is not suitable to say that the meaning-generality of sound is the subject—even though this appears to the mind of the opponent—because the meaning-generality is permanent. The meaning-generality is permanent because it is not put together from causes and conditions; it comes from the clear and knowing mind (*sems sel rig*).

If the predicate of the probandum and the reason are impermanent things, then the subject must definitely be an impermanent thing. However, it is not necessarily the case that if the subject is a thing, the predicate of the probandum and the reason must necessarily be impermanent things. For example, "The subject, a pot, is an object of knowledge because of being suitable as an object of mind." Here, both object of knowledge and object of mind are permanent, but this is a correct sign.[65]

If, when stating a reason, the qualification of the subject by the reason had to be established with respect to just whatever was the basis of debate, there would be no point in [Dignāga and Dharmakīrti] dividing subjects into the two—mere subjects and basal subjects.

When refuting the self (*ātman*) and principal (*pradhāna*) [of the Sāṃkhya system], it is necessary that these themselves be refuted; therefore, they must be taken as the basis of debate [subject] of the autonomous syllogism (*rang rgyud kyi sbyor ba, svatantraprayoga*). At that time, even though those subjects are refuted by the signs which establish them to be non-things [i.e., non-existent], there is no fault; for, just that is the correct means of developing an inference realizing the thesis—that self, principal and so forth do not exist. Therefore, the omniscient Kay-drup says:

> Regarding such a reason, the [thesis] being proven is a composite of the subject and [its] definite non-existence. Therefore, since the very non-establishment of the subject is a proof that the thesis is established by valid cognition, there is no fault. Although [something] is not an established base, there is no contradiction in its being a subject that someone desires to know about, and with respect to which the reason is ascertained. It is like the fact that, despite not being an established base, it is not contradictory for something to be a concordant example with respect to which the pervasion is ascertained. Therefore, [Dignāga's indicat-

ing the division into basal and mere subjects by] saying "own base" indicates that a reason is faulty if it negates a basal subject which is an established base; it does not indicate that a reason which merely negates the existence of a [mere] subject is faulty.

For example, there is no fault in a reason refuting the mere existence of a self-sufficient self or of the principal.[66]

Therefore, only the self, principal, and so forth are taken as the [refuted] subject; the meaning-of-the-term of these is not taken as the [refuted] subject. The omniscient Gyel-tsap says:

> The opponent, having mistaken the self-sufficient person and the appearance of such to be the same, wishes to know [whether or not such a person exists]. The sign [or reason] is established by valid cognition in relation to the meaning-of-the-term which is a [mental] appearance.

Unlike Kay-drup, Gyel-tsap considers that both the self and its image are the subject because they appear undifferentiably to the mind of the opponent. This means that the subject here consists of both a basal subject—the image—and a mere subject—the self-sufficient self.[67]

If the self-sufficient person were not taken as the subject, the self of persons itself would not be refuted. Since the opponent is operating within apprehending the [self-sufficient person] and its [mental] image as one, there is no fault of the meaning-of-the-term being unsuitable as the subject. Therefore, with regard to whatever is a correct sign, the subject about which knowledge is sought necessarily is an established base [because at least the image involved is an established base], but whatever is the subject about which knowledge is sought in relation to a correct sign is not necessarily an established base [because, for example, a self-sufficient person does not exist].

In the opinion of Geshe Belden Drakba, whatever is a subject *is* necessarily an established base. This would mean that the

> meaning-generality of a self-sufficient person is the only subject of a syllogism stating "The subject, a self-sufficient person, does not inherently exist because of being neither one with nor different from its mental and physical aggregates." However, according to Geshe Belden Drakba, whatever is a stated subject is not necessarily a subject, that is, it does not necessarily possess the qualities of the predicate of the probandum and the reason. This is because whatever is a subject must possess qualities, but if something does not exist—like the substantially self-sufficient self of persons—it cannot have qualities. That which has the qualities of not inherently existing and not being the same as or different from its aggregates is, in his view, the meaning-generality of a self-sufficient self. There are many systems of assertion on this. Some, unlike Geshe Belden Drakba, assert that whatever is the subject of a correct reason is *not* necessarily an established base. In that case, the self-sufficient self of persons could be considered the subject of a syllogism.[68]

Since the assertions of the two spiritual sons of the foremost omniscient [Tsong-ka-ba] are very profound, how could someone like myself make a presentation saying, "This one is right and that one is not?" However, the foremost Tsong-ka-ba himself clearly speaks about the meaning of this topic in his *Notes on (Śāntarakṣita's) "Ornament to the Middle Way"*. His explanation accords in large part with the latter's [Gyel-tsap's], and since it effectively bestows understanding, I will present it just as stated, down to the letter. Tsong-ka-ba's *Notes on (Śāntarakṣita's) "Ornament"* [9a.5] says:

> With respect to the meaning of Dignāga's statement [quoted on p. 173 above], Dharmakīrti's *Commentary on (Dignāga's) "Compendium on Valid Cognition"* says:
>
> These abiding as the conventions of objects which are
> An object inferred [the thesis being proven] or a means of inference [proof]
> Are designated in dependence on what are established as different for the mind.

Accordingly, there are [some] bases [subjects] which must be impermanent things; [for example] in the proofs of sound as impermanent by [the sign of being a] product and of fire existing on a [smoky] mountain pass by the sign of smoke, the two [subjects], sound and mountain pass, [are necessarily impermanent things]. The images which are the appearance to thought as opposite from these two are the actual bases of refutation and proof. Sound and mountain pass themselves are not the actual bases because they do not actually appear to the thought which makes a refutation or proof, and because [if they did actually appear as in complete engagement, then] when one feature was established, all its features would [absurdly] be established simultaneously.

> The proof of sound as impermanent and so forth is done in relation to the image of sound which appears to thought. If sound itself were posited as the actual basis of proof, there would be the fault that in establishing sound's impermanence one would simultaneously establish all its other features, because actual impermanent sound would be an object of direct perception and thus an object of complete engagement.

Nevertheless, the bases of the appearance of such images are [actual] sound and mountain pass; therefore, the bases [of debate in these cases] are necessarily impermanent things.

As for cases in which the basis, the subject, need not be an [impermanent] thing, even when [non-existents such as] the principal, Īśvara and so forth are taken as the basis of debate, the opposite of non-principal and non-Īśvara appear to thought. In observing that [image], these are established as "non-things" [that is, non-existent]. Therefore, with this [type of] basis, there is no fault of the other party not having [a subject he] wishes to know about or the challenger not having [a subject about which he] wishes [the opponent] to generate an inference. It can be refuted that the basis of the appearance [the principal] exists as a thing by reason of its being empty of the ability to perform a function; it can be refuted that the basis of the appearance [Īśvara] truly exists by reason of its being neither truly one nor truly many. When such refutation is done, the two reasons are established in relation to the appearances as opposite from non-principal and opposite from non-Īśvara. Just such [an image] is designated as the subject in relation to which the predicate is posited as its predicate and the subject in relation to which the reason is posited as its property. Thus there is no fault of the property of the subject not being established due to the refutation of the mere subject.

When one proves that sound is impermanent by [the sign of being a] product, the mere appearance which is the appearance as opposite from non-sound does not exist as a thing and thus the sign—product—is not established in relation to it, but must be established in relation to the sound which is the [image's] basis of appearance. This is due to the fact that things (*dngos po, abhāva*) are being taken as the sign and as the predicate.

When being empty of performing a function, or not being one or many are taken as signs, both the basis of the appearance [the principal and Īśvara] and the mere appearances [the images of the principal and Īśvara respectively] are established as those signs.

> Both the principal itself and its image are empty of being able to perform a function; similarly, both Īśvara and the image of Īśvara are neither truly one nor truly many.[69]

When those bases of appearance are established as being those signs, even though [those bases] are refuted, the mere appearance [or image of the subject under debate] serves as the subject on which the two qualities—the predicate being proven and the property of the subject—depend. This is the condensed essence [of the topic]; it should be known extensively from Kamalaśīla's *Illumination of the Middle Way*.

These statements are very weighty and of great import; thus, they need to be interpreted in detail. To do so here, however, would obscure the topic at hand [the selflessness of persons], so I will not write [more]. If it should be meaningful, I hope to explain it elsewhere.

To summarize, if one pieces together the explanations by the three, the father [Tsong-ka-ba] and sons [Gyel-tsap and Kay-drup], when the sign and predicate are mere eliminations [non-affirming negatives], the basis which is the subject need not be an established base. Therefore, "self," "principal," and so forth may be posited as subjects. When an inference is generated in the continuum of the opponent, the sign is actually established in relation to the meaning-of-the-term, and the stated subject is refuted through [that] sign. Hence there is no fault; [such a subject] is wholly beneficial for developing an inference realizing selflessness. Furthermore, the meaning-of-the-term which is the actual basis of proof and refutation can be posited as an imputed subject.

For example, in the syllogism "The subject, the principal, is a non-thing because of lacking the ability to perform a function," the actual subject is the principal itself; the mental image or meaning-of-the-term is the imputed subject.

The proof of sound as impermanent by [the sign of being a] product is a different case [because here if the subject is not existent, the presence of the sign in the subject cannot be established]. For since the sign [product] and the predicate [impermanent thing] are [impermanent] things, it is not suitable to establish them in relation to sound's meaning-of-the-term [which, as a mental image, is permanent]. This is the unblemished thought of the three, the foremost father [Tsong-ka-ba] and his spiritual sons [Gyel-tsap and Kay-drup].

These assertions are common to all Buddhist systems from Sautrāntika on up [Cittamātra, Svātantrika, and Prāsaṅgika]. However, a few qualifications are needed for Prāsaṅgika with respect to establishing the sign, subject, and meaning [predicate].

In the Prāsaṅgika system an inferential cognizer is not necessarily generated in dependence on stating a correct reason; a consequence (*thal 'gyur, prasaṅga*) can be sufficient.[70]

The mode of explanation of this in Kamalaśīla's *Illumination of the Middle Way* and so forth will be discussed later [in the Svātantrika chapter].[71]

Establishing the Pervasion of the Sign

[With respect to ascertaining that whatever is neither one in nature with nor different in nature from its own aggregates does not inherently exist] the valid cognizer which ascertains one nature and different natures to be explicit contradictories (*dngos 'gal*) [that is, a dichotomy] in the sense of being contradictories of mutual exclusion (*phan tshun spangs 'gal*) ascertains that the inverted reason pervades the predicate being negated.

> Basic syllogism: "The subject, a self-sufficient person which is not merely imputed to the collection or continuum of its aggregates, is without inherent existence because of being neither one in nature with nor different in nature from its aggregates." The valid cognizer which ascertains same and different natures to be mutually exclusive also understands that whatever exists must be either one or the other; that is the meaning of their being explicit contradictories or a dichotomy. This valid cognizer thereby understands that whatever inherently exists must be the same as or different from its aggregates. This is known as ascertainment of the counter pervasion.
>
> In the non-Prāsaṅgika systems, it is asserted that one can generate an inference in dependence on a consequence, but not in dependence on a consequence *alone*. According to Prāsaṅgika, it is sufficient to say, to a suitable opponent, "It follows that the subject, sound, is not a product because it is permanent." This will cause the opponent to understand that sound is in fact a product. The other systems maintain, however, that it is not sufficient to end the discussion with the above consequence; the opponent must also be told that "The subject, sound, is not permanent because it is a product." It is only in dependence on this statement that an inferential understanding of sound as impermanent will be generated in the mind of the opponent.[72]

Through the functioning of this valid cognizer together with the valid cognizer which ascertains [the sign as] a property of the subject [i.e., which ascertains that a self-sufficient person is neither one in nature with, nor different in nature from, its aggregates] the forward pervasion is ascertained. This is an ascertainment of the sign [of not being truly one or truly different] as absent from the dissimilar class [of inherently existent phenomena] and existing only in the similar class [of that which does not inherently exist].

The counter pervasion is: "Whatever is inherently existent is necessarily either inherently one or inherently many." Whatever is neither truly one nor truly many is necessarily not inherently existent. When this is ascertained explicitly, the forward pervasion is implicitly established. More precisely, when the sign is explicitly ascertained as absent from the dissimilar class it is implicitly ascertained as existing only in the similar class.

The Sign as a Property of the Subject

Those with sharp faculties establish through direct perception that the aggregates and the self-sufficient person are not different in nature. Those with dull faculties [i.e., non-Buddhists who posit that the aggregates and person *are* different and thus need to rely on reasons in order to realize that they are *not* different] ascertain this through an inference which depends on a sign which is a non-observation of a nature.

A sharp person has good discrimination and sees directly that a self-sufficient person is not a separate entity from the aggregates. A duller person reasons that the subject, a self-sufficient person which is not included among the aggregates, is not different in nature from the aggregates because of not being observed by a valid cognizer to be so.[73]

It is difficult to decide which type of direct perception ascertains that the self-sufficient person and aggregates are not one in nature. In terms of ordinary persons, it cannot be mental direct perception, because that is a consciousness to which phenomena appear without being ascertained.[74] It cannot be yogic direct perception [because the realizer is not yet a Superior]. Yet, it is said that the sharp person can directly understand that a self-sufficient self, one related with the aggregates in the manner of a person standing inside a house, does not exist.

In terms of reasoned understanding, a self-sufficient self would be independent and permanent; the aggregates are other-powered and impermanent. Thus how could such a self and its aggregates be of one nature? In this way one can understand that the self-sufficient self is not one nature with the aggregates. Whatever is self-sufficient must operate under its own power but the aggregates arise from actions and afflictions and thus are not independent.[75]

> If there were a self different from the aggregates, it should be observed by valid cognition. Thus, one can say that there is no self which is different from its aggregates because such is not observed by valid cognition. Among types of reasoning, this is a non-observation sign.

The statement of a reason which establishes [the person and aggregates] as not being one in nature is: The aggregates in one's own continuum are not one in nature with a self-sufficient person because they are impermanent and powered by other [phenomena which are their causes]. The sign entails the predicate because a self-sufficient person is necessarily permanent and self-powered [in that it does not depend on other phenomena as causes].

To establish the sign [of being impermanent and other-powered as a property of the subject]: The subject, the aggregates in one's own continuum, are other-powered because they are aggregated through [contaminated] actions and afflictions. The subject [of the syllogism, the aggregates in one's own continuum] are impermanent because of being products.

With respect to the establishment of the pervasion [that whatever is a product is necessarily impermanent] it must be established in dependence on a sign of non-dependence on an undermining sign which is a proof of the counter-pervasion. I will not elaborate on this.

> A sign of non-dependence which is a proof of the forward pervasion is: The subject, a product, is impermanent [or empty of being permanent] because of being momentary. How can it be established that whatever is a product is necessarily impermanent? This pervasion is established through a sign of non-dependence as follows:
>
> The subject, a product, is impermanent because of being momentary.
>
> This is called a reason of non-dependence because product is here proven to be impermanent by the sign of being momentary. Its being momentary does not need to depend on any further cause. From the very first, momentary phenomena are impermanent. To be impermanent means to be established as an entity of disintegration. This impermanence is present from the first instant of the phenomenon's existence. It does not depend on any-

> thing else. For this reason, the above is a sign of non-dependence.
>
> An undermining sign which is a proof of the counter-pervasion is: The subject, a permanent phenomenon, is empty of the ability to perform functions serially or simultaneously because it cannot undergo or precipitate change of any kind. One could also put as the undermining reason in this syllogism, "...because of being empty of performing a function." If the subject, a permanent phenomenon, were able to function, then this would undermine its being permanent.[76]

It is certainly necessary with respect to this reason of the lack of being one and many to know in detail the mode of establishing the sign as a property of the subject as well as the pervasion and to know the presentation of whether this is a [reasoning] establishing a meaning or a convention and so forth.

Nowadays, although most authors of textbooks on the Middle Way and the Perfection of Wisdom have written ever so many pages about this reasoning, it is rare to find one who has penetrated the essential meaning just as it is. Thus, in following them, those of small mind, who blindly run after [the words] of others, recite "reasoning of one and many" like the northern [uncultured Avahoes] reciting *Maṇi* [the mantra of Avalokiteśvara, *oṃ maṇi padme hūṃ*]; how could they understand the meaning just as it is? Just a short presentation of these [points] will be given in the Svātantrika chapter. We will now return to the general subject matter.

CHAPTER EIGHT
THE FOUR NOBLE TRUTHS (126.10)

The main path is just the wisdom realizing selflessness. Furthermore, this [Sautrāntika] system asserts that the wisdom realizing selflessness explicitly realizes conditioned things [specifically, the mental and physical aggregates] as devoid of a self [that is, devoid of a substantially existent person]; it implicitly realizes the non-affirming negation which is the negative of self [that is, the absence of a substantially existent person].

According to Sautrāntika, only impermanent phenomena can appear to a direct perceiver. Therefore, selflessness—being permanent—can only be realized indirectly or implicitly by the yogic direct perceiver which is the wisdom realizing selflessness. The higher systems differ, maintaining the possibility of an explicit realization of emptiness.

A brief Sautrāntika explanation of the sixteen aspects of [the four noble truths] is as follows.

The four noble truths are: true sufferings, true sources of suffering, true cessations of suffering, and true paths which lead to liberation—the state of final freedom from suffering.[77] Each of the four has four sub-topics which, when contemplated, overcome misconceptions connected with that truth. The truth of suffering is a truth because it exists just as Buddha described it. It is a Superior truth because only Superiors can directly realize suffering. Their perception of suffering is like someone with a [strand of] hair in the eye; for ordinary people, however, perception of suffering is like a [strand of] hair in the palm of the hand—it goes unnoticed.

The Four Truths are the central teaching of Buddha. If one understands their mode of abiding, one will understand that liberation and omniscience can be attained in dependence on them. The actions that cause birth as a human and so forth are extremely hidden and cannot be understood through mere reasoning. However, the four truths are not like that; one can understand, on the basis of reason, that liberation and omniscience are possible because the means to attain them exist.[78]

The four misconceptions associated with true sufferings are the conceptions of [the mental and physical aggregates] as:
1. permanent,
2. pleasant,
3. clean,
4. self.[79]

The antidotes to these four [misconceptions are meditations on true sufferings] as:
1. impermanent,
2. miserable,
3. empty,
4. selfless.

> The self or person which is the enjoyer of the aggregates is empty of being a self-sufficient person and for this reason is not clean. Although our own and others' bodies are unclean, not perceiving them as such we think of them as pure and desirable. This desire would never arise if their nature were understood to be suffering. If flesh is pinched, it hurts; this is a sign that its nature of suffering is ready to manifest at any time. The objects around us are also sources of suffering; even those that are temporarily pleasing will yield suffering when they inevitably disappear.
>
> The aggregates, which are impermanent because they arise in dependence on causes, are empty of being a self-sufficient person, but due to the misconception of conceiving that such a person exists one comes to believe that the aggregates are clean, pleasant, permanent, and possessed of a self.[80]

The reasons [by which the aggregates can be understood as qualified by the above] respectively are as follows. The appropriated aggregates are:

1. impermanent because they are momentary and disintegrating,
2. miserable because they are empowered by what is other than themselves, namely, contaminated actions and afflictions,
3. empty because they are empty of being a [substantially existent] self which is an entity other [than the aggregates],
4. selfless because there is no self which is its own entity [in the sense of being under its own power].

The four misconceptions associated with the true sources are that suffering is:

1. causeless [as in the Nihilist (*Cārvāka*) assertion that suffering arises causelessly like the sharpness of thorns, the "eyes" of a peacock feather, and so forth which are not made by anyone],
2. produced from only a single cause [such as the fundamental nature asserted by the non-theistic Sāṃkhyas as the cause of all phenomena],[81]
3. made through [temporary] changes in the [permanent nature] of the Sound-Brahman,[82]
4. made under the supervision of [a creator of the world such

as] Īśvara and so forth [as asserted by the theistic Sāṃkhyas, etc.].

The antidotes to these four misconceptions [are meditation on true sources—contaminated actions and craving—as]:

1. causes,
2. sources,
3. strong producers,
4. conditions.

The proofs [by which true sources—contaminated actions and craving—can be understood as qualified by the above four] are that contaminated actions and craving are:

1. causes because they are the roots of the suffering which is their effect,
2. sources because they produce all types of suffering again and again,
3. strong producers because they generate suffering with great force,
4. conditions because the craving for cyclic existence[83] is a cooperative condition of suffering; [contaminated actions are the substantial cause of suffering].

The four misconceptions associated with true cessations are that:

1. there is utterly no liberation,
2. only a contaminated state is liberation,

> Non-Buddhists think that the concentrations and absorptions of the form and formless realms are liberation and that the preparations for these are paths of liberation. Because these states actually are still within cyclic existence, one must eventually fall from them. At such a time the non-Buddhist wrongly concludes that liberation does not exist.[84]

3. there is a liberation superior to the cessation of all suffering,
4. although temporary liberation exists, final liberation does not.

The antidotes to these four misconceptions [are meditation on true cessations as]:

1. cessations,
2. pacifications,

3. highly auspicious,
4. definitely liberating.

The proofs, respectively, are as follows. A state of separation which is a total extinguishment of suffering by the power of its antidote is:

1. a cessation because it is a state of separation which is an abandonment of that suffering,
2. a pacification because it is a state of separation which is an abandonment of the [unpeaceful] afflictions,
3. highly auspicious because it is a liberation in relation to which there is nothing more beneficial or blissful,
4. definitely liberating because it is a liberation which, once attained, has the quality of never being reversed.

The four misconceptions associated with true paths are that:

1. final paths to liberation do not exist at all,
2. correct paths to liberation [such as the yogic direct perceiver realizing the aggregates as empty of a self-sufficient self] are not paths to liberation,
3. the wisdom realizing selflessness understands its object mistakenly,
4. the wisdom realizing selflessness is not a final extinguisher of suffering.

The antidotes to these four misconceptions are [meditation on true paths as]:

1. paths,
2. suitable,
3. achievings,
4. deliverers.

The reasons are as follows. The wisdom consciousness directly realizing selflessness is:

1. a path because it causes one to proceed to liberation,
2. suitable because it is the actual antidote to afflictions,
3. an achiever because it realizes the nature of the mind, unmistakenly,
4. a deliverer because it unquestionably causes one to pass to a permanent state.

CHAPTER NINE
FRUITS (128.4)

There are no Hearers or Solitary Realizers who [as the Vaibhāṣikas claim] fall from their abandonment [of all afflictions] and realization [of selflessness]. A Bodhisattva superior is necessarily in meditative equipoise.

There are no Bodhisattva Superiors abiding in the wisdom subsequent to meditative equipoise, for a Bodhisattva who achieves the heat (*drod, uṣmagata*) level of the path of preparation will in that same meditative session pass through the remaining paths and reach liberation. The remaining paths are (*1*) the path of preparation, (*2*) the path of seeing—at which point a Bodhisattva becomes a Superior—and (*3*) the path of meditation. Only the Cittamātrins and above posit both meditative equipoise and the wisdom subsequent to it in relation to Bodhisattva Superiors.

Most [Sautrāntikas] assert that the continuum of matter [body] and mind is severed when the three [Hearer, Solitary Realizer, and Bodhisattva attain] a nirvana without remainder (*lhag med myang 'das, anupadhiśeṣa-nirvāṇa*). However, I wonder whether further distinctions are needed on this with regard to the Sautrāntikas Following Reasoning.

Jang-gya probably means that the Sautrāntika Followers of Reasoning, like the Cittamātra Followers of Reasoning, assert that the mind does not cease in the nirvana without remainder. For, both follow the Seven Treatises on Valid Cognition which make this assertion. The Cittamātrins say that any mind is a connecting mind—that is, any mind connects to the next moment of mind. Jang-gya indicates that this should be investigated because it may be that the Sautrāntikas posit that a mind without desire does not connect to the next moment. If the mind of an Arhat does not connect to a subsequent moment of mind, then at death he becomes nonexistent. If it does connect, it is like lighting one candle with another.[85] The Followers of Reasoning agree with the Followers of Scripture that the mental and physical continuums of Hearers and Solitary Realizers are severed at the time of nirvana without remainder but maintain that the continuums of Bodhisattva Arhats, that is Buddhas, are not.[86]

[The Sautrāntikas] assert both Truth and Form Bodies as

Buddhas. Vaibhāṣikas do not have a presentation of the Enjoyment Body (*longs sku, saṃboghakāya*). Further, because they—unlike the Mahāyāna—assert that Buddha attained nirvana in that very life as Prince of the Śākya clan, the Vaibhāṣikas consider that his body of that lifetime was established through previous afflicted actions. Thus, they consider his body to be a truth of suffering whereas the Mahāyāna considers it to be an Emanation Body (*sprul sku, nirmāṇakāya*). Some scholars assert that, according to the Vaibhāṣikas, Buddha "merely withdrew a creation of his body from the sight of some trainees when he passed from suffering" [i.e., entered *parinirvāṇa*] and did not actually vanish completely. Gön-jok-jik-may-wang-bo rejects this assertion on behalf of the Vaibhāṣika, however.

According to the Vaibhāṣikas, the physical body of a Buddha is not an object of refuge. Rather, the Buddha Jewel which is an object of refuge is the wisdom of extinction of the obstructions and the wisdom that the obstructions will not be produced again.[87]

They assert that [among all the teachings spoken by Buddha] a wheel of doctrine is only the wheel of doctrine of the four truths, and they assert both scriptural and realizational wheels of doctrine.

Unlike the Vaibhāṣikas, who assert only a scriptural wheel of doctrine, the Sautrāntikas consider the path of seeing—when the four noble truths are cognized directly—as a realizational wheel of doctrine.[88]

According to the Mahāyāna, all Buddha's spoken words are wheels of doctrine. Realizational wheels of doctrine according to some scholars, can occur either before or after entering the path; others say that these exist in the continuums only of those who have entered the path of accumulation. A wheel of the teaching or a wheel of realization is so called because it goes from the continuum of one person to another and another.[89]

The three-fold repetition of the four [noble] truths and the mode of the twelve-aspected turning [of the wheel of doctrine] is unlike [that explained by the Vaibhāṣikas].

Buddha explained the entity, activity to be done, and the successful completion of that activity with respect to each of the four noble truths, making twelve aspects.

[In the first repetition when Buddha] said, "These are true

sufferings," and so forth, that was the cycle about the entities [of the four truths]. [When in the second repetition] Buddha stated that [true sufferings] are to be known, [true sources] are to be abandoned, [true cessations] are to be actualized, and [true paths] are to be cultivated, that was the cycle about the activity to be done. [When in the third repetition] Buddha stated that [true sufferings] had been understood, [true sources] abandoned, [true cessations] actualized and [true paths] cultivated, that was the cycle about completion. Those are also the twelve aspects. For the most part this [presentation] is the same for the Sautrāntikas and above.

> The Vaibhāṣikas are not included because they present knowledge, eye, intelligence, and wisdom[90] with regard to the entities of the four truths, the activities to be done, and the fruit of those activities.[91]

It was renowned among earlier [scholars] that because the two schools propounding [truly existent external] objects [Vaibhāṣika and Sautrāntika] do not assert the Mahāyāna as [Buddha's] word, they do not accept Mahāyāna sutras—such as the doctrinal wheel of signlessness in the middle [wheel of Buddha's] word—as an instance of a wheel of doctrine. The foremost father [Tsong-ka-ba] and his spiritual sons also assert this to be correct in relation to Vaibhāṣikas and Sautrāntikas but only *in general*. However, it should be asserted in accordance with the omniscient Gyel-tsap's statements in his *Commentary on (Śāntideva's) "Engaging in the Bodhisattva Deeds," Commentary on (Maitreya's) "Sublime Science,"* and so forth that some Hearer sects which arose after the father Nāgārjuna and his spiritual sons did assert the *Perfection of Wisdom* and so forth to be [valid] sutras.

Nevertheless, it does not seem correct to explain the following stanza from [the third chapter of] Dharmakīrti's *Commentary on (Dignāga's) "Compendium on Valid Cognition"* as a Sautrāntika interpretation of the thought of a *Perfection of Wisdom Sutra*:

> All definitions such as of the aggregates and so forth

> Having the feature of [being] agents [of defining]
> Are also not real.[92]
> They too [assert] that those [definitions] are without [their own] nature.

Dharmakīrti's *Commentary on (Dignāga's) "Compendium on Valid Cognition"* states that Sautrāntikas accept the meaning of the *Perfection of Wisdom* sutras where it is stated that all phenomena are without own-nature. According to Prāsaṅgika-Mādhyamika, this means without inherent existence. However, the Sautrāntikas assert inherent existence. Therefore, regarding this, some say that Sautrāntikas assert as follows: The aggregates, constituents, and sources have many mentally fabricated factors (*sgro btags gyi cha*); that is, their activities, definitions and definiendums. From this point of view, the Sautrāntikas assert phenomena to be not established by way of their own nature (*rang gyis mtshan nyid gyis ma grub pa*); however, Tsong-ka-ba explains that the meaning of this quote does not refer to the objects and agents of the aggregates themselves but to the objects and agents of definiendum and definition being imputed by thought. Both Sautrāntikas and Cittamātrins agree that the activities of definitions and definiendums are imputed by thought, but there is no need to posit that they, therefore, have a common interpretation of the *Perfection of Wisdom Sutras* because the Hearer sects—Vaibhāṣika and Sautrāntika—do not accept the *Perfection of Wisdom Sutras* as the word of Buddha.[93]

In their commentaries on [Dharmakīrti's *Commentary on (Dignāga's) "Compendium on Valid Cognition"*] at this point, Devendrabuddhi and [Prajñakaragupta], the author of the *Ornament Commentary* (*Pramāṇavārttikālaṃkāra*), do state that [this position] is common to the Proponents of Truly Existent External Objects. However, the foremost father [Tsong-ka-ba] and his spiritual sons state that [their identification] means that even the Sautrāntikas accept the mere meaning indicated by this stanza [i.e., that definition and definiendum do not ultimately exist; it does not mean that the Sautrāntikas interpret the *Perfection of Wisdom Sutras* in this way, as the Cittamātrins do]. Also, Kay-drup refuted Yam-ri's explanation that [the reference of "too" in the stanza] is to a Lower Vehicle mode of assertion. Furthermore, both Gyel-tsap and Kay-drup explain that the words "They too" in the last line indicate a second type of Cittamātrin interpreter of this stanza [not a Hīnayāna one]. In particular, the *Great Purification of Forgetfulness Regarding Valid Cognition*, which was written down by Gyeltsap in accordance with the speech of the foremost [Tsong-ka-ba] clearly states:

> [Dharmakīrti] is mentioning another mode of interpretation when he says, in commenting on the meaning of this stanza, that it is suitable to explain the thought of non-inherent existence in the third stanza as also being like this. It is not correct to apply this to the Sautrāntikas because most Hearer sects do not assert Mahāyāna sutras as the word [of Buddha], and therefore, it is not that they have to explain the thought [of the *Perfection of Wisdom Sutras*, etc.]. Furthermore, the term "too" in the phrase "They too [assert] that these [definitions] are without [their own] nature" includes a previous [assertion], and, therefore, clearly it is the Cittamātrins' own system.

Thus when, after quoting this verse in his *Essence of the Good Explanations, A Treatise Differentiating the Interpretable and the Definitive*, the foremost omniscient [Tsong-ka-ba] says that [this position] is also common to Hearer sects [and not just Cittamātrin], he means that it is suitable even for Hearer sects to assert the point being indicated, i.e., this mode of the aggregates and so forth as being without their own nature [in the sense of their non-ultimacy as definitions and definiendums]. However, [Tsong-ka-ba] is not explaining that the [Cittamātrin] mode of interpretation of the thought of the *Perfection of Wisdom* [which is based on the *Unravelling of Thought Sutra*] is shared with the Hearer sects [in the sense that the latter have such an interpretation of the *Perfection of Wisdom*].

Śāntasrakṣita's own *Commentary on the "Ornament to the Middle Way"* explains that the Hearer sects assert that the statement [in a *Perfection of Wisdom Sutra*] that "all phenomena are non-things and non-produced" refers to the paucity and lowliness [of impermanent phenomena], and Kamalaśīla's *Commentary on the Difficult Points of the "Ornament"* does indeed explain that as a Hearer sect's explanation of the thought of the *Perfection of Wisdom Sutras*, but these are clearly Hearer sects which arose after Nāgārjuna.

> For example, a person having little money is sometimes described as having none; this is a demeaning exaggeration of his circumstances. Similarly, a person without any good qualities may be described as "not human." In the same way, later Sautrāntikas consider it an exaggeration to state that all phenomena are non-produced. The actual situation is that (1) there are more non-products than products and (2) even with regard to products, production is posited for only a tiny moment at the beginning of their continuums. Thus, although products are fewer in number and production is relatively short, it is an exaggeration to say that all phenomena are non-things and that there is no [production] at all. According to later Sautrāntikas, Buddha's statement in the *Perfection of Wisdom* requires interpretation in this way.[94]

Kamalaśīla explains that the Vatsiputriyas consider the statement "all phenomena are selfless" to refer to the absence of a self which is another entity from the [mental and physical] aggregates, but he does not state that such is the two Hearer sects' interpretation of the thought of the Perfection of Wisdom class of sutras. Rather, he is describing the interpretation of passages on selflessness in scriptures renowned among Hearer sects themselves.

In this [Sautrāntika] system it is not asserted that whatever is a bundle of doctrine is necessarily a wheel of doctrine; therefore, although one or two [Sautrāntikas subsequent to Nāgārjuna] accept Mahāyāna sutras such as the *Perfection of Wisdom*, these sutras need not be asserted as wheels of doctrine [even for them]. Not only that, except for the sutra passages on the three-fold repetition and twelve aspects of the four noble truths, no other Hīnayāna sutra is asserted as a wheel of doctrine. This can be known through the Vaibhāṣika and Sautrāntika mode of explaining the name and meaning of "wheel of doctrine."

Therefore, in these systems the word of Buddha is not necessarily a wheel of doctrine. Also, the measure of a bundle of doctrine is to be taken as the teaching of a complete antidote to each of the [afflicted] deeds, there being 21,000 such deeds in relation to each of the three poisons [predominant desire, hatred, or ignorance] as well as [deeds connected with the existence of all three poisons] in equal proportion. These [84,000] bundles of doctrine are asserted as included within the form aggregate [because they are sound, which is form].

As was explained above [in reference to Kamalaśīla on page 195], there are one or two interpretations—bent slightly from the literal meaning—of statements on truthlessness and so forth. Nevertheless, for the most part the two Hearer sects assert that whatever is Buddha's word is necessarily only of definitive meaning. Still, Bhāvaviveka's *Blaze of Reasoning* explains that there are those who accept both definitive [sutras] and those requiring interpretation.

Notes

PART I: INTRODUCTION

1. See Anne C. Klein, *Knowledge and Liberation* (Ithaca: Snow Lion Publications, 1986), pp. 15-27, 38-46, 84-88. The historical relationship of Sautrāntika to Mādhyamika is indeed complex. David Ruegg in *The Literature of the Mādhyamaka School of Philosophy in India* (Wiesbaden: Otto Harrassowitz, 1981), p. 59, n.175 points to Bodhibhadra's statement that Sautrāntikas could be regarded as Mahāyānists. Tsong-ka-ba uses the term Sautrāntika-Mādhyamika in his *Middling Exposition of the Stages of the Path* (Dharamsala: Shes rig par khang, 1968), p. 193b.6-194a.1. (See also n.5 p. 213 below.)

2. In the Gomang (*sGo-mang*) College of Drebung (*'Bras-spung*) Monastic University "The Collected Topics" (*bsDus sgrva*) are studied for four years and "Awareness and Knowledge" (*bLo rig*) and "Signs and Reasoning" (*rTags rigs*) for one year each. In Loseling (*bLo-gsal-gling*), also a college of Drebung, only one year is devoted to "The Collected Topics" and, as at Gomang, a year each is spent on "Awareness and Knowledge" and "Signs and Reasoning." For more on Drebung curricula, see Elizabeth Napper, *Mind in Tibetan Buddhism* (Ithaca: Snow Lion Publications, 1980), p. 161.

In the Jay *(Byes)* College of Sera (*Se-rva*) Monastic University, three years are spent on "The Collected Topics." See Geshe Lhundup Sopa, *Lectures in Tibetan Culture* (Dharamsala: Library of Tibetan Works & Archives, 1983), p. 42.

3. For instance, the brief Collected Topics Text (*bsDus-grva*) by Loseling's Jam-bel-drin-lay (*'Jam-dpal-'phrin-las-yon-tan-rgya-mthso*) makes its connection to Dharmakīrti explicit; like the Ra-dö text it does so by opening each topic with a quote from the *Commentary on (Dignāga's) "Compendium on Valid Cognition"* (*Tshad ma rnam 'grel, Pramāṇavārttika*) See Jam-bel-drin-lay, *bsDus grva'i don kun bsdus pa legs bshad mkhas pa'i dga' ston* (Mundgod: Drebung Loseling Printing Press, 1978).

4. For further discussion of how Gelukbas came to develop and define this system, see Klein, *Knowledge and Liberation*, pp. 19–22, 29–32, 41–44, 48–49. (See also note 6 below.)

5. For an explanation of debate format and a translation of debates that begin the study of "The Collected Topics" see Daniel Perdue, "Practice and Theory of Philosophical Debate in Tibetan Buddhist Education," (Ann Arbor: University Microfilms, 1983).

6. The Dalai Lama II, Gendun Gyatso (*dGe'dun-rgya-mtsho*, 1476-1542) observes that all three Buddhist vehicles "propound tenets established through their own scriptures and reasoning." *Boat Entering the Ocean of Tenets* [*Grub mtha' rgya mtshor 'jug pa'i gru rdzings*], Varanasi: Ye-ses-stobs-ldan, 1969, pp. 3, 11-24; and in his own discussion of Sautrāntika he divides them into Followers of Scripture and Reasoning, pp. 20-21.

Another Tenet text from about this same period, by Jay-tshun-chö-gyi-gyal-tsen (*rJe-btsun-chos-gyi-rgyal-mtshan*, 1469–1546) also uses this division of Sautrāntika in his *Presentation of Tenets* (*Grub mtha' rnam bzhag*), (Sbag-sa: s.n., 196-) p. 4a.4. Thus the two-fold division of Sautrāntika, and with it the term *Sautrāntikas Following Reasoning* was present from virtually the beginning of Gelukba studies on tenets.

7. For example, Kay-drup's (*mKhas-grub, 1384-1438*) *Clear-*

ing Away Mental Darkness, An Ornament of Dharmakīrti's "Seven Treatises on Valid Cognition" (*Tshad ma sde bdun gyi rgyan yid kyi mun sel*), Toh. 5501; and Gyel-tsap's (*rGyal-tshab*, 1364-1432) *Teachings on Valid Cognition* (*Tshad ma'i Lam Khrid*) (Varanasi: Ye-ses-stobs-ldan, 1969). One could argue that these are similar in type to Tibetan texts on Mādhyamika which comment on Candrakīrti or Nāgārjuna, but the fact that the structure of these works is not strongly governed by the Indian text, and that here the text commented upon is not elaborating the same system as the commentator, mitigates against this. Because they are topically focused works outside the context of a general presentation of tenets, I see them as belonging to the third category of Sautrāntika texts discussed here.

8. My long-time mentor on Mādhyamika, Prof. Jeffrey Hopkins, has suggested that Tibetan scholarship can support the translation of this title as "Supplement to (*Nāgārjuna's*) 'Treatise on the Middle Way'." [See Hopkins, *Meditation on Emptiness* (London Wisdom Publications, 1983), pp. 868–871.] As he points out, Candrakīrti's intent was to supplement, and thereby introduce the student to Nāgārjuna's text. Since both of these purposes are for the sake of entering into understanding, and because the Tibetan *'jug pa* (*avatāra*) literally means "entrance" in the sense of entering into or gaining an understanding of Nāgārjuna's thought, I have here chosen to translate the title as *Entrance to (Nāgārjuna's) 'Treatise on the Middle Way'*.

9. It appears that this classification had no importance, if indeed it existed, outside Gelukba. It is not mentioned in the Sautrāntika chapter of the 14th century *bka'-gdams-pa* text on tenets, the *blo gsal grub mtha'* by dBus-pa-blo-gsal, a compiler of Tibetan Cannonical materials of sNar-thang monastery (See Mimaki: 1979, p. 176); and, for tr., Mimaki, 1980, pp. 145ff). Moreover, the Sa-gya-ba Dak-tsang (*rTag-tshang-lo-tsa-ba*, b. 1405) does not mention it in his extensive discussion of tenets (see *Knowledge and Liberation*, pp. 24–25, 40–41, 51). Also, the discussion by Long-chen-rab-jam (*kLong-chen-rab-'byams*, 1308-1363) in his *Precious Treasury of the Supreme Vehicle* (*Grub-*

pa'i-mtha' rin-po-che mdzod), a major text on tenet systems in the Nyingma tradition includes a brief segment on Sautrāntika (Th.A. 108.5ff.) which does not mention the categories of specifically characterized (*rang mtshan, svalakṣaṇa*) and generally characterized (*spyi mtshan, sāmānyalakṣaṇa*) phenomena so central to Gelukba discussions on Sautrāntika and to their division of it into Followers of Scripture and Reasoning. Like Dak-tsang (who however does consider these categories in elaborating Sautrāntika), Long-chen-ba makes no mention of Sautrāntika sub-systems.

10. Gön-chok-jig-may-wang-bo, (*dKon-mchog-'jigs-med-dbang-po*, 1728–1791), *Grub pa'i mtha'i rnam par bzhag pa rin po che'i phreng ba* (Mundgod, India: Dre-Gomang Buddhist Cultural Association, 1980), p. 14; see also the translation by Geshe Sopa and Jeffrey Hopkins in *Practice and Theory of Tibetan Buddhism* (London: Rider, 1976), p. 92.

11. Among Gelukbas the next best-known medium-length tenets text is probably that by Tu-gen Lo-sang-chö-gyi-nyi-ma (*Thu'u bkvan blo-bzang-chos-kyi-nyi-ma*, 1737–1802), *Mirror of the Good Explanations Showing the Sources and Assertions of All systems of Tenets* (*Grub mtha' thams cad kyi khungs dang 'dod tshul ston pa legs shad shel gyi me long*) (Sarnath: Chhos Je Lama, 1963). For a list of Gelukba texts included in the tenet genre see Jeffrey Hopkins, *Emptiness Yoga* (Ithaca: Snow Lion Publications, 1987), p. 458-59. For a discussion of the importance of the Tenet genre in Tibetan literature as a whole, and a summary of available Tenet texts, see Mimaki, *bLo gsal grub mtha'* (Kyoto: Zinbun Kagaku Kenkyuso, 1982), pp. 1-12. For concordances of extant editions of *Grub mtha' chen mo* and *lCang skya grub mtha'* see Mimaki: 1982, pp. 257-275.

12. See Klein, *Knowledge and Liberation*, Chapter II. Moreover, several tenets central to Gelukba's formulation of Sautrāntikas Following Reasoning are unique to them; see *Knowledge and Liberation*, pp. 34–52, 178–182.

13. For further discussion of Jam-yang-shay-ba's major Indian sources on Prāsaṅgika, see Hopkins, *Meditation on Emptiness*, pp. 569–572; for a translation of a portion of Jam-yang-

shay-ba's presentation of Prāsaṅgika from his *Great Exposition of Tenets* (*Grub mtha' chen mo*) see the same volume, pp. 584–697.

14. Jam-yang-shay-ba, *Grub mtha' chen mo*, 1a.4–2b.5; see also Nga-wang-bel-den (*Ngag-dbang-dpal-ldan*, b. 1797) *Annotations for (Jam-yang-shay-ba's) 'Great Exposition of Tenets', Freeing the Knots of the Difficult Points, Precious Jewel of Clear Thought* (*Grub mtha' chen mo'i mchan 'grel dka' gnad mdud grol blo gsal bces nor*) from *kha* of Sautrāntika section.

15. See Klein, *Knowledge and Liberation*, pp. 35–46.

16. Nga-wang-bel-den (a.k.a. Bel-den-chö-jay) also includes an important discussion of this issue in the Sautrāntika section of his *Explanation of the Meaning of "Conventional" and "Ultimate" in the Four Systems of Tenets* (*Grub mtha' bzhi'i lugs kyi kun rdzob dang don dam pa'i don rnam par bshad pa*) (New Delhi: Lama Guru Deva, 1972), p. 40.3ff.

17. For the diverse meanings of "substantially established" in Sautrāntika see Klein, *Knowledge and Liberation*, pp. 52–55; for a concise description of the Prāsaṅgika meaning of selflessness see Hopkins, *Meditation on Emptiness*, pp. 35–41.

18. See Klein, *Knowledge and Liberation*, Chapter IV.

19. For a detailed discussion of the object negated in Gelukba Prāsaṅgika discussions of emptiness, see Elizabeth Napper, *Dependent-Arising and Emptiness* (London: Wisdom Publications, 1989).

20. See Klein, *Knowledge and Liberation*, pp. 141–182.

21. *Ibid.*, pp. 27–32; 40–46.

22. Masaaki Hattori, tr., *Dignāga on Perception*, Harvard Oriental Series ed. by Daniel H. H. Ingalls (Cambridge: Harvard University Press, 1968), pp. 26–27 (verse 4cd); refer also to p. 25 (3c) and pp. 89–90, n. 39 and n. 40. Dignāga here argues that direct perception (*mngon sum, pratyakṣa*) observes a multiplicity of objects without "conceptually constructing a unity" and thus that his definition of direct perception as free from conceptual construction is consonant with the *Abhidharmakośa*. This argument is obviously important for the Gelukba formulation of Sautrāntikas Following Reasoning, in

which objects of direct perception are held to be synonymous with specifically characterized phenomena (*rang mtshan, svalakṣaṇa*), and with all impermanent things.

23. This is explicitly asserted by several major Gelukba scholars. In this volume, see Jang-gya, *Presentation of Tenets* (*Grub mtha'i rnam bzad*) (Sarnath: Pleasure of Elegant Sayings Press, 1979), p. 124; Tib. p. 98.14. Similar statements are found in: Pur-bu-jok (*Phur-bu-lcog*), *Magical Key to the Path of Reasoning* (*bsDus grva'i rnam bzhad rigs lam 'phrl gi sde mig*) (Buxa: n.p., 1965), p. 10.3; also, Bel-den-chö-jay, *Explanation of "Conventional" and "Ultimate"*, pp. 34.lff; also, the *Collected Topics of Ra-dö* (*Rva-stod bsDus grva*) (Dharamsala, India: Damchoe Sangpo, Library of Tibetan Works and Archives, 1980), pp. 10.3–11.3. For additional discussion of the interpretive steps involved in their definition of ultimate truth as "ultimately able to perform a function" see Klein, *Knowledge and Liberation*, pp. 50–88.

24. Den-dar, Tib. p. 153.8; see trans. p. 46 above. Because of the epistemological and ontological importance of this understanding of "specific characteristics" the terms *rang mtshan* (*svalakṣaṇa*) and *spyi mtshan* (*sāmānyalakṣaṇa*), usually translated as "particular" and "universal," are here translated throughout as "specifically characterized phenomenon" and "generally characterized phenomenon."

25. *Ibid.*, p. 158.4ff; trans. p.47 above. For a discussion of differences in interpretation between Gelukba scholars such as Den-dar-hla-ram-ba and the Sagyaba Dak-tsang, see Klein, *Knowledge and Liberation*, Chapter II.

26. *Ibid.*, p. 159.2ff.; trans. p. 47 above.

27. *Ibid.*, p. 178.6ff; trans. p 56 above.

28. *Ibid.*, p. 179.1; trans. p. 56 above.

29. *Ibid.*, p. 181.1ff.; trans. p. 56 above.

30. Jang-gya, Tib. p. 100.3; trans. p. 127 above.

The distinction made here between an impermanent object which appears to thought and a permanent appearing object of thought is perhaps no more difficult than Frege's famous claim that "the concept horse is not a concept, it is an object." See for example Peter Geach and Max Black, eds., *Translations from the Philosophical Writings of Gottlob Frege* (Oxford, Basil Blackwell, 1960), p. 46; see also the subsequent critique of this in John R. Searle, *Speech Acts* (Cambridge: The University Press, 1969), pp. 97ff. and also Chapter 4, "Reference as a Speech Act," pp. 72ff. However, unlike Frege, who has been called the first important western philosopher since Descartes to reject the primacy of questions regarding how and what we know, the classic Indo-Tibetan Buddhist scholarship has taken just such epistemological questions to be foundational to soteriology as well as to philosophy. An in-depth comparative analysis of elements in current linguistic philosophy with the epistemological concerns of Indo-Tibetan scholarship may well be the next step in our exploration of these materials.

31. Jang-gya, Tib, p. 100.3, trans. p. 127 above, see also Jang-gya Tib, p. 107.17ff., trans. p. 142 above.

32. The question of how well language can express philosophical subtleties, not to mention actual objects, is of course also important to current thinking in philosophy of language. The distinction between ordinary language and the philosophical reconstruction of language was never an explicit issue in Tibet, despite the existence of a sophisticated philosophical language and syllogistic debate which early became the unique property of trained scholastics. Nevertheless, the construction of a less defective language *qua* language was never attempted, probably because such defects as attracted the attention of these philosophers were understood to characterize all language. Hence, "ordinary" language, though in practice often eschewed, was never criticized as "vague" in the manner of Leibniz, Russell or Carnap. The focus was on the fallacies incumbent upon all thought and language, which were seen as similar in operating via exclusion. For further discussion of Gelukba Sautrāntika positions on this, see Klein, *Knowledge and Liberation*, pp. 126–133 and 143–144.

33. *Pramāṇasamuccaya*, 2a-b; see Hattori, *Dignāga on Perception*, p. 24.

34. *Pramāṇavārttika*, P5709, Vol. 130, 88-3-3. For discussion of the importance of this passage to Gelukba interpretations, and Jam-yang-shay-ba's use of it, see Klein, *Knowledge and Liberation*, pp. 81–84.

35. The wider cultural significance of Tibet's emphasis on oral commentary and oral debate has yet to be studied. Walter Ong has referred to similar styles of interaction as a rational form of masculine ceremonial combat. Ong observes, "During the romantic age, academic education was all but exclusively focused on defending a position (thesis) or attacking the position of another person." (Walter Ong, "Review of Brian Vickers' *Classical Rhetoric in English Poetry*," *College English*, February 1972, quoted by Adrienne Rich, *On Lies, Secrets and Silence* (New York: Norton, 1979), p. 138. From my own observation, this style is quite different from the patient exposition typical of oral commentary. The former interaction largely takes place among peers and encourages what has recently been called the "separate knowing" described by Piaget, Kohlberg, and Perry, which is characterized by an experienced objectivity, or separation from, the ideas known and discussed. The interaction with ideas that takes place through the intervention of a recognized scholar in the role of giving commentary is different. First, the interaction is not between equals, but between student and Teacher. Second, this interaction is often experienced as "personal" in ways that debate is not: students often appear visibly moved by respect for the speaker and the material, so that the relationship between knower and known is less "other" than in debate. For further discussion of separate and connected styles of knowing as part of a developmental process, see Belenky et al., *Women's Ways of Knowing* (New York: Basic Book Publishers, 1986), pp. 103ff.

36. José Cabezón made a similar point in a paper delivered at the August, 1987 meeting of the International Association of Buddhist Studies.

PART II
A. SPECIFICALLY AND GENERALLY CHARACTERIZED PHENOMENA

1. Although the precise boundaries of "Gelukba" as a religious and philosophical entity are not always clear, there is little ambiguity in my use of the term here: it indicates that the texts and persons whose oral commentary is translated here are associated with monastic institutions widely known in Tibet as "Gelukba." For a discussion of some of the issues involved in considering Gelukba or any other Tibetan Buddhist order as an actual unit of discourse, see Leonard van der Kuijp, "Miscellanea Apropos of the Philosophy of Mind in Tibet: Mind in Tibetan Buddhism," *The Tibet Journal*, spring 1985, Vol. X, No. 1, pp. 32–43.

2. For more on the intermingled history of Mongolia and Tibetan religious orders, see David Snellgrove and Hugh Richardson, *A Cultural History of Tibet* (New York: Praeger, 1968), pp. 148ff. and especially 183ff. [Reprinted in Boulder: Prajna Press, 1980]; see also R. A. Stein, *Tibetan Civilization*, reprint of 1962 edition (Stanford: Stanford Press, 1972), pp. 77–83, and W. D. Shakabpa, *Tibet—A Political History* (New Haven and London, 1967).

3. *Collected gSung 'bum of Bstan-dar-Lha-ram of A-lag-sha* (New Delhi: Lama Guru Deva, 1971).

4. This is the *Nere udqa-yi todotqayci saran-u gegen gerel kemegdekii donkiyan-u bicig orusiba/Brda'-yig ming don gsal-bar-byed-pa'i zla-ba'i-'od-snang*, in 139 folios. Cited in Lokesh Chandra, *Materials for a History of Tibetan Literature* (New Delhi: International Academy of Indian Culture, 1983), pp. 21–23.

5. This is his *Annotations to ('Jig-may-ling-ba's) "Treasury of Excellence"* (*Yon tan mdzod kyi mchan 'grel/Yon tan rin po che'i mdzod kyi dka' 'gnad rdo rje'i rgya mdud 'grol byed legs bshed ser gyi thur ma*) in 613 folios, (sNga-'gyur-rNying ma, 'Jam dbyangs mkhyen brdze: n.p., n.d.). Gene Smith, formerly head of the Library of Congress in India, has reported this as the opinion of Ven. Dingo Khenze Rinbochay, who published the

commentary in approximately 1979. The Nyingma historian Khetsun Sangpo Rinbochay concurred that its author is the Mongolian Den-dar-hla-ram-ba, adding that toward the end of his long life Den-dar-hla-ram-ba is said to have become a practitioner of Nyingmaba.

6. For discussion of this position, apparently unique to Gelukba, see Klein, *Knowledge and Liberation*, pp. 45–46.

7. There are also mistaken non-conceptual consciousnesses. See Elizabeth Napper, *Mind in Tibetan Buddhism* (Ithaca: Snow Lion Publications, 1980 and London: Rider & Co., 1980). Compare with Ryle's statement that "...it is certainly improper to speak of a mistaken sensation." [Gilbert Ryle, *The Concept of Mind*, reprint (New York: Barnes and Noble, 1976), p. 237.]

8. Discussed in Klein, *Knowledge and Liberation*, pp. 148–149; 170–171, and 204–216.

9. See "Naming" in *Knowledge and Liberation*, especially pp. 204–216.

10. *Ibid.*, pp. 52–55.

11. In this section through to the "Application of Names," oral commentary is from Jambel Shenpen Rinbochay.

12. See Napper, *Mind in Tibetan Buddhism*, pp. 51–52. The four causes of error are errors existing in the (1) object (*yul, viṣaya*), (2) basis (*rten, āśraya*), (3) place (*gnas, sthāna*), or (4) immediately preceding condition (*de ma thag rkyen, samantara-pratyaya*).

13. When a term such as *bum pa ma yin pa las log pa* is in the subject position its translation will be hyphenated as in "opposite-from-non-pot is a negative phenomenon." When such a term appears in the predicate position as a modifier, hyphens are not used. For example, "A mental image of pot is an appearance as opposite from non-pot" or "It is not opposite-from-non-pot which appears to direct perception according to Gomang; rather, the pot which is opposite from non-pot appears." See Perdue, "Debate in Tibetan Buddhist Education," Part III (forthcoming from Wisdom Publications).

14. Compare with David Hume, who attributes a similar error to the confusion between identity and diversity. "We have

a distinct idea of an object that remains invariable. . .and this idea we call that of *identity* or *sameness.* We have also a distinct idea of several different objects existing in succession. . .and this [functions as]. . .a notion of diversity. . . ." The amalgamation of these two is ". . .the cause of the confusion and mistake [of inappropriately construing continuity], and makes us substitute the notion of identity, instead of that of related objects." David Hume, *A Treatise of Human Nature*, Book I, ed. L. A. Selby Bigge (Oxford, 1888 and 1896), pp. 253–254. [Thanks to Karen Carr and P. J. Ivanhoe for piquing my interest in Hume, and Lee Yearley for reminding me of it.]

15. Next section begins at p. 177.2 of the Tibetan.

16. The *Minds and Awareness* (*bLo rig*) texts agree that thought has a referent object. According to Jambel Shenpen Rinbochay however, terms also have referent objects (*zhen yul*). A term is also related with its object (*yul, viṣaya*) and its explicit objects of expression (*dngos su brjod bya*). The meaning-generality, or mental image, which is the explicit object of expression of a term, as well as an appearing object (*snang yul, pratibhāsa-viṣaya*) of thought, is not the referent object of that term; rather, the actual object represented is so designated.

To put this another way, a direct perceiver does not have a referent object because, for example, an eye consciousness perceiving yellow does not have the thought, "This is yellow." The thought consciousness apprehending yellow, however, does conceive in this way, and yellow is its referent object. However, Jambel Shenpen is suggesting that even though a term has no conception, it does have a referent object. The term expressing pot, for example, has pot as its referent object.

17. This line, which reads *rtag pa med pa* should read *rtag pa la med pa* [Jambel Shenpen Rinbochay].

18. This and the remainder of the indented oral commentary to Den-dar is from Denma Lochö Rinbochay.

B. POSITIVE AND NEGATIVE PHENOMENA

1. It is doubtful that nuns or female practitioners ever engaged in debate in significant numbers. The late Gomang Geshe Gedun Lodrö firmly stated that nuns had not debated in Tibet. However, Denma Lochö Rinbochay, in teaching the particularly abstruse topic of "substantial phenomena and phenomena which are isolates" (*rdzas chos ldog chos*) in Pur-bu-jok's *Collected Topics* (*bsDus grva*), observed that certain monks had created this topic so as to gain a debating victory over a group of clever nuns who, apparently, were invincible on the standard topics of the day. Most likely, customs varied considerably over time and place, as they do today. In 1980, at the relocated Gomang College in Mundgod, India, neither male nor female laypersons were allowed to participate in the debating courtyard. That same year Kensur Yeshay Tupden, abbot emeritus of Loseling College, also in Mundgod, encouraged western laywomen to join in debating there. Since approximately the mid-70's, both lay and ordained men and women debate in Dharamsala, India, as they do in Tibetan monastic or study centers in Switzerland and elsewhere.

For a discussion of the syllogistic debate format, see Daniel Perdue, "Practice and Theory of Philosophical Debate in Tibetan Buddhist Education" (Ph.D., University of Virginia, 1983). See also note 35 above.

2. A frequent feature of the Collected Topics genre is its subdivision of each topic into three parts: (1) refutation of errors (*'khrul ba 'gag*), (2) presentation of the text's own position (*rang lugs bzhag*), and (3) elimination of objections (*rdzod pa spong*). The first section of the Gomang text can be read as combining the functions of the first and third of these.

3. The topic of positive and negative phenomena, and the associated issue of exclusion (*gzhan sel, anyāpoha*) is discussed in the Ra-dö *Collected Topics* in the context of quotations from Dharmakīrti's chapters on inference (*rang don [rjes dpag], svarthānumāna*) and direct perception (*mngon sum, pratyakṣa*). In their works on the Collected Topics, Ra-dö and Pur-bu-jok

include this topic in the "great path of reasoning" (*Rigs lam che ba*) portion of their texts. For an analysis of Gelukba views on this topic, see Klein, *Knowledge and Liberation*, Chapters V-VII.

4. See chapters IV and IX, "Conceptual Thought" and "Conceptuality and Wisdom" in Klein, *Knowledge and Liberation*. See also note 6 below.

5. *dngos po, bhāva*. "Thing" is defined as "that which is able to perform a function" and therefore the word "functioning" has been added into the translation for clarity.

6. My translation of *'gag pa* incorporates the word "phenomenon" to distinguish Gelukba's use of the term from scholarship which describes the theory of exclusion as a theory of *language* rather than, as here, fundamentally a categorization of objects known made on the basis of how they are known. For an argument that *apoha* is a theory of language and meaning see Dhirendra Sharma, *The Differentiation Theory of Meaning in Indian Logic* (The Hague: Mouton, 1969), especially pp. 11–12 (discussed in *Knowledge and Liberation*, p. 159ff.). For a relevant discussion of Bhartṛhari's theory of language *vis à vis* Dignāga (with references also to Quine and Anscombe), see B. K. Matilal, *Perception* (Oxford: Clarendon Press, 1986), pp. 386–398. For an overview of how Gelukba scholarship on negative phenomena fits into the larger context of Indian work on *apoha*, see *Knowledge and Liberation*, pp. 144–149, and 178–182. See also note 17 below.

For Gelukbas, the presence or absence of a phenomenon is not a factor in distinguishing negative from positive phenomena. Dhirendra Sharma however suggests such a criterion in "The Paradox of Negative Judgment and Indian Logic," *Vishveshvaranand Indological Journal* Vol. 9, No. 4 (*1966*), p. 113.

7. The translation spells out statements which the text renders only in the syllogistic ellipses characteristic of debate. Thus, the translation completes, whereas the text does not, statements of entailment (*thal 'gyur, prāsaṅga*), pervasion (*khyab ba, vyāpti*) and the establishment of reasons (*phyogs chos, pakśa-*

dharma).

8. The Tibetan word for space has two syllables: *nam mkha'*. Therefore, the text literally says "because (1) *nam mkha'* is the actual name and (2) neither *nam* nor *mkha'* are negative syllables. . . ."

9. the text actually reads "a phenomenon which has a negative syllable *at the end* of its actual name" but this is, no doubt, an inadvertent change from the phrase "as a part of" which appears throughout this debate.

10. The text here merely says "You cannot accept the initial consequence."

11. The text on p. 456.9 mistakenly reads *rtogs pa'i rdogs pas* instead of *rtogs pa'i togs pas* and *khyod ma yin par* instead of *khyod la yin par.*

12. See J. F. Staal, "Negation and the Law of Contradiction in Indian Thought," *Bulletin of the School of Oriental and African Studies*, Vol. 25, Part I, (1962), pp. 56–57.

13. The text makes the second part of this sentence a statement of reason but the format indicates it to be a statement of entailment.

14. The word "phenomenon" is added for clarity.

15. Here "to be under its own power" means that a phenomenon is not merely imputed by thought; thus, whatever is a positive phenomenon which is under its own power is necessarily a functioning thing. Gomang is unique among Gelukba colleges in asserting that whatever is permanent is necessarily a negative phenomenon.

16. The text mistakenly omits "not" (p. 462.3).

17. The term here translated as "non-affirming negative" (*med dgag, prasajya-pratiṣedha*) is translated by B. K. Matilal as "verbally bound negative." This name signifies for him, as the Tibetan does for Gelukba, that "the negating act simply rejects. . . it does not impute anything positively." (*Perception*, pp. 399–400) However, Gelukba interpretations of negatives, as discussed in the system of Sautrāntikas Following Reasoning and as used in their Mādhyamika analysis, would disagree with Matilal's characterization (p. 67) of Nāgārjuna's

negative dialectic as resulting in "no position." (See also Hopkins, *Meditation on Emptiness*, pp. 471–473, 492–3.) There is, moreover, a subtle but important connection between Matilal's point here and his subsequent characterization (p. 399) of non-affirming/verbally bound negatives as an act of "illocutionary negation in the speech-act theory of Searle." Searle notes that he himself uses Austin's term "illocutionary" advisedly since he does not accept Austin's distinction between locutionary and illocutionary acts. (Searle, *Speech Acts* (Cambridge: The University Press, 1969), p. 23) The Gelukba emphasis however, and the soteriological context in which Gelukbas place Nāgārjunian analysis, leads us rather to characterize the statements which express such negatives as what Austin calls perlocutionary acts, a category Matilal himself adduces in a most useful manner (p. 25). As Gelukbas understand it, the Nāgārjunian denial of, for example, any production from self, other, both or neither, is *not* simply an illocutionary act containing propositions about the nature of production, nor does it signify an inability to make assertions regarding production. Rather, the purpose is to achieve a particular effect on the listener. (For the Gelukba understanding of that effect, see *Meditation on Emptiness*, pp. 57–59 and pp. 549–559; see also Klein, *Knowledge and Liberation*, Chapter IX.) This function arguably makes it, in Austin's terminology, a perlocutionary act. A further complexity here is that the "listener" affected by such analysis may also be the "speaking" subject, insofar as this analysis forms the core of important forms of solitary contemplation. However, whether the words are given by oneself to oneself, or by a teacher to a student, the purpose, as this tradition understands it, is the same: to foster recognition of the simple absence—the mere emptiness—of such a concretely describable form of production.

18. The text mistakenly repeats this reason (p. 466.1).

NOTES TO JANG-GYA SECTION

1. Lokesh Chandra, *Materials for a History of Tibetan Literature* (New Delhi: International Academy of Indian Culture, 1963), Part I, pp. 36–38.

2. See Klein, *Knowledge and Liberation*, Chapter I.

3. See Chapter III, "Direct Perception" in Klein, *Knowledge and Liberation*.

4. See note 17 p. 211 above.

5. The Sthavira Bodhibhadra, a disciple of Mahāmati of Somapurī, was a Tantric master of Vikramaśīla and reputed to be a Bodhisattva. For more biographical information and a list of works attributed to him, see Tāranātha, *History of Buddhism in India*, translated from the Tibetan by Lama Chinpa Alaka, edited by Devi Prasad Chattopadhyayaya (Simla: Indian Institute of Advanced Study, 1970), pp. 18, 300–301, 327, and 429.

David Ruegg notes that in the *Jñānasarasamuccayanāmanibhandhana* [Explanation of *(Āryadeva's) "Compendium of Wisdom"*] (49a–b) Bodhibhadra "states that Sautrāntikas too may be regarded as Mahāyānists" and notes too that late eighth-century Tibetan scholars in fact used the term "Sautrāntika-Mādhyamika." See Ruegg, *The Literature of the Mādhyamaka School of Philosophy in India* (Weisbaden, Otto Harrassowitz, 1981), p. 59 n.176. Tsong-ka-ba too uses this term in his *Middling Exposition of the Stages of the Path* (*Lam rim 'bring*) (Dharamsala: Shes rig par khang, 1968), p. 193b.6–194a.1. Later texts on tenets however, such as those by Gön-jok-jig-may-dbang-bo, Jang-gya, and Jam-yang-shay-ba do not take up this category.

6. Lati Rinbochay, oral commentary.

7. *Dharmaskhanda* is the first of the Seven Treatises of Knowledge (*mNgon pa sde bdun*).

8. See Sopa and Hopkins, *Practice and Theory*, p. 93; Dre-Gomang Cultural Association Tibetan edition, pp. 21–32.

9. Denma Lochö Rinbochay, oral commentary.

10. *Ibid.*

11. Lati Rinbochay, oral commentary.
12. Geshe Jampel Thando, discussion.
13. *Ibid.*
14. "As suitable to be mixed" is intended to describe the manner in which thought apprehends its object; it does not refer to a process of decision.
15. Denma Lochö Rinbochay, oral commentary.
16. Geshe Tshultrim Puntsok, discussion. Clearly, Jang-gya is turning his attention to the problem of classifying an understanding which is not language-based and which therefore can be common to animals, pre-verbal children and adult humans. For a contemporary argument for the difference between language and understanding, see Saugstad, *A Theory of Language and Understanding* (Oslo: Universitetsforlaget, 1980), *passim* but especially pp. 44–49.
17. See p. 147 for discussion of the four types of isolates.
18. Lati Rinbochay, oral commentary.
19. *Ibid.*
20. More technically, non-one with pot; thereby excluding golden pot, which is a pot, but is not one with pot.
21. In the chapter on Vaibhāṣika.
22. Denma Lochö Rinbochay, oral commentary.
23. Earlier only three characteristics were mentioned, however, no difference of meaning is intended here.
24. Denma Lochö Rinbochay, oral commentary.
25. For a brief explanation of undermining reasons, see p. 185.
26. Denma Lochö Rinbochay, oral commentary.
27. Geshe Belden Drakba, oral commentary.
28. Denma Lochö Rinbochay, oral commentary.
29. See Klein, *Knowledge and Liberation*, p. 244, n. 28.
30. Denma Lochö Rinbochay, oral commentary.
31. P5709 Vol. 130, 78-5-6.
32. Lati Rinbochay, oral commentary.
33. Geshe Belden Drakba, oral commentary.
34. Denma Lochö Rinbochay, oral commentary.
35. *Ibid.*

36. For a pertinent discussion of atomist theory in India, see B. K. Matilal, *Perception*, pp. 359–371.

37. In the Peking edition of this text (Vol. 146, 115.3-5) translated from Sanskrit into Tibetan by Śāntibhadra, this line reads *thogs bcas gzugs min yod ma yin*. In the translation of Jetāri's commentary by Kanakaśrīmitra, this line is quoted as Jang-gya has it: *thogs pa med pa'i gzugs yod min*. Their meanings are the same.

38. This text has not yet been identified.

39. Denma Lochö Rinbochay, oral commentary.

40. Lati Rinbochay, oral commentary.

41. See Hopkins, *Meditation on Emptiness*, p. 232.

42. Geshe Belden Drakba, oral commentary.

43. Lati Rinbochay, oral commentary.

44. Lati Rinbochay and Denma Lochö Rinbochay, oral commentary.

45. For further explanation of this point, see Sopa and Hopkins, *Practice and Theory*, p. 79. For the wider Indian context here see Matilal, *Perception*, pp. 248–251.

46. For a summary of these three types of aspected direct perception see Klein, *Knowledge and Liberation*, pp. 108–110.

47. Jambel Shenpen Rinbochay, oral commentary.

48. For a more detailed discussion of inference see Napper, *Mind in Tibetan Buddhism*. Chapter II.

49. For a discussion of these divisions of inferential consciousnesses, see Napper, *Mind in Tibetan Buddhism*, pp. 76–82.

50. All examples in this chapter are taken from Katherine Rogers, "The Topic of Signs and Reasoning" (M. A., University of Virginia, 1980). See Rogers also for detailed explanations of the types of reasonings mentioned by Jang-gya.

51. In other presentations of reasonings this is called an "effect sign proving the self-reverse of a cause" (*rgyu rang ldog sgrub gyi 'bras rtags yang dag*) but the meaning is the same.

52. In another way, nature signs which are free of qualification are divided into (1) those expressed by a term which directly expresses its agent and (2) those expressed by a term which indirectly expresses its agent.

53. This sixth illustration and category are not mentioned by Pur-bu-jok.

54. See Hopkins, *Meditation on Emptiness*, pp. 273–274.

55. Jang-gya discusses this on p. 90.4ff. The five are mentioned in Vasubhandu's *Treasury* as follows: appearing form-base, I.9–14; main mind base, II.34; accompanying mental factor base, II. 23–24; non-associated compositional factor base, II. 35–48; and non-product base, I.5–6.

56. See Jang-gya, 91.4. the Vaibhāṣikas assert only forty-six mental factors and fourteen non-associated compositional factors; they also set forth a three-fold division of non-products: uncaused spaces, analytical cessations, and non-analytical cessations.

57. See Hopkins, *Meditation on Emptiness*, pp. 107ff.

58. For a discussion of differences characterizing the three paths see Tsong-ka-ba, *Tantra in Tibet* (London: Allen & Unwin, 1977), pp. 173–188, and pp. 210ff.

59. For an extensive discussion see Hopkins, *Meditation on Emptiness*, pp. 292ff.

60. For further reasoning proving selflessness as discussed in Gelukba Prāsaṅgika, see Hopkins, *Meditation on Emptiness*, pp. 175–196.

61. Lati Rinbochay, oral commentary.

62. Denma Lochö Rinbochay, oral commentary.

63. *Ibid.*

64. Geshe Belden Drakba, oral commentary.

65. *Ibid.*

66. Lati Rinbochay, oral commentary.

67. Denma Lochö Rinbochay, oral commentary.

68. Geshe Belden Drakba, oral commentary.

69. Lati Rinbochay, oral commentary.

70. Denma Lochö Rinbochay, oral commentary. For a discussion of consequences (*prasaṅga*) see Hopkins, *Meditation on Emptiness*, pp. 443–454.

71. For a translation and exposition of this chapter see Donald S. Lopez, *A Study of Svātantrika* (Ithaca: Snow Lion Publications 1987). For a focus on Indian Svātantrika via

Jñāngarbha see M. David Eckel, *Jñānagarbha's Commentary on the Distinction Between the Two Truths* (Albany: SUNY Press, 1987).

72. Geshe Belden Drakba, oral commentary.

73. Denma Lochö Rinbochay, oral commentary.

74. For further discussion of problems in interpreting the function of the sixth consciousness see Masatoshi Nagatomi, "Mānasa-pratyakṣa: A Conundrum in the Buddhist Pramāṇa System," in *Sanskrit and Indian Studies*, eds. M. Nagatomi, B. K. Matilal, J. M. Masson, and R. Dimock (Boston: Reidel, 1980), pp. 243–259.

75. Geshe Belden Drakba, oral commentary.

76. *Ibid.*

77. For discussion of the four truths see Hopkins, *Meditation on Emptiness*, pp. 285–304.

78. Geshe Belden Drakba, oral commentary.

79. The text cites these four in a different order: clean, pleasant, permanent, and self. However, according to Geshe Belden Drakba, that order is for the sake of easy pronunciation in Tibetan. The order that accords with the listing of antidotes given by Geshe Belden Drakba is given in the translation.

80. Lati Rinbochay, oral commentary.

81. For discussion of Sāṃkhya see Sopa and Hopkins, *Practice and Theory*, p. 58ff; also, Hopkins, *Meditation on Emptiness*, p. 352ff.

82. Pan-chen Sö-nam-drak-ba's *General Meaning Commentary on "Ornament,"* p. 72a. gives the third misconception here as "conceiving the nature to be permanent and the states impermanent" (*rang bzhin rtag la gnas skabs mi rtag par 'dzin pa*).

83. *Srid* here means cyclic existence (Geshe Belden Drakba, oral commentary).

84. Lati Rinbochay, oral commentary.

85. Geshe Belden Drakba, oral commentary.

86. Lati Rinbochay, oral commentary.

87. Sopa and Hopkins, *Practice and Theory*, pp. 89–90.

88. Lati Rinbochay, oral commentary.

89. Geshe Belden Drakba, oral commentary.

90. *Rig pa, mig, blo* and *shes pa*. The Pāli order and wording is slightly different: *chakkhu, jnana, panna, and vijja.*

91. Denma Lochö Rinbochay, oral commentary.

92. Definitions and their definiendums—the former being defining agents and the latter the objects of the activity of definition—do not exist by way of their own nature but are imputed by thought.

93. Geshe, Belden Drakba, oral commentary.

94. Denma Lochö Rinbochay, oral commentary.

NOTES: JANG-GYA TIBETAN TEXT

Notes indicate where changes have been made in the Sautrāntika chapter from the *Presentation of Tenets* by Jang-gya (*Grub mtha'i rnam bzhag*) published in Sarnath, Varanasi at the Pleasure of Elegant Sayings Press in 1970; also indicated are discrepancies with the edition edited by Lokesh Chandra and published by Sharada Rani in New Delhi, 1977. Preferences, if any, are indicated.

1. *la* added in accordance with the Delhi edition.
2. Delhi edition has *grags ces.*
3. Changed from *dbye ba lung* to *dbye ba la lung* in accordance with the Delhi edition.
4. Delhi edition has Ku-ma-ra-ta.
5. Changed from *'dar* to *'dir* in accordance with Delhi.
6. Delhi reads *zhes.*
7. Delhi reads *zhes.*
8. Delhi incorrectly reads *sgrub bya.*
9. Delhi incorrectly reads *snang ngo de nyid.*
10. Delhi incorrectly reads *yin las.*
11. Here and throughout, Delhi edition spells this *brda'* whereas Sarnath edition consistently reads *brda.*
12. *byung* changed to *byang* by editor.
13. *rang gis* changed to *rang gi* by editor.

* Thanks to Craig Preston for making the initial listing of discrepancies between the two editions.

14. Delhi erroneously reads *brjod byed.*

15. Delhi reads *de ka'i thad.*

16. pp. 104 and 105 erroneously transposed in Sarnath edition.

17. Delhi erroneously reads *rtogs pa'i.*

18. Delhi omits the *ni.*

19. Changed from *grub po'i* to *grub bo'i* by editor.

20. Changed from *dngos pong da* to *dngos po dang* in accordance with Delhi.

21. Delhi erroneously reads *brtags pa'i.*

22. Delhi reads *mtha' bcad pa'i.*

23. Delhi reads *rtsigs su.*

24. Delhi reads *shags.*

25. Changed from *gyis* to *gyi* by editor.

26. Delhi erroneously reads *ltan.*

27. Delhi erroneously reads *bsgrub byed.*

28. Changed from *med pas* to *med par* by editor. Delhi erroneously reads *ed pa.*

29. Changed from *byas pa dang* to *byas p'ang* in accordance with Delhi.

30. Changed from *thams cad brtag pa* to *thams cad pa rtag pa* in accordance with Delhi edition.

31. Delhi erroneously reads *spangs spangs pa'i.*

32. Delhi erroneously reads *brtag.*

33. Changed from *skad cig gam* to *sakd cig ma* in accordance with Delhi.

34. Delhi erroneously reads *phug.*

35. Delhi consistently reads *'gag pa* for Sarnath's *'gags pa.*

36. Delhi consistently reads *ltos nas* for Sarnath's *bltos nas.*

37. Changed from *bltos par* to *ltos sar* in accordance with Delhi edition.

38. Changed as in note 37.

39. *sol* changed to *sel* by editor.

40. Delhi consistently reads *bsgrub pa* for Sarnath's *sgrub pa.*

41. Delhi reads *bgag shul.*

42. Changed from *shis rab* to *shes rab* in accordance with Delhi edition.

43. Delhi erroneously reads *brtags.*

44. Changed from *'bul ba'i* to *phul ba'i* in accordance with Delhi.

45. Changed from *gru mtha'* to *grub mtha'* by editor.

46. Delhi erroneously reads *brtags par.*

47. Changed from *'dzod 'grel* to *mdzod 'grel* by editor.

48. Delhi erroneously reads *btags pa'i.*

49. Changed from *bltas pa'i* to *ltas pa'i* in accordance with Delhi.

50. Delhi reads *rtsigs pa.*

51. Delhi reads *gegs.*

52. *mthong* added in accordance with Lati Rinbochay. Delhi appears different but illegible here.

53. Delhi erroneously reads *sgor.*

54. Changed from *kyis* to *kyi* in accordance with Delhi.

55. Changed from *kyis* to *kyi* in accordance with Delhi.

56. Changed from *kyis* to *kyi* in accordance with Delhi.

57. Changed from *na* to *ni* by editor.

58. *che* added in accordance with Delhi.

59. Delhi reads *bskyed byed.*

60. Changed from *phye ma* to *phyi ma* in accordance with Delhi.

61. Changed from *byed brag* to *bye brag* in accordance with Delhi.

62. Changed from *yad ches* to *yid ches* in accordance with Delhi.

63. Delhi reads *gar bar.*

64. Delhi erroneously reads *med pa.*

65. Changed from *dang du bral* to *dang gcig du bral* by editor.

66. Delhi reads *gsungs.*

67. Delhi reads *ces.*

68. Delhi reads *'gag pa.*

69. Delhi erroneously reads *gya noms.*

70. Delhi reads *gsum ka'i.*

71. Delhi erroneously reads *rig pa'i.*

72. Delhi erroneously reads *bsgom mo.*

73. Delhi reads *ya ma ris.*

74. Delhi reads *kha med.*
75. *kyang* added in accordance with Delhi.
76. Delhi reads *dkyogs.*

Glossary

English	*Sanskrit*	*Tibetan*
abiding	sthāna	gnas pa
actual	sākṣāt	dngos
affirming negative	paryudāsprati-ṣedha	ma yin dgag
affixing the appellation		brda 'sbyar ba
affliction	kleśa	nyon mongs
aggregate	skandha	phung po
aggregation		'dus pa
alternative	koṭi	mu
Amitayus	amitayus	tshe dpag med
analytical cessation	pratisaṃkhyā-nirodha	so sor brtags 'gog
antidote	pratipakṣa	gnyen po
appearance	pratibhāsa	snang ba
appearing object	pratibhāsaviṣaya	snang yul
appellation	saṃketa	brda
apprehend	grahaṇa	'dzin pa
apprehended object	*grahyaviṣaya	gzung yul, gzung don

English	*Sanskrit*	*Tibetan*
apprehending aspect	grāhakākāra	'dzin rnam
apprehension aspect	grāhyākāra	bzung rnam
Āryadeva	āryadeva	'phags-pa-lha
Asaṅga	asaṅga	thogs-med
ascertain	niścaya	nges pa
aspect	ākāra	rnam pa
attribute	viśeṣa	khyad par
autonomous syllogism	svatantraprayoga	rang rgyud kyi sbyor ba
Avalokitavrata	avalokitavrata	spyan-ras-gzigs-brtul-zhugs
Avalokiteśvara	avalokiteśvara	spyan-ras-gzigs
awareness	buddhi	blo
basal subject		rang rten gyi chos can
base	āśraya	rten
basis of affixing		'jug gzhi
Bhāvaviveka	bhāvaviveka	legs-ldan-'byed
Blessed One	bhagavān	bcom ldan 'das
Bodhibhadra	bodhibhadra	byang-chub-bzang-po
Bodhisattva	bodhisattva	byang chub sems dpa'
causal condition	hetupratyaya	rgyu rkyen
calm abiding	śamatha	zhi gnas
cause	hetu	rgyu
challenger (in debate)		snga rgol
Cittamātra	cittamātra	sems tsam
collection		tshogs pa
collection generality		tshogs spyi
color	varṇa	kha dog
common	sādhārna	thun mong

English	*Sanskrit*	*Tibetan*
common locus	samānādhikaraṇa	gzhi mthun
compassion	karuṇā	snying rje
complete engager	*vidhipravṛtti-buddhi	sgrub 'jug gi blo
composite		bsags pa
compositional factor	saṃskāra	'du byed
conception of a self of phenomena	dharmātmagrāha	chos kyi bdag'dzin
concordant example	sadṛṣṭānta	mthun dpe
condition	pratyaya	rkyen
consciousness	jñāna/vijñāna	shes pa/rnam par shes pa
consequence	prasaṅga	thal 'gyur
constituent	dhātu	khams
continuum	samtāna	rgyud
contradictory	virodha	'gal ba
convention	vyavahāra	tha snyad
conventional truth	saṃvṛtisatya	kun rdzob bden pa
conventionally existent	saṃvṛtisat	kun rdzob du yod pa/tha snyad du yod pa
cooperative condition	sahakāripratyaya	lhan cig byed rkyen
correct reason	*saṃyakliṅga	rtags yang dag
counter pervasion	vyatirekavyāpti	ldog khyab
definiendum	lakṣya	mtshon bya
definition	lakṣaṇa	mtshan nyid
designation		brda'
Devendrabuddhi	devendrabuddhi	lha-dbang-blo
Dharmakīrti	dharmakīrti	chos-kyi-grags-pa
Dignāga	dignāga	phyogs-glang
direct perceiver/direct perception	pratyakṣa	mngon sum

English	*Sanskrit*	*Tibetan*
discipline	vinaya	'dul ba
discrimination	samjñā	'du shes
disintegration	vināśa	'jig pa
dissimilar class		mi mthun phyogs
dominant condition	adhipatipratyaya	bdag rkyen
effect	phala	'bras bu
effect sign proving a general cause		rgyu'i spyi sgrub kyi 'bras rtags
effect sign proving a particular cause		rgyu'i khyad par sgrub kyi 'bras rtags
effect sign proving a preceding cause		rgyu sngon song sgrub kyi'bras rtags
effect sign proving an actual cause		rgyu dngos sgrub kyi 'bras rtags
effect sign which is a means of inferring causal attributes		rgyu chos rjes dpog gi bras rtags
eliminative engager	*apohapravṛtti-buddhi	sel 'jug gi blo
empowering condition	adhipatipratyaya	bdag rkyen
emptiness	*śūnyata	stong pa nyid
Enjoyment Body	longs sku	saṃbhogakāya
entity	vastu	ngo bo
established/proven	siddha	grub pa
established basis		gzhi grub
established through its own power	svairīsiddhi	rang dbang du grub pa
evolute	parināma/vikāra	rnam 'gyur
exclusion	apoha	sel ba

English	*Sanskrit*	*Tibetan*
Exemplifiers	dārśṭāntika	dpe ston pa
existence	sat	yod pa
experience		myong ba
explicit	sākṣāt	dngos
explicit object of expression		dngos gyi brjod bya
explicit realization		dngos rtogs
explicitly suggest		dngos su 'phen pa
eye sense power	cakṣurindriya	mig dbang
factor	amṣa/bhāga	cha
factually concordant	anvartha	don mthun
factually other		don gzhan
feature	viśeṣa	khyad par
feeling	vedanā	tshor ba
For Destroyer	arhan	dgra bcom pa
Followers of Reasoning	*nyāyānusārin	rigs pa'i rje su 'brangs pa
Followers of Scripture	*āgamānusārin	lung gi rjes su 'brangs pa
form	rūpa	gzugs
form aggregate	rūpaskandha	gzugs gyi phung po
Four Noble Truths	catvāry-āryasatyāni	bden pa bzhi
fruit	phala	'bras bu
functioning thing (that which is able to perform a function)	bhāva, *kriyāśakta, *kriyāsamarta, arthakriya-kāritva	don byed mus pa/ dngos po
generality	sāmānya	spyi
generally characterized thing		dngos por 'gyur ba'i spyi mtshan

English	*Sanskrit*	*Tibetan*
generally characterized phenomenon	sāmānyalakṣaṇa	spyi mtshan
Half-Eggists		sgo nga phyed tshal ba
heat	uṣmagata	drod
Hearer	śrāvaka	nyan thos
hidden phenomenon	parokṣa	lkog gyur
hue		tshon
illustration		mtshan gzhi
illustration-isolate		gzhi ldog
immediately preceding condition	samanantarapratyaya	de ma thag rkyen
impermanent	anitya	mi rtag pa
impermanent thing	bhāva/anityadharma	dngos po mi rtag pai chos
implicitly suggest		zhugs la 'phen pa
imputedly established	*prajñaptisiddhi	btags du grub pa
imputedly existent	*prajñaptisat	btags yod
incontrovertible	avisaṃvādin	mi slu ba
inference	anumāna	rjes dpag
inference by the power of the fact	*vastu-bala-anumāna	dngos stobs rjes dpag
inference through belief	*āpta-anumāna	yid ches rjes dpag
inference through renown	*prasiddha-anumāna	grags pa'i rjes dpag
inherent existence	svabhāvasiddhi	rang bzhin gyis grub pa
instance, manifestation	vyākti	gsal ba
isolate	vivartana	ldog pa

English	*Sanskrit*	*Tibetan*
Knowledge	abhidharma	chos mngon pa
latency	vāsanā	bag chags
liberation	mokṣa/vimokṣa	thar pa
Mādhyamika	mādhyamika	dbu ma pa
manifest phenomenon	abhimukhī	mngon gyur
matter	kanthā	bem po
meaning/object	artha	don
meaning-generality	arthasāmānya	don spyi
meaning isolate	*arthavivartana	don ldog
meaning-of-the-term	śabdārtha	sgra don
meditative absorption	samāpatti	snyoms 'jug
mental and physical aggregates	skandha	phung po
mental application	mānaskara	yid la byed pa
mental direct perceiver	mānasapratyakṣa	yid kyi mngon sum
mental exclusion	buddhyātmakānyā-poha	blo'i gzhan sel
mental factor	caitta	sems byung
mentally fabricated factor		sgro btag gyi cha
merely propounded subject, mere subject		chos can 'ba' zhig pa
method	upāya	thabs
mind of complete engagement	*viddhipravṛtti-buddhi	grub 'jug gi blo
mind of partial engagement	*apohapravṛtti-buddhi	sel 'jug gi blo
minute particle	paramāṇu	rdul phra rab
mistaken	bhrānta	'khrul ba

English	*Sanskrit*	*Tibetan*
mix, associate		'dres pa
mode of abiding		gnas lugs
mode of subsistence		sdod lugs, gnas lugs
moment	kṣaṇa	skad cig
momentary	kṣaṇika	skad cig ma
mutual	anyonya	phan tshun
mutual exclusion	anyonyaparihara-virodha	phan tshun spangs 'gal
Nāgārjuna	nāgārjuna	klu-grub
name	nāma, saṃketa	ming, brda
natural existence	svalakṣaṇa-siddhi	rang gi mtshan nyid kyis grub pa
nature	prākṛti	rang bzhin
nature sign	*svabhāva-liṅga	rang bzhin kyi rtags
nature sign that is free of qualification		khyad par dag pa pa'i rang bzhin kyi rtags
nature sign that relates to a qualification		khyad par ltos pa pa'i rang bzhin kyi rtags
nature sign which implies [a qualification or agent which is another substantial entity]		khyad par kyi chos rdzas gzhan 'phen pa'i rang bzhin kyi rtags
nature sign which implies [a qualification or agent which is not another substantial entity]		rdzas gzhan ma yin pa 'phen pa'i rang bzhin kyi rtags

English	*Sanskrit*	*Tibetan*
negative/negative phenomenon	pratiṣedha	dgag pa
negative, affirming	paryudāsaprati-ṣedha	ma yin dgag
negative, non-affirming	prasajyaprati-ṣedha	med dgag
nine successive meditative absorbtions	navānupūrvavihār-asamāpatti	mthar gyis gnas pa'i snyoms par 'jug pa dgu
nirvana without remainder	anupadhiśeṣa-nirvāṇa	lhag med myang ngan las 'das pa
noble/superior	ārya	'phags pa
non-affirming negative	prasajyapratiṣedha	med dgag
non-associated compositional factor	viprayukta-saṃskāra	ldan min 'du byed
non-conceptual	nirvikalpaka	rtog med
non-observation sign	*anupalabdaliṅga	ma dmigs pa'i rtags
non-observation sign of the non-appearing	*apratibhāsa-anupalab-dhiliṅga	mi snang ba ma dmigs pa'i rtags
non-obstructive	apratihata, apratigha	thogs pa med pa
non-mistaken	abhrānta	ma 'khrul ba
Non-Pluralists		sna tshogs gnyis med pa
non-revelatory form	avijñaptirūpa	rnam par rig byed ma yin pa'i gzugs
non-thing	abhāva	dngos med

English	*Sanskrit*	*Tibetan*
object	viṣaya	yul
object being proved	sādhya	bsgrub bya
object condition	ālambanapratyaya	dmigs rkyen
object of comprehension	prameya	gzhal bya
object of engagement	*pravṛttiviṣaya	'jug yul
object of expression	abhidheya, vācyam	brjod bya
object of knowledge	jñeya	shes bya
object of negation	pratiṣedhya	dgag bya
object of operation		'jug yul
object of the mode of apprehension		'dzin stangs kyi yul
objective exclusion	arthātmaka-svalakṣaṇa-anyāpoha	don rang mtshan gyi gzhan sel
obscured	saṃvṛti	kun rdzob
observed object condition	ālambana-pratyaya	dmigs rkyen
odor	gandha	dri
one substantial entity	ekadravya	rdzas gcig
one substantial type		rdzas rigs gcig
one substantiality of establishment and abiding		grub bde rdzas gcig
opposite	vyatireka	log pa
other-exclusion	anyāpoha	gzhan sel
other-knower	*anyasaṃvedanā	gzhan rig
partial engager	*apohapravṛtti-buddhi	sel 'jug gi blo

English	*Sanskrit*	*Tibetan*
path	mārga	lam
path of seeing	darśanamārga	mthong lam
perfection	pāramitā	phar phyin
permanent	nitya	rtag pa
pervastion/positive pervasion	anvayavyāpti	rjes khyab
phenomenon imputed by thought		rtog pas btags tsam gyi chos
phenomenon-source	dharmāyatana	chos kyi skye mched
phrase/word	vacana	tshig
place	sthana	gnas
positive phenomenon	vidhi	sgrub pa
power of the thing	*vastubala	dngos stobs
Prāsaṅgika	prāsaṅgika	thal 'gyur pa
predicate of the probandum	sādhyadharma	bsgrub bya'i chos
predicate of the negandum		dgag bya'i chos
proponents of true existence	bhāvavādin	dngos smra ba
principal	pradhāna	gtso bo
product	saṃskṛta, kṛta	'dus byas, byas pa
production	utpatti	skye ba
property of the subject	pakṣadharma	phyogs chos
proponents of an equal number of subjects & objects		gzung 'dzin grangs mnyam pa
pure thing	vastumātra	dngos po dag pa
reality	dharmatā	chos nyid

English	*Sanskrit*	*Tibetan*
realize	adhigamana	rtogs pa
referent object	*adhyavasaya-viṣaya	zhen yul
reflection	pratibiṃba	gzugs brnyan
reverse	vivartana, vyatireka	ldog pa
Sāṃkhya	sāṃkhya	grangs can pa
Śāntarakṣita	śāntarakṣita	zhi-ba-'tsho
Sautrāntika	sautrāntika	mdo sde pa
self-isolate	vivartana	rang ldog
self-knower	svasaṃvedanā	rang rig
self of persons	pudgalātman	gang zag gi bdag
self of phenomenon	dharmātman	chos kyi bdag
selflessness	nairātyma	bdag med
selflessness of persons	pudgalanairātmya	gang zag gi bdag med
selflessness of phenomenon	dharmanairātmya	chos kyi bdag med
self sufficient		rang rkya ba
sense direct perceiver	*rūpagrahanendriyapratyakṣa	gzugs 'dzin dbang mngon
Sequential Non-Pluralists		rim gyis ba'i sna tshogs gnyis med pa
sets of discourses/ sets of sutras	sutrānta	mdo sde
shape	samsthāna	dbyibs
sign	liṅga	rtags
sign of non-dependence		ltogs med kyi rtags
sign of observation of a contradictory object		'gal zla dmigs pa'i rtags
sign of sameness entity	svabhāva-liṅga	rang bzhin gyi rtags

English	*Sanskrit*	*Tibetan*
sign which is a non-conservation of a related object		'brel zla ma dmigs pa'i rtags
sign which is a non-observtion of the suitable to appear		snang rung ma dmigs pa'i rtags
similar aspect		'dra rnam
similar class		mthun phyogs
similar example	sadṛṣṭānta	mthun dpe
small particle		rdul phran
Solitary Realizer	pratyekabuddha	rang sangs rgyas
sound	śabda	sgra
source	āyatana	skye mched
space	ākāśa	nam mkha'
special insight	vipaśyanā	lhag mthong
specifically charac-terized phenomenon	svalakṣaṇa	rang mtshan
stated subject	*vāda-dharmin	smra ba'i chos can
subsequent cognizer	*pariccinna-jñāna	bcad shed/dpyad shes
substantial entity	dravya	rdzas
substantial entity establishment and abiding		grub bde rdzas gcig
substantially established	dravyasiddha	rdzas su grub pa
substantially existent	dravyasat	rdzas yod
substratum		khyad gzhi
suggest		'phen
suitable to be mixed		'dres rung

English	*Sanskrit*	*Tibetan*
superimposition	āropa	sgro 'dogs
supreme mundane qualities	laukikāgrya-dharma	'jig rten pa'i chos kyi mchog
syllogism	prayoga	sbyor ba
tangible object/ object of touch	sprastavya	reg bya
tenet	siddhānta	grub mtha'
term	śabda	sgra
term generality	śabdasāmānya	sgra spyi
terminology	saṃketa	brda
thesis	pratijñā	dam bca'
thing	bhāva	dngos po
thirty-seven harmonies with enlightenment		byang phyogs so bdun
thought/thought consciouisness	kalpanā	rtog pa
three modes	trirūpa	tshul gsum
truly existent	*satyasat	bden par yod pa
type generality	*gotrasāmānya	rigs spyi
two truths	satyadvaya	bden pa gnyis
ultimate truth	paramārthasatya	don dam bden pa
ultimately established phenomenon	paramārtha-siddhidharma	don dam du grub ba'i chos
ultimately existent	paramārthasat	don dam par yod pa
uncommon	asādharaṇa	thun mong ma yin ba
uncommon cause	asadharaṇa-hetu	thun mong ma yin ba'i rgyu

English	*Sanskrit*	*Tibetan*
unconditioned	asaṃskṛta	'dus ma byas
undermining sign		gnod pa can gyi rtags
Vaibhāṣika	vaibhāṣika	bye brag smar ba
Vasubandhu	vasubandhu	dbyig-gnyen
valid cognizer/ prime cognizer	pramāṇa	tshad ma
Vinītadeva	vinītadeva	dul-ba-lha
yogic direct perceiver	yogipratyakṣa	rnal 'byor mngon sum

Bibliography of Works Cited

Abbreviations

P: *Tibetan Tripitaka* (Tokyo-Kyoto: Tibetan Tripitaka Research Foundation, 1956)

Toh: *A Complete Catalogue of the Tibetan Buddhist Canons*, ed. by Prof. Hakuji Ui, and *A Catalogue of the Tohoku University Collection of Tibetan Works on Buddhism*, ed. by Prof. Yensho Kanakura (Sendai, Japan, 1934 and 1953)

Bibliography

1. TIBETAN AND SANSKRIT SOURCES

Asaṅga (Thogs-med), 4th Century
Compendium of Knowledge
Abhidharmasamuccaya
mNgon pa kun btus
P550, Vol. 112

Avalokitavrata (sPyan-ras-gzigs-brtul-zhugs), probably 8th Century
Commentary on (Bhāvaviveka's) "Lamp for Nāgārjuna's

'Wisdom' "
Prajñāpradīpaṭīkā
Shes rab sgron ma'i rgya cher 'grel pa
P5259, Vol. 96-97

Bel-den-chö-jay, *see* Nga-wang-bel-den

Bhāvaviveka (Legs-ldan-'byed), c. 400 A.D.
Blaze of Reasoning, Commentary on the "Heart of the Middle Way"
Madhyamakahṛdayavṛttitarkajvālā
dbU ma'i snying po'i 'grel pa rtog ge 'bar la
P5256, Vol 96

Bodhibhadra (Byang-chub-bzang-po), 16th Century
Explanation of (Āryadeva's) "Compendium of Wisdom"
Jñānasārasamuccayanāmanibandhana
Ye shes snying po kun las btus pa shes bya ba'i bshad sbyar
P5252, Vol. 95

Chim-jam-bel-yang (mChims-'jam dpal-dbyangs)
Ornament of Knowledge, Commentary on the Chapters of (Vasubandhu's) "Treasury of Knowledge"
Chos mngon pa'i mdzod kyi tshig le'ur byas pa'i grel pa mngon pa'i rgyan
Text from Gomang Library of Drebung Monastery, Mundgod, India, from blocks available to them.

Chö-gyi-gyel-tsen (Chos-kyi-rgyal-mtshan), 1469-1446
Presentation of Tenets
Grub mtha'i rnam gzahg
Boxa: s.n., 196–.

Dak-tsang (sTag-tshang-lo-tsa-ba Shes-rab-rin-chen), b. 1405
Ocean of Good Explanations, Explanation of "Freedom from Extremes Through Understanding All Tenets"
Grub mtha' kun shes nas mtha' bral grub pa zhes bya ba'i bstan bcos rnam par bshad pa legs bshad kyi rgya mtsho
Thim-phu: Kun-gzang-stobs-rgyal, 1976

Den-dar-hla-ram-ba (bsTan-dar-lha-ram-pa), b. 1759
Introduction to the General Meaning of (Dharmakīrti's) "Commentary on (Dignāga's) 'Compendium on Valid Cognition' "

rNam 'grel spyi don rdzom 'phro
Collected *gSung 'bum* of Bstan-dar Lha-ram of A-lag-sha, Vol. Ka
New Delhi: Guru Deva, 1971
Annotations to (Jig-may-ling-pa's) "Treasury of Excellence"
Yon tan mdzod kyi mchan 'grely/Yon tan rin po che'i mdzod kyi dka' gnad rdo rje'i rgya mdud 'grol byed legs bshad gser gyi thur ma
Ngagyur Nyingma, Jamyang Khentse: n.p., n.d.,
Presentation of Generally and Specifically Characterized Phenomena
Rang mtshan spyi mtshan gyi rnam zhag
Collected *gSung 'bum* of Bstan-dar Lha-ram of A-la-sha, Vol. Ka
New Delhi: Guru Deva, 1971
Devendrabuddhi (Lha-dbang-blo)
Commentary on (Dharmakīrti's) "Commentary on (Dignāga's) 'Compendium on Valid Cognition' "
Pramāṇavārttikapañjikā
Tshad ma rnam 'grel gyi dka' 'grel
P5709, Vol. 130
Dharmakīrti (Chos-kyi-grags-pa), 7th Century
Seven Treatises on Valid Cognition
Analysis of Relations
Saṃbandhaparīkṣāvṛtti
'Brel pa brtag pa'i rab tu byed pa
P5713, Vol. 130
Ascertainment of Valid Cognition
Pramāṇaviniścaya
Tshad ma rnam par nges pa
P5710, Vol. 130
Commentary on (Dignāga's) "Compendium on Valid Cognition"
Pramāṇavārttikakārikā
Tshad ma rnam 'grel gyi tshig le'ur byas pa
P5709, Vol. 130
Drop of Reasoning

Nyāyabinduprakaraṇa
Rigs pa'i thigs pa zhes bya ba'i rab tu byed pa
P5711, Vol. 130
Drop of Reasons
Hetubindunāmaprakaraṇa
gTan tshigs kyi thigs pa zhes bya ba rab tu byed pa
P5712, Vol. 130
Proof of Other Continuums
Saṃtānāntarasiddhināmaprakaraṇa
rGyud bzhan grub pa zhes bya ba'i rab tu byed pa
P5716, Vol. 130
Reasoning for Debate
Vādanyāyanāmaprakaraṇa
rTsod pa'i rigs pa zhes bya ba'i rab tu byed pa
P5715, Vol. 130

Dignāga (Phyogs-glang), 5th Century
Commentary on "Examination of Objects"
Ālambanaparīkṣāvṛtti
dMigs pa brtag pa'i 'grel pa
P5704, Vol. 130
Compendium on Valid Cognition
Pramāṇasamuccaya
Tshad ma kun las btus pa
P5700, Vol. 130
Examination of Objects of Observation
Ālambanaparīkṣā
dMigs pa brtag pa
P5703, Vol. 130

Dharmottara (Chos-mchog)
Commentary on (Dharmakīrti's) "Compendium on Valid Cognition"
Pramāṇviniścayaṭīka
Tshad ma rnam par nges pa'i 'grel bshad
P5727, Vol. 136

Ge-dun-gya-tsho (dGe-'dun-rgya-mtsho), Dalai Lama II, 1476-1542
Boat Entering the Ocean of Tenets

Grub mtha' rgya mtshor 'jug pa'i gru rdzins zes bya ba'i bstan bcos
Varanasi: Ye-ses-stobs-ldan, 1969

Gön-chok-jik-may-wang-bo (dKon-mchog-'jigs-med-dbang-po), 1728-1791

Precious Garland of Tenets/Presentation of Tenets, A Precious Garland
Grub pa'i mtha'i rnam par bzhag pa rin po che'i phreng ba
Mundgod, India: Dre-Gomang Buddhist Cultural Association (Printed by Dre-Loseling Press), 1980

Gyel-tsap (rGyal-tshab), 1364-1432

Commentary on (Dharmakīrti's) "Ascertainment of Valid Cognition"
rNam nges ṭik chen
Tashi Lunpo blockprint, n.d.

Commentary on (Maitreya's) "Sublime Science" / Commentary on (Maitreya's) "Mahāyāna Treatise on the Sublime Science"
Thek pa chen po rgyud bla ma'i ṭīkkā
Toh. 5434

Commentary on (Śāntideva's) "Engaging in the Bodhisattva Deeds"
Byang chub sems dpa'i spyod pa la 'jug pa'i rnam bshad rgyal sras 'jug ngogs
Toh. 5436

Explanation of (Dharmakīrti's) "Commentary on (Dignāga's) 'Compendium on Valid Cognition'"
Tshad ma rnam 'grel gyi tshig le'ur byas pa'i rnam bshad thar lam phyin ci ma log par gsal bar byed pa
Sarnath, Varanasi: Pleasure of Elegant Sayings Press, Vol. I, 1974, Vol. II, 1975
Toh. 5450

Eradication of Forgetfulness Regarding the Chapter on Direct Perception in (Dharmakīrti's) "Commentary on (Dignāga's) 'Compendium on Valid Cognition'"
mNgon sum le'u'i brjed byang
Toh. 5448

Great Eradication of Forgetfulness Regarding Valid Cognition

Tshad ma'i brjed byang chen mo
Toh. 5438
Illumination of the Thought, An Extensive Commentary on (Dharmakīrti's) "Ascertainment of Valid Cognition"
bsTan bcos tshad ma rnam nges kyi ṭik chen dgongs pa rab gsal
Toh. 5453-4
Teachings on Valid Cognition
Tshad ma'i lam khrid
Varanasi: Ye-ses-stobs-ldan, 1969

'Jam-dpal-phrin-las
Compendium on the Meaning of the Collected Topics, a Good Explanation Indicating the Joy of Sages
bsDus grva'i don kun bsdus pa'i legs bshad mkhas pa'i dga' ston
Mundgod, India: Drepung Loseling Printing Press, 1978

Jam-bel-sam-pel, Geshe ('Jam-dpal-bsam-'phel, dGe-bshes), d. 1975
Presentation of Awareness and Knowledge, Composite of All the Important Points, Opener of the Eye of New Intelligence
Blo rig gi rnam bzhag nyer mkho kun 'dus blo gsar mig 'byed
Modern blockprint, n.p., n.d.

Jam-yang-chok-hla-ö-ser ('Jam-dbyangs-phyogs-lha-'od-zer), about 15th century
Collected Topics of Ra-dö
Rva stod bsdus grva
Dharamsala, India: Damchoe Sangpo, Library of Tibetan Works and Archives (Printed at Jayyed Press, Ballimaran, Delhi), 1980.

Jam-yang-shay-ba ('Jam-dbyangs-bzhad-pa), 1648-1721
Final Analysis of (Dharmakīrti's) "Commentary on Dignāga's 'Compendium on Valid Cognition' "
Tshad ma rnam 'grel gyi mtha' dpyod
Collected Works of 'Jam-dbans-bźad-pa
New Delhi: Ngawang Gelek Demo, 1972
Great Exposition of the Middle Way/Analysis of (Candrakīr-

ti's) "Entrance to the Middle Way," Treasury of Scripture and Reasoning, Thoroughly Illuminating the Profound Meaning [of Emptiness], Gateway for the Fortunate
dbU ma la 'jug pa'i mtha' dpyod lung rigs gter mdzod zab don kun gsal skal bzang 'jug ngogs
Buxador: Gomang, 1967
Presentation of Awareness and Knowledge
bLo rig gi rnam bzhag
The Collected Works of 'Jam-dbyans-bzad-pa'i-rdo-rje
New Delhi: Ngawang Gelek Demo, 1973 Vol. 15
Great Exposition of Tenets/Explanation of 'Tenets,' Sun of the Land of Samantabhadra Brilliantly Illuminating All of Our Own and Others' Tenets and the Meaning of the Profound [Emptiness], Ocean of Scripture and Reasoning Fulfilling All Hopes of All Beings
Musoorie: Dalama, 1962
Grub mtha chen mo/Grub mtha'i rnam bshad gzhan grub mtha' kun dang sab don mchog tu gsal ba kun bzang shing gi myi ma lung rigs rgya mtsho skye dgu'i re ba kun skong
Presentation of Tenets, Roar of the Five-Faced [Lion] Eradicating Error, Precious Lamp Illuminating the Good Path to Omniscience
Grub mtha'i rnam par bzhag pa 'khrul spong gdong lnga'i sgra dbyangs kun mykhyen lam bzang gsal ba'i rin chen sgron me
Folio printing in India, no publication data.
Jang-gya (lCang-skya Rol-pa'i-rdo-rje), 1717-1786
Presentation of Tenets/Clear Exposition of the Presentations of Tenets, Beautiful Ornament for the Meru of the Subduer's Teaching
Grub pa'i mtha'i rnam par bzhag pa gsal bar bshad pa thub bstan lhun po'i mdzes rgyan
Sarnath, Varanasi: Pleasure of Elegant Sayings Press, 1970
Jetāri (dGra-las-rgyal-ba)
Work on the Texts of the Sugata
Sugatamatvibhāṅgakārikā

bDer gshegs gzhung gi rab byed
P5867, Vol. 146

Jñānaśrīmitra
Arrayed Treatise of Jñānaśrīmitra
Jñānaśrīmitranibandhāvali
ed. with Introduction by Anantalal Thakur, Tibetan Sanskrit Series, Patna: Jayaswal Research Institute, 1961

Kamalaśīla, 8th Century
Commentary on the Difficult Points of (Śāntarakṣita's) "Compendium on Suchness"
Tattvasaṃgrahapañjikā
De kho na nyid bsdus pa'i dks' 'grel
P5765, Vol. 138

Kay-drup (mKhas-grub), 1384-1438
Clearing Away Mental Darkness [with Respect to the Seven Treatises]/An Ornament of Dharmakīrti's "Seven Treatises on Valid Cognition," Clearing Away Mental Darkness
sDe bdun yid kyi mum sel/Tshad ma sde bdun gyi rgyan yid kyi mun sel
Toh. 5501

Nga-wang-bel-den (Ngag-dbang-dpal-ldan), b. 1797
Annotations for (Jam-yang-shay-ba's) "Great Exposition of Tenets," Freeing the Knots of the Difficult Points, Precious Jewel of Clear Thought
Grub mtha' chen mo'i mchan 'grel dka' gnad mdud grol blo gsal bces nor
Sarnath, Varanasi: Pleasure of Elegant Sayings Press, 1964
Explanation of the Meaning of "Conventional" and "Ultimate" in the Four Tenet Systems
Grub mtha' gzhi'i lugs kyi kun rdzob dang don dam pa'i don rnam par bshad pa
New Delhi: Guru Deva, 1972

Nga-wang-dra-shi (Ngag-dbang-bkra-shis), 1648-1721
The Collected Topics by a Spiritual Son of Jam-yang-shay-ba
Sras bsdus grva
n.p., nd. (available from Gomang College, Mundgod, India)

Prajñākaragupta (Shes-rab-'byung-gnas-sbas-pa)

"Ornament" Commentary

Pramāṇavārttikālaṃkāra

Tshad ma rnam 'grel gyi rgyan

P5719, Vol. 132

Pur-bu-jok (Phur-bu-lcog Byams-pa-rgya-mtsho), 1825-1901

"Explanation of the Presentation of Objects and Object Possessors as well as Awareness and Knowledge" in Magical Key to the Path of Reasoning, Presentation of the Collected Topics Revealing the Meaning of the Treatises on Valid Cognition

Yul yul can dang blo rig gi rnam par bshad pa *in* Tshad ma'i gzhung don 'byed pa'i bsdus grva'i rnam bzhag rigs lam 'phrul gyi sde mig

Buxa: n.d., 1965

The Topic of Signs and Reasonings from the "Great Path of Reasoning" in *The Magic Key to the Path of Reasoning, Presentation of the Collected Topics Revealing the Meaning of the Texts on Valid Cognition*

Tshad ma'i gzhung don 'byed ba'i bsdus grva'i rnam gzhag rigs lam 'phrul gyi sde mig

Buxa: n.d. 1965

Pūrṇavardhana (Gang-ba-spel-ba), about 8th Century

Commentary on Vasubandhu's "Treasury of Knowledge," An Investigation of the Characteristics

Abhidharmakośaṭīkālakṣaṇānusārininīma

Chos mngon pa'i mdzod kyi 'brel bshad mtshan nyid kyi rjes su 'brang ba shes bya ba

P5594, Vol. 117

Sagya Paṇḍiṭa (Sa-skya Pandita Kun-dga'-rgyal-mtshan), 1182-1251

Treasury of Reasoning

Tshad ma rigs pa'i gter

The Complete Works of the Great Masters of the Sa-skya Sect of Tibetan Buddhism, Vol. 5, 155.1-1.167.2.1

Tokyo: Toyo Bunko, 1968

Śākyabuddhi/Śākyamati (Śakya-blo)

Explanation of (Dharmakīrti's) "Commentary on (Dignāga's)

'Compendium on Valid Cognition' "
Pramāṇavārttikaṭīkā
rNam 'grel shad
P5718, Vol. 131
Śāntideva (Zhi-ba-lha), 8th Century
Engaging in the Bodhisattva Deeds
Bodhisattvacaryāvatāra
Byang chub sems dpa'i spyod pa la 'jug pa
P5272, Vol. 99
Śāntarakṣita (Zhi-ba-'tsho), 8th Century
Commentary on the "Ornament to the Middle Way"
Madhyamakālaṃkāravṛtti
dbU ma'i rgyan gyi grel ba
P5285, Vol. 101
Compendium on Suchness
Tattvasaṃgrahakārikā
De kho na nyid bsdus pa'i tshing le'ur byas pa
P5764, Vol. 138; See also Gaekward Oriental Series, ed. E. Krishnamacharya, 2 Vols. (Baroda, 1926); also, with *Pañjikā* of Kamalaśīla, ed. by Swami Dwarikadas Shastri in 2 vols., Varanasi: Bauddha Bharati, 1968.
Ornament to the Middle Way
Madhyamakālaṃkāra
dbU ma rgyan gyi tshig le'ur byas pa
P5284, Vol. 101
Śāriputra
Aggregate of Phenomena
Dharmaskandha
Chos kyi phung po
Taisho 1537
Sera Jetsun Chö-gyi gyel-tsen, (Sera rJe-bstun-chos-kyi-rgyal-mtshan), *see* Chö-gyi-gyel-tsen
So-nam Drak-ba, Pan-chen (Bsod-nams-grags-pa), 1478-1554
The Collected Works (*gsung 'bum*) of Pan-Chen
Bsod-nams-grags-pa Literature Series, Karnataka: Drepung Loseling Library Society, 1982
Tsong-ka-ba (Tsong-kha-pa), 1357-1419

Door of Entry to the Seven Treatises
Sde bdun la 'jug pa'i sgo
Sarnath, Varanasi: Pleasure of Elegant Sayings Press, 1972
Essence of the Good Explanations, Treatise Discriminating What is to be Interpreted and the Definitive
Drang ba dang nges pa'i don rnam par phye ba'i bstan bcos legs bshad snying po
P6142, Vol. 153
Middling Exposition of the Stages of the Path
Lam rim 'bring
P6002, Vol. 152
Also: Dharamsala, Shes rig par khang, 1968
Notes on (Śāntarakṣita's) Ornament to the Middle Way
dbU ma rgyan gyi zin bris
Blockprint, n.p., n.d.

Vasubandhu (dbYig-gnyen), 4th Century
Explanation of the "Treasury of Knowledge"
Abhidharmakośabhāṣya
Chos mngon pa'i mdzod kyi bshad pa
P5591, Vol. 115; Skt. ed. by Swami Dwarikadas Shastri, Varanasi: Bauddha Bharati, 1972
Treasury of Knowledge
Abhidharmkośakārikā
Chos mngon pa'i mdzod kyi tshig le'ur byas pa
P5590, Vol. 115

Yaśomitra (rGyal-po'i-sras Grags-pa'i-shes-gnyen), probably 8th Century
Commentary to (Vasubandhu's) "Treasury of Knowledge"
Chos mngon pa'i mdzod kyi 'grel bshad
P5593, Vol. 116

II. WORKS IN ENGLISH AND FRENCH

Ayer, Sir Alfred J.
The Problem of Knowledge
Middlesex, England: Penguin Books, 1984 [1956 reprint]

Bareau, André
Les sectes boudhiques du Petit Véhicule
Saigon: Bulletin de l'École Francaise d'Extrême Orient, 1955
Barlingay, S. S.
A Modern Introduction to Indian Logic
Delhi: National Publishing House, 1965
Belenky, Clinchy, Goldberger, and Tarule
Women's Ways of Knowing
New York: Basic Books, 1986
Cabezón, José
"The Development of a Buddhist Philosophy of Language and its Culmination in Tibetan Mādhyamika Thought"
Dissertation, Univ. of Wisconsin, 1987
Chandra, Dr. Lokesh
Materials for History of Tibetan Literature
New Delhi: International Academy of Indian Culture, 1963
Coward, Harold G.
Sphoṭa Theory of Language
Delhi: Motilal Banarsidass, 1980
Dasgupta, Surendranath
A History of Indian Philosophy, Vol. I
Cambridge: University Press, 1957
Datta, D. M.
The Six Ways of Knowing
Calcutta: University of Calcutta Press, 1960 (originally published in 1932 in Great Britain)
Eckel, M. David
Jñānagarbha's Commentary on the Distinction between the Two Truths
Albany: SUNY Press, 1987
Frauwallner, Erich
History of Indian Philosophy, Vol. II; tr. by V. M. Bedekar
Delhi: Motilal Banarsidass, 1973
"Landmarks": Landmarks in the History of Buddhist Logic
Wiener Zeitschrift fur die Kunde des Sud-und Ost-Asiens, Bd. V [1961], pp. 125-148

Gön-chok-jik-may-wang-bo (dKon-mchog-'jigs-med-dbang-po), 1728-91
"Precious Garland of Tenets" translated in Sopa & Hopkins, *Practice and Theory of Tibetan Buddhism*
London: Rider & Co., 1976
Hattori, Masaaki
Dignāga on Perception
Cambridge, MA: Harvard University Press, 1968
"*Apoha* and *Pratibhā*"
Sanskrit and Indian Studies, M. Nagotomi, B. K. Matilal, J. M. Masson, and R. Dimock, eds.
Boston, MA: D. Reidel, 1979
Hiriyanna, M
Outlines of Indian Philosophy
London: George Allen & Unwin, 1932
Hopkins, P. Jeffrey
Meditation on Emptiness
London: Wisdom Publications, 1983
Hume, David
A Treatise of Human Nature
Book I, ed. L. A. Selby Bigge
Oxford, 1888
Iida, Shotaro
Reason and Emptiness, A Study in Logic and Mysticism
Tokyo: The Hokuseido Press, 1980
"*Āgama* (Scripture) and *Yukti* (Reason) in Bhāvaviveka"
Kyoto: Heirakuji-shoten,
Kanakura Festschrift, October, 1966
Ingalls, D. H. H.
Materials for the Study of Navya-Nyāya Logic
Cambridge: Harvard Oriental Series, 1951, Vol. 40
Iyengar, H. H. R.
"*Bhartṛhari and Dinnāga*"
Journal of the Bombay Branch, Royal Asiatic Society
New series 26 Bombay: 1950, pp. 147-149
Jam-bel-sam-pel, Geshe ('Jam-dpal-bsam-phel, dGe-gshes), d. 1975

Presentation of Awareness and Knowledge
trans., ed., Elizabeth Napper, with commentary by Lati Rinbochay in *Mind in Tibetan Buddhism*
London: Rider & Co., 1980

Jayatilleke, K. N.
Early Buddhist Theory of Knowledge
London: George Allen & Unwin, 1968

Jha, Ganganatha, tr.
"The Tattvasangraha of Śāntarakṣita with the Commentary of Kamalaśila"
Gaekwad Oriental Series Vols. 80 and 83
Baroda: Oriental Institute, 1937 and 1929

Kajiyama, Yuichi
An Introduction to Buddhist Philosophy: An Annotated Translation of the Tarkabhāsā of Mokśakāragupta
Kyoto, Memoirs of the Faculty of Letters, Kyoto University, No. 10, 1966
"Three Kinds of Affirmation and Two Kinds of Negation in Buddhist Philosophy"
Wiener Zeitschrift fur die Kunde Sudasiens und Archiv fur Indische Philosophie, 1973

Keith, Arthur Berriedal
Indian Logic and Atomism
New York: Greenwood Press, 1968

Klein, Anne C.
Knowledge and Liberation
Ithaca: Snow Lion, 1986

Matilal, Bimal K.
Epistemology, Logic, and Grammar in Indian Philosophical Analysis
The Hague and Paris: Mouton, 1971
Perception
Oxford: Clarendon Press, 1986

Mikogami, E.
"Some Remarks on the Concept of *Arthakriyā*"
Journal of Indian Philosophy, 7, (1979), pp. 79-94

Mimaki, Katsumi

La Réfutation Bouddhique de la Permanence des Choses (Sthirasiddhidūṣaṇa) et *La Preuve de la Momentanéité des Choses (Kṣaṇabhaṅgasiddhi)*
Paris: Institut de Civilisation Indienne (1976)

Blo gsal grub mtha
Kyoto: Zinbun Kagaku Kenkyusyo, Université de Kyoto, 1982

"Le Chapitre du *Blo gsal grub mtha'* sur les Sautrāntika, Presentation et édition," Zinbun n. 15 (1979)

"Le Chapitre du *Blo gsal grub mtha'* sur les Sautrāntika, un essai de traduction," Zinbun, n. 16. (1980)

Mookerjee, Satkari

The Buddhist Philosophy of Universal Flux
Delhi: Motilal Banarsidass, 1975 (First published 1935)

Mookerjee, S. and Nagasaki, Hojun, translators

The Pramāṇavārttikam of Dharmakīrti, An English Translation of the First Chapter with the Autocommentary and with Elaborate Comments, Kārikās I-LI
Nalanda: Nava Nalanda Mahavihara, 1964

Nagatomi, Masatoshi

A Study of Dharmakīrti's Pramāṇavārtika, An English Translation and Annotation of the Pramāṇavārttika, Book I (Pramāṇasiddhi); Doctoral Thesis, Harvard University, June 1957

"Arthakriyā"
The Adyar Library Bulletin, Dr. V. Raghavan Felicitation Volume, 1967-68, XXXI-XXXII, (Adyar, Madras) p. 52-72

"The Framework of the Pramāṇavārttika, Book I"
Journal of the American Oriental Society, Vol. 79, No. 4. Oct-Dec., 1959, pp. 263-266

"Mānasa-pratyakṣa: A Conundrum in the Buddhist Pramāṇa System"
Sanskrit and Indian Studies, M. Nagatomi, B. K. Matilal, J. M. Masson, and R. Dimock, eds.
Boston: D. Reidel, 1980

Ong, Walter
"Review of Brian Vickers' *Classical Rhetoric in English Poetry*," in *College English*, February, 1972

Potter, Karl H.
Presuppositions of Indian Philosophies
Englewood Cliffs, New Jersey: Prentice-Hall, Inc., 1963

Rich, Adrienne
On Lies, Secrets, and Silence
New York: W. W. Norton & Company, 1979

Ruegg, David Seyfort
The Literature of the Mādhyamaka School of Philosophy in India
Weisbaden: Otto Harrassowitz, 1981

Ryle, Gilbert
The Concept of Mind
New York: Barnes & Noble, 1949

Rogers, Katherine
Tibetan Logic: A Translation with Commentary of Pur-bu-jok's "The Topic of Signs and Reasonings from the 'Great Path of Reasoning' " in the *Magic Key to the Path of Reasoning, Explanation of the Collected Topics Revealing the Meaning of the Texts on Valid Cognition*
M. A., University of Virginia, 1980

Śankarācārya
The Bṛhadāranyaka Upaniṣad with the Commentary of Śankarācārya
trans. by Swami Madhvananda,
Calcutta: Advaita Ashram, 1965

Saugstad, Per
A Theory of Language and Understanding
Oslo: Universitetsforlag, 1980

Searle, John R.
Speech Acts
Cambridge: The University Press, 1969

Sharma, Dhirendra
The Differentiation Theory of Meaning in Indian Logic
Paris and The Hague: Mouton, 1969

"The Paradox of Negative Judgement and Indian Logic"
Vishveshvaranand Indological Journal, Vol. 9, No. 4, 1966

Shastri, Dharmendra Nath
Critique of Indian Realism: A Study of the Conflict Between the Nyāya-Vaiśeṣika and the Buddhist Dignāga School
Agra, India: Agra University, 1964

Smart, Ninian
The Philosophy of Religion
New York: Oxford University Press, 1979

Snellgrove, David and Richardson, Hugh
A Cultural History of Tibet
Boulder: Prajna Press, 1980 (reprint)

Sopa, Geshe Lhundup
Lectures in Tibetan Culture
2 Vol., Dharamsala: Library of Tibetan Works and Archives, 1983

Sopa and Hopkins
Practice and Theory of Tibetan Buddhism
London: Rider & Co., 1976

Staal, J. F.
"Negation and the Law of Contradiction in Indian Thought"
Bulletin of the School of Oriental and African Studies, Vol. 25, Part I, 1962

Stcherbatsky, F. Th.
Buddhist Logic
New York: Dover Publications, Inc., 1962 (First published 1930)

Steinkellner, Ernst
Verse-Index of Dharmakīrti's Works (Tibetan Versions)
Wien: Arbeitskreis für Tibetische und Buddhistiche Studien Universität Wien, 1977

Streng, Federick J.
Emptiness: A Study in Religious Meaning
Nashville: Abingdon Press, 1967

Tāranātha
History of Buddhism in India

tr. from the Tibetan by Lama Chimpa and Alaka Chattopadhyaya
ed. by Debiprasad Chattopadhyaya
Simla: Indian Institute of Advanced Study, 1970

Tripathi, C. L.
The Problem of Knowledge in Yogācāra Buddhism
Varanasi: Bharat-Bharati, 1972

Tsong-ka-pa
Tantra in Tibet
trans., and ed. Jeffrey Hopkins
London: George Allen & Unwin, 1977

van der Kuijp, Leonard W. J.
Contributions to the Development of Tibetan Buddhist Epistemology
Weisbaden: Franz Steiner Verlag, Alt-und Neu-Indische Studien herausgegeben vom Seminar für Kultur und Geschichte Indiens an der Universität (Hamburg) 26, 1983

"Phya-Pa Chos-Kyi Seng-Ge's Impact on Tibetan Epistemological Theory"
Journal of Indian Philosophy, Vol. 5, 1978

Wayman, Alex
Calming the Mind and Discerning the Real, From Tsong-ka-pa's Lam Rim Chen Mo
New York: Columbia University Press, 1978; reprint New Delhi: Motilal Banarsidass, 1979

Warder, A. K.
Indian Buddhism
New Delhi: Motilal Banarsidass, 1970

Wylie, Turrell
"A Standard System of Tibetan Transcription"
Harvard Journal of Asian Studies, Vol. 22, 1959, 261-267

Yamaguchi, Susumu
"*Ālaṃbanaparikṣā* with *Vṛtti* of Dignāga, Tibetan version" in *Seshin Yuishiki no Genten Kaimei*
Kyoto, 1953

Zwilling, Leonard

"Dharmakīrti on *Apoha*" Ph.D. Dissertation, University of Wisconsin, 1976

"Saskya Paṇḍita's Version of *Pramāṇavārttikam* III.3—A Case Study on the Influence of Exegesis upon Translation in Tibet"
Studies in Indian Philosophy, A Memorial Volume in Honour of Pandit Sukhalalji Sanghvi
L.D. Series 84, Dalsukh Malvania and Nagin J. Shah general editors
Ahmedbad: L.D. Institute of Indology, 1981

"Some Aspects of Dharmakīrti's Ontology Reconsidered"
KAILASH, A Journal of Himalayan Studies
Kathmandu: Ratna Pustak Bhandar, Vol. III, No. 3, 1975

Index

Commentators

GESHE BELDEN DRAKBA, Loseling College, Drebung; Professor and Head Librarian at Tibet House, New Delhi. He is the author of *Legs bshad dad pa'i mdzas rgyan: dbang po rno rdul gyi dad pa skye tshul* (*The Well Stated Ornament of Faith: How Faith Develops in those of Sharp Minds*) (Mundgod, India: Drebung Loseling Library, 1979). He was a Visiting Lecturer in the Department of Religious Studies, University of Virginia, in 1986. He comments here on Jang-gya's "Chapter on Sautrāntika."

DENMA LOCHÖ RINBOCHAY, a Geshe of Loseling College, lives and teaches in Dharamsala, North India, and spent a year as Visiting Lecturer at the University of Virginia in 1978. He comments here on Jang-gya's discussion of Sautrāntika and Den-dar-hla-ram-pa's *Generally and Specifically Characterized Phenomena*.

JAMBEL SHENPEN RINBOCHAY, a Geshe of Jangdzay College, Ganden and abbot emeritus of Gyumay Tantric College, was a Visiting Lecturer in the University of Virginia in 1981. In 1984 he was appointed Preceptor of Ganden (Ganden Triba). He comments here upon the Gomang *Collected*

Topics section on "Positive and Negative Phenomena" and on Den-dar-lha-ram-ba's *Generally and Specifically Characterized Phenomena.*

LATI RINBOCHAY, a Geshe of Shardzay College, Ganden, was abbot and head teacher at his college between 1979 and 1985. For a year and a half prior to this he was a Visiting Lecturer at the University of Virginia. Currently living and teaching in Dharamsala at the request of the Dalai Lama, he comments here on Jang-gya's "Chapter on Sautrāntika."

KENSUR YESHAY TUPDEN, a Geshe of Loseling College, Drebung, was abbot of that college for ten years following the institution's relocation in Mundgod, India. He was a Visiting Lecturer in Virginia in 1985 and again in 1987; in 1984 and 1986 he was Resident Teacher at the Tibetan Buddhist Learning Center in Washington, N.J. Until his death in 1988 he lived in Mundgod where he was the senior resident scholar and teacher at Loseling College. His comments formed the background for much of the current translation.

PART III
THE TIBETAN TEXTS

Selections from

Presentation of Specifically and Generally Characterized Phenomena

by Den-dar-hla-ram-ba

156 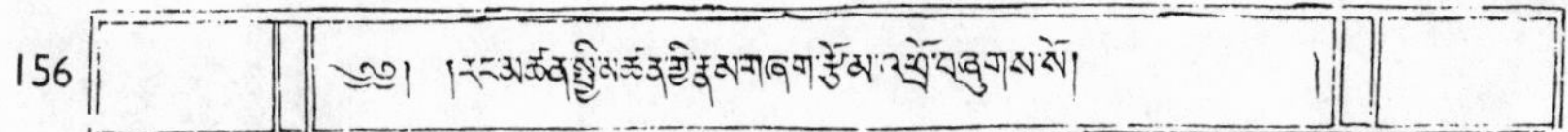

༄༅། །རང་མཚན་སྤྱི་མཚན་གྱི་རྣམ་གཞག་རྩོམ་འཕྲོ་བཞུགས་སོ། །

157

༄༅། །དཀའ་གི་དབང་ཕྱུག་ཕྱི་ལ་མཛོད་འཛམ་དཔལ་བཞད་བྱུང་ས། །གྲོ་གྲོས་བཟང་པོའི་དགོངས་གྲུབ་མཆོག་སྟེར་བཞུས། །དེས་འབྱུང་བྱང་སེམས་ཡང་དག་ལྟ་བ་དང་། །རིམ་གཉིས་མཐར་ཕྱིན་དཔལ་ལྡན་བླ་མས་སྤྲོས། །རིགས་པ་སྨྲ་བའི་ཆོས་སྒྲ་སྒྲོག་པ་ཡིས། །རྒྱ་ནག་སྨྲ་བའི་སྤྱི་ངན་སྒྲོ་གས་རིད། །དེ་དང་ཆབས་ཅིག་ཡང་དག་ལྟ་བ་ཡིས། །ཡིད་ཅན་འདྲེན་པ་ཁས་ཕྱོགས་སྣང་ཡབ་སྲས་རྒྱལ། །ཚད་མའི་གཞུང་ལུགས་རྒྱ་མཚོ་ལུང་རིགས་ཀྱི། །ཐབས་འཕྲིང་གཡོ་ལྡན་དོན་མཚར་སྒྲུབ་མོ་ཅན། །གང་ཞིག་བལྟ་བར་འདོད་དན་འདྲེན་ནི་དང་། །ལམ་པ་ཏྲ་ཀུ་འདི་ནི་བསྟེན་པར་གྱིས། །དེ་ཡང་དེ་ར་ཚད་མའི་བསྟན་བཅོས་ལ་ཉེ་བར་འཇུག་པའི་ཡན་ལག་དག་ཞིག་བཤད་པར་བྱ་བ་ལ། རང་མཚན་བཤད་པ།

158

༄༅། །སྤྱི་མཚན་བཤད་པ། བརྗོད་སྦྱོར་ཚུལ་བཤད་པ་དང་། ཞར་ལ་ཆོས་ཅན་དང་ཆོས་བརྗོད་ཀྱི་སྒྲ་བཤད་པའོ། །དང་པོ་རང་མཚན་བཤད་པར་བྱ་བ་ལ། རྟོག་པས་བཏགས་ཙམ་མ་ཡིན་པར་རང་གི་ཐུན་མོང་མ་ཡིན་པའི་སྡོད་ལུགས་སུ་གྲུབ་པའི་དངོས་པོ། རང་མཚན་གྱི་མཚན་ཉིད། མཚན་གཞི་ནི། མངོན་སུམ་ཚད་མའི་སྣང་ཡུལ་ཏེ་བུམ་པ་ལྟ་བུའོ། །དེ་ལ་རང་མཚན་ཞེས་བྱ་སྟེ། རང་དངོས་སུ་སྣང་བའི་མངོན་སུམ་ལ་སྣང་བའི་ཆོས་གཞན་དང་འཆར་བ་ལ་མི་ལྟོས་པར་འཆར་བའི་མཚན་ཉིད་ཅན་ཡིན་པའི་ཕྱིར་རོ། །རང་མཚན་དང་དོན་དམ་མཚན་གཉིས་ལ་ཁྱད་པར་མེད་ཅིང་། དོན་རང་མཚན་ཞེས་པ་ནི་དོན་དངོས་གནས་པ་དམ་དོན་རྣལ་མ་ཞེས་པའི་དོན་ནོ། །དེ་ཉིད་དངོས་སུ་འཇལ་བའི་མངོན་སུམ་གྱི་གཞལ་

159

རྒྱུ་བཞི་པོ་གང་གིས་ཀྱང་མ་བསླད་པའི་མ་འཁྲུལ་བའི་ཤེས་པ་ཡིན་པས་མདོ་སྡེ་པས་འདོད་དུ་ཆོང་། དེ་ཡང་རང་མཚན་རྣམས་བློ་དོན་དམ་པ་མངོན་སུམ་མ་འཁྲུལ་བ་འི་ངོར་གྲུབ་པས་ན་དོན་དམ་པར་གྲུབ་པ་དང་དེ་ངོར་བདེན་པས་ན་དོན་དམ་བདེན་པ་ཡང་ཡིན་ཞིང་། འདི་པའི་ལུགས་ཀྱི་རང་མཚན་གྱི་སྡོད་ལུགས་ནི་རང་གི་གནས་ལུགས་སུ་གྲུབ་པ་ཡིན་པས། མངོན་སུམ་ཕྱིས་དེ་གཞལ་བ་བདེ་ཡུལ་གྱི་གནས་ལུགས་དེ་ཡང་གཞལ་བ་ཡིན་པ་དེའི་ཕྱིར། དབུ་མ་འཇུག་པའི་རྣམ་བཤད་དགོངས་པ་རབ་གསལ་ལས། མདོ་སྡེ་པས་ཚད་མའི་གཞལ་བྱར་རྟོག་པ་ནི་གཞལ་བྱའི་སྡོད་ལུགས་ཚད་མས་རྟོགས་པའི་དོན་ཡིན་ཞེས་གསུངས་ཤིང་དེའི་ཕྱིར། དངོས་སྨྲ་བས་རང་མཚན་གྱི་དོན་ལྡོག་ཏུ་གང་འདོད་པ་ཐལ་འགྱུར་པས་དོན་དམ་དཔྱོད་པའི་རིགས་པའི་དཔྱད་བྱར་འདོད་ཙམ་པ་ཡང་དེ་ཡིན་ནོ། །དེས་ན་བློ་དོན་དམ་པ་མངོན་སུམ་མ་འཁྲུལ་བའི་ངོར་བདེན་པའི་དངོས་པོ་རང་མཚན་གྱི་དོན་ལྡོག་ཡིན་ཞིང་། ཡུལ་དུས་རང་བཞིན་མ་འདྲེས་པའི་དངོས་པོ་རང་མཚན་གྱི་གཞི་ལྡོག་ཡིན་ནོ། །འོ་ན་ཡུལ་དུས་རང་བཞིན་མ་འདྲེས་པའི་དོན་གང་ཞེ་ན། དེ་ནི་ཡུལ་དུས་རང་རང་བཞིན་འདྲེས་པ་མ་ཉམས་པའི་རྟོག་པའི་འཛིན་སྟངས་ཀྱི་བཀླག་ཕྱོགས་ལ་ཡིན་པས་ཐོག་མར་འདི་ཤེས་པ་གལ་ཆེ་བས། དེ་རྟུང་ཟད་བརྗོད་པར་བྱ་བ་ལ། དཔེར་ན་བུམ་པའི་ཐ་སྙད

160

༄༅། །མི་ཤེས་པ་ཞིག་གིས་ཤར་ཕྱོགས་སུ་གསེར་གྱི་ལྟོ་ལྡིར་བ་མཐོང་ནས་འདི་ཅི་ཡིན་ཞེས་འདྲི་བ་ན། པ་རོལ་པོས་འདི་བུམ་པའོ་ཞེས་སྨྲས་པའི་ཚེ་ཉན་པ་པོའི་རྒྱུད་ལ་བུམ་པ་ཞེས་བརྗོད་པའི་སྒྲ་དེའི་རྗེས་སུ་འབྲང་ནས་གསེར་གྱི་ལྟོ་ལྡིར་འདི་བུམ་པའོ་སྙམ་དུ་འཛིན་པའི་རྟོག་པ་སྐྱེ་ཞིང་། རྟོག་པ་དེའི་འཛིན་སྟངས་ཀྱི་ངོར་གསེར་གྱི་ལྟོ་ལྡིར་བ་དེ་བུམ་པ་ཡིན་པར་སྣང་བ་ཡིན་པས་བུམ་པ་མ་ཡིན་པ་ལས་ལོག་པར་ཡང་སྣང་བ་ཡིན་ཞིང་། བུམ་པ་མ་ཡིན་པ་ལས་ལོག་པར་སྣང་བ་དེ་ཉིད་བུམ་པའི་སྒྲ་དོན་ཡིན་ཡང་རྟོག་པ་དེས་བུམ་པ་རང་མཚན་པར་འཁྲུལ་ནས་སྣང་བའི་ཕྱིར་རྟོག་པ་དེ་ལ་སྣང་བཏགས་གཅིག་ཏུ་འདྲེས་ནས་སྣང་བ་ཞེས་བྱའོ། །འདིའི་སྣང་བ་ནི་བུམ་པ་དོན་རང་མཚན་པ་དང་བཏགས་པ་ནི་བུམ་པའི་སྒྲ་དོན་ནོ། །དེའི་ཕྱིར་རྟོག་པ་དེས་གསེར་བུམ་བུམ་པ་མ་ཡིན་པ་ལས་ལོག་པར་སྣང་བའི་སྒྲ་དོན་ཉིད་སྣང་བའི་ཕྱིར་རོ། །བུམ་པ་རང་མཚན་པ་དངོས་སུ་མི་སྣང་བར་སྒྲ་དོན་ལོན་སྣང་ཡུལ་དུ་བྱས་པ་ཡིན་ནོ། །དེ་ནས་གང་ཟག་དེས་ནུབ་ཕྱོགས་སུ་ཟངས་ཀྱི་ལྟོ་ལྡིར་བ་མཐོང་བ་ན་བརྡ་ལ་བརྟེན་ནས་དགོས་པར་དེ་ཉིད་བུམ་པ་ཡིན་ནོ་སྙམ་དུ་འཛིན་པའི་རྟོག་པ་སྐྱེ་ཞིང་། རྟོག་པ་དེའི་སྣང་ངོར་ཤར་ཕྱོགས་སུ་མཐོང་བའི་གསེར་བུམ་གྱི་སྟེང་གི་བུམ་པ་ཡིན་པའི་ཆ་ཐམས་ཅད་ནུབ་ཀྱི་ཟངས་བུམ་ལ་ཡང་ཡོད་པར་སྣང་བཞིན་རྒྱུ་ལ་འདི་ནི······

161 རྟོག་པ་ལ་ཡུལ་འདྲེས་པར་སྣང་བའི་ཚུལ་ལོ། །དེ་བཞིན་དུ་སྔ་དྲོ་གསེར་བུམ་མཐོང་ནས་ཕྱི་དྲོ་ཟངས་བུམ་མཐོང་བ་ན། སྔ་དྲོ་མཐོང་བའི་གསེར་བུམ་གྱི་ཆ་ཐམས་ཅད་ཕྱི་དྲོའི་ཟངས་བུམ་ལ་ཡང་ཡོད་པར་སྣང་བ་ནི་དུས་འདྲེས་པར་སྣང་བའི་
ཚུལ་ལོ། །ཡང་གསེར་བུམ་གྱི་སྟེང་གི་བུམ་པ་ཡིན་པའི་ཆ་དང་ཟངས་བུམ་གྱི་སྟེང་གི་བུམ་པ་ཡིན་པའི་ཆ་གཉིས་གཅིག་ཏུ་སྣང་བ་ནི་རང་བཞིན་འདྲེས་པར་སྣང་ཚུལ་ཡིན་པས། རྟོག་པ་དེས་བུམ་པའི་གསལ་བ་མཐའ་དག་གི་སྟེང་གི་…
བུམ་པ་ཡིན་པའི་ཆ་ཐམས་ཅད་གཅིག་ཏུ་སྣང་བ་ཡང་ཡིན་ནོ། །བུམ་པའི་གསལ་བ་ཞེས་པ་བུམ་པའི་བྱེ་བྲག་ལ་གོ་བར་བྱའོ། །མདོར་ན་རྟོག་པས་སྔ་ཕྱི་གཅིག་ཏུ་འཛིན་ཚུལ་ནི། དཔེར་ན་ཕར་ཕྱིན་ལྷས་སྦྱིན་འདི་ནི་ཞེས་ངོ་ཤེས་
པ་ལྟ་བུ་དེ་སྔ་ཕྱི་གཅིག་ཏུ་འཛིན་པའི་རྟགས་ཡིན་ནོ། །བུམ་འཛིན་རྟོག་པ་ལ་བུམ་པའི་ཧྲུལ་ཕྲ་རབ་དང་སྐད་ཅིག་མའི་ཆ་སོགས་དངོས་སུ་མི་སྣང་བར་བུམ་པའི་ཧྲུལ་ཕྲན་ཚོགས་པའི་རགས་པ་དང་སྐད་ཅིག་སྔ་ཕྱིའི་རྒྱུན་གྱི་སྤྱི་དོན་དེ་དག
བུམ་པར་སྣང་བ་ཡིན་ཏེ། དཔེར་ན་རྒྱ་སྐྱུང་ཞིག་ཏུ་བཀལ་བ་ན་མི་དེའི་ལྷམ་རྒྱུས་ཁྱེར་ནས་ཡུན་རིང་སོང་ཡང་མི་དེས་རྒྱ་སྐྱུང་དེ་ལ་མཇལ་བ་མ་རྫོགས་ནས་ངའི་ལྷམ་ཁྱེར་བའི་ཁྱུ་འདིའོ་ཞེས་སྨྲས་ཀྱང་། དོན་ལ་ལྷམ་ཁྱེར་བའི་ཁྱུ་རྒྱུན་ཐལ
ཟིན་ཅིང་རྟོག་པས་རྫས་རྒྱུན་ལྡན་ཕྱི་དག་གི་སྤྱི་དོན་གཅིག་ཏུ་སྣང་བ་དེ་ལ་ཞེན་པའི་དབང་གིས་དེ་སྐད་སྨྲས་སོ། །དབང་ཤེས་ལ་དེ་ལྟ་བུ་སྤྱི་དོན་མི་སྣང་བར་ཡུལ་རང་མཚན་པ་དེ་དང་རྫས་ཆ་སོ་སོར་དབྱེར་མེད་པའི་ཧྲུལ་ཕྲ་རབ་དང་ཡུལ

162 ཨཾ། ཨཱུཾ། ཁྲི། ཏི།
༄༅། །དེའི་མི་རྟག་པ་དང་སྐད་ཅིག་མ་སོགས་ཇི་བཞིན་སྣང་བ་ཡིན་ཏེ། རྒྱ་སྐྱུང་དེ་ལ་མིག་གིས་བལྟས་པའི་ཚེ་དབྱེ་རང་ལ་སྣང་བཞིན་པའི་རྒྱུ་ཧྲུལ་ཕྲ་རབ་དང་དེའི་སྐད་ཅིག་མ་དང་མི་རྟག་པ་ཇི་བཞིན་སྣང་བས་མ
གཏོགས་སྤྱིར་སོང་བའི་རྒྱུ་རྡུལ་དང་སྐྱར་འབབ་འགྱུར་གྱི་རྒྱུ་རྡུལ་གང་ཡང་མི་སྣང་བའི་ཕྱིར། འོན་བུམ་པའི་ཧྲུལ་ཕྲ་རབ་དང་བུམ་པ་མི་རྟག་པ་ཕྲ་བའི་མི་རྟག་པ་མ་ཡིན་ནམ་དེ་སོ་སྐྱེའི་དབང་ཤེས་ལ་ཅི་ལྟར་སྣང་ཞེ་ན། དེ་དག་ཤིན་ཏུ
ཕྲ་བ་ཡིན་ཡང་བུམ་པ་དང་གྲུབ་བདེ་དབྱེར་མེད་ཀྱི་རྫས་གཅིག་ཡིན་པའི་རྒྱུ་མཚན་གྱིས་དེ་ལྟར་སྣང་བ་ཡིན་ཏེ། རང་དོན་ལེའུ་ལས། དོན་གྱི་རང་གི་ངོ་བོ་གཅིག །ཁྱད་ཉིད་མངོན་སུམ་ཡིན་པ་ལ། །ཚད་མ་གཞན་གྱིས་བརྟག་བྱ་གང་། །
མ་མཐོང་ཆ་གཞན་ཅི་ཞིག་ཡོད། །ཅེས་དང་། དེ་ཕྱིར་དངོས་པོ་མཐོང་བ་ཡིས། །ཡོན་ཏན་མཐའ་དག་མཐོང་བ་ཉིད། །ཅེས་གསུངས་པའི་ཕྱིར། ཁྱབ་སྟེ། ལུང་དེས་བུམ་འཛིན་དབང་ཤེས་སྐྱེ་བ་རྟག་ཡིན་པས་བུམ་པ་སྣང་དུས་ན…
བུམ་པ་དང་གྲུབ་བདེ་དབྱེར་མེད་ཀྱི་རྫས་གཅིག་པ་ཐམས་ཅད་སྣང་དགོས་པར་བཤད་ཅིང་། དེ་ཡང་དབང་ཤེས་དེ་ལ་བུམ་པའི་ཧྲུལ་ཕྲ་རབ་རེ་རེ་བ་མི་སྣང་ཡང་ཧྲུལ་མང་པོ་འདུས་པ་འབྱར་དུ་ཚོགས་པའི་ཧྲུལ་དུམ་སྣང་བ་ལ་འགལ་བ་མེད་དེ།
དཔེར་ན་ཁྱུ་…ཚུར་སྣང་བ་ལ་སོ་སོར་མི་ལྟ་ཚོགས་སྣང་དགོས་པ་བཞིན་ནོ། །དེ་སྐད་དུ། མདོ་ནས་སྡུམ་འབྱུང་ལས། ཁྱད་པར་སྐྱེ་འགྱུར་མང་པོ་དག །ཅིག་ཅར་བློ་ཡི་རྒྱུར་འགྱུར་ཡང་། །རྒྱ་ལ་བདག་གི་ཅི་ཞིག་ཡོད། །ཅེས་གསུངས་པའི་ཕྱིར།

163 བུམ་པ་དང་བུམ་པ་མི་རྟག་པ་གཉིས་གྲུབ་བདེ་དབྱེར་མེད་ཀྱི་རྫས་གཅིག་པའི་དོན་ནི། བུམ་པ་དང་སྐྱེ་འགག་གནས་གསུམ་དུས་མཉམ་ཞིང་། བུམ་པའི་རྫས་གང་ཡིན་པ་དེ་ཉིད་བུམ་པ་མི་རྟག་པའི་རྫས་ཀྱང་ཡིན། བུམ་པ་མི་རྟག་པའི་རྫས་གང་ཡིན
པ་དེ་ཉིད་བུམ་པའི་རྫས་ཀྱང་ཡིན་པའི་ཕྱིར་ན་མངོན་སུམ་གཅིག་ལ་གཅིག་སྣང་ནས་གཅིག་ཤོས་མི་སྣང་བ་མི་སྲིད་པའི་རྒྱུ་མཚན་གྱིས་བུམ་འཛིན་དབང་ཤེས་ལ་བུམ་པ་མི་རྟག་པར་ཡང་སྣང་བ་ཡིན་ནོ། །འོན་སྒྲ་འཛིན་དབང་མངོན་གྱིས་སྒྲ་མངོན
སུམ་དུ་རྟོགས་པ་ལྟར་སྒྲ་མི་རྟག་པ་ལ་ངེས་པ་འདྲེན་པར་འགྱུར་ལ། དེ་ལྟར་ན་སྒྲ་མི་རྟག་པར་སྒྲུབ་པའི་རྟགས་དང་རྗེས་དཔག་དོན་མེད་པར་འགྱུར་རོ་ཞེ་ན། སྐྱོན་མེད་དེ། སྒྲ་འཛིན་དབང་མངོན་གྱིས་སྒྲ་དང་རྫས་ཆ་སོ་སོར་དབྱེར་མེད་པའི་ཁྱད་ཆོས་དེ
རང་མངོན་སུམ་དུ་མཐོང་ཡང་མཐོང་བ་ལྟར་ངེས་པ་འདྲེན་པར་བྱེད་པ་ལ་ནང་གི་རྐྱེན་རྟག་པར་ཞེན་པའི་བག་ཆགས་འཐུག་པོ་ཡོད་པ་དང་། ཕྱིའི་རྐྱེན་རིགས་འདྲ་ཕྱི་མ་མཚམས་སྦྱོར་བར་མཐོང་བའི་དབང་གིས་དེ་ལྟར་ཆ་འགའ་ཞིག་ལ་ངེས་པ…
འདྲེན་མི་ནུས་པ་གང་ཞིག །གལ་ཏེ་དེ་ལྟ་བུའི་འགལ་རྐྱེན་མེད་ན་བུམ་འཛིན་དབང་ཤེས་ཀྱིས་ཀྱང་རང་གི་སྣང་ཡུལ་འགའ་ཞིག་གི་མི་རྟག་པ་ལ་ངེས་པ་འདྲེན་པའི་སྐབས་ཡོང་སྲིད་པའི་ཕྱིར། དང་པོ་གྲུབ་སྟེ། དཔེར་ན་ལྷས་སྦྱིན་གྱི་སྟེང་ན་ལྷས་སྦྱིན
བོང་བུམ་ཡིན་པ་དང་། ལྷས་སྦྱིན་སེམས་ཅན་ཡིན་པ་དང་མི་ཡིན་པ་དང་ལྷས་སྦྱིན་ཡིན་པའི་ཆ་ཚང་དུས་ཡོད་ཀྱང་། ལྷས་སྦྱིན་རྒྱུད་རིང་པོ་ནས་འཚོང་བ་མཐོང་བའི་ཚེ་མིག་ཤེས་ཀྱིས་ཁྱད་ཆོས་དེ་དག་མངོན་སུམ་དུ་མཐོང་ཡང་། ཡུལ་རྒྱུད་རིང་བའི

164 ཨཾ། ཨཱུཾ། ༡༤། ཏི།
༄༅། །རྐྱེན་གྱིས་དང་པོར་གོང་བུར་ལྷམ་དུ་སྐྱོ་འདོགས་ཤིང་། དེ་ནས་ཐག་ཉེ་རུ་སླེབ་པའི་ཚེ་རིམ་གྱིས་སེམས་ཅན་ཡིན་པ་དང་མི་ཡིན་པ་དང་ལྷས་སྦྱིན་ཡིན་པར་ངེས་པ་ལྟར། བུམ་འཛིན་དབང་མངོན་དེས་ཀྱང་
བུམ་པའི་བྱས་མི་རྟག་ལ་སོགས་པའི་ཁྱད་ཆོས་དེ་དག་མངོན་སུམ་དུ་མཐོང་ཡང་། འགལ་རྐྱེན་བྱུང་བའི་རིགས་འདྲ་ཕྱི་མ་སྐད་ཅིག་གཞན་དང་མཚམས་སྦྱོར་བར་མཐོང་བའི་དབང་གིས་བུམ་པ་སྐད་ཅིག་གིས་འཇིག་པའི་མི་རྟག་པ་ལ་ངེས་པ་འདྲེན…
མི་ནུས་པ་བཞིན་ཡིན་པའི་ཕྱིར། གཉིས་པ་གྲུབ་སྟེ། དེ་ལྟ་བུའི་འགལ་རྐྱེན་མེད་ན་བུམ་འཛིན་དབང་མངོན་འགའ་ཞིག་གིས་རང་ཡུལ་མི་རྟག་པ་ལ་ངེས་པ་འདྲེན་པ་ཡང་ཡོད་པའི་ཕྱིར་ཏེ། བུམ་པ་སྐད་ཅིག་ཐ་མ་མཐོང་བའི་དབང་ཤེས་དེས་རང…
ཡུལ་གྱི་བུམ་པ་མི་རྟག་པ་ལ་ངེས་པ་འདྲེན་ནུས་པའི་ཕྱིར། རྟགས་དེར་ཐལ། མར་མེ་སྐད་ཅིག་ཐ་མ་འཛིན་པའི་དབང་མངོན་གྱིས་དེ་ལྟར་ངེས་པ་འདྲེན་པའི་ཕྱིར་ཏེ། མངོན་སུམ་ལེའུ་ལས། སྤྱི་ཡི་རྟེན་ནི་གྲུབ་པ་ན། །སྤྱི་ནི་ཉིད་ནི་གྲུབ་པ་ཡིན། །
ཞེས་གསུངས་པའི་ཕྱིར། ལུང་དེའི་དོན་ཡོད་དེ། དེ་ལྟ་བུའི་འགལ་རྐྱེན་མེད་ཅིང་མཐུན་རྐྱེན་ཚང་ན་བུམ་པའི་སྤྱི་མི་རྟག་པ་དེ་ཡི་རྟེན་དུ་གྱུར་པའི་བུམ་པ་དེ་ནི་མངོན་སུམ་གྱིས་གྲུབ་པ་ན། སྤྱི་མི་རྟག་པ་དེ་ཉིད་ནི་མངོན་སུམ་དེས་གྲུབ་པ་ཡིན་ཞེས་པའི
དོན་ཡིན་པའི་ཕྱིར། དེའི་རྒྱུ་མཚན་འཆད་པ་ལ། དེ་ཉིད་ལས། འདི་ལྟར་རྟགས་མེད་ཅེས་བར་གྱི། །སྐྱེ་བོས་ཕྱི་དབུང་བ་དང་ནི། །འབྲེལ་མེད་མར་མེ་ལ་སོགས་ཀྱི། །ངེས་པ་མཐོང་བས་ཡོངས་གཅོད་ཉིད། །ཅེས་གསུངས་པའི་ཕྱིར།

165 ལུང་དེའི་དོན་ཡང་ཡོད་དེ། འདི་ལྟར་རིགས་འདྲ་འི་རྒྱུན་མཐོང་བ་ལས་རྟག་པར་འཁྲུལ་བའི་རྒྱུ་མཚན་ནི་འདྲ་མེད་ན་རྟགས་ལ་སྙོམས་པ་མེད་པར་མཁས་པ་ནས་བྱིས་པའི་བར་གྱི་སྐྱེ་བོས་རིགས་འདྲ་ཕྱི་མ་ཕྱིས་སུ་འབྱུང་བ་གཞན་དང་ནི་མཚན་ས···
སྐྱུར་བའི་འབྲེལ་བ་མེད་པའི་ཨར་མི་སྐད་ཅིག་ཐམས་ཅད་མངོན་སུམ་གྱིས་མཐོང་ན། དེ་ལ་སོགས་ཀྱི་མི་རྟག་པ་དང་འཇིག་པ་མངོན་སུམ་གྱིས་མཐོང་བས་ཡོངས་སུ་གཅོད་ནུས་པ་ཉིད་ཅེས་པའི་དོན་ཡིན་པའི་ཕྱིར། དེའི་ཕྱིར་ས་སྐད་ཅིག་ཐམས་མི་རྟག
པ་དེ་རགས་པའི་མི་རྟག་པ་ཡིན་ནོ། །འོན་ལས་སེ་སྐད་ཅིག་ཐ་མའི་སྐྱེ་རྒྱུ་བའི་མི་རྟག་པ་ཅི་ལྟར་འཇོག་ཅེ་ན། དེ་ཡོད་དེ། ས་སྐད་ཅིག་ཐ་མ་སྐྱེས་ཙམ་ནས་འཇིག་པའི་ཆོས་ཅན་གྱི་མི་རྟག་པ་ཕྲ་བའི་ཚུལ་དེ་ཕྲ་བའི་མི་རྟག་པ་ཡིན་པའི
ཕྱིར། ཡང་ལུང་དེ་རིམ་རྟག་གི །བློ་གྲོས་ཆེན་པོས་མཐོང་ཉིད་ལས། །རྣམ་པ་ཐམས་ཅད་ངེས་པར་བྱེད། །ཅེས་པའི་དོན་ལ་ དེ་དང་ས་མང་པོས་བློ་གྲོས་ཆེན་པོ་དེ་འཕགས་པ་ལ་བྱས་ནས་འཕགས་པས་གང་ཞིག་མངོན་སུམ་དུ་མཐོང་ན···
དེ་ལ་ངེས་པ་འདྲེན་པས་ཁྱབ་པས་འཕགས་རྒྱུད་ཀྱི་མངོན་སུམ་ལ་སྣང་ལ་མ་ངེས་པ་མེད་ཟེར་རོ། །དེ་ལ་ཁ་ཅིག་གིས། རྣམ་མཁྱེན་མི་རྟག་པར་རྟོགས་པའི་སློབ་པའི་རྒྱུད་ཀྱི་རྣལ་འབྱོར་མངོན་སུམ་ཆོས་ཅན། རྣམ་མཁྱེན་མངོན་སུམ་དུ···
མཐོང་བར་ཐལ། རྣམ་མཁྱེན་མི་རྟག་པར་མངོན་སུམ་དུ་མཐོང་བ་གང་ཞིག །དེ་གཉིས་གྲུབ་བདེ་དབྱེར་མེད་ཀྱི་རྫས་གཅིག་ཏུ་ཁྱེད་ཀྱིས་འདོད་པའི་ཕྱིར། འདོད་ན། རྣམ་མཁྱེན་མངོན་སུམ་དུ་རྟོགས་པའི་སེམས་ཅན་ཡོད་པར་ཐལ་ལོ། ། །

ཨ ཨཱཿ 166 ཧཱུྃ ཧྲཱིཿ

༄༅། །དེས་ན་རྣམ་མཁྱེན་དང་རྣམ་མཁྱེན་མི་རྟག་པ་གཉིས་གྲུབ་བདེ་རྫས་གཅིག་ཡིན་གྱི་གྲུབ་བདེ་དབྱེར་མེད་ཀྱི་རྫས་གཅིག་མ་ཡིན་ཟེར་རོ། །ཁ་ཅིག །མེའི་ཁ་དོག་མེ་དང་རྫས་ཐ་དད་ཟེར་བ་མི་འཐད་དེ། མེའི་
ཁ་དོག་མེ་དང་རྫས་གཅིག་ཡིན་པའི་ཕྱིར་ཏེ། དཔེར་ན། སྨྱུ་གུའི་ཁ་དོག་སྨྱུ་གུ་དང་རྫས་གཅིག་ཡིན་པའི་ཕྱིར། རྟགས་གྲུབ་སྟེ། རྗེ་ཤེས་རྣམ་པ་ཤད་རིགས་པའི་རྒྱ་མཚོ་ལས། སྨྱུ་གུའི་ཁ་དོག་དང་དབྱིབས་སོགས་སྨྱུ་གུའི་བདག་ཉིད་ཡིན་
པས་དེ་དེའི་ངོ་བོ་ཞེས་བྱའོ། །ཞེས་གསུངས་པའི་ཕྱིར། ཁྱབ་སྟེ། སྨྱུ་གུའི་ཁ་དོག་སྨྱུ་གུའི་བདག་ཉིད་དང་ངོ་བོ་གཅིག་ཡིན་པ་དེ་གཉིས་བདག་ཉིད་གཅིག་ཏུ་གྲུབ་ལ། བདག་ཉིད་གཅིག་པའི་རྫས་གྲུབ་ལ་རྫས་གཅིག་པ་དགོས་པའི་ཕྱིར་རོ། །
དེར་མ་ཟད་མེ་དང་མེའི་ཁ་དོག་གཉིས་གྲུབ་བདེ་རྫས་གཅིག་པ་ཡང་ཡིན་ཏེ། ཚད་མ་རྣམ་ངེས། གྲུབ་པ་ནི་ཚོགས་མ་ཐོབ་པ་ལས་འབྲེལ་བའོ། །བདེ་བ་ནི་ཐོབ་པ་རྗེས་སུ་འཇུག་པའོ། །ཞེས་གསུངས་པ་ལྟར་སྐྱེ་འགག་གནས་གསུམ་གཅིག
པ་གྲུབ་བདེ་རྫས་གཅིག་པའི་དོན་ཡིན་པ་གང་ཞིག །མེ་དང་དེའི་ཁ་དོག་གཉིས་སྐྱེ་འགག་གནས་གསུམ་དུས་མཉམ་ཞིང་རྫས་གཅིག་པ་ཡང་ཡིན་པའི་ཕྱིར་རོ། །འོན་ཀྱང་དེ་གཉིས་གྲུབ་བདེ་དབྱེར་མེད་ཀྱི་རྫས་གཅིག་ཡིན་མིན་ལ་སྒོ་ཚོགས
བློ་སྟེ། ཁ་ཅིག །དེ་གཉིས་གྲུབ་བདེ་དབྱེར་མེད་ཀྱི་རྫས་གཅིག་མ་ཡིན་ཏེ། མེ་མངོན་སུམ་དུ་སྣང་ན་མེའི་ཁ་དོག་སྣང་བས་མ་ཁྱབ་པའི་ཕྱིར། དེར་ཐལ། དཀྱུས་ལོང་གི་ལུས་ཤེས་ལ་མེ་སྣང་བ་གང་ཞིག །མེའི་ཁ་དོག་མི་སྣང་བའི་ཕྱིར་ཟེར།

167 དེ་ལ་འོ་ན། དཀྱུས་ལོང་གི་ལུས་ཤེས་དེ་ལ་མེ་དམར་པོ་སྣང་བར་ཐལ། དེ་ལ་མེ་སྣང་བ་གང་ཞིག །དམར་པོ་མ་ཡིན་པའི་མེ་མེད་པའི་ཕྱིར་ཟེར་ན། ཁ་ཅིག་གིས་འདོད་ཟེར། ལ་ལས་མ་ཁྱབ་སྟེ། མེ་དམར་པོ་ཁ་དོག་ཡིན་པའི་ཕྱིར། དེ་ལ་ན་མི་སྣང
ཟེར། འདི་ལ་ཁོ་ན་རེ། ཤིང་རིང་པོ་དབྱིབས་ཡིན་པར་ཐལ། མེ་དམར་པོ་ཁ་དོག་ཡིན་པའི་ཕྱིར། རིགས་པ་མཚུངས་སོ་ཟེར་ན། ཁ་ཅིག་གིས་མ་ཁྱབ་ཟེར། འདོད་ན། དཀྱུས་ལོང་གིས་ཤིང་རིང་ཐུང་གི་དབྱེ་བ་མངོན་སུམ་དུ་འཇལ་མི་ནུས་པར
འགྱུར་རོ་ཞེ་ན། འདི་ལྟར་བཤད་པར་བྱ་སྟེ། ཤིང་རིང་པོ་ཤིང་ཡིན་པའི་ཕྱིར་ལུས་ཤེས་ཀྱི་རེག་བྱ་ཡིན་པའི་རྒྱུ་མཚན་གྱིས་ལོང་བ་རྣམས་ཀྱིས་དེ་ར་རིང་ཐུང་གི་ཁྱད་པར་མངོན་སུམ་དུ་འཇལ་ནུས་པ་དེ་ཡིན་ལ། འོན་ཀྱང་ཤིང་རིང་པོའི་དབྱིབས་དེ···
དབྱིབས་ཡིན་གྱི་ཤིང་མ་ཡིན་ཞིང་། ཤིང་རིང་པོ་དེ་ཤིང་ཡིན་པས་ལུས་ཤེས་ཀྱི་རེག་བྱ་ཡིན་ཞེས་ཅིས་ཀྱང་ཁས་ལེན་དགོས་ཏེ། དཔེར་ན་བུམ་པའི་དོན་བྱེད་ནུས་པ་ཤས་སུ་གྱུར་པའི་མགྲིན་པ་རིང་བ་བུམ་པ་ཡིན་གྱི་མགྲིན་པ་རིང་བའི···
དབྱིབས་བུམ་པ་མིན་པ་བཞིན་ཡིན་པའི་ཕྱིར་ཏེ། ལྷག་མཐོང་ཆེན་མོ་ལས། ལྟོ་བ་ལྡིར་བ་དང་མགྲིན་པ་རིང་བ་སོགས་དེ་ནི་བུམ་པ་ཡིན་པར་འདོད་ཀྱི། ལྟོ་བ་ལྡིར་བ་སོགས་ཀྱི་དབྱིབས་བུམ་པར་མི་འདོད་དེ། ཞེས་གསུངས་པའི་ཕྱིར། ཡང་
ཁ་ཅིག །མིག་ཤེས་རབ་ཅན་གྱིས་ལྗན་པའི་འཚང་ན་གནས་པའི་དུང་ལ་ལག་པས་རེག་ནས་རེ་ཞེས་པ་དུང་དཀར་པོ་མངོན་སུམ་དུ་རྟོགས་ཟེར་ན། མིག་དང་མ་ལྡན་པས་དེ་ལྟར་ངེས་པ་དུང་མངོན་སུམ་དུ་རྟོགས་ཀྱང་དུང་དཀར་པོ་མངོན་སུམ་དུ་མ་རྟོགས་ཟེར་

ཨ 168 ཧཱུྃ ཧྲཱིཿ

༄༅། །མོད་ཀྱི་ འོན་ཀྱང་འདི་སྐོར་ལ་རྒྱལ་དབང་ལྔ་པས་དུང་དཀར་སེར་པོར་སྣང་བའི་དབང་ཤེས་དུང་གི་ཁ་དོག་ལ་འཁྲུལ་ཡང་དབྱིབས་ལ་མ་འཁྲུལ་ཞེས་བཞེད་ལ། དེའི་རྒྱུ་མཚན་ནི་དུང་སེར་པོར་སྣང་བའི་མིག་ཤེས་དང···
དཀར་པོར་སྣང་བའི་མིག་ཤེས་གཉིས་ལ་སྣང་བའི་དུང་གི་དབྱིབས་ལ་མི་འདྲ་བ་མེད་པའི་ཕྱིར་དང་། སེར་པོར་སྣང་བའི་མིག་ཤེས་དེ་ལ་བརྟེན་ནས་ཀྱང་དུང་དཀར་པོ་ཐོབ་ནུས་པའི་ཕྱིར་ཞེས་དགོངས་ལ། རྒྱལ་ཚབ་རྗེ་སོགས་དེ་མི་འཐད···
ཅེས་བཞེད་དེ། རྣམ་ངེས་ཊཱིཀ་ཆེན་དགོངས་པ་རབ་གསལ་ལས། དབྱིབས་ནི་ཁ་དོག་ལས་རྫས་ཐ་དད་པའི་དོན་བྱེད་ནུས་པས་ཡིན་པས། ཁ་དོག་ལ་འཁྲུལ་ན་དབྱིབས་ལ་མ་འཁྲུལ་བར་ག་ལ་འགྱུར། དུང་གི་སྣ་ཡང་དབྱིབས་ཀྱི་ཁྱད་པར
ཅན་གྱི་ཁ་དོག་ལ་འཇུག་ལ། དུང་ཐོབ་པ་ཡང་ཚད་མ་གཞན་ལ་བརྟེན་པ་ཡིན་གྱི་སེར་པོར་འཛིན་པ་ལས་ནི་མ་ཡིན་ནོ། །ཞེས་གསུངས་སོ། །འདིའི་དུང་གི་སྣ་དབྱིབས་ཀྱི་ཁྱད་པར་ཅན་གྱི་ཁ་དོག་ལ་འཇུག་ཅེས་པ་ལ་ཁོ་བོ་མོས་ཤིང
གྱིས་དཔག་ན། དུང་མངོན་སུམ་དུ་རིག་ན་འཁྲུལ་བའི་རི་མོ་ཙམ་གྱི་ཁྱད་པར་དུ་བྱས་པའི་དཀར་པོ་རིག་པས་ཁྱབ་ཅེས་པ་ཨེ་ཡིན་ལྟམ་དུ་དོགས་སོ། །རྒྱལ་དབང་ལྔ་པའི་བཞེད་པ་འགོག་པའི་རིགས་པ་དངོས་ནི། དབྱིབས་ཀྱི་རྫུལ་ཁ་དོག་གི
རྫུལ་ལ་བརྟགས་པ་ཙམ་ཡིན་པས་ཁ་དོག་ནི་རྫུལ་མ་སྣང་བར་དབྱིབས་རང་དབང་བར་སྣང་དུ་མི་རུང་ཞིང་། དེས་ན་དུང་དཀར་སེར་པོར་སྣང་བའི་དབང་ཤེས་ཆོས་ཅན། ཁྱོད་ལ་དུང་དཀར་པོའི་དབྱིབས་སྣང་བར་ཐལ། ཁྱོད་དུང་གི་དབྱིབས

169 ལ་སྣང་བ་འཛུག་གི་བློ་ཡིན་པ་གང་ཞིག། དུང་གི་དཀར་པོ་དང་དབྱིབས་གཉིས་གྲུབ་བདེ་རྫས་གཅིག་ཡིན་པའི་ཕྱིར། འདོད་མི་ནུས་ཏེ། ཚོན་ལྟ་དུང་དཀར་པོའི་དབྱིབས་སུ་སྣང་བར་དུང་སེར་པོའི་དབྱིབས་སྣང་བ་གང་ཞིག། སེར་པོའི་དུང་
གཞི་མི་གྲུབ་པའི་ཕྱིར་ཞེས་འགོག་པར་མཛད་དོ། །དེ་ཡང་དུང་གི་དབྱིབས་ཁ་དོག་གཉིས་གྲུབ་བདེ་དབྱེར་མེད་ཀྱི་རྫས་གཅིག་ཏུ་འདོད་མི་འདོད་ཉིད་དཔྱད་པ་རྟག་པར་བྱ་བ་ཁོ་ནའོ། །འོན་ཀྱང་དེ་ལ་འདི་དཔྱད་པར་བྱ་སྟེ། སྨིག་རྒྱུ་ཆུར་
སྣང་བའི་དབང་ཤེས་རྒྱུ་ལ་འཁྲུལ་ཡང་སྐྱོ་ཞིང་འཁྱུག་པའི་ཆ་ལ་ཚད་མར་སོང་ཞེས་མཁས་གྲུབ་རྗེས་གསུངས་ཤིང་། ཐག་ཁྲ་སྦྲུལ་སྣང་གི་དབང་ཤེས་ཐག་ཁྲའི་ཁ་དོག་གི་རྣམ་པ་ལ་ཚད་མར་སོང་ཞེས་ས་པཎ་གྱིས་གསུངས་པས། དངག
རང་ལུགས་སུ་ཁས་ལེན་རུང་ནི་གཞན་གྱིས་སྐྱོན་ཤིང་འགྲོ་བར་སྣང་བའི་དབང་ཤེས་སྟོང་པའི་སྐྱོན་ཤིང་ལ་འཁྲུལ་ཡང་རྟོན་ཤིང་སྐྱོན་པོ་ཡིན་པ་ལ་ཚད་མར་སོང་ཞེས་སྨྲ་བ་མི་འཐད་དེ་ས་ཅི་ལྟར་འགོག་རིགས། དེ་གཉིས་རིགས་པ
མཚུངས་པས་སོ་ཞེ་ན། དེའི་ལན་ཅུང་ཟད་སྨྲ་ནུས་མོད་ཀྱང་རེ་ཞིག་འཕྲུང་འཕྱུར་གྱི་མཁས་པ་རྣམས་ལེགས་པར་བཤད་ལ་རྟོག་དཔྱོད་གནང་བའི་ཆེད་དུ་བཏང་སྙོམས་སུ་བཞག་གོ །ཡང་ཐལ་ཆེ་བ་དག་གིས། མེ་ལུས་ཤེས་ཀྱི་རིག་བྱ
ཡིན་པས་སོ་སྐྱེའི་མིག་ཤེས་ལ་མི་སྣང་། མེའི་ཁ་དོག་མིག་ཤེས་ཀྱི་གཟུང་བྱ་ཡིན་པས་སོ་སྐྱེའི་ལུས་ཤེས་ལ་མི་སྣང་ཟེར་ཞིང་། དེ་བཞིན་དུ་མཁས་པའི་གསུང་ལས་བྱུང་བ་ཡང་ཡོད་ལ། དེའི་རྒྱུ་མཚན་ནི་གཟུགས་འཛིན་དབང་

༄༅། །ཤེས་ལྟ་བུ་ལ་རང་གི་ངོ་བོ་གསལ་རིག་གི་ཆ་དང་། གཟུགས་ཀྱི་རྣམ་ལྡན་དུ་སྐྱེ་བའི་ཆ་དང་། གཟུགས་འཛིན་ནུས་ཀྱང་སྒྲ་སོགས་འཛིན་མི་ནུས་པའི་ཆ་གསུམ་ཡོད་པ་ལས་དང་པོ་ནི་དེ་མ་ཐག་རྐྱེན་གྱི་ལག
རྗེས་དང་། གཉིས་པ་ནི་དམིགས་རྐྱེན་གྱི་ལག་རྗེས་དང་། གསུམ་པ་ནི་བདག་རྐྱེན་གྱི་ལག་རྗེས་ཡིན་པའི་རྒྱུ་མཚན་གྱིས་གཟུགས་འཛིན་མིག་ཤེས་ཀྱིས་གཟུགས་ཁོ་ན་སྣང་ཞིང་རེག་བྱ་སོགས་མི་སྣང་བའི་ཁྱད་པར་དེ་འདྲ་བྱུང་བ་ཡིན
170 ཞེས་སྨྲའོ། །དེ་ལྟར་དོན་ལ་གནས་ཤས་ཆེ། འོན་ཀྱང་དོགས་སློང་གི་རྒྱུ་ལ་ཅུང་ཟད་སྨྲ་བར་བྱ་བ་འདི་སྐད། འོན་སོ་སྐྱེའི་མིག་ཤེས་ལ་མེ་མི་སྣང་བར་ཐལ། མེ་ལུས་ཤེས་ཀྱི་རིག་བྱ་ཡིན་པའི་ཕྱིར། རྟགས་ཁས། འདོད་ན།
དེ་ལ་གཏར་མེ་མི་སྣང་བར་ཐལ། འདོད་པའི་ཕྱིར། འདོད་ན། མར་མེའི་རྩེ་མོ་ཁྲ་ཁྲོར་བར་སྣང་བའི་དབང་ཤེས་ལ་ཡང་མར་མེ་མི་སྣང་བར་ཐལ། དེ་འདྲའི་དབང་ཤེས་མིག་ཤེས་ལས་གཞན་དུ་མི་འཐད་པའི་ཕྱིར། དེ་ཡང་འདོད་ན།
སྡེ་བདུན་གྱི་རྒྱན་ཡིད་ཀྱི་མུན་སེལ་ལས། མར་མེའི་རྩེ་མོ་ཁྲ་ཁྲོར་བར་སྣང་བའི་དབང་ཤེས་ཀྱིས་ཀྱང་མར་མེའི་རྩེ་མོ་མངོན་སུམ་དུ་མཐོང་བར་སྤྱོད་པས་གྲུབ་པོ། །ཞེས་གསུངས་པ་དང་ཅི་ལྟར་མི་འགལ། དེ་ལ་མར་མེའི་རྩེ་མོ
མཐོང་ཡང་མར་མེ་མ་མཐོང་ཞེས་ཤེས་ལྡན་སུ་ཞིག་སྨྲ། གཞན་ཡང་སོ་སྐྱེའི་མིག་ཤེས་ལ་ཆུ་མི་སྣང་བར་ཐལ། ཆུ་ལུས་ཤེས་ཀྱི་རིག་བྱ་ཡིན་པའི་ཕྱིར། འདོད་ན། དེ་ལ་རྣག་དང་ཁྲག་ཀྱང་མི་སྣང་བར་ཐལ། དེ་དག་ལུས་ཤེས

ཀྱི་རིག་བྱ་ཡིན་པའི་ཕྱིར། འདོད་ན། ཡི་དྭགས་ཀྱི་མིག་ཤེས་ལ་རྣག་དང་ཁྲག་མི་སྣང་བར་ཐལ། སོ་སྐྱེའི་མིག་ཤེས་ལ་དེ་དག་མི་སྣང་བའི་ཕྱིར། རྟགས་ཁས། འདོད་ན། རྗེའི་གསུང་དང་འགལ་བར་དོགས་ཏེ། དབུ་མ་འཇུག
པའི་རྣམ་བཤད་དགོངས་པ་རབ་གསལ་ལས། ཡི་དྭགས་ལ་ཆུ་ཀླུང་རྣག་ཁྲག་ཏུ་སྣང་བ་ནི་དེའི་མིག་ཤེས་ལ་སྣང་བ་ཡིན་པས་གཟུགས་ཀྱི་སྐྱེ་མཆེད་དུ་བཞག་དགོས་སོ། །ཞེས་གསུངས་པའི་ཕྱིར། གཞན་ཡང་། སྟོང་ཐུན
171 སྐལ་བཟང་མིག་འབྱེད་ལས། དཔེར་ན་ཆུ་ཀླུང་དང་དེའི་འོག་གཞི་རི་ས་གཉིས་ལས། མིའི་མིག་ཤེས་ཆུ་ལ་ཚད་མར་སོང་གི་འོག་གཞི་རི་ས་ལ་ཚད་མར་མ་སོང་། ཡི་དྭགས་ཀྱི་མིག་ཤེས་འོག་གཞི་རི་ས་ལ་ཚད་མར་སོང་གི་ཆུ་ལ་ཚད
མར་མ་སོང་ངོ་། །ཞེས་གསུངས་པ་དང་། དངོས་སྨྲ་བའི་འདོད་པ་བརྗོད་པའི་སྐབས་ཀྱི་ལམ་རིམ་ཆེན་མོ་ལས་ཀྱང་། རྟོག་པ་དང་བྲལ་ཞིང་མ་འཁྲུལ་བའི་ཤེས་པ་ནི་མངོན་སུམ་ཉིད་དུ་འདོད་དོ། །དེ་ལ་མ་འཁྲུལ་བ་ནི་ཡུལ་གྱི་རང་གི
མཚན་ཉིད་ཇི་ལྟར་གནས་པ་ལྟར་འཛིན་པར་བྱེད་པས། དབང་པོའི་ཤེས་པའི་མངོན་སུམ་ལྔ་ཀས་རང་མཚན་འཛིན་ལ་བསན། གཟུགས་ལ་སོགས་པའི་རང་གི་མཚན་ཉིད་ནི་མངོན་སུམ་ལྔ་པོ་དེ་དག་གི་གཞལ་བྱ་ཡིན་པས། དེ་དག
ཚད་མར་འགྲོ་ས་ཡང་ཡུལ་ལྔ་པོ་དེའི་རང་གི་མཚན་ཉིད་ཡིན་པར་འདོད་དོ། །ཞེས་གསུངས་པའི་ཕྱིར། དེ་ལ་ཁོ་ན་རེ། ལུང་དེ་དག་གི་དོན་ཁྱོད་ཀྱིས་སྨྲ་བ་ལྟར་མ་ཡིན་ཟེར། འོ་ན་ཅི་ཡིན་ཞེ་ན། སྟོང་ཐུན་གྱི་དོན་ནི། ཡི་དྭགས་ཀྱི་མིག་ཤེས

༄༅། །ངེས་ས་ལ་མངོན་སུམ་ཚད་མར་སོང་བ་མ་ཡིན་ཡང་སའི་ཁ་དོག་ལ་མངོན་སུམ་ཚད་མར་སོང་བའི་སྟོབས་ཀྱིས་ས་ལ་ངེས་ཤེས་འདྲེན་ནུས་པས་ན་དེ་ལ་ཚད་མར་སོང་ཞེས་བཤད་པ་ཙམ་ཡིན
ཏེ། དཔེར་ན་བུམ་པས་དག་པའི་ས་ཕྱོགས་འཛིན་པའི་དབང་མངོན་དེ་བུམ་མེད་ལ་མངོན་སུམ་ཚད་མ་དང་རྗེས་དཔག་བཅད་ཤེས་གང་ཡང་མ་ཡིན་ཡང་། ས་ཕྱོགས་ལ་ཚད་མར་སོང་བའི་སྟོབས་ཀྱིས་བུམ་མེད་ལ་ངེས་པ་འདྲེན་པའི་རྒྱུ་མཚན
172 ཀྱིས་བུམ་མེད་ལ་ཚད་མར་སོང་ཞེས་བཤད་ཆོག་པ་བཞིན་ཡིན་པའི་ཕྱིར། དེ་ལ་ན་གཟུགས་སོགས་དོན་ལྔ་དབང་ཤེས་ལྔའི་ཡུལ་དུ་སོ་སོར་ངེས་པའི་ཕྱིར་ལུས་ཤེས་ཀྱི་རིག་བྱ་ཡིན་ན་མིག་ཤེས་ལ་མི་སྣང་བ་དགོས་པའི་ཕྱིར། དེ་ཡང
ཡིན་ཏེ། བུམ་པ་རྟོགས་པའི་ལུས་ཤེས་ཀྱིས་བུམ་པའི་གཟུགས་དང་། ཁ་དོག་སོགས་མཐོང་བ་མ་ཡིན་པའི་ཕྱིར། དེ་ལྟར་ཡང་ཁས་ལེན་དགོས་ཏེ། རྣམ་འགྲེལ་ཊཱིཀ་ཆེན་རིགས་པའི་རྒྱ་མཚོ་ལས། སྣང་བའི་ཁྱད་པར་དང་བྲལ་བའི
མུན་པའི་ནང་དུ་བུམ་པ་ལ་ལག་པས་རེག་པའི་སྐབས་སུ་བུམ་པའི་རེག་བྱ་མངོན་སུམ་དུ་འཛིན་པའི་ལུས་ཤེས་ཆོས་ཅན། ཁྱོད་ཀྱིས་བུམ་པ་མངོན་སུམ་དུ་མཐོང་བར་ཐལ། བུམ་པའི་རེག་བྱ་མངོན་སུམ་དུ་མཐོང་བ་གང་ཞིག།
དེ་གཉིས་གྲུབ་བདེ་རྫས་གཅིག་ཡིན་པའི་ཕྱིར། འདོད་ན། བུམ་གཟུགས་མངོན་སུམ་དུ་མཐོང་བར་ཐལ་ལོ། །འདོད་ན། གཟུགས་འཛིན་དབང་ཤེས་ཡིན་ན་མིག་ཤེས་ཡིན་པས་མ་ཁྱབ་པར་ཐལ་ལོ། །ཞེས་གསུངས་པའི་ཕྱིར

173 ཟེར་ན། དེ་ལྟ་བུ་ལང་ཏེ་ཀ་ཆེན་དུ་ཞུ་བར་ཤེས་གྲུ་རེ་བཞིན་བཞུགས་པ་པོ་ལོ་སྐད་དུས་སུ་མཐོང་ནུས་ཅི་ཡང་གཏོང་ལ་མ་ཐུང་བར་བཏང་སྙོམས་སུ་བཞག་ལ། དཔེར་ན་ཚོད་ཀྱིས་དེ་དྲང་ས་པ་ལེགས་མེད། འོན་ཀྱང་གསུང་དེའི་སྐབས་ཟིན་
ཚོད་ལྟར་ན། དེ་ལྟ་བུ་བུམ་པ་མངོན་སུམ་དུ་འཛིན་པའི་ལུས་ཤེས་ཀྱིས་བུམ་པ་ཡང་མ་མཐོང་བུམ་པའི་གཟུགས་ཁྲང་མ་མཐོང་ཟེར་དགོས་པར་མངོན་པ་ཡང་། དེ་ལྟར་ཐལ་བ་ཡིན་ན་ཚ་ཞིང་སྲེག་པ་མངོན་སུམ་དུ་རིག་པའི་ལུས་ཤེས་མེད་...
ཟེར་དགོས་པ་འདྲ་ཡང་ན་དེས་མི་མ་མཐོང་ཟེར་དགོས་སམ། གལ་ཏེ་དེ་ལྟར་ཡིན་ན་ནི་མཐོང་བའི་ལུས་ཤེས་གཏན་མེད་དུ་འགྱུར་རོ། །འོན་ལུང་དེའི་དོན་གང་ཡིན་ཞེ་ན། དེ་ནི་བུམ་པ་མངོན་སུམ་དུ་མཐོང་ན་བུམ་གཟུགས་མངོན་
སུམ་དུ་མཐོང་བར་ཐལ་བ་འཕངས་པའི་ཡུལ་ནི། གྲུབ་བདེ་རྫས་གཅིག་པ་དང་འགྲུབ་བདེ་ཕྱེར་མེད་ཀྱི་རྫས་གཅིག་པ་གཉིས་གཅིག་ཏུ་འཁྲུལ་བའི་རྩོལ་བ་ཡིན་ལ། རྩོལ་བ་དེ་ལ་བུམ་པའི་གཟུགས་འཛིན་པའི་དབང་ཤེས་ཡིན་ན་
གཟུགས་འཛིན་དབང་ཤེས་སུ་ཐལ་ཞེས་རིག་པས་ཕུལ་ནས། དེ་ནས་ལུས་ཤེས་མིག་ཤེས་སུ་ཐལ་དུ་འགྱུར་པའི་རིགས་པ་ཡིན་གྱི། དེ་ལྟ་མ་ཡིན་པར་བུམ་པའི་རེག་བྱ་མངོན་སུམ་དུ་འཛིན་པའི་ལུས་ཤེས་ཀྱིས་བུམ་པ་མཐོང་བར་
ཐལ་བ་འཕངས་པ་མ་ཡིན་ནམ་སྙམ་མོ། །འོན་ཀྱང་སྔོན་ཁུང་གི་བུམ་པ་ལ་ལག་པས་རེག་པའི་སྔོན་ལ་བུམ་པ་རྟོགས་པའི་ལུས་ཤེས་དེས་བུམ་པའི་གཟུགས་མ་མཐོང་གསུངས་པ་དེ་ལེགས་པ་བཤད་ལྡན་མེད་པ་ཡིན་ཏེ། དེ་ལྟར་ཟེར

174 ༄༅། །དགོས་པའི་རྒྱུ་མཚན་ནི། བུམ་པའི་གཟུགས་ཞེས་བརྗོད་པའི་སྒྲ་དེ་བུམ་པ་དང་བུམ་པའི་གཟུགས་གཉིས་གཞི་མཐུན་དུ་བརྗོད་པའི་སྒྲ་མ་ཡིན་པར། བུམ་པའི་གཟུགས་ཞེས་བརྗོད་པའི་སྒྲ་དེས་བུམ་པའི་དྲི་རོ་...
རེག་བྱ་རྣམས་ལས་བུམ་པའི་གཟུགས་ཐ་དད་དུ་ཕྱེ་སྟེ་རང་འཛིན་མིག་ཤེས་སྐྱེད་པའི་ནུས་མཐོང་མ་ཡིན་པའི་ནུས་པ་ཅན་དུ་སྟོན་པར་བྱེད་ཅིང་། དེ་བཞིན་དུ་ཙནྡན་གྱི་དྲི་ཞེས་བརྗོད་པའི་སྒྲས་ཀྱང་ཙནྡན་ཙམ་བརྗོད་པ་མ་ཡིན་པར་རང་འཛིན་སྣ་ཤེས་
སྐྱེད་པའི་ནུས་པའི་ཁྱད་པར་ཐུན་མོང་མ་ཡིན་པར་གོ་བར་བྱེད་པའི་ཕྱིར་རོ། །དེའི་ཕྱིར་... ཙནྡན་གྱི་དྲི་འཛིན་པའི་དབང་ཤེས་ཡིན་ན་སྣ་ཤེས་ཡིན་དགོས་པ་ལྟར། བུམ་པའི་གཟུགས་འཛིན་པའི་དབང་ཤེས་ཡིན་ན་མིག་ཤེས་ཡིན་...
དགོས་པར་བསྒྲུབས་པས་སྔོན་ཁུང་གི་བུམ་པ་ལ་ལག་པས་རེག་པའི་སྔོན་བུམ་པ་རྟོགས་པའི་ལུས་ཤེས་དེ་བུམ་པ་མཐོང་ཡང་བུམ་པའི་གཟུགས་མ་མཐོང་བ་ཡིན་ནོ། །གལ་ཏེ་ཡིན་ན་ཚ་ཞིང་སྲེག་པ་མངོན་སུམ་དུ་འཛིན་པའི་ལུས་...
ཤེས་ཀྱིས་ཁྱང་མེ་གཏན་ནས་མ་མཐོང་ཟེར་དགོས་པས་དེ་ལྟར་ན་མེ་མཐོང་བའི་ལུས་ཤེས་སོ་སོ་སྐྱེ་བོའི་རྒྱུད་ལ་གཏན་མེད་དུ་འགྱུར་རོ། །དགེ་ཚོད་ཀྱི་འདོད་པ་བརྗོད་དགོས་སོ་ཞེ་ན། ཁོ་བོ་ལ་ཡང་སྔ་མའི་ལེགས་པ་བཤད་པ་ལ་ཆེར
བསྒུབས་ནས་ལེགས་པ་བཤད་གསར་པས་བསྒྲུབ་མཐའ་འཆལ་བའི་གདེངས་མེད་ཀྱང་དེ་ཞིག་སེམས་ལ་ཤར་ཚོད་ཅིག་སྨྲ་ན། རེག་བྱ་ཡིན་ན་སོ་སྐྱེའི་མིག་ཤེས་ལ་མི་སྣང་བ་དགོས་ན། ཐུ་རྩོལ་གྱིས་ཕྱིར་རྩོལ་མངོན་སུམ་དུ་མ་མཐོང་ཟེར་...

175 དགོས་པས་དེ་ལྟར་ན་མངོན་སུམ་དང་འགལ་བས། ཕྱིར་རྩོལ་མཐོང་གི་མངོན་སུམ་ལ་དབང་ཡིད་རང་རིག་གསུམ་ལས་རང་རིག་གིས་མཐོང་དོན་མེད་ལ་ཡིད་མངོན་ཡང་ཐལ་ཆེར་སྣང་ལ་མ་ངེས་པ་ཡིན་པས་དབང་ཤེས་ཀྱིས་མཐོང་དགོས
ཤིང་དེ་ཡང་མིག་ཤེས་ལས་གཞན་དུ་མི་འཐད་པས། དེས་ན་ཐུ་རྩོལ་དེའི་རྒྱུད་ཀྱི་མིག་གི་རྣམ་པར་ཤེས་པ་དང་མཚུངས་ལྡན་གྱི་འདུ་ཤེས་དེ་ལ་གཟུགས་ཀྱི་འདུ་ཤེས་དང་། ཐོགས་པའི་འདུ་ཤེས་དང་། སྣ་ཚོགས་ཀྱི་འདུ་ཤེས་གསུམ་ཡོད
པས་ཐོགས་པའི་འདུ་ཤེས་དེས་ཕྱིར་རྩོལ་སོགས་འགྲོ་བའི་རིགས་རྟོགས་པ་འདྲ་ཡིན་སྙམ་སྟེ། རྣམ་པར་གཏན་ལ་དབབ་པ་བསྡུས་པ་ལས། དེ་ལ་སྔོན་པོ་ལ་སོགས་པའི་ཁ་དོག་འཛིན་པར་བྱེད་པ་ནི་གཟུགས་ཀྱི་འདུ་ཤེས་སོ། །
འགྲོ་བ་ཐོགས་པར་འཛིན་པར་བྱེད་པ་ནི་ཐོགས་པའི་འདུ་ཤེས་སོ། །བུད་མེད་དང་སྐྱེས་པ་དང་ཁང་ཁྱིམ་དང་ཤིང་ལ་སོགས་པ་ཐ་དད་པར་འདོགས་པར་བྱེད་པ་ནི་སྣ་ཚོགས་ཀྱི་འདུ་ཤེས་ཏེ། ཞེས་གསུངས་པའི་ཕྱིར། གལ་ཏེ་དེ་ལྟར་ཁས་ལེན་ན་ཡང
ས་རྒྱུ་ལྟ་སོགས་མིག་ཤེས་ཀྱི་སྣང་ཡུལ་ལས་གཟུང་ཡུལ་ཡིན་ཞེས་རྣམ་པ་ཀུན་ཏུ་ཁས་ལེན་མི་རུང་བས། དེས་ན་དམུས་ལོང་གི་རྒྱུད་ཀྱི་ཚ་སྲེག་སྣང་བའི་ལུས་ཤེས་ཆོས་ཅན། མེའི་གཟུགས་འཛིན་པའི་དབང་ཤེས་ཡིན་པར་ཐལ། མེའི
གཟུགས་འཛིན་པ་གང་ཞིག །དབང་ཤེས་ཡིན་པའི་ཕྱིར་ན་མ་ཁྱབ། དཔེར་ན་སྒྲ་ཡུལ་གྱི་མིག་ཤེས་ཆོས་ཅན། སྒྲ་འཛིན་དབང་ཤེས་ཡིན་པར་ཐལ། སྒྲ་འཛིན་པ་གང་ཞིག །དབང་ཤེས་ཡིན་པའི་ཕྱིར་ན་མ་ཁྱབ་ཟེར་དགོས་པ་ལྟ་བུའམ། ཡང་ན

176 ༄༅། །ཚེ་བདུན་ཡོད་ཀྱི་སྨན་སེལ་ལས། ཤེས་པ་དེས་བཟུང་བའི་ཡུལ་ཡིན་པས་གཟུང་ཡུལ་དུ་འགྱུར་དགོས་པ་ཉིད་ཡིན་ཏེ། ཞེས་གསུངས་པ་ལྟར་མེ་ཆོས་ཅན། ཐུ་རྩོལ་མཐོང་གི་མིག་ཤེས་ཀྱི་གཟུང་བྱ་ཡིན་པར་ཐལ།
མིག་ཤེས་དེས་བཟུང་བའི་ཡུལ་ཡིན་པའི་ཕྱིར་ན། མ་ཁྱབ་ཟེར་དགོས་སོ། །ཡང་རྣམ་པ་གཅིག་ཏུ་ན། མངོན་པ་མཛོད་ལས། འཇིག་རྟེན་གྱི་ནི་ཐ་སྙད་དུ། །ཁ་དོག་དབྱིབས་ལ་ས་ཞེས་བརྗོད། །ཅེས་གསུངས་པ་ལྟར། མེ་ལ་སོགས་པ
མིག་གིས་མཐོང་ཞེས་བརྗོད་མི་རིགས་ཏེ། དེ་དག་རེག་བྱ་ཡིན་པའི་ཕྱིར་ཞེ་ན། དེ་ལྟ་ཡིན་མོད་ཀྱི་འཇིག་རྟེན་གྱི་ཐ་སྙད་དུ་མེའི་ཁ་དོག་མཐོང་བ་ལ་མེ་མཐོང་ཞེས་ཐ་སྙད་བྱེད་པ་ལྟར། རྟ་དང་བ་ལང་སོགས་མིག་ཤེས་ཀྱི་གཟུང་བྱ་མིན་ཡང
དེ་དག་གི་དབྱིབས་དང་ཁ་དོག་མིག་ཤེས་ཀྱིས་མཐོང་བས་བ་ལང་སོགས་མངོན་སུམ་དུ་རྟོགས་པའི་གོ་ཆོད་དོ། མིག་ཤེས་དེས་བ་ལང་སོགས་ལ་དེས་ཤེས་འདྲེན་པའི་ཕྱིར་ཞེས་འདོད་པའམ། དེ་ལྟར་འདོད་པའི་ཚེ་ན་འང་གང་ཟག་དེས་བ
ལང་མངོན་སུམ་དུ་རྟོགས་ཀྱང་དེའི་རྒྱུད་ལ་བ་ལང་མངོན་སུམ་དུ་རྟོགས་པའི་བློ་མེད་ཟེར་བའམ། ཡང་ན་མིག་ཤེས་དེས་བ་ལང་དངོས་སུ་རྟོགས་ཀྱང་བ་ལང་དེའི་དངོས་གཞལ་མིན་ཟེར་དགོས་སམ། གང་ལྟར་ཡང་། རང་དོན་ལེའུར།
[illegible] མངོན་སུམ་ལེའུར། [illegible] གལ་ཏེ་དེ་[illegible] ཅེས་པའི་སྐབས་[illegible]

177 ཁ་ཟབ་འདོགས་པའི་ཐུས་བ་ཡང་མིག་ཤེས་ལ་སྣང་བར་བཤད་པས་ས་རྒྱུ་ལ་སོགས་པའི་གཟུགས་རགས་པ་ཅི་ལྟར་མི་སྣང་ཞེས་དོགས་སློང་གི་རྒྱུ་ལ་དུ་ལན་ལོབ་མངབ་བྱས་པ་ཡིན་པས་དབྱེད་པར་འཚལ། །
གཉིས་པ་སྤྱི་མཚན་བཤད་པར་བྱ་བ་ལ། རང་ངོས་ནས་གྲུབ་པའི་གནས་ལུགས་ཀྱི་ངོ་བོ་མ་ཡིན་པར་རྟོག་པས་བཏགས་ཙམ་དུ་གྲུབ་པ་སྤྱི་མཚན་གྱི་མཚན་ཉིད། མཚན་གཞི་ནི། ཡུལ་དུས་རང་བཞིན་འདྲེས་པར་འཛིན་པའི་རྟོག་པའི་སྣང་
ཡུལ་ཏེ་བུམ་འཛིན་རྟོག་པ་ལ་བུམ་པ་མ་ཡིན་པ་ལས་ལོག་པར་སྣང་བ་ལྟ་བུའོ། །དེ་ཆོས་ཅན། སྤྱི་མཚན་ཞེས་བྱ་སྟེ། བུམ་པ་རང་གི་ངོ་བོའི་སྟེང་ནས་རྟོག་པ་བར་ཐུབ་མེད་པར་སྤྱིའི་སྒོ་ནས་རྟོགས་པའི་མཚན་ཉིད་ཅན་ཡིན་པའི་ཕྱིར་རོ། །འདི་རི་སྤྱི་
ཞེས་པ་ནི་གསེར་བུམ་ལྟ་བུ་ཞིག་གི་སྤྲ་དོན་ལ་བྱ་ཞིང་། སྤྲ་དོན་དེ་ཡང་གང་ལ་བྱ་སྟེ་ལྟམ་ནུམ་འཛིན་རྟོག་པ་ལ་གསེར་བུམ་བུམ་པ་མ་ཡིན་པ་ལས་ལོག་པར་སྣང་བ་དེ་ལ་བྱའོ། །དེ་ཆོས་ཅན། སྤྱི་ཞེས་བྱ་སྟེ། བུམ་པའི་གསལ་བ་རྣམས་ཀྱི་
སྤྱི་ཡིན་པའི་ཕྱིར་དང་། གསེར་བུམ་ཟངས་བུམ་སོགས་ཀྱང་བྱེད་ཀྱི་བྱེ་བྲག་ཡིན་པའི་ཕྱིར་དང་། གསེར་བུམ་ཟངས་བུམ་སོགས་བུམ་འཛིན་རྟོག་པ་ལ་བུམ་པར་སྣང་བ་ཡང་ཡིན་པའི་ཕྱིར་རོ། །དེ་ལ་རྟོག་པས་སྣང་ཚུལ་དང་སྒྲས་བརྗོད་ཚུལ་
གཉིས་དགོས་པས་དེ་གཉིས་བ་བཤད་པར་བྱ་བ་ལ། དང་པོ་རྟོག་པས་སྣང་ཚུལ་ནི། དཔེར་ན་ལྷ་ཁང་ཞིག་གི་ནང་དུ་གསེར་གྱི་བུམ་པ་ཞིག་ཤེས་ཀྱིས་མཐོང་ནས། དེ་ནས་ཡུལ་གཞན་དུ་ཕྱིན་པ་ན་སྔར་གྱི་གསེར་བུམ་དེའི་དབྱིབས་དང་ཁ་དོག་

178 ཨ ༄༅། །སོགས་བློ་དོན་བཀྲལ་མ་མེ་ནར་འཆར་ཞིང་། དེ་ལྟར་ཤར་བའི་བློ་དེ་ནི་རྟོག་པ་ཡིན་གྱི་མངོན་སུམ་མ་ཡིན་ལ། རྟོག་པ་དེ་ལ་ཤར་བའི་སྣང་བ་དེ་ཡང་གསེར་བུམ་གྱི་དོན་སྤྱི་ཡིན་གྱི་གསེར་བུམ་དངོས་མ་ཡིན་ནོ། །གལ་ཏེ
ཡིན་ན་སྔར་གྱི་གསེར་བུམ་དེ་ཉིད་ཞིག་ནས་བཅོམ་ནས་གཟུགས་གཞན་དུ་བསྒྱུར་ཡོད་ནའང་དེ་ཉིད་ཇི་བཞིན་སྣང་དགོས་པ་ལས་དེ་མི་སྣང་བའི་ཕྱིར་རོ། །ཡང་ན་རྟོག་པ་ལ་སྣང་བ་དེ་བུམ་པ་དངོས་ཡིན་ན། སྣང་བ་དེས་ཆུ་སྐྱོར་བ་ལ་སོགས་པའི་དོན
བྱེད་ནུས་པར་འགྱུར་ལ། དེ་ལྟ་ན་བུམ་འཛིན་རྟོག་པ་གར་ཡོད་དུ་བུམ་པ་ཡོད་པར་འགྱུར་བས་སུས་ཀྱང་བུམ་པ་བསལ་འཚོལ་བར་མི་འགྱུར་རོ། །དེས་ན་རྟོག་པ་དེ་སྣང་ཡུལ་ལ་འཁྲུལ་བ་ཡིན་ཏེ། རང་ལ་གསེར་བུམ་བུམ་པར་སྣང་བ་དེ་བུམ་པ
མ་ཡིན་པ་བཞིན་དུ་བུམ་པར་སྣང་བ་ཡིན་པའི་ཕྱིར། ཞེན་ཡུལ་ལ་མ་འཁྲུལ་བ་ཡིན་ཏེ། རྟོག་པ་དེའི་འཛིན་སྟངས་ལ་གསེར་བུམ་བུམ་པའི་ལྟ་མ་དུ་ཞེན་པ་ཡོད་ཀྱི་སྣང་བ་དེ་ཉིད་བུམ་པའི་ལྟ་མ་དུ་ཞེན་པ་མེད་པའི་ཕྱིར། དཔེར་ན་མི་ཞིག
གིས་རང་གི་བཞིན་ལ་དྲི་མ་ཡོད་མེད་རྟོགས་འདོད་ནས་མེ་ལོང་ལ་བལྟས་པའི་ཚེ། མེ་ལོང་ནང་གི་གཟུགས་བརྙན་དེ་ཉིད་རང་གི་ངོ་བཞིན་དུ་སྣང་ཞིང་། སྣང་བ་དེ་ལ་བརྟེན་ནས་རང་གི་བཞིན་ཉིད་རྟོགས་པར་འགྱུར་གྱི་གཟུགས་བརྙན་དེ
ཉིད་རང་གི་བཞིན་ཡིན་ནོ་སྙམ་དུ་ཞེན་པ་མེད་པ་ལྟར། བུམ་འཛིན་རྟོག་པ་དེས་བུམ་པའི་གཟུགས་བརྙན་སྣང་བའི་སྒོ་ནས་བུམ་པ་ལ་ཞེན་པར་བྱེད་ཀྱི་བུམ་པའི་གཟུགས་བརྙན་དེ་ཉིད་དུ་བུམ་པ་ཡིན་པར་ཞེན་པ་མེད་པའི་ཕྱིར་རོ། །དེ་ལྟར

179 གོ་དེ་ནི་བུམ་འཛིན་རྟོག་པས་བུམ་པ་དངོས་སུ་མ་ཟིན་ནི་པར་བུམ་པའི་དོན་སྤྱི་དངོས་སུ་ཟིན་ཅིང་། བུམ་པ་ཞེས་བརྗོད་པའི་སྒྲས་ཀྱང་བུམ་པ་དངོས་སུ་མ་བརྗོད་པར་བུམ་པའི་སྒྲ་སྤྱི་དངོས་སུ་བརྗོད་པ་ཡིན་མོད། འོན་ཀྱང་དེ་དག་ལ་བརྟེན
ནས་བུམ་པ་དང་མཚན་བལྟོས་མེད་དུ་ཐོབ་པའི་རྒྱུ་མཚན་གྱིས་བུམ་འཛིན་རྟོག་པས་བུམ་པ་དངོས་སུ་རྟོགས་པ་དང་བུམ་པ་ཞེས་བརྗོད་པའི་སྒྲས་བུམ་པ་དངོས་སུ་བརྗོད་པར་ཁས་ལེན་དགོས་ཏེ། དེ་ལྟ་མ་ཡིན་ན་རང་མཚན་ཡིན་ན་རྟོག་པའི་ཤུགས་ཡུལ
ཡིན་དང་བསྟན་བཅོས་ཀྱི་ཤུགས་བསྟན་ཡིན་པས་ཁྱབ་ལེན་དགོས་པར་འགྱུར་རོ། །བུམ་འཛིན་རྟོག་པས་བུམ་པ་དངོས་སུ་རྟོགས་པའི་རྒྱུ་མཚན་མཐར་ཐུག་པ་ནི། དང་པོར་བུམ་འཛིན་ནི་དེ་ལུས་སྐྱེ་བ་ན་བུམ་པར་ཞེན་པའི་བག་ཆགས་བཞག
ཅིང་། བག་ཆགས་དེ་སྨིན་པ་ན་གསེར་བུམ་ལ་སོགས་པ་བུམ་པར་འཛིན་པའི་རྟོག་པ་སྐྱེ་ཞིང་། རྟོག་པ་དེས་གསེར་བུམ་བུམ་པ་མ་ཡིན་པ་ལས་ལོག་པར་སྣང་བ་ལ་བརྟེན་ནས་བུམ་པ་རང་མཚན་པ་ཐོབ་པའི་འབྲས་བུ་ཅན་ཡིན་པས།
དོན་ན་རྟོག་པ་དེ་མཐུན་བཅས་ཆེར་མཐར་མངོན་སུམ་ལ་ཐུག་པ་ཡིན་ཏེ། ནམ་མཁའ་འཛིན་པའི་རྟོག་པ་ཡང་ཐོགས་པའི་རེག་བྱ་འཛིན་པའི་མངོན་སུམ་ལ་ཐུག་པ་ཡིན་པའི་ཕྱིར་རོ། །ཁ་ཅིག་གིས། རྟོག་པ་ཡིན་ན་སྣང་ཡུལ་ལ་འཁྲུལ
བས་མ་ཁྱབ་པར་ཐལ། ཤེས་བྱ་འཛིན་པའི་རྟོག་པས་ཤེས་བྱའི་དོན་སྤྱི་ཤེས་བྱ་ཡིན་པར་སྣང་བ་གང་ཞིག ཤེས་བྱའི་དོན་སྤྱི་ཤེས་བྱ་ཡིན་པའི་ཕྱིར་ཟེར་ན། མ་ཁྱབ་སྟེ། དེ་ཙམ་གྱིས་དེ་ལྟ་བུ་རྟོག་པ་དེས་སྣང་ཡུལ་ལ་མ་འཁྲུལ་བ་ཡིན་པར

180 ཨ ༄༅། །སྒྲུབ་མི་ནུས་པའི་ཕྱིར་ཏེ། རྟོག་པ་ལ་ཡུལ་དེའི་དོན་སྤྱི་སྣང་བ་ནི་དོན་སྤྱི་དེ་ཉིད་དོན་དེ་ཡི་ངོ་བོ་ལྟ་བུར་སྣང་བ་དང་། དོན་སྤྱི་དོན་དེ་དང་གཅིག་ལྟ་བུར་སྣང་བ་དང་། དོན་སྤྱི་དོན་དེ་མ་ཡིན་པ་ལས་ལོག་པ་ལྟ་བུར་སྣང་བ
གསུམ་ཡོད་པ་གང་ཞིག ཤེས་བྱ་འཛིན་པའི་རྟོག་པ་ལ་ཤེས་བྱའི་དོན་སྤྱི་ཤེས་བྱ་དང་གཅིག་ཏུ་སྣང་བ་དེ་ཡོད་པས་རྟོག་ །དེ་སྣང་ཡུལ་ལ་འཁྲུལ་པ་ཡིན་པའི་ཕྱིར། དང་པོ་ཡིན་ཏེ། རྣམ་འགྲེལ་ལས། དེ་ལ་ངོ་བོ་ཕྱི་རོལ་དང་། །གཅིག
ལྟ་གཞན་ལས་ལོག་ལྟ་བུར། །སྣང་བ་གང་ཡིན་བཏག་པ་ཡི། །ཡན་ལག་མེད་ཕྱིར་དེ་ཉིད་མིན། །ཞེས་གསུངས་པའི་ཕྱིར། དེས་ན་རྟོག་པ་ཡིན་ན་དོན་སྤྱི་དོན་དུ་འཁྲུལ་བས་མ་ཁྱབ་ཀྱང་དོན་སྤྱི་དོན་དང་གཅིག་ཏུ་འཁྲུལ་བས་ཁྱབ་བོ་ ... ན
ཤེགས་པར་མངོན་ནོ། །འོ་ན་སྒྲ་མི་རྟག་པར་རྟོགས་པའི་རྗེས་དཔག་དང་། སྒྲ་རྟག་པར་འཛིན་པའི་སྒྲོ་འདོགས་གཉིས་ལ་བསླུ་མི་བསླུའི་ཁྱད་པར་མེད་པར་ཐལ། དེ་གཉིས་ཀ་འཁྲུལ་ཤེས་སུ་ཁྱད་པར་མེད་པའི་ཕྱིར་ཞེ་ན། དེ
གཉིས་འཁྲུལ་ཤེས་སུ་འདྲ་ཡང་རྗེས་དཔག་ལས་འཇུག་ཡུལ་ཐོབ་ནུས་ཤིང་། སྒྲོ་འདོགས་ལས་འཇུག་ཡུལ་ཐོབ་མི་ནུས་པའི་ཕྱིར། དཔེར་ན་ནོར་བུའི་འོད་ལ་ནོར་བུར་འཛིན་པ་དང་མར་མེའི་འོད་ལ་ནོར་བུར་འཛིན་པ་གཉིས་འཁྲུལ
བར་འདྲ་ཡང་ནོར་བུའི་འོད་ལས་ནོར་བུ་ཐོབ་ནུས་ཤིང་། མར་མེའི་འོད་ལས་ནོར་བུ་ཐོབ་མི་ནུས་པ་བཞིན་ཡིན་པའི་ཕྱིར། དེ་ཉིད་ལས། རྗེས་དཔག་དེ་སྐད་བཤད་དེ་བཞིན། །འཁྲུལ་བར་འདྲ་ཡང་གཞན་ལྟ་མིན། །མར་མེའི་འོད

181 ལས་ཅེར་བུ་བཞིན། །ཞེས་གསུངས་པའི་ཕྱིར། སྣ་ཚོགས་སེལ་བ་ལས་འཇུག་ཚུལ་འདི་ལེགས་པར་ཤེས་དགོས་ཏེ། ཏིཀ་ཆེན་ལས། བུམ་པ་ཞེས་བརྗོད་པའི་སྒྲའི་དངོས་ཀྱི་བརྗོད་བྱ་རྫས་སུམ་གྲུབ་ཀྱང་། དེས་དངོས་སུ་བརྗོད་པ་ཡིན་ན་རྫས་སུམ་
གྲུབ་མི་དགོས་པའི་ཚུལ་འདི་ནི། ཕྱི་བདུན་གྱི་ཐུན་མོང་མ་ཡིན་པའི་ཁྱད་ཆོས་ཡིན་པར་ཤེས་པར་བྱ་ལ། ཞེས་གསུངས་པའི་ཕྱིར། ཐུན་མོང་མ་ཡིན་པའི་ཁྱད་ཆོས་ཞེས་པ་སྡེ་བདུན་མ་རྟོགས་གཞུང་གཞན་གང་ལས་ཀྱང་མ་བྱུང་བའི་དོན་
ནོ། །དེས་ན་བུམ་འཛིན་མངོན་སུམ་སྒྲུབ་འཇུག་ཡིན་ནས་བུམ་པ་མ་ཡིན་པ་རྣམས་པར་བཅད་པ་ཙམ་གྱི་སྒོ་ནས་མ་གཞལ་བར་བུམ་པའི་རྣམ་པ་དེ་བཞིན་གཏད་པའི་སྒོ་ནས་གཞལ་ལ། བུམ་འཛིན་རྟོག་པ་སེལ་འཇུག་ཡིན་པས་བུམ་པའི་
རྣམ་པ་དེ་ལྟ་བ་གཏད་པའི་སྒོ་ནས་མ་གཞལ་བར་བུམ་པ་མ་ཡིན་པ་ལས་ལོག་པར་སྣང་བ་ཙམ་གྱིས་བུམ་མིན་རྣམ་པར་བཅད་པའི་སྒྲོ་བཏགས་པ་འབའ་ཞིག་གཞལ་བ་ཡིན་པས། རྟོག་པ་དེ་ལ་བུམ་པ་དངོས་སུ་དེས་ཡུལ་དུ་སོང་ཡང་སྣང་
ཡུལ་དུ་མ་ཐུར་ལ། བུམ་པའི་དོན་སྤྱི་སྣང་ཡུལ་དུ་སོང་ཡང་དེས་ཡུལ་དུ་མ་ཐུར་བ་ཡིན་ནོ། །དེ་ལྟར་རྟོག་པས་སྣང་བཏགས་གཉིས་གཅིག་ཏུ་བསྲེས་ནས་སྒྲོ་བཏགས་པའི་ཆོས་སྣང་ཡུལ་དུ་བྱས་པའི་རྒྱུ་མཚན་གྱིས། གྲངས་ཅན་པའི་འདོད་པ་
འགོག་པའི་སྐབས་སུ་སྤྱི་གཙོ་བོ་ཆོས་ཅན། རྣམ་འགྱུར་སྣ་ཚོགས་ཀྱི་ཉེར་ལེན་དུ་མེད་དེ། རྣམ་འགྱུར་སྣ་ཚོགས་ཀྱི་ཉེར་ལེན་དུ་མ་དམིགས་པའི་ཕྱིར་ཞེས་ཚིག་ཟིན་ལ་གཙོ་བོ་ཉིད་ཆོས་ཅན་དུ་བཀོད་ན་འང་། ཕྱི་རོལ་དེས་གཙོ་བོ་དང་དེ་འཛིན་པའི་

182 ཨ། ཨཱུཾ། ཧཱུྃ། ཧྲཱིཿ
༄༅། །རྟོག་པ་ལ་གཙོ་བོར་སྣང་བ་གཉིས་གཅིག་ཏུ་བསྲེས་ནས་ཞེན་འདོད་ཞུགས་པའི་རྒྱུ་མཚན་གྱིས་གཙོ་བོ་ནི་དོན་སྤྱི་ཆོས་ཅན་དུ་སོང་བའི་གནད་ཀྱང་དེ་ཡིན་ནོ། །འོན་ཀྱང་སྒྲུབ་བྱེད་འདིའི་ཤེས་འདོད་ཆོས་ཅན་ཡོད་
ཀྱང་ཕྱོགས་ཆོས་ནི་ཤེས་འདོད་ཆོས་ཅན་ཡིན་ན་ཡོད་པས་མ་ཁྱབ་བོ། །འདི་ལ་སྤྱི་ཁྱབ་མང་ཡང་རེ་ཞིག་བཞག་གོ །གཉིས་པ་སྒྲས་བརྗོད་ཚུལ་བཤད་པ་ལ། བུམ་པ་ཞེས་བརྗོད་པའི་སྒྲ་བུམ་པའི་མིང་དུ་ཐ་སྙད་དང་བརྡའ་
གསུམ་ག་ཡིན་པས་དེ་གསུམ་མི་འགལ་ལ་ཡང་། དགོས་པའི་དབང་གིས་ཕྱོགས་རྣམས་སོ་སོར་ཕྱེ་ན། དགོས་པ་གང་གི་ཕྱིར་ཞེ་ན། བུམ་པ་ཞེས་བརྗོད་པའི་སྒྲ་ཆོས་ཅན། མིང་ཞེས་བྱ་སྟེ། དོན་ལྡོག་ལྡོག་པ་ལ་ཐོག་མར་འཇོག་པར་བྱེད་པ་འམ་
གྲོད་པར་བྱེད་པའི་ཕྱིར། དེ་ཆོས་ཅན། ཐ་སྙད་ཞེས་བྱ་སྟེ། ལྡོག་ལྡོག་པ་དེ་རྒྱུད་གཞན་གྱི་དོན་བྱེད་ནུས་པ་ཡིན་པས་རྒྱུ་ལྡོག་པ་ལ་མ་ལོ་ཞིང་། གདུང་མ་འདོགས་པ་ལ་མི་མཐོ་བར་ཤེས་པའི་ཆེད་ཡིན་པའི་ཕྱིར། དེ་ཆོས་ཅན། བརྡའ་ཞེས་བྱ་སྟེ།
ལྡོག་ལྡོག་པ་བུམ་པ་ཡིན་པར་ཐ་སྙད་སྦྱོར་ཤེས་པའི་ཆེད་དུ་འདོད་པས་སྦྱར་བ་ཡིན་པའི་ཕྱིར། དེ་ལྟར་ལྡོག་ལྡོག་པ་ལ་བུམ་པའོ་ཞེས་བརྡ་སྦྱར་བ་ལ་བརྟེན་ནས་ལྡོག་ལྡོག་པ་འདི་ནི་བུམ་པའོ་སྙམ་དུ་ཐ་སྙད་ཐོགས་ཤེས་པ་འབྱུང་ཞིང་དེ་ལ་
བུམ་པའི་མིང་དོན་གྱི་འབྲེལ་བ་དེས་པ་ཞེས་བྱ་བ་ཡང་ཡིན་པས། དེས་ན་མིང་སྦྱོར་རྟོག་པ་ཡིན་ན་བརྡ་དུས་སུ་སྦྱར་བའི་མིང་དེ་དང་། ཕྱིས་ཐ་སྙད་དུས་སུ་མཐོང་བའི་དོན་གཉིས་གཅིག་ཏུ་བསྲེ་བར་བྱེད་པའི་བདག་ཉིད་ཅན་ཡིན་

83 དགོས་སོ། །ཕྱི་རྒྱ་ནི་གོ་བ་བརྡའ་ལ་ལྟོས་ཤིང་བརྡའ་ནི་དོན་གྱི་དབང་ལ་ཡང་སྦྱོར་རུང་སྟེ། དཔེར་ན་ཀ་ཡི་ཞེས་བརྗོད་པ་ན། ཡུལ་དབུས་པ་དག་གིས་དུས་བརྗོད་པར་གོ་ལ། ཡུལ་འགྲོ་ལྡིང་བ་དག་གིས་སྔོན་པ་བརྗོད་པར་གོ་ཡང་བྱེད་ས་སུ
དབུས་པ་དག་གིས་དུས་བརྗོད་པར་མཐོང་བ་ན་ཕྱར་གྱི་གོ་བ་དེ་ལོག་ནས་དུས་བརྗོད་པར་ཡང་གོ་བའི་ཕྱིར། རྗོད་བྱེད་ཀྱི་སྒྲ་རྣམས་འདོད་པ་ཙམ་གྱིས་འཇུག་པ་ཡིན་ནོ། །དེའི་ཕྱིར་བུམ་པ་ཞེས་བརྗོད་པའི་སྒྲ་དེ་ལ་འདོད་རྒྱལ་གྱི་སྒྲ་ཞེས་བྱ་སྟེ།
ཐོག་མར་བརྡའ་སྦྱོར་བ་པོས་འདོད་པའི་དབང་གིས་རང་གར་ལྟོ་ལྡིར་བ་ལ་བུམ་པ་ཞེས་བརྡའ་སྦྱར་ཞིང་དེ་ལ་བརྟེན་ནས་བུམ་པ་ཞེས་པ་ལྟོ་ལྡིར་བའི་དངོས་མིང་དུ་རྒྱལ་ཞིང་། ཕྱིས་སུ་གཞན་དག་གིས་མིང་གཞན་བཏགས་ཀྱང་དེའི་དངོས་མིང་
དུ་གྲགས་ན་གྲུབ་པ་ཡིན་པའི་ཕྱིར་རོ། །དེ་ལྟར་བུམ་པ་ཞེས་པའི་སྒྲ་བརྗོད་འདོད་ཀྱིས་ཐོག་མར་བརྡར་སྦྱར་བའི་དབང་གིས་ལྟོ་ལྡིར་བའི་དངོས་མིང་དུ་གྲགས་ཤིང་། གཞན་གྱི་དངོས་མིང་དུ་གྲགས་མ་གྲུབ་པའི་དབང་གིས་བུམ་པ་ཞེས་
པའི་སྒྲ་ལྟོ་ལྡིར་བའི་དངོས་མིང་དུ་ལས་ཀྱི་གཞན་གྱི་དངོས་མིང་མ་ཡིན་ནོ། །འོན་ཀྱང་བུམ་པའི་སྒྲ་དེ་ལྟོ་ལྡིར་བ་ལས་གཞན་ལ་སྦྱར་དུ་མི་རུང་བ་མ་ཡིན་ཏེ། སྣམ་བུ་ལ་ཡང་བུམ་པའོ་ཞེས་མིང་སྦྱར་ན་ཡང་བར་སྐབས་སུ་གོ་ནུས་པའི་དབང་
གིས་སྣམ་བུ་ལ་བུམ་པའི་དོན་སྤྱི་ཡང་འཆར་རུང་བའི་ཕྱིར། དེའི་ཕྱིར་བུམ་པ་ཞེས་པ་ལྟོ་ལྡིར་བའི་སྟེང་དུ་དངོས་དབང་གིས་མ་གྲུབ་པ་ཡིན་ནོ། །མདོར་ན་རྟོག་པའི་སྣང་ཡུལ་གང་ཡིན་རྗོད་བྱེད་གང་གིས་ཀྱང་བརྗོད་དུ་རུང་བས་གྲགས

184 ཨ། ཨཱུཾ། ཧཱུྃ། ཧྲཱིཿ
༄༅། །རྟགས་ཡང་དག་འབད་མེད་དུ་འགྲུབ་བོ། །ཕྱིར་བརྡའ་དང་ཐ་སྙད་དོན་གཅིག །ཐ་སྙད་དེ་ལ་གསུམ་ཡོད་དེ། བུམ་པའོ་སྙམ་པ་ལྟ་བུ་བློའི་ཐ་སྙད་དང་། བུམ་པ་ཞེས་བརྗོད་པ་ལྟ་བུ་ངག་གི་ཐ་སྙད་དང་། བུམ་པ་ཡིན་
པར་ལག་པ་སོགས་ཀྱིས་བརྡའ་བྱས་པ་ལྟ་བུ་ལུས་ཀྱི་ཐ་སྙད་དང་གསུམ་ཡོད་པའི་ཕྱིར། ཕྱི་དང་གཞི་མཐུན་གྱི་ཐ་སྙད་སྦྱོར་ཚུལ་ལ། གྲངས་ཅན་པས་ཀྱི་གཙོ་བོ་ཆ་མེད་པའི་རྟག་དངོས་ཞེས་པ་གཅིག་གསལ་བ་རྣམས་ཀྱི་སྤྱིར་འདོད་ཅིང་།
གསལ་བ་རྣམས་གནས་སྐབས་ཐ་དད་ཀྱང་སྤྱི་གཙོ་བོའི་ངང་དུ་རང་བཞིན་གཅིག་པས་སྤྱི་གསལ་གཉིས་རྫས་གཅིག་ཏུ་འདོད་ལ། བྱེ་བྲག་པས་དེ་གཉིས་རྫས་ཐ་དད་དུ་འདོད་དོ། །རང་ལུགས་ལ། དེ་གཉིས་རྫས་གཅིག་དང་ཐ་དད་
གང་ཡང་མ་ཡིན་ཏེ། དེ་གཉིས་དངོས་པོ་མ་ཡིན་པའི་ཕྱིར། བུམ་པ་མ་ཡིན་པ་ལས་ལོག་པ་ལྟ་བུ་དངོས་པོ་ཡིན་པའི་སྤྱི་ཡོད་ཀྱང་། སྤྱི་ལ་བརྡའ་སྦྱར་བས་གསལ་བ་མཐའ་དག་གོ་བར་འགྱུར་བའི་ཕྱིར་དེ་ལ་རྟོག་པའི་སྣང་ཡུལ་གཙོ་
ཆེ་ཞིང་། དེ་ཡང་གསེར་གྱི་ལྟོ་ལྡིར་བ་འདི་ནི་བུམ་པའོ་ཞེས་བརྡའ་སྦྱར་བའི་ཚེ་བུམ་འཛིན་རྟོག་པ་ལ་བུམ་པ་མ་ཡིན་པ་ལས་ལོག་པར་སྣང་བ་དེ་ལ་བུམ་པའི་བརྡའ་སྦྱར་བ་ཡིན་པས། དེའི་ཚེ་ཉན་པ་པོའི་རྒྱུད་ལ་གསེར་གྱི་ལྟོ་ལྡིར་བ་དེ་
ཉིད་བུམ་པ་ཡིན་པར་མཚོན་པའི་སྣང་བ་སྐྱེད་ནུས་ཤིང་། སྣང་བ་དེ་ལ་བུམ་པའི་མཚན་མ་ཞེས་བྱ་བ་ཡིན་པས་མཚན་མ་དེ་ལ་བརྟེན་ནས་གསེར་གྱི་ལྟོ་ལྡིར་བ་དེ་ནི་བུམ་པའོ་ཞེས་མིང་དང་མིང་ཅན་འབྲེལ་བར་ཤེས་པའི་སྒོ་ནས་གསེར་གྱི་ལྟོ་

185 ཕྱིར་བ་དེ་ཉིད་བུམ་པ་ཡིན་པར་ཐ་སྙད་འདོགས་ཤེས་པ་བསྐྱེད་ཅིང་། དེ་ལ་བུམ་པ་རྟོགས་པ་ཡིན་ནེར་རོ། །དེའི་ཕྱིར་ཐེ་བྲག་སྒྲ་བས་སྒྲ་མིང་ལ་འཇུག་མིང་མཚན་མ་ལ་འཇུག་མཚན་མ་ལས་དོན་རྟོགས་པར་འདོད་པའི་དོན་ཡང་དེ
ཡིན་ནོ། །མདོར་ན་བུམ་པ་ཞེས་བརྗོད་པའི་སྒྲས་བུམ་པ་རང་མཚན་པ་དངོས་སུ་བརྗོད་མི་ནུས་པར་བུམ་པའི་སྒྲ་སྤྱི་དངོས་སུ་བརྗོད་ཅིང་། སྒྲ་སྤྱི་བརྗོད་པ་དེ་ཡིས་བུམ་པའི་མིང་བརྗོད་པ་ཡིན་པས་མིང་དེ་ལ་བརྟེན་ནས་སྤྱི་ཕྱིར་བ་བུམ་པ
ཡིན་པར་མངོན་ནས་བུམ་པ་རྟོགས་པ་ཡིན་ནོ། །འོ་ན་བུམ་པ་ཞེས་བརྗོད་པའི་སྒྲས་བུམ་པ་རང་མཚན་པ་དངོས་སུ་བརྗོད་མི་ནུས་པའི་རྒྱུ་མཚན་ཅི་ཡིན་ཞེ་ན། བུམ་པ་རང་མཚན་པ་ཞེས་པའི་བུམ་འཛིན་མངོན་སུམ་ལ་སྣང་བ་ལྟར་གྱི་བུམ
པའི་དབྱིབས་དང་ཁ་དོག་ལ་སོགས་ད་ལྟར་བ་དེ་ཡིན་ལ། དེ་ཉིད་སྒྲ་སྒྲས་བརྗོད་པའི་དུས་སུ་སྔར་གྱི་དབྱིབས་དང་ཁ་དོག་འགགས་ནས་མེད་པའི་ཕྱིར་དེ་དེ་ལྟ་བཞིན་བརྗོད་པར་ག་ལ་ནུས། གལ་ཏེ་ནུས་ན་བུམ་འཛིན་མངོན་སུམ་ལ་བུམ་པ
སྣང་དུས་ན་བུམ་པའི་མི་རྟག་པ་ཡང་སྣང་བ་ཡིན་པས་དེ་ཡང་དངོས་བརྗོད་པར་འགྱུར་ལ། དེ་ལྟར་ན་བུམ་པའི་སྒྲ་སྒྲུབ་འཇུག་ཏུ་འགྱུར་རོ། །གྲངས་ཅན་པས་རྗོད་བྱེད་ཀྱི་སྒྲ་རྣམས་སྒྲུབ་འཇུག་ཏུ་འདོད་པ་ཡིན་པས་བུམ་པ་ཞེས་བརྗོད་པའི
སྒྲས་བུམ་པ་མི་རྟག་པར་ཡང་བརྗོད་པར་འདོད་ཅིང་། དེ་བཞིན་དུ་བྱས་པ་དང་མི་རྟག་པ་གཉིས་རྫས་གཅིག་ཡིན་པས་བྱས་པ་ཞེས་པའི་སྒྲས་མི་རྟག་པ་ཡང་བརྗོད་ནེར་རོ། །ཕྱིར་བྱས་པའི་རྫས་ལས་ལོགས་སུ་མི་རྟག་པ་དང་མི་རྟག་པའི

ཚ ཚད་མ། བརྒྱ་དྲུག

186 ༄༅། །རྫས་ལས་ལོགས་སུ་བྱས་པ་འཛིན་རྒྱུ་མེད་པས་དེ་གཉིས་རྫས་གཅིག་ཏུ་རང་གཞན་གཉིས་ཀས་འདོད་དོ། །དེ་ལ་གྲངས་ཅན་པས་ཁྱེད་ཅག་གིས་དེད་ལ་སྒྲ་མི་རྟག་པར་སྒྲུབ་པའི་ཚེ་རྟགས་སུ་བཀོད
པའི་བྱས་པ་དེ་མི་རྟག་པའི་རྫས་སུ་གྱུར་པའི་བྱས་པ་ཡིན་ནམ། འོན་ཏེ་རྟོག་པས་བཏགས་པ་ཙམ་གྱི་བྱས་པ་ཡིན། ཕྱི་མ་ལྟར་ན་རྟགས་དེ་མ་གྲུབ་པའི་རྟགས་སུ་འགྱུར་ལ། དང་པོ་ལྟར་ན་སྒྲ་ཆོས་ཅན་མི་རྟག་སྟེ་བྱས་པའི་ཕྱིར
ཞེས་བཀོད་པ་ན་བྱས་པའི་ཕྱིར་ཞེས་པའི་ཚིག་དེས་ཀྱང་མི་རྟག་པ་བརྗོད་པ་ཡིན་པས། དེས་ན་དམ་བཅའ་བའི་ཕྱོགས་གཅིག་རྟགས་སུ་བཀོད་པར་འགྱུར་རོ་ཞེ་ན། དོགས་པ་དེ་ནི་སྒྲ་རྟོག་སྒྲུབ་འཇུག་ཏུ་འདོད་པའི་དབང་གིས་བྱུང་བ
ཡིན་པས། རང་ལུགས་ལ་སྒྲ་རྟོག་སེལ་འཇུག་ཡིན་པའི་རྒྱུ་མཚན་གྱིས་ངོ་བོ་གཅིག་ལ་ལྡོག་པ་ཐ་དད་པའི་རྣམ་གཞག་སེལ་དོན་འཛིན་པའི་ཚུལ་ལེགས་པར་སྒྲུབ་པའི་སྒོ་ནས་ལན་གདབ་དགོས་པས་དེའི་ཚུལ་ནི་འདི་ལྟ་སྟེ།
དཔེར་ན་བྱས་པ་ཞེས་པའི་སྒྲས་མ་བྱས་པ་སེལ་ནས་བྱས་པ་ཡིན་པར་བརྗོད། དེ་འཛིན་པའི་རྟོག་པས་བྱས་པ་མ་ཡིན་པ་ལས་ལོག་པར་སྣང་བའི་ཕྱིར་བྱས་པ་མ་ཡིན་པ་སེལ་ནས་བྱས་པ་ཡིན་པར་སྣང་བ་ཡིན་པས་སྒྲ་རྟོག་གཉིས
ལ་སེལ་བས་འཇུག་པ་ཞེས་བྱའོ། །དེའི་ཕྱིར་བྱས་པ་ཞེས་པའི་སྒྲས་བྱས་པ་མ་ཡིན་པ་ལས་ལོག་པར་བརྗོད་ཀྱང་མི་རྟག་པ་མ་ཡིན་པ་ལས་ལོག་པར་མ་བརྗོད། མི་རྟག་པ་ཞེས་བརྗོད་པའི་སྒྲས་ཀྱང་མི་རྟག་པ་མ་ཡིན་པ་ལས

187 ལོག་པར་བརྗོད་ཀྱང་བྱས་པ་མ་ཡིན་པ་ལས་ལོག་པར་མ་བརྗོད་པའི་ཕྱིར་བྱས་པ་མ་ཡིན་པ་ལས་ལོག་པ་དང་མི་རྟག་པ་མ་ཡིན་པ་ལས་ལོག་པ་གཉིས་སྒྲས་བརྗོད་ཚུལ་ལ་ལྟོས་ཏེ་ཐ་དད་དུ་གྲུབ་པས་ན་བྱས་པ་དང་མི་རྟག་པ་གཉིས་ལྡོག་པ
ཐ་དད་ཅེས་པའི་དོན་དེ་ཡིན་ནོ། །འོན་ཀྱང་བྱས་པའི་ངོ་བོ་གང་ཡིན་པ་དེ་ཉིད་མི་རྟག་པའི་ངོ་བོ་ཡང་ཡིན་ལ། མི་རྟག་པའི་ངོ་བོ་གང་ཡིན་པ་དེ་ཉིད་བྱས་པའི་ངོ་བོ་ཡང་ཡིན་པའི་ཕྱིར་བྱས་པ་དང་མི་རྟག་པ་གཉིས་ངོ་བོ་གཅིག་ཡིན་ཡང་། བྱས་པ་ཞེས
པའི་སྒྲས་མི་རྟག་པ་དངོས་སུ་མ་བརྗོད། མི་རྟག་པ་ཞེས་པའི་སྒྲས་ཀྱང་བྱས་པ་དངོས་སུ་མ་བརྗོད། སྒྲ་དེའི་རྗེས་སུ་འབྲངས་པའི་རྟོག་པས་ཀྱང་གཅིག་གི་ཡུལ་དུ་གྱུར་པ་ཅིག་ཤེས་ཀྱིས་དངོས་སུ་མི་འཛིན་པའི་ཕྱིར་རོ། །དེས་ན་བྱས་པ་ཞེས
བརྗོད་པ་ན་ཕ་རོལ་པོས་བྱས་པ་ཙམ་ཞིག་གོ་ཡི་མི་རྟག་པ་མི་གོ་བའི་ཕྱིར་བྱས་མི་རྟག་གཉིས་ལྡོག་པ་ཐ་དད་ཀྱང་ངོ་བོ་གཅིག ..... པའི་ཚུལ་འདི་གྲངས་ཅན་པས་རྟོག་དཀའ་བ་ཡིན་ནོ། །དེའི་ཕྱིར་སྒྲ་ཆོས་ཅན། མི་རྟག་སྟེ། བྱས་པའི
ཕྱིར་ཞེས་འགོད་པའི་ཚེ་རྟགས་སུ་སོང་བའི་བྱས་པ་དང་བསྒྲུབ་བྱའི་ཆོས་སུ་སོང་བའི་མི་རྟག་པ་གཉིས་ངོ་བོ་གཅིག་ཡིན་ཡང་། རྟགས་བྱས་པ་བརྗོད་པའི་སྒྲས་བསྒྲུབ་བྱའི་ཆོས་མི་རྟག་པ་མ་བརྗོད་པའི་ཕྱིར་དམ་བཅའ་བའི་ཕྱོགས
གཅིག་སྟེ་མི་རྟག་པ་རྟགས་སུ་འགོད་པར་ཐལ་བའི་སྐྱོན་མེད་དོ། །དེ་བཞིན་དུ་གཞི་མཐུན་དུ་འཇོག་པ་ཡང་སྒྲ་རྟོག་གི་སེལ་དོན་འཛིན་པ་ཡིན་ཏེ། དཔེར་ན་མེ་ཏོག་གཅིག་ཨུཏྤལ་དང་སྔོན་པོ་གཉིས་ཀ་ཡིན་པར་བརྗོད་འདོད་ནས་མེ་ཏོག་དེ

ཚ ཚད་མ། བརྒྱ་བརྒྱད

188 ༄༅། །ཞི་ཨུཏྤལ་སྔོན་པོ་ཞེས་བརྗོད་པའི་ཚེ་ན། མེ་ཏོག་གཅིག་པུ་དེའི་སྟེང་དུ་ཨུཏྤལ་མ་ཡིན་པའི་སྔོན་པོ་དང་སྔོན་པོ་མ་ཡིན་པའི་ཨུཏྤལ་རྫས་ཐ་དད་པ་གཉིས་མེད་ཀྱང་། ཨུཏྤལ་སྔོན་པོ་ཞེས་པའི་སྒྲའི་གདངས
ལ་ཨུཏྤལ་དང་སྔོན་པོ་གཉིས་རིམ་གྱིས་ཐོས་པ་ལྟར། ཉན་པ་པོའི་རྒྱུད་ལ་ཨུཏྤལ་དང་སྔོན་པོ་གཉིས་ཐ་དད་དུ་སྣང་བའི་རྟོག་པ་སྐྱེ་ཞིང་། སྣང་བ་དེ་ལ་བརྟེན་ནས་མེ་ཏོག་གཅིག་པུ་དེ་ཉིད་ཨུཏྤལ་དང་སྔོན་པོའི་གཞི་མཐུན་ཡིན་པར་གོ
བའི་ཕྱིར། དེ་ལྟར་གོ་བའི་རྒྱུ་མཚན་ཡོད་དེ། དེའི་ཚེ་ཉན་པ་པོའི་རྒྱུད་ཀྱི་རྟོག་པ་དེ་ལ་ཨུཏྤལ་མ་ཡིན་པ་ལས་ལོག་པ་དང་སྔོན་པོ་མ་ཡིན་པ་ལས་ལོག་པ་གཉིས་ཚོགས་སྣང་བའི་རྒྱུ་མཚན་གྱིས་ཡིན་པའི་ཕྱིར། དེའི་ཕྱིར་རྟོག་པ་ལ་ལྡོག
པ་གཉིས་ཚོགས་སྣང་བ་དེ་ལ་ལྟོས་ཏེ་གཞི་མཐུན་དུ་འཛིན་པ་མ་གཏོགས་མེ་ཏོག་གཅིག་པུ་དེའི་སྟེང་དུ་ཨུཏྤལ་དང་སྔོན་པོའི་རྫས་ཐ་དད་དུ་དོན་དམ་པར་མེད་པའི་ཕྱིར་རོ། །མདོར་ན་བསྒྲུབ་བྱ་སྒྲུབ་བྱེད་དང་ཆོས་དང་ཆོས་ཅན་གྱི
ཐ་སྙད་ཐམས་ཅད་རྟོག་པའི་སྣང་ངོར་བརྟེན་ནས་བྱེད་པ་མ་གཏོགས་རང་མཚན་ལ་བྱེད་ན། སྒྲའི་སྟེང་དུ་མི་རྟག་པ་སྒྲུབ་པའི་ཚེ་དང་པོར ... སྒྲ་ལས་བརྟོག་པའི་དོན་སྒྲ་ཕྱིར་མེད་གསར་དུ་གྲུབ་པ་ལྟ་བུ་ཞིག། དེའི་རྗེས
སུ་སྒྲའི་སྟེང་དུ་བྱས་པ་དང་མི་རྟག་པ་གཉིས་རིམ་གྱིས་ངེས་པའི་ཚེ་བྱས་པ་དང་མི་རྟག་པ་འཁར་གཞོང་ལ་རྒྱ་ཕྱུག་བརྟེན་པ་ལྟར་རམ་སྟུམ་བུ་དཀར་པོ་དམར་པོར་སོང་བ་ལྟར་དང་པོར་བྱས་པ་དང་དེའི་རྗེས་སུ་མི་རྟག་པ་ཕྱིར་མེད་གསར་དུ

189 གྲུབ་པ་ལྟ་བུར་སྣང་བས། སྤྱི་འདི་རིམ་པ་འདི་ནི་དོན་རང་མཚན་ལ་མི་འཐད་དེ། སྒྲ་སྤྱི་ས་ཅན་ནས་བྱས་མི་རྟག་གི་ངོ་བོར་དུས་མཉམ་དུ་སྐྱེས་ཟིན་པས་སོ། །མདོར་ན་མངོན་སུམ་རྣམས་ནི་སྒྲུབ་འཇུག་དང་རྟོག་པ་རྣམས་སེལ་འཇུག......
ཡིན་པའི་དོན་ནོ། །དཔེར་ན་སྔོན་འཛིན་དབང་མངོན་གྱིས་སྔོན་པོ་སྣང་བ་ན་སྔོན་པོ་དང་དེ་ནི་གཅིག་པའི་ཁྱད་ཆོས་རྣམས་རང་གི་ཡུལ་དུ་སྒྲུབ་པ་སྟེ་རྫས་སུ་སྣང་བའི་ཚུལ་གྱིས་ཁྱད་ཆོས་དེ་དག་སྣང་བའི་ཕྱིར་ན་སྔོན་པོ་རང་མཚན་པ་སྣང་ངོ་། སྔོན
འཛིན་རྟོག་པས་སྔོན་པོ་སྣང་བ་ན་ཁྱད་ཆོས་དེ་དག་རང་གི་ཡུལ་དུ་སེལ་བ་སྟེ་ཤར་བསལ་བའི་ཚུལ་གྱིས་ཁྱད་ཆོས་དེ་དག་མི་སྣང་བར་རྗེས་ཙམ་རྣམ་པར་བཅད་པའི་སྒྲོ་བཏགས་པའི་ཆོས་སྣང་བ་ཡིན་པའི་ཕྱིར་རོ། །གཞན་ཡང་སྒྲ་ལ་ཞེན
ཡུལ་མེད་པས་ཞེན་པའི་བརྗོད་བྱ་མེད་ཅེ་ན་མེད། སྒྲ་རྗེས་འདོད་ཀྱི་རྟོག་པས་བུམ་པ་བརྗོད་པར་བྱའི་སྐབས་ནས་བུམ་པ་ཞེན་པའི་ཡུལ་དུ་བཞག་ནས་བརྗོད་པས་ཉན་པ་པོས་བུམ་པ་འཁྲུལ་མེད་དུ་གོ་བའི་རྒྱུ་མཚན་དེ་ལ་བློག་པས་སྒྲའི
ཞེན་པའི་བརྗོད་བྱ་ཡོད་ཅེ་ན་རྣམ་གོ་རྒྱུ་ཡོད་དོ། །ཡང་བུམ་པ་མ་ཡིན་པ་ལས་ལོག་པ་བུམ་པའི་དོན་རང་མཚན་གྱི་གཞན་སེལ་ཡིན་པའི་རྒྱུ་མཚན་གྱིས་བུམ་པ་མ་ཡིན་པ་ལས་ལོག་པ་དངོས་པོ་ཡིན་བྱས་པ་ལ། ཁོ་ན་རེ། དེ་མི་འཐད་པར
ཐལ། བུམ་པ་མ་ཡིན་པ་ལས་ལོག་པ་རྟག་པ་ཡིན་པའི་ཕྱིར། མ་གྲུབ་ན། བུམ་པ་ཆོས་ཅན། ཁྱོད་མ་ཡིན་པ་ལས་ལོག་པ་རྟག་པ་ཡིན་པར་ཐལ། ཁྱོད་ཡིན་པ་རྟག་པ་ཡིན་པའི་ཕྱིར། མ་གྲུབ་ན། བུམ་པ་ཆོས་ཅན། ཁྱོད་ཡིན

190 ༄༅། །པ་རྟག་པ་ཡིན་པར་ཐལ། ཁྱོད་ཡིན་པ་ཡོད་པའི་ཕྱིར་ཞེ་ན། འདི་ནི་སྐྱེ་བཟླ་བ་ཀྱི་རིགས་པའི་འགྲོས་ཤིག་ཡིན་ཡང་། བུམ་པ་མ་ཡིན་པ་ལས་ལོག་པ་དངོས་པོ་ཡིན་ཟེར་ན་གཞུང་དང་མཐུན་པར
སེམས་སོ། །ཡང་ཁོ་ན་རེ། ཁྱོད་ཀྱིས་བྱས་པ་ཞེས་བརྗོད་པའི་སྒྲས་བྱས་པ་མ་ཡིན་པ་ལས་ལོག་པར་བརྗོད་ཟེར་བ་མི་འཐད་དེ། གལ་ཏེ་འཐད་ན་བྱས་པ་ཞེས་བརྗོད་པའི་སྒྲ་ཆོས་ཅན། བྱས་པ་མ་ཡིན་པ་ལས་ལོག་པ་དངོས་སུ
བརྗོད་པར་ཐལ། བྱས་པ་མ་ཡིན་པ་ལས་ལོག་པ་དངོས་སུ་བརྗོད་པའི་ཕྱིར། འདོད་ན། བྱས་པ་དངོས་སུ་འཛིན་པའི་རྟོག་པ་ཆོས་ཅན། བྱས་པ་མ་ཡིན་པ་ལས་ལོག་པ་དངོས་སུ་འཛིན་པར་ཐལ། བྱས་པ...... བརྗོད་པའི
སྒྲས་དེ་ལྟར་བརྗོད་པ་གང་ཞིག །སྒྲ་རྟོག་གཉིས་འཇུག་པ་མཚུངས་པའི་ཕྱིར་ནམ་ཁྱབ། འདོད་ན། བྱས་པ་མ་ཡིན་པ་ལས་ལོག་པ་ཆོས་ཅན། བྱས་པ་དང་གཅིག་ཡིན་པར་ཐལ། བྱས་པ་དངོས་སུ་འཛིན་པའི་རྟོག་པའི་དངོས
ཡུལ་ཡིན་པའི་ཕྱིར་ཟེར་རོ། །འོན་ཀྱང་སྒྲ་རྟོག་གཉིས་འཇུག་པ་མཚུངས་ཞེས་གྲགས་མོད་དེ་ལ་འདི་ལྟར་བྱེད་པར་བྱ་སྟེ། དེ་ན་སྒྲ་གང་དང་གང་གིས་གང་ཞིག་དངོས་སུ་བརྗོད་ན་རྟོག་པས་ཀྱང་དེ་ལྟ་ར་དངོས་སུ་འཛིན་པས་ཁྱབ་པ
ཐལ། སྒྲ་རྟོག་གཉིས་འཇུག་པ་མཚུངས་པའི་ཕྱིར། འདོད་ན། པཎ་ཆེན་བསོད་ནམས་གྲགས་པས། ཚད་མས་འཇུག་ཚུལ་དང་སྒྲ་རྗེས་ཚུལ་མི་འདྲ་བར་བསྒྲུབ་སྟེ། རྟག་ན་མ་བྱས་པས་ཁྱབ་ཅེས་པའི་སྒྲས་བྱས་པ་རྟག་པ་ལ་མེད་པལ

191 བརྗོད་ཀྱང་། རྟག་ན་མ་བྱས་པས་ཁྱབ་པ་འདྲེལ་བ་འདི་ཚད་མས་བྱས་པ་རྟག་པ་ལ་མེད་པར་མཐོང་བའི་ཕྱིར། ཞེས་གསུངས་ཤིང་། དེ་བཞིན་དུ་ཀུན་མཁྱེན་འཇམ་དབྱངས་བཞད་པས་ཀྱང་། སྒྲ་རྟོག་གཉིས་རང་ཡུལ་ལ་སེལ
འཇུག་ཡིན་པར་མཚུངས་ཀྱང་། རྟག་པ་བྱས་སྟོང་དུ་རྟོགས་པའི་རྗེས་དཔག་གིས་བྱས་པ་རྟག་པ་ལ་མེད་པར་མཐོང་ཀྱང་། རྟག་པ་ལ་བྱས་པ་མེད་པར་སྟོན་པའི་སྒྲ་དེས་བྱས་པ་རྟག་པ་ལ་མེད་པར་སྟོན་པ་སོགས་རིགས་པའི
ཕྱིར་བ་གཅེས་སོ། །ཞེས་གསུངས་པའི་ཕྱིར། འདི་གོ་བདེ་བར་བརྗོད་ན། རྟག་པ་ཡིན་ན་མ་བྱས་པ་ཡིན་པས་ཁྱབ་ཅེས་བརྗོད་པའི་སྒྲས། བྱས་པ་རྟག་པ་ལས་སྟོང་པར་བརྗོད་ཀྱང་། རྟག་ན་མ་བྱས་པས་ཁྱབ་པར་འཛིན་པའི་རྟོག་པས།
བྱས་པ་རྟག་པས་སྟོང་པར་མ་འཛིན་ཞེས་པའི་དོན་ནོ། །དེས་ན་སྒྲ་རྟོག་གཉིས་རང་ཡུལ་ལ་སེལ་བས་འཇུག་པ་ཙམ་མཚུངས་ཀྱང་སྒྲས་གང་བརྗོད་པ་ཐམས་ཅད་རྟོག་པས་དེ་ལྟར་དུ་འཛིན་པའི་ངེས་པ་མེད་པའི་ཚུལ་ཤེས་པར
བྱའོ། །གསུམ་པ་བཤད་སྦྱོར་ཚུལ་བཤད་པ་ལ། བ་ལང་ལ་བཤད་སྦྱོར་བའི་དབང་དུ་བྱས་ན། བ་ལང་མ་ཡིན་པ་ལས་ལོག་པ་དེ་ལ་སྤྱི་ཞེས་བྱ་ཞིང་། བ་ལང་དཀར་ནག་དང་ཁྲ་བོ་ལ་སོགས་པ་དེའི་གསལ
བ་ཡིན་ལ། དེ་ལྟ་བུའི་སྤྱི་དང་གསལ་བ་གཉིས་རྫས་གཅིག་པ་དང་། སྤྱི་དེ་ཉིད་རང་གི་གསལ་བ་ཀུན་ལ་ཁྱབ་པ་ཡང་ཡིན་ནོ། །དེ་ལ་ནང་པ་སངས་རྒྱས་པ་དང་ཕྱི་རོལ་པ་གྲངས་ཅན་པ་གཉིས་ཀས་སྤྱི་ཞེས་པ་ཙམ་ཁས་ལེན་པ...

192 ༄༅། །མཐུན་ཡང་སྤྱི་དེའི་ངོས་འཛིན་ལ་མི་མཐུན་ཏེ། སངས་རྒྱས་པ་དག་གིས་སྤྱི་དེ་ལ་རིགས་སྤྱི་དང་ཚོགས་སྤྱི་ཞེས་གཉིས་སུ་གྲགས་པ་ལས་འདིར་རིགས་སྤྱི་སྟེ་བ་ལང་མ་ཡིན་པ་ལས་ལོག་པའི་གཞན
སེལ་ཏེ་བ་མིན་རྣམ་པར་བཅད་པ་དེ་ཉིད་བ་ལང་གི་གསལ་བ་རྣམས་ཀྱི་སྤྱི་ཡིན་པར་འདོད་ཅིང་། གྲངས་ཅན་པས་བྱེ་བྲག་ཐམས་ཅད་ལ་ཁྱབ་པའི་གཙོ་བོ་ཞེས་བྱ་བའི་སྤྱི་རྟག་པའི་དངོས་པོ་ཞིག་ཡོད་པ་དེ་བ་ལང་གི་གསལ་བ་རྣམས
ཀྱི་སྤྱི་ཡིན་ཟེར། གཞན་ཡང་བ་ལང་དཀར་ནག་ལ་ལྟ་བུ་གཅིག་ལ་བརྡ་སྦྱར་བས་དེའི་རིགས་ཅན་ལྷག་མ་ཀུན་བ་ལང་དུ་གོ་བ་དང་། བརྡ་སྦྱར་བའི་དགོས་པ་ཡང་ཐ་སྙད་གོ་བའི་ཆེད་ཡིན་པ་སངས་རྒྱས་པ་དང་གྲངས་ཅན་པ་གཉིས
ཀས་འདོད་པ་མཐུན་ཡང་། དེ་ལྟར་གོ་བའི་རྒྱུ་མཚན་ལ་མི་མཐུན་ཏེ། སངས་རྒྱས་པ་དག་གིས་ཐོག་མར་བ་ལང་དཀར་ནག་ལ་ལྟ་བུ་ཞིག་གཞིར་བཟུང་ནས་འདི་བ་ལང་ངོ་ཞེས་བརྡ་སྦྱར་བ་ན། གོང་བུ་དེ་ཉིད་ནག་དང་སྐྱ་ཁྲ་ལ་ལ
སོགས་པ་འདུས་པའི་བདག་ཉིད་ཡིན་ཡང་རྒྱུ་མཚན་དུ་བྱས་ནས་བ་ལང་མ་ཡིན་པ་ལས་ལོག་པ་ལ་བརྡ་སྦྱར་ཞིང་། དེ་ཉིད་བ་ལང་གི་གསལ་བ་མཐའ་དག་ལ་རྗེས་སུ་འགྲོ་བའི་རྒྱུ་མཚན་གྱིས་ཡིན་ཟེར། གྲངས་ཅན་པས
བ་ལང་ཞེས་པའི་སྒྲ་དེ་སྒྲུབ་འཇུག་ཡིན་པས་བ་ལང་དང་ངོ་བོ་གཅིག་པ་ཐམས་ཅད་བརྗོད་དགོས་པའི་ཕྱིར་བ་སྤྱི་རྟག་དངོས་དེ་ཡང་དེས་བརྗོད་པ་ཡིན་པས། དེས་ན་ཐོག་མ་དཀར་ནག་ལ་ལྟ་བུ་གཅིག་གཞིར་བཟུང་ནས་འདི་བ་ལང་ངོ་...

ཞིང་བརྡར་གྱུར་བའི་བསྒྱུ་རྟག་དངོས་དེ་ལ་ཡང་བརྡར་གྱུར་བ་ཡིན་པས། སྤྱི་གཙོ་བོ་དེ་ཉིད་བ་ལང་གི་གསལ་བ་མཐའ་དག་ལ་ཁྱབ་ཡོད་པའི་རྒྱུ་མཚན་གྱིས་སྤྱིས་བ་ལང་ནག་སྒྲུར་མཐོང་བའི་རྒྱུ་མཚན་གཞན་གང་ཡང་བས་མི་དགོས
པར་བ་ལང་ངོ་ཤེས་རྒྱུ་ཡི་བ་ཡིན་ཟེར། གྲངས་ཅན་པས་སྤྱི་གཙོ་བོ་དེ་ཆ་མེད་དང་རྟག་པའི་དངོས་པོར་ཁས་བླངས་ཤིང་། དེའི་སྟེང་དུ་བསྒྱུ་རྟག་དངོས་དང་ཤིང་གི་སྤྱི་རྟག་དངོས་ཟེར་བ་སོགས་འདོགས་ཁྱད་དེ་དག་བླུས་བརྗོད་ཚུལ་ལ་ལྟོས་ཏེ……
193 ལྟོས་པ་ཐུ་དང་དུ་འཛིན་པའི་ཚུལ་དེམ་ཤེས་པའི་དབང་གིས་བསྒྱུ་རྟག་དངོས་དེ་ཉིད་རང་གི་གསལ་བ་རྣམས་ལ་རྗེས་སུ་འགྲོ་བའི་ཚེ་ན་བ་ལང་ཁྲ་བོའི་རང་བཞིན་གང་ཡིན་པ་དེ་ཉིད་བ་ལང་ཁྲ་ཡུའི་རང་བཞིན་ཡང་ཡིན་ལ། ཁྲ་ཡུའི་རང……
བཞིན་གང་ཡིན་པ་དེ་ཉིད་ཁྲ་བོའི་རང་བཞིན་ཡིན་པར་སྨྲ་དགོས་པ་ཐུབ་པ་ཡིན་པས། རྣམ་འགྲེལ་ལས་ཀྱི་གཞུང་གོང་དེ་གྲངས་ཅན་པ་ལ་གནོད་བྱེད་སྟོན་པ་ཡིན་ནོ། །དེ་ཡང་ཅན་པོས་སྤྱི་པས་རྡུལ་ཕྲ་རབ་ཆ་མེད་དུ་འདོད་པ་དང
གྲངས་ཅན་པས་སྤྱི་གཙོ་བོ་ཆ་མེད་དུ་འདོད་པ་གཉིས་མི་འདྲ་ཡང་དོན་མི་འདྲ་སྟེ། རྡུལ་ཕྲ་རབ་ཆ་མེད་དུ་འདོད་པའི་དོན་ནི་རང་གི་བདག་ཉིད་དུ་གྲུབ་པའི་རང་ཡིན་པའི་ཆ་རྣམ་མེད་པའི་དོན་ཡིན་ལ། གཙོ་བོ་ཆ་མེད་པའི་དོན་ནི་རང་གི་གསལ་བ་རྣམས་ལ……
རྗེས་སུ་འགྲོ་བའི་ཕྱོགས་པའི་ཆ་རྣམ་མེད་པའི་དོན་ནོ། །ཉན་ཐོས་སྡེ་པའི་ལུགས་ལ་རྡུལ་ཕྲ་རབ་ཆ་མེད་ཡིན་ཡང་སྤྱི་ཡིན་པ་མིང་གལ་ཏེ། ཤར་ནུབ་ལ་སོགས་པའི་རྡུལ་ཕྲ་རབ་རྣམས་ཅིའི་སྤྱི་ཡིན་པའི་ཕྱིར་རོ། །གཞན་ཡང་ཙན་དན་དང་ཨ་ག་རུ་དང……

༄༅། །སྤྱི་པ་གསུམ་རྗེས་འགྲོ་དང་བཅས་མཚུངས་ཅད། ཙན་དན་དང་ཨ་ག་རུ་གཉིས་ལ་རིགས་གཅིག་པའི་བློ་སྐྱེ་ལ། ཙན་དན་དང་ལྕུག་མ་གཉིས་ལ་རིགས་གཅིག་པའི་བློ་མི་སྐྱེ་བའི་རྒྱུ་མཚན་ཅི་ཡིན་ཞེ་ན། དེ་ལ་གྲངས་ཅན
པས་ཤིང་གི་སྤྱི་གཙོ་བོ་དེས་བྱེད་པ་ཡིན་ཏེ། ཤིང་གི་སྤྱི་དེ་ཉིད་ཙན་དན་དང་ཨ་ག་རུ་གཉིས་ལ་ཐུན་མོང་དུ་རྗེས་སུ་འགྲོ་ལ་ལྕུག་མ་ལ་རྗེས་སུ་མི་འགྲོ་བའི་རྒྱུ་མཚན་གྱིས་ཡིན་ཟེར། འདིས་གཙོ་བོ་ཡོད་པར་སྒྲུབ་པའི་རིགས་པ་གཅིག་བསྟན
པ་ཡིན་པས་དེ་བཤད་ཞེན། ཤིང་གི་གསལ་བ་ཙན་དན་དང་ཨ་ག་རུ་སོགས་དང་ལྕུག་མའི་གསལ་བ་གསེར་ལྕུག་ཟངས་ལྕུག་སོགས་ཆོས་ཅན། དེ་དག་སོ་སོར་མ་འདྲེས་པར་རིགས་གཅིག་ཏུ་གོ་བའི་རྒྱུ་ཞིག་ཡོད་དགོས་ཏེ། དེ་མེད་ན་དེ……
194 ལྟར་གོ་བ་མི་སྲིད་པའི་ཕྱིར། དེས་ན་འབྲས་བུ་སྣ་ཚོགས་སོ་སོར་བྱེད་པ་པོའི་རྒྱུ་ཞིག་ཡོད་པར་གྲུབ་ཅིང་རྒྱུ་དེ་སྤྱི་གཙོ་བོ་ལས་གཞན་དེ་མིན་ཐར་བའི་ཕྱིར་ཟེར་རོ། །སྤྱི་དེའི་ངོ་བོ་གང་ཞེ་ན། རྫ་བྲག་ཐམས་ཅད་ཀྱི་རང་བཞིན་གཅིག་ཏུ་འདྲེས
པའི་མི་གསལ་བའི་དངོས་པོ་ཞིག་ཡིན་ཞིང་། རྫ་བྲག་རྣམས་དེ་ཉིད་གསལ་བར་བྱེད་པས་ན་གསལ་བ་ཞེས་བྱའོ་ཞེས་ཟེར། རང་ལུགས་ལ་དེ་བཀག་ནས་ཤིང་མ་ཡིན་པ་ལས་ལོག་པའི་གཞན་སེལ་དེ་ཉིད་ཙན་དན་དང་ཨ་ག་རུ་གཉིས་ལ
ཐུན་མོང་དུ་རྗེས་སུ་འགྲོ་ཞིང་བ་ལང་ལ་རྗེས་སུ་མི་འགྲོ་བས་ཡིན་ཟེར། འོན་ཀྱང་དེ་ཙམ་གྱིས་རིགས་གཅིག་ཏུ་འཛིན་མི་ནུས་ཏེ། གལ་ཏེ་ནུས་ན་མི་དང་བ་ལང་གཉིས་ཆོས་ཅན། རིགས་གཅིག་ཡིན་པར་ཐལ། སེམས་ཅན་ཡིན་པ་ལས

ལོག་པའི་གཞན་སེལ་དེ་གཉིས་ལ་ཐུན་མོང་དུ་རྗེས་སུ་འགྲོ་བའི་ཕྱིར། དེས་ན་རིགས་གཅིག་ཏུ་འཛིན་བྱེད་ནས་ཞར་སྒྲུག་པ་བཞི། བརྡ་ལ་བྱང་བ་དག་གིས་ཡིད་གཏད་པའི་རྫས་ལ་སྒྱུ་མཐོང་ཙམ་ཉིད་ནས་འདུ་བར་འཛིན་པའི་བློ་དང་གིས
སྐྱེ་བར་འགྱུར་བའི་ཆོས་གཉིས་ལ་རིགས་གཅིག་ཏུ་འཛིན་པ་ཡིན་པས། དེས་ན་བ་ལང་དཀར་ཟལ་དང་ནག་སྒྲུར་གཉིས་ཆོས་ཅན། རིགས་གཅིག་ཡིན་ཏེ། བརྡ་ལ་བྱང་བའི་སྐྱེས་བུ་དག་གིས་མཐོང་ཙམ་ཉིད་ནས་དེ་དག་གི་བློ་ལྡན་སྐྱེས
ལ་འདྲ་བར་སྣང་བའི་ཕྱིར། དཀར་ཟལ་དང་རྟ་མ་པ་གཉིས་ཆོས་ཅན། རིགས་གཅིག་མ་ཡིན་ཏེ། དེ་ལྟ་བུའི་བློ་ལྡན་སྐྱེས་ལ་འདྲ་བར་མི་སྣང་བའི་ཕྱིར། དེ་ལྟར་འདྲ་བ་དང་མི་འདྲ་བར་སྣང་བའི་རྒྱུ་མཚན་ཡང་ཡོད་དེ། ནང་གི་རྐྱེན་དབྱེ་བ་མེད
195 རྣམས་དཀར་ཟལ་དང་ནག་སྒྲུར་གཉིས་ལ་ཐུན་མོང་དུ་བ་ལང་དུ་ཞེས་རིགས་གཅིག་ཏུ་མངོན་པར་བརྗོད་པའི་བག་ཆགས་གསོས་པ་ཤས་ཆེ་ལ། དཀར་ཟལ་དང་རྟ་མ་པ་གཉིས་ལ་དེ་ལྟ་བུའི་རིགས་གཅིག་ཏུ་འཛིན་པའི་མངོན་བརྗོད་ཀྱི་བག
ཆགས་དང་སྤྲས་མི་ཆེ་བའི་ཕྱིར་དང་། ཕྱི་རོལ་རྐྱེན་དཀར་ཟལ་དང་ནག་སྒྲུར་གཉིས་ཞིག་དང་སྐྱ་ཤ་ལ་སོགས་དང་ལྡན་པར་མཚུངས་ལ། དཀར་ཟལ་དང་རྟ་མ་པ་གཉིས་དེ་ལྟ་བུའི་ཁྲ་ཆོས་དང་ལྡན་པར་མི་མཚུངས་པ་ཡིན་པའི་ཕྱིར། དེས་ན་ཟང་བ
ལང་དཀར་ནག་གཉིས་བ་ལང་མ་ཡིན་པ་ལས་ལོག་པར་མཚུངས་པའི་སྒོ་ནས་དེ་གཉིས་སྐྱེ་རིགས་གཅིག་པ་ཡང་ཡིན་པས་དེ་གཉིས་ལ་རིགས་གཅིག་པའི་བློ་སྐྱེ་བ་ཡིན་ནོ། །དཔེར་ན་མི་རྣམས་ཀྱི་ཁ་དོག་སྣ་ཚོགས་ཡོད་ཀྱང་ཡིན་མིའི……

༄༅། །ཁ་དོག་ནག་པོར་མཚུངས་པའི་སྒོ་ནས་ཀྱི་བ་མ་རྣམས་རིགས་གཅིག་ཏུ་སྣང་བ་བཞིན་ནོ། །དེའི་ཕྱིར་རིགས་གཅིག་པ་ལ་ལྡོག་རིགས་གཅིག་པ་དང་རྫས་རིགས་གཅིག་པ་གཉིས་པས། དང་པོ་ནི་གསེར་བུམ
དང་ཟངས་བུམ་གཉིས་ལྟ་བུ་སྟེ། དེ་གཉིས་བུམ་པ་མ་ཡིན་པ་ལས་ལོག་པ་ཡིན་པར་མཚུངས་པའི་ཕྱིར་ལྡོག་རིགས་གཅིག་པ་ཞེས་བྱའོ། །གཉིས་པ་ནི་ནས་འབྲུ་གཅིག་ལས་སྐྱེ་བའི་ནས་འབྲུ་ཕྱི་མ་གཉིས་ལྟ་བུ་སྟེ། དེ་གཉིས་ཉེར་ལེན་ནས……
འབྲུ་གཅིག་ལས་སྐྱེ་བར་མཚུངས་པའི་ཕྱིར་རྫས་རིགས་གཅིག་པ་ཡིན་ཡང་རྫས་གཅིག་མ་ཡིན་ཏེ། གཅིག་པ་ཀ་ཅིག་ཤེས་ཁེགས་པས་མཐའ་པའི་ཕྱིར་རོ། །དེས་མཚོན་ནས་རྫས་ཞེས་པ་དེ་ལ་དབྱེ་ན་དོན་བྱེད་ནུས་པས་ཡོན་ཏན……
196 རྗེས་གཞན་གྱི་རྟེན་བྱེད་པའི་རྫས་ཞེས་པ་དེ་དང་། གྲངས་ཅན་པ་སོགས་རང་རྒྱུད་པའི་རྫས་ཡོད་ཅེས་པའི་རྫས་དེ་དང་། སྔོན་དགག་པ་རྣམས་ཀྱིས་རྫས་ཀྱི་རང་བཞིན་བརྗོད་པའི་རྒྱ་ཅན་པའི་རྫས་དེ་དང་། བསྡུས་གྲྭ་པ་རྣམས་ཀྱིས་རྫས་ཆོས་ལྡོག
ཆོས་ཞེས་པའི་རྫས་དེ་དང་། བྱེ་བྲག་སྨྲ་བ་འདུས་མ་བྱས་གསུམ་རྫས་སུ་སྨྲ་བའི་རྫས་དེ་དང་། ཡང་ན་གི་སློང་ལ་ལའི་སྤྱི་བ་བརྫས་པ་གཅིག་ཅེས་པའི་རྫས་དེ་དང་། མདོ་སྡེ་པས་གདུང་འདོགས་ཀྱི་དོན་བྱེད་ནུས་པ་རྫས་ཡོད་ཆོས་གསུམ་ཚང
བ་ཞེས་པའི་རྫས་དེ་དང་། སེམས་ཙམ་པས་སྔོན་པོ་དང་སྔོན་འཛིན་ཚད་མ་གཅིག་ཤེས་གཉིས་རྫས་གཅིག་ཅེས་པའི་རྫས་དེ་དང་། དབུ་མ་པས་རྫས་གྲུབ་ཁས་མི་ལེན་ཞེས་པའི་རྫས་དེ་རྣམས་ལ་སོ་སོར་གོ་རྒྱུ་ཡོད་པ་གོ་རིམ་ཆགས་པས་ཁ་ཟེ……

197 དཔང་པོ་རྟོལ་བས་མཛེ་བཞིན་བརྗོད་པའི་རྗེས་འབྲེགས་ཐང་། ཞེ་ན་ཅག་ཤེས་རབ་ཆེ་བ་དག་གིས་མཐའ་ཚོད་པར་བྱེས་ཤིག ། དེ་ལྟར་བ་ལ་འདོད་ཀ་ར་བལ་ལ་ལྟ་བུ་གཅིག་གཞིར་བཟུང་ནས་གོང་བུ་འདི་ནི་བ་ལང་དོ་ཞེས་བརྗོད་འགྱུར་བའོ།
གོང་བུ་དེ་ཉིད་ནོག་སོགས་འདུས་པའི་བདག་ཉིད་ཡིན་པ་རྒྱུ་མཚན་དུ་བྱས་ནས་བ་ལང་གི་བརྡར་སྦྱར་བ་ཡིན་པའི་གནད་ཀྱིས། བ་ལང་ནག་ཐྲ་ར་པ་ང་ནོག་སོགས་འདུས་པའི་བདག་ཉིད་ཡིན་པས་ན་བ་ལང་མཐའ་དག་རིགས་གཅིག་པ་ཡིན་ནོ།
འོན་ཀར་ཞལ་གཞིར་བཟུང་ནས་དེ་བ་ལང་གི་བརྡར་སྦྱར་བའི་བརྡ་དེ་འཇུག་ཡུལ་དེ་གང་ལ་བྱ་ཞེ་ན། དེའི་ཚེ་དཀར་ཞལ་དེ་ཉིད་བ་ལང་གི་བརྡར་སྦྱར་བའི་གཞི་ཡིན་གྱི་འཇུག་ཡུལ་མ་ཡིན་ཏེ། བ་ལང་ཞེས་པའི་སྒྲའི་འཇུག་ཡུལ་ཡིན་ན
བ་ལང་འཛིན་པའི་རྟོག་པའི་འཛིན་སྟངས་ཀྱི་ཡུལ་ཡིན་དགོས་པས་དེའི་ཞེན་ཡུལ་དུ་ཡང་འགྱུར་བའི་ཕྱིར་རོ། །དེས་ན་བ་ལང་ཞེས་པའི་བརྡའི་དངོས་ཀྱི་འཇུག་ཡུལ་ནི་བ་ལང་དང་བ་ལང་མ་ཡིན་པ་ལས་ལོག་པ་གཉིས་ཡིན་ཏེ། ལྟེ་བརྟན
རྒྱན་ཡིད་ཀྱི་མུན་སེལ་ལས། བ་ལང་ཞེས་པའི་བརྡ་འདི་དཀར་ཞལ་ལ་གཞིར་བྱས་ནས་སྦྱར་བ་འདི་ཚེ། བརྡ་དེའི་ཡུལ་ཀྱི་གཙོ་བོ་ནི་བ་ལ་ངང་བ་ལང་མ་ཡིན་པ་ལས་ལོག་པ་རིགས་ཞེན་སེལ་གཉིས་ཡིན་ལ། དཀར་ཞལ་བ་ལང་མ་ཡིན་པ་ལས་ལོག
པར་སྣང་བའི་སྒྲ་དོན་ལ་ཡང་བརྡའི་ཡུལ་ཚམ་དུ་འགྱུར་བ་ཡིན་ནོ། །ཞེས་གསུངས་པའི་ཕྱིར། དཔྱད་ཡིན་ཏེ། དེ་རབ་རྒྱུ་མི་རྟག་པ་ནི་ཞེས་བརྗོད་པ་འི་ཚེ་སྒྲ་དེ་ནི་མི་རྟག་པ་ཞེས་པ་འི་སྒྲ་སྦྱོར་བའི་གཞི་ཡིན་གྱི་མི་རྟག་པ་ཞེས་པའི་སྒྲའི་འཇུག་ཡུལ་...

ཚ། སྐྱེ།

198 སྒྲ་གཉིས། ༢༩ ༄༅། །མ་ཡིན་པ་བཞིན་ནོ། །དེ་ལ་ཁོ་ན་རེ། འོ་ན་དཀར་ཞལ་གཞིར་བཟུང་ནས་འདི་བ་ལང་ངོ་ཞེས་བརྡར་བྱས་པའི་ཚེ་ན། ཉེར་བ་པོའི་རྒྱུད་ལ་དཀར་ཞལ་བ་ལང་ཡིན་པར་འཛིན་པའི་རྟོག་པ་སྐྱེ་འམ་མི་སྐྱེ། སྐྱེ་ན་
ཞེ་ན། དེ་ལྟ་བུ་དཀར་ཞལ་བ་ལང་ཡིན་པར་འཛིན་པའི་རྟོག་པ་ཚོས་ཅན། དཀར་ཞལ་དང་བ་ལང་གི་ཚོགས་དོན་ཡང་འཛིན་པར་ཐལ། སྒྲ་མི་རྟག་པར་འཛིན་པའི་རྟོག་པས་སྒྲ་དང་མི་རྟག་པའི་ཚོགས་དོན་འཛིན་པ་གང་ཞིག །སྒྲ་རྟོག
གཉིས་འཇུག་པ་མཚུངས་པའི་ཕྱིར་ཞེན། དེའི་ལན་ལ་རང་རེའི་མཁས་པ་རྣམས། སྐྱོན་དེ་མེད་དེ། སྒྲ་མི་རྟག་པར་སྒྲུབ་པའི་དགོས་པ་ནི། སྒྲའི་སྟེང་དུ་མི་རྟག་པ་བསྒྲུབ་པའི་ཚེད་ཡིན་པས་དེ་སྒྲུབ་ཀྱི་བསྒྲུབ་བྱ་རྟོགས་ནས་ཆོས་དང་ཆོས
ཅན་གྱི་ཚོགས་དོན་ལ་ཞུགས་དགོས་ཤིང་། དཀར་ཞལ་གཞིར་བཟུང་ནས་བ་ལང་གི་བརྡའ་སྦྱར་བའི་དགོས་པ་ནི། ཐ་སྙད་ཀྱི་དུས་སུ་གཟུར་སོགས་པ་ལ་ངང་ཡིན་པར་གོ་བའི་ཚེད་དུ་བརྡ་སྦྱར་བ་ཡིན་གྱི། དཀར་ཞལ་དང་བ་ལང་མ
ཡིན་པ་ལས་ལོག་པའི་ཚོགས་དོན་ཤེས་པའི་ཚེད་དུ་བརྡ་འབྱུས་པ་མ་ཡིན་པས་རྟོག་ཉེས་དེ་ཚེས་ལ་ནམ་རྫོད་དོ། །ཨ་རོ་ཙ་ན་ཐ་རྟོག་གི་དགོས་ཡུལ་དུ་གཞན་སེལ་མེད་པར་རང་མཚན་ཁོ་ན་མི་ འདུག་ནས། བརྡ་སྦྱར་བའི་ཚེན་ཡང་གཞན་སེལ
ལ་བརྡ་མ་བྱས་པར་རང་མཚན་ཁོ་ན་ལ་སྦྱར་བ་ཡིན་ན། བ་ལང་གི་བརྡ་ཐོགས་མར་དཀར་ཞལ་ལ་སྦྱོར་བའི་ཚེ་དཀར་ཞལ་གྱི་རྗེས་གཅིག་པུ་ལ་བརྡ་བྱས་པར་འགྱུར་བ་ཞིང་། དེ་ལྟར་ན་ཕྱིས་ནག་ཐྲ་མཐོང་བ་ན་འདི་བ་ལང་ངོ་ཞེས་བྱ...

199 སྔར་བྱ་མ་མེད་པར་ཐལ། ཕྱིར་བརྡ་འབྱུར་དུས་ཀྱི་དཀར་ཞལ་དེ་ཉིད་ཐ་སྙད་དུས་ཀྱི་ནག་ཐྲ་ལ་རྗེས་འགྲོ་མི་བྱེད་པའི་ཕྱིར། དེར་ཐལ། ཕྱིར་བརྡ་འབྱུར་དུས་ཀྱི་དཀར་ཞལ་དེ་ཉིད་ཐ་སྙད་ཀྱི་དུས་སུ་འགག་ནས་མེད་པའི་ཕྱིར་རོ། །འོན་ཅིག་ཅེད་...
རང་ལ་ཡང་ཉེས་པ་དེ་མི་འདྲ་གྱི་གསང་ཞེ་ན། མི་འདྲ་སྟེ། བ་ལང་མ་ཡིན་པ་ལས་ལོག་པའི་གཞན་སེལ་ཏེ་བ་མི་ཉམས་པར་རྟག་དངོས་ལ་བརྡ་བྱས་པ་ཡིན་ནས་དེ་ཉིད་དེའི་རྗེས་སུ་མ་འགགས་པར་ཡོད་པའི་ཕྱིར་རམ། ཡང་ན་དེའི་ཚེ་...
རྟོག་པ་ལ་དཀར་ཞལ་བ་ལང་མ་ཡིན་པ་ལས་ལོག་པར་སྣང་བའི་སྒྲ་དོན་མ་འགགས་པར་ཡོད་པའི་ཕྱིར་རོ། །དེ་བཞིན་དུ་རིགས་གཏེར་ལས། རང་མཚན་སོ་སོར་ངེས་པའི། །མཐའ་ཡས་ཕྱིར་ན་བརྡ་འམི་ནུས། །ཐ་སྙད་བྱེད་པའི་ཚེ་ན
ཡང་། །དང་པོའི་རང་མཚན་ཉེ་བར་དཀའ། །ཞེས་གསུངས་སོ། །དེ་དོན་ནི་བ་ལང་ཞེས་པའི་བརྡའ་བ་ལང་རང་མཚན་པ་དངོས་སུ་བརྗོད་ན་བ་ལང་མཐའ་ཡས་པའི་ཕྱིར་དེ་ལྟར་བརྡ་སྦྱོར་མི་ནུས་ལ། ནུས་སུ་ཆུག །ན་ཡང་བརྡའ་འདུས་ཀྱི་བ
ལང་དེ་ཉིད་ཐ་སྙད་ཀྱི་དུས་སུ་ཡུལ་དུས་རང་བཞིན་གཞན་དུ་འགྱུར་ཡོད་པས་ཐ་པོའི་བ་ལང་དེ་ཉིད་རྗེ་བཞིན་ཉེ་དཀའ་ཞེས་པའི་དོན་ནོ། །གཞན་ཡང་ཁོ་ན་རེ། ཐོག་མར་དཀར་ཞལ་ལ་བ་ལང་གི་བརྡར་སྦྱར་བའི་ཚེ་ན་གསུར་ལ་བ་ལང་གི
བརྡ་སྦྱར་རམ་མ་སྦྱར། གལ་ཏེ་བརྡར་སྦྱར་བ་ཡིན་ན། བ་ལང་ཞེས་པའི་སྒྲ་ཚེས་ཅན། ཕྱི་འཇུག་ཡིན་པར་ཐལ། ནག་ཐྲ་སོགས་བ་ལང་གི་གསལ་བ་མཐའ་དག་བ་ལང་ཡིན་པར་བརྗོད་པའི་ཕྱིར། འོན་ཏེ་བརྡའ་མ་སྦྱར་བ་ཡིན་ན་ཐ་སྙད་ཀྱི་

ཚ། མཚོ།

200 སྒྲ་གསུམ། ༣༠ ༄༅། །དུས་སུ་ནག་ཐྲ་ལ་བ་ལང་དུ་གོ་བ་ཅི་ལྟར་ཡིན་ཞེ་ན། བཤད་པར་བྱ་སྟེ། ཐོག་མར་བརྡ་འབྱུར་བའི་དུས་སུ་ནག་ཐྲ་ལ་བ་ལང་གི་བརྡའ་དངོས་སུ་མ་སྦྱར་ཡང་ཐ་སྙད་ཀྱི་དུས་སུ་དེ་བ་ལང་དུ་མི་གོ་བའི་སྐྱོན་མེད་དེ། ཐོག
མར་བ་ལང་གི་བརྡའ་སྦྱར་བའི་ཚེ་བ་ལང་མ་ཡིན་པ་ལས་ལོག་པ་སྣ་བ་མིན་རྣམ་པར་བཅད་པ་ལ་བརྡའ་བྱས་པ་ཡིན་པས། དེའི་ཚེ་ཉན་པ་པོའི་རྒྱུད་ལ་ནོག་དང་རྐོག་ཤལ་ལ་སོགས་པ་འདུས་པའི་གོང་བུ་འདི་ལྟ་བུ་ལ་བ་ལང་ཞེས་བྱ་སྙད
ཐོགས་པ་རེད་སྙམ་དུ་དཀར་ཞལ་བ་ལང་ཡིན་པར་འཛིན་པའི་རྟོག་པ་སྐྱེ་ཞིང་། རྟོག་པ་དེའི་ཞེན་ངོར་ཉམས་པ་ར་ནག་ཐྲ་རྣམས་ཐོང་བ་ན་གོང་བུ་འདི་ཡང་ནོག་དང་རྐོག་ཤལ་ལ་སོགས་པ་འདུས་པ་ཡིན་པའི་ཕྱིར་བ་ལང་དོ་སྙམ་དུ་གོ་བར
འགྱུར་བ་ཡིན་པའི་ཕྱིར་རོ། །དེ་ལ་ཁོ་ན་རེ། དེ་ལྟར་ན་འོན་ཟླུམ་པ་འདི་ནི་མི་རྟག་པའོ་ཞེས་བརྗོད་པ་ན་མི་རྟག་པ་མ་ཡིན་པ་ལས་ལོག་པ་ལ་ཡང་བརྡ་འབྱས་པར་ཐལ། འདོད་པའི་ཕྱིར། འདོད་ན། ཉིང་པ་པོ་དེས་ཕྱིས་སུ་སྒྲ་ཐོས་པ
ན་སྒྲ་འདི་ཡང་མི་རྟག་པ་ཡིན་པར་གོ་བར་འགྱུར་བས། དེ་ལྟར་ན་སྒྲ་མི་རྟག་པར་སྒྲུབ་པའི་གཏན་ཚིགས་དང་རྗེས་དཔག་དོན་མེད་པར་འགྱུར་རོ་ཞེན། དེ་ལྟར་ཐལ་བའི་སྐྱོན་མེད་དེ། སྤྱི་ལ་བརྡའ་སྦྱར་བས་དེའི་བྱེ་བྲག་ཀུན་གོ་བར...
འགྱུར་ཞེས་པ་དེ་པ་མ་ཁ་སང་ཅམ་ཡིན་གྱི་ཁྱབ་མཐའ་བཟུང་བ་མ་ཡིན་ཏེ། གལ་ཏེ་ཁྱབ་མཐའ་བཟུང་ན་རང་ལུགས་ལ་ཡང་སྤྱར་བ་ལང་རྒྱུད་དུའི་སྟེང་དུ་བ་ལང་གི་བརྡའ་སྦྱོར་ཐང་། ཁྱིམ་སུ་བ་ལང་ཆེན་པོ་མཐོང་བ་ན་ཆེ་རྒྱུང་གི་དབང་གིས

201 འབྲུ་ལ་ཞུགས་པ་ལ་ཡང་དུ་མི་གོ་བ་ཡང་གྲོད་པའི་ཕྱིར། དེ་འདྲ་སྤྲོད་སྐབས་སྟོན་དུ་མེད་མོད་དོན་གྱིང་དེ་འདྲ་བ་དེས་བ་ལང་ཆེན་པོའི་སྟོང་དུ་ནོག་དང་སློག་ཤལ་ལ་སོགས་པ་འདུས་པའི་གོང་བུ་མངོན་སུམ་ཚད་མས་མཐོང་བ་ཡིན་པས་བ་ལང་གི
དོན་སྤྱི་གསལ་སྣང་བ་རྟོགས་ཟིན་གྱིང་། དེ་ལ་བ་ལང་གི་ཐ་སྙད་ཙམ་སྦྱོར་མི་ཤེས་པ་ཡིན་པས་དེ་ཤེས་པའི་ཆེད་དུ་ཐ་སྙད་འབའ་ཞིག་སྒྲུབ་པའི་གཏན་ཚིགས་འགོད་པ་དོན་དང་བཅས་པ་ཡིན་ནོ། །དེ་ལ་ཐ་སྙད་འབའ་ཞིག་སྒྲུབ་པའི་ཚུལ་ཡང
ཡོད་དེ། སོག་པ་གཉིས་ཀྱི་ཕ་སོར་ཤ་འབུར་པོ་ཡོད་པའི་གོང་བུ་ཆེན་པོ་འདི་ཆོས་ཅན། བ་ལང་ཡིན་ཏེ། ནོག་དང་སློག་ཤལ་ལ་སོགས་པ་འདུས་པའི་བདག་ཉིད་ཡིན་པའི་ཕྱིར་ཞེས་དགོད་པར་བྱ་ཞིང་། དེའི་ཚེ་སྦྱོར་བ་དེའི་ཕྱོགས་ལས
ལ་བརྟེན་ནས་ཀོ་ལེ་བ་དེས་སྔར་མངོན་སུམ་དུ་མཐོང་ཟིན་པའི་དོན་ལས་ལྐོག་པའི་དོན་གསར་དུ་རྟོགས་རྒྱུ་མེད་ཅིང་། དེ་ལ་བ་ལང་ངོ་ཞེས་པའི་སྒྲ་བརྗོད་ཤེས་པ་ཙམ་དང་རྟོགས་པས་བྱང་བ་ལང་ངོ་སྙམ་དུ་ཐ་སྙད་གསར་དུ་འདོགས་ཤེས
པ་ཙམ་བྱུང་བ། སྦྱོར་བ་དེས་ཐ་སྙད་འབའ་ཞིག་སྒྲུབ་ཅེས་པའི་དགོས་པ་གྲུབ་པ་ཡིན་པས། དེའི་ཕྱིར་སྦྱོར་བ་དེ་ནི་ནོག་སོགས་འདུས་པའི་གོང་བུ་དེ་བ་ལང་གི་རྒྱུ་མཚན་ནས་དོན་དུ་མ་གོ་བ་ལ་བ་ལང་གི་ཐ་སྙད་ཙམ་སྒྲུབ་པའི་ཆེད་དུ་བཀོད་པ
ཡིན་ནོ། །དེས་མཚོན་ནས་ཐ་སྙད་འབའ་ཞིག་སྒྲུབ་པའི་གཏན་ཚིགས་ཐམས་ཅད་ཀྱི་དོན་དེ་ལྟར་དུ་ཤེས་པར་བྱའོ། །གཞན་ཡང་བུམ་པ་མི་རྟག་པར་ངེས་ནས་ཕྱིས་སྒྲ་ཐོས་པ་ན་སྒྲ་མི་རྟག་པར་མི་གོ་བའི་རྒྱུ་མཚན་གཞན་ཡང་ཡོད་དེ།

ཚ་སྡུ། ཉེར་བཞི། ཕྱི།

202 ༄༅། །ཕྱིར་བུམ་པ་ལ་རིགས་འདྲའི་རྒྱུན་མཐུད་རྒྱུ་ཡོད་པས་ལོ་དང་ཟླ་བའི་བར་དུ་གནས་པའི་རྒྱུན་ཡོད་ལ། སྒྲ་ལ་དེ་ཙམ་གནས་པའི་རྒྱུན་མེད་པར་མངོན་སུམ་གྱིས་གྲུབ་པས་བུམ་པ་དེ་སྒྲ་ལ་ལྟོས་ཏེ་མི་རྟག་པར
ངེས་སླ་བས་ཡིན་པ་དང་། འོན་ཀྱང་གྲུབ་མཐའ་སྨྲ་བ་རྒྱུད་བསླད་པའི་ལོག་རྟོག་གི་དབང་གིས་བུམ་པ་མི་རྟག་པར་སྔོན་ལ་ངེས་ནས་དེའི་རྗེས་སུ་སྒྲ་མི་རྟག་པར་ངེས་དགོས་པ་ཡང་ཡོད་པའི་ཕྱིར། ལོག་རྟོག་གཙོ་བོ་ནི་ཞེ་ན། སྒྲ་སྒྲོགས
བྱེ་བྲག་པས། རྫས་དང་ཡོན་ཏན་ལས་དང་སྤྱི། །བྱེ་བྲག་འདུ་བ་རྣམ་པ་དྲུག །ཅེས་པའི་ཚུལ་གྱིས་ཤེས་བྱ་ཐམས་ཅད་དོན་ཚིག་དྲུག་ཏུ་འདུ་བར་འདོད་ཅིང་། དེའི་ནང་གི་རྫས་དེ་ལ། འབྱུང་བཞི་ཡིད་དང་ནམ་མཁའ་དང་། །དུས
ཕྱོགས་བདག་ཉིད་རྣམ་པ་དགུ། །ཞེས་པའི་ཚུལ་གྱིས་དགུ་ཡོད་པར་འདོད་ལ། ཡོན་ཏན་ལ་ཉི་ཤུ་རྩ་བཞི་ཡོད་ཅིང་དེ་དག་གི་རྫས་དགུ་པོ་དག་ལ་ཅི་རིགས་པར་བརྟེན་པར་འདོད་ཅིང་། དེའི་ནང་ནས་སྒྲ་ནི་ནམ་མཁའ་ཁོ་ནའི
ཡོན་ཏན་ཡིན་གྱི་རྫས་གཞན་པ་དག་ལ་མི་བརྟེན་ནོ་ཞེས་ཟེར། །ཅིའི་ཕྱིར་རྫས་གཞན་ལ་མི་བརྟེན་ཅེ་ན། གང་སྐྱེ་འཇིག་དང་ལྡན་པ་དེ་འགའ་ཞིག་ལ་བརྟེན་པས་ཁྱབ། དཔེར་ན་བུམ་རས་མ་བཞིན། སྒྲ་ཡང་སྐྱེ་འཇིག་བྱེད་པ་ཡིན་ནོ
ཞེས་པའི་རིགས་པ་ལ་བརྟེན་ནས་སྒྲ་དེ་ནི་རྫས་ཞིག་ལ་བརྟེན་པར་གྲུབ་ལ། དེ་ས་སོགས་འབྱུང་བ་བཞི་ལ་བརྟེན་པ་མ་ཡིན་ཏེ། གལ་ཏེ་བརྟེན་ན་ས་སོགས་གར་ཡོད་དུ་སྒྲ་ཡོད་དགོས་པ་ལ་དེ་མེད་པའི་ཕྱིར་དང་། སྒྲ་ཐོས་པའི་ཚེ

203 ཀང་ས་སོགས་ལས་ལོགས་སུ་ཆད་པར་ཐོས་པའི་ཕྱིར་རོ། །བདག་ལ་བརྟེན་པའི་ཡོན་ཏན་ཡང་མ་ཡིན་ཏེ། བདག་གཞན་རྒྱུན་མེད་པ་དེ་ལོངས་སྤྱོད་བྱ་ཡིན་པའི་ཕྱིར་རོ། །ཕྱོགས་དུས་ཡིད་གསུམ་གྱི་ཡོན་ཏན་ཡང་མ་ཡིན་ཏེ
རྣ་བའི་གཟུང་བྱ་ཡིན་པའི་ཕྱིར་རོ། །དེས་ན་ནམ་མཁའ་གོ་འབྱེད་པའི་ཐོག་སུ་རེག་བ་ཀག་པའི་སྟོང་སངས་ལ་སྒྲ་གྲགས་ཀྱི་རྗེས་ཡི་གོ་ད་བུ་རྫ་བུའི་ནང་དུ་སྒྲ་མི་གྲགས་པའི་ཕྱིར་སྒྲ་ནི་ནམ་མཁའི་ཡོན་ཏན་ཁོ་ན་ཡིན་ནོ། །དེ་ཡང་ནམ
མཁའ་ག་ར་ཡོད་དུ་སྒྲ་ཡང་དེ་བཞིན་དུ་ཁྱབ་པ་ཡོད་ཅིང་རྟེན་ནམ་མཁའ་རྟག་པ་ཡིན་པས་བརྟེན་པ་སྒྲ་ཡང་རྟག་པ་ཡིན་པར་གྲུབ་བ་ལ། བུམ་པ་ནི་དེ་ལྟ་མ་ཡིན་ཏེ། རྟེན་འབྱུང་བ་བཞི་ལ་བརྟེན་པའི་རྫས་རགས་པ་ཡིན་པས་མི་རྟག
པ་ཡིན་པར་འདོད་དོ། །དེ་ལྟར་གྲུབ་མཐའི་དབང་གིས་སྒྲ་མི་རྟག་པར་ངེས་པའི་སྔོན་དུ་བུམ་པ་མི་རྟག་པར་ངེས་དགོས་པའི་གང་ཟག་ཁ་ཅིག་ཡོད་ཁྱད་པར་དེ་ལྟར་ཡོད་པ་ལ་ལྟོས་ནས། གང་བྱས་ན་མི་རྟག་པ་ཡིན་པས་ཁྱབ། དཔེར
ན་བུམ་པ་བཞིན། སྒྲ་ཡང་བྱས་པ་ཡིན་ནོ་ཞེས་བུམ་པ་མཐུན་དཔེར་བཀོད་པ་ཡིན་གྱི་སྒྲ་ངེས་དཀའ་སླ་ཡོད་པའི་དབང་གིས་མ་ཡིན་པའི་ཚུལ་ཤེས་པར་བྱའོ། །ཞར་ལ་ཆོས་ཅན་དང་ཆོས་བརྗོད་ཀྱི་སྒྲ་བཤད་པར
བྱ་བ་ལ། ཆོས་ཅན་བརྗོད་པའི་སྒྲ་ནི་དོན་དེ་ཉིད་ཁྱད་གཞི་ལྟ་བུར་སྟོན་པར་བྱེད་ཅིང་། འདི་དང་ཁྱད་པར་གཞན་མི་སྤོང་བའི་སྒྲ་དོན་གཅིག །མཚན་གཞི་ནི། བུམ་པ་མི་རྟག་པ་ཞེས་བརྗོད་པའི་སྒྲ་ལྟ་བུའོ། །དེ་ཆོས་ཅན། ཆོས་ཅན་བརྗོད་པའི

ཚ། སྡུ། ཉེར་ལྔ། ཕྱི།

204 ༄༅། །སྒྲ་ཞེས་བྱ་སྟེ། བུམ་པ་མི་རྟག་པའི་ཁྱད་གཞི་ལྟ་བུར་ཉན་པ་པོའི་བློ་ཡུལ་དུ་འཕངས་པའི་ཕྱིར། དེ་ལ་ཁྱད་པར་གཞན་མི་སྤོང་བའི་སྒྲ་ཞེས་ཀྱང་བྱ་སྟེ། དེའི་ཚེ་བུམ་པ་དེ་ཉན་པ་པོའི་བློ་ངོར་ཀ་བ་དང
སྣམ་བུ་སོགས་ཆོས་གཞན་གྱི་རྟེན་དུ་རུང་བ་མི་སྤོང་བའི་ཚུལ་གྱིས་འཕངས་པས་སོ། །ཆོས་བརྗོད་ཀྱི་སྒྲ་ཞེས་པ་དོན་དེ་ཉིད་ཁྱད་ཆོས་ལྟ་བུར་སྟོན་པར་བྱེད་ཅིང་། འདི་དང་ཁྱད་པར་གཞན་སྤོང་གི་སྒྲ་དོན་གཅིག །མཚན་གཞི
ནི་བུམ་པའི་མི་རྟག་པ་ཞེས་བརྗོད་པའི་སྒྲ་ལྟ་བུའོ། །དེ་ཆོས་ཅན། ཆོས་བརྗོད་ཀྱི་སྒྲ་ཞེས་བྱ་སྟེ། བུམ་པ་མི་རྟག་པ་ཁྱད་ཆོས་ལྟ་བུར་བློ་ཡུལ་དུ་འཕངས་པའི་ཕྱིར་དང་། ཁྱད་པར་གཞན་སྤོང་གི་སྒྲ་ཡང་ཡིན་ཏེ། བུམ་པའི
མི་རྟག་པ་ཞེས་རྣམ་དབྱེ་དྲུག་པའི་སྒྲས་བརྗོད་པ་ན་མི་རྟག་པ་དེ་ཀ་བའི་མི་རྟག་པ་ཡིན་པ་སྤོང་བའི་ཚུལ་གྱིས་འཕངས་པས་སོ། །དེ་ལ་ཁ་ཅིག་ན་རེ། བུམ་པ་མི་རྟག་པའོ་ཞེས་བརྗོད་པའི་ཚེ་བུམ་པ་ཁྱད་གཞི་རང་འཕང་ལས་མོད།
བུམ་པའི་མི་རྟག་པའོ་ཞེས་བརྗོད་པའི་ཚེ་མི་རྟག་པ་ཁྱད་གཞི་རང་འཕང་སུ་ཚུལ་དེ་ཇི་ལྟར་ཡིན་ཞེ་ན། རྣམ་བཤད་རིགས་པའི་རྒྱ་མཚོ་དང་གསེར་ཕྲེང་གཉིས་ཀར། བ་ལང་གི་རྟ་མ་ཡིན་ཞེས་པའི་སྒྲ་ལ་དཔེར་བརྗོད་མཛད
ཀྱང་། དེ་ལས་དང་པོ་བས་འཇུག་དཀའ་བས་དེ་ཉིད་གོ་སླ་བའི་དཔེ་གཞན་གྱི་སྒོ་ནས་བཤད་པར་བྱ་བ་ལ། དཔེར་ན་སྒྲ་གཅན་ཞེས་པ་དེ་ལུས་དང་མགྲིན་སོགས་ཀྱི་ཚོགས་པ་ལ་བཏགས་པ་མ་ཡིན་པར་མགོ་ཙམ་ལ་བཏགས

205 པ་ཡིན་པས། དེའི་ཚེ་སྒྲ་གཅན་གྱི་མགོ་ཞེས་རྣམ་དབྱེ་དྲུག་པའི་སྒྲས་བརྗོད་བྱ་ཉན་པ་པོའི་བློ་ཡུལ་དུ་མགོ་ཁྱད་གཞི་དང་སྒྲ་གཅན་ཁྱད་ཆོས་སུ་གོ་བར་བྱེད་པ་ལས་འགལ་བ་ཞིབ་མེད་དེ། དེའི་ཚེ་མགོ་མི་གཏོགས་པའི་སྒྲ་གཅན་
ཞེས་པ་ལོགས་སུ་མེད་པའི་ཕྱིར་རོ། །དེའི་ཕྱིར་སྒྲ་གཅན་གྱི་མགོ་ཞེས་པའི་སྒྲ་དེས་ཉན་པ་པོའི་བློ་ཡུལ་དུ་མགོ་དེ་ལྟར་དང་མི་འདྲ་མགོ་ལས་ཁྱད་པར་དུ་བྱེ་ནས་སྒྲ་གཅན་གྱི་ཁྱད་ཆོས་སུ་འཕངས་པ་ནས་ཆོས་བརྗོད་ཀྱི་སྒྲ་ཞེས་བྱའོ། །
དེ་ཡང་ལེགས་པར་བཤད་གསེར་ཕྲེང་ལས། ཕྱིར་བརྟག་རྣམས་ཉན་པ་པོའི་ཤེས་འདོད་དང་རྗེས་སུ་མཐུན་པར་སྨྲ་བ་པོས་བརྗོད་འདོད་ཀྱི་ཀུན་ནས་བསླང་སྟེ་དགོས་པ་འགའ་ཞིག་གི་ཕྱིར་དུ་སྦྱོར་བ་ཡིན་ལ། ཞེས་གསུངས་པ་ལྟར་
རྗོད་བྱེད་ཀྱི་སྒྲ་རྣམས་ཡུལ་དེའི་དངོས་པོའི་གནས་ཚོད་ཀྱི་དབང་གིས་མ་ཡིན་པར་སྨྲ་བ་པོའི་བརྗོད་འདོད་དང་ཉན་པ་པོའི་ཤེས་འདོད་ལ་རག་ལས་པའི་རྒྱུ་མཚན་གྱིས་དོན་གཅིག་ཉིད། ལ་ལར་ཁྱད་གཞི་དང་ལ་ལར་ཁྱད་ཆོས་སུ་སོང་
བ་ཡིན་པས། དོན་མདོར་བསྡུ་... ན་ཉན་པ་པོས་དོན་དེ་ཉིད་ཁྱད་གཞིར་བྱས་མ་བྱས་དང་། དོན་དེ་ལ་ཤེས་འདོད་ཞུགས་མ་ཞུགས་ཀྱི་ ཁྱད་ཡིན་ནོ། དཔེར་ན་སྒྲ་གཅན་ཞེས་པ་དེ་ཅི་ཞིག་ཡིན་པ་ཤེས་པར་འདོད་ནས་དྲིས་པ
ན་ སྨྲ་བ་པོས་སྒྲ་གཅན་ མགོ་ཡིན་ཞེས་སྨྲ་ན་ཉན་པ་པོས་སྒྲ་གཅན་ལ་ཤེས་འདོད་གཏོད་ན་ཡོད་པ་མ་གཏོགས་ཆོས་གཞན་ཤེས་པར་མི་འདོད། ཡང་མགོ་ཞེས་པ་བྲིས་ནས་དེ་ཅི་ཞིག་གི་མགོ་ཡིན་པ་ཤེས་པར་འདོད་ནས

ཀ། སུམ་ རྟགས་ ཕྱི།

06 ༄༅། །དྲིས་པ་ན། སྒྲ་གཅན་གྱི་མགོ་ཞེས་སྨྲ་བའི་ཚེ་ཉན་པ་པོས་མགོ་གཙོ་བོར་ཤེས་པར་འདོད་ཀྱི་སྒྲ་གཅན་གཙོ་བོར་ཤེས་འདོད་མེད་པ་བཞིན་ཡིན་པས། དེའི་ཕྱིར་ཁྱད་གཞི་ཁྱད་ཆོས་སུ་སོང་ཞེས་པའི་དོན་ཉན་པ་པོས་གཞི
གང་ལ་གཙོ་བོར་ཤེས་འདོད་ཡོད་མེད་ལ་ལྟོས་པ་དེ་ཙམ་མ་གཏོགས་ཡུལ་གྱི་ངོས་ནས་ཁྱད་གཞི་ཁྱད་ཆོས་ལོག་ལོག་པོ་དེ་ལྟར་མེད་པའི་ཚུལ་གོ་བར་གྱིས། སྐབས་འདིར་ཆོས་དང་ཆོས་ཅན་དེ་ལྟར་གཏན་ལ་ཕབ་པ་འདི་དགོས་པ་ནི། མུ་སྟེགས
བྱེ་བྲག་པ་དག་གིས། རྣམ་དབྱེ་དྲུག་པའི་སྒྲ་ནི་ལྡན་སྦྱོར་གྱི་རིལ་བ་ལྟ་བུ་ཆོས་དང་ཆོས་ཅན་རྫས་ཐ་དད་པ་ཁོ་ན་ལ་སྦྱོར་བར་འདོད་དེ། སྒྲའི་བསྟན་བཅོས་དག་ལས། ཐ་དད་པ་ལ་ནི་དྲུག་པའོ་ཞེས་བྱུང་བས་སོ། །ཞེས་ཟེར། རང་ལུགས
ལ་ཆོས་དང་ཆོས་ཅན་རྫས་གཅིག་པ་ལ་འང་རྣམ་དབྱེ་དྲུག་པའི་སྒྲ་ཤིན་ཏུ་སྦྱོར་རུང་སྟེ། སྨྲ་བ་པོས་དོན་གཅིག་ཉིད་ཁྱད་གཞི་ལྟ་བུར་གོ་བར་བྱེད་འདོད་པ་དང་ཁྱད་ཆོས་ལྟ་བུར་གོ་བར་བྱེད་འདོད་པའི་ཀུན་ནས་སློང་བ་རྩོམ་གྱིས་ཆོས
དང་ཆོས་ཅན་གྱི་བརྡ་འབྱུམ་པར་ཟད་ཀྱི་དོན་གྱི་དབང་གིས་དེ་ལྟ་མ་ཡིན་པའི་ཚུལ་ཤེས་པར་བྱ་བའི་ཆེད་དུ་ཆོས་དང་ཆོས་ཅན་བརྗོད་པའི་སྒྲ་རྒྱས་པར་བཤད་པ་ཡིན་ནོ། །གཞན་ཡང་རང་དོན་ལེའུ་ལས། གཉིས་ཀས་གཅིག་གཅིག་
བརྗོད་མེད་ཕྱི། །ཞེས་པའི་དོན་དུ་བསམས་ནས། ཁ་ཅིག་གིས། བུམ་པ་མི་རྟག་ཅེས་པའི་སྒྲ་དང་བུམ་པའི་མི་རྟག་ཅེས་བརྗོད་པའི་སྒྲ་གཉིས་ཀ་ས་བུམ་པ་བརྗོད་པར་འདོད་ལ། རྒྱུ་འདི་ནི་སྔ་བདུན་ཕྱོད་ཀྱི་ཐུན་མོང་དུ་སྒྲ་མི་རྟག་ཅེས་...

207 བརྗོད་པའི་ངག་གིས་སྒྲ་ཡང་བརྗོད་མི་རྟག་པ་ཡང་བརྗོད་པར་གསུངས་པ་དང་མཐུན་མོད། དེ་ལ་སློབ་དཔོན་ལེགས་ལྡན་ ན་རེ། བུམ་པ་དེ་བུམ་པ་མི་རྟག་ཅེས་པའི་སྒྲས་ངོས་སུ་བརྗོད་ན། བུམ་པ་དེ་བུམ་པ་མི་རྟག་པར་འཛིན་པའི་རྟོག་པའི་ཞེན
སྟངས་ཀྱི་ཡུལ་ཡིན་དགོས་པས། དེ་ལྟར་ན་སྒྲ་མི་རྟག་པར་རྟོགས་པའི་རྗེས་དཔག་གིས་ཀྱང་སྒྲ་དང་སྒྲ་མི་རྟག་པ་གཉིས་ཀ་རྟོགས་ཟེར་ན་དགོས་པས་དེ་ལྟར་མི་འཐད་ཅེར་བ་ནི་འདོད་ཚུལ་དུ་མ་ཞིག་སྣང་བས་བློ་གྲོས་དང་ལྡན་པ་དག་གིས་དཔྱད། འོན
ཀྱང་བུམ་པ་མི་རྟག་ཅེས་བརྗོད་པའི་སྒྲས་བུམ་པ་བརྗོད་པར་ཁས་ལེན་པའི་ཚེ་བུམ་པ་མེད་ཅེས་པའི་སྒྲས་བུམ་པ་བརྗོད་པར་ཁས་ལེན་ནམ། ནོ་ཀ་ཆེན་རིགས་པའི་རྒྱ་མཚོ་དང་དོན་སྤྱི་འགལ་བས་དེ་ལྟ་བུ་གཏན་ཁས་ལེན་མི་རུང་ངོ། །དེ་ཡང
བུམ་པ་མི་རྟག་གི་ཐ་དད་ལྟ་བུ་ནི་འདོད་པས་བརྡ་གང་སྦྱར་གྱི་རྗེས་སུ་འགྲོ་བ་མ་ཡིན་པར་ཡུལ་གྱི་དངོས་པོའི་གནས་ཚོད་དང་མཐུན་པའི་ཆོས་ཡིན་པས་རྟོག་པས་བཏགས་ཙམ་ཡིན་ཡང་འདོད་པ་ཙམ་གྱིས་བཞག་ནུས་པ་མ་ཡིན་ལ། རི་བོང
ཅན་ལྟ་བ་ཡིན་པ་དེ་ཟླ་བའི་གནས་ལུགས་སུ་གྲུབ་པའི་ཆོས་མ་ཡིན་ཡང་སྐྱེས་བུས་འདོད་པ་ཙམ་གྱིས་བཞག་པ་ལྟར་འཇིག་རྟེན་གྲགས་པའི་ཆོས་ཡིན་པའི་རྒྱུ་མཚན་གྱིས་འདོད་པ་ཙམ་གྱིས་བཞག་པའི་ཆོས་ཞེས་བྱའོ། །ཐག་ཁྲ་སྦྲུལ་ལ་ཡིན
པ་དེ་སྦྲུལ་གྱི་གནས་ལུགས་སུ་གྲུབ་པ་མ་ཡིན་པར་མ་ཟད་བློ་ལོག་ཤེས་ཀྱིས་བཞག་པ་ཡིན་པས་འདོད་པས་བཞག་པའི་ཆོས་མ་ཡིན་ནོ། །དེ་དག་གི་རྒྱུ་མཚན་མཐར་ཕྱུག་པ་ནི། ཕྱིར་རྗོད་བྱེད་ཀྱི་སྒྲ་རྣམས་བརྡ་ལ་བརྟེན་ནས་དོན་གོ་བར

ཀ། ཚད་མ་ ༣

༄༅། །ཇི་ཙམ་ཅིང་། བརྡ་ལ་ཡང་སྐྱེས་བུའི་འདོད་པ་ལ་རག་ལས་ཤིང་། སྐྱེས་བུའི་འདོད་པ་ལ་མཐའ་མེད་པའི་ཕྱིར་གང་ཅི་ཡང་རུང་བ་བརྗོད་པར་འདོད་པའི་རྒྱུ་མཚན་གྱིས་ཟླ་བ་ཞེས་བརྗོད་པའི་སྒྲ་དེས་ཆོས་ཐམས་ཅད
བརྗོད་པ་ལ་འགལ་བ་མེད་པ་ཡིན་ནོ། །ཞེས་པ་འདི་ནི་སྐལ་ལྡན་བུམ་བཟང་ཐམས་པ་གླིང་དུ་དཔར་དུ་བསྒྲུབས་པའོ།། མངྒ་ལཾ ། །

TIBETAN TEXT

"Positive and Negative Phenomena"

from

The Collected Topics by
A Spiritual Son of Jam-yang-shay-ba

by Nga-wang-dra-shi

(I)

༄༅། །ཚད་མའི་དགོངས་འགྲེལ་གྱི་བསྟན་བཅོས་
ཆེན་པོ་རྣམ་འགྲེལ་གྱི་དོན་གཅིག་ཏུ་དྲིལ་བ་བློ་
རབ་འབྱེད་ཚད་མ་གསུམ་དུ་སྟོན་པ་ལེགས་
བཤད་ཆེན་པོ་མཁས་པའི་མགུལ་རྒྱན་
སྐལ་བཟང་རེ་བ་ཀུན་སྐོང་ཞེས་
བྱ་བ་བཞུགས་སོ།།

དགག་སྒྲུབ་ཀྱི་རྣམ་བཞག་བཤད་པ་
ལ༔ ཁ་ཅིག་ན་རེ། དངོས་པོ་ཡིན་ན་སྒྲུབ་
པ་ཡིན་པས་ཁྱབ་ཟེར་ན། སྒྲ་མི་རྟག་པ་ཆོས་
ཅན། སྒྲུབ་པ་ཡིན་པར་ཐལ། དངོས་པོ་ཡིན་
པའི་ཕྱིར། ཁྱབ་པ་ཁས། འདོད་ན། སྒྲ་མི་རྟག་
པ་ཆོས་ཅན། སྒྲུབ་པ་མ་ཡིན་པར་ཐལ། དགག་
པ་ཡིན་པའི་ཕྱིར། དེར་ཐལ། རང་དངོས་སུ་
རྟོགས་པའི་བློས་རང་གི་དགག་བྱ་དངོས་སུ་བཅད་
ནས་རྟོགས་དགོས་པའི་ཆོས་ཡིན་པ་གང་ཞིག།
རང་ཞེས་བརྗོད་པའི་སྒྲས་རང་གི་དགག་བྱ་
དངོས་སུ་བཅད་ནས་བརྗོད་དགོས་པའི་ཆོས་
ཡིན་པའི་ཕྱིར། རྟགས་གཉིས་པ་གྲུབ་སྟེ།
སྒྲ་མི་རྟག་ཞེས་བརྗོད་པའི་སྒྲས་སྒྲ་རྟག་པ་
ཡིན་པ་ཆོག་ཟིན་པ་དངོས་སུ་བཅད་ནས་སྒྲ་
མི་རྟག་པར་བརྗོད་པར་བྱེད་པ་ཡིན་པའི་ཕྱིར།
དེ་འཛིན་པའི་བློ་ལ་ཡང་རིགས་འགྲེ། ཁ་ཅིག་
ན་རེ། རང་གི་དངོས་མིང་གི་མཐར་མེད་ཚིག་
སྦྱར་བའི་ཆོས་ཡིན་ན། མེད་ དགག་ཡིན་
པས་ཁྱབ་ཟེར་ན། སངས་རྒྱས་ཚེ་དཔག་མེད་
ཆོས་ཅན། དེར་ཐལ། དེའི་ཕྱིར། ཁྱབ་པ་ཁས།

མ་གྲུབ་ན། སངས་རྒྱས་ཚེ་དཔག་མེད་ཆོས་
ཅན། དེ་ར་ཐལ། སངས་རྒྱས་ཚེ་དཔག་མེད་
ཞེས་བརྗོད་པའི་སྒྲ་དེ་ཁྱེད་ཀྱི་དངོས་མིང་
ཡིན་པ་གང་ཞིག །དེའི་མཐར་མེད་ཚིག་སྒྱུར་
ཀ་ཨ་ཛེ་ཉ་སུ་མ་ཏུ་གྲུབ་པ་ ཡིན་པའི་ཕྱིར།
ཛ་བར་འདོད་ན། སངས་རྒྱས་ཚེ་དཔག་མེད་
ཆོས་ཅན། མེད་དགག་མ་ཡིན་པར་ཐལ། དངོས་
པོ་ཡིན་པའི་ཕྱིར། མ་ཁྱབ་ན་ཁྱབ་པ་ཡོད་པར་
ཐལ། མེད་དགག་ཡིན་ན་རྟག་པ་ཡིན་པས་
ཁྱབ་པའི་ཕྱིར། ཁ་ཅིག་ན་རེ། དགག་པ་ཡིན་
ན་རང་གི་དངོས་མིང་ལ་དགག་ཚིག་སྒྱུར་བའི་
ཆོས་ཡིན་པས་ཁྱབ་ཟེར་ན། ནམ་མཁའ་ཆོས་
ཅན། རང་གི་དངོས་མིང་ལ་དགག་ཚིག་སྒྱུར་
བའི་ཆོས་ཡིན་པར་ཐལ། དགག་པ་ཡིན་པའི་
ཕྱིར། ཁྱབ་པ་ཁས། མ་གྲུབ་ན། ནམ་མཁའ་
ཆོས་ཅན། དགག་པ་ཡིན་པར་ཐལ། མེད་
དགག་ཡིན་པའི་ཕྱིར། མ་གྲུབ་ན། ནམ་མཁའ་
ཆོས་ཅན། མེད་དགག་ཡིན་པར་ཐལ། ཐོག

རེག་བཅད་ཚམ་གྱི་མེད་དགག་ཡིན་པའི་ཕྱིར།
དེར་ཐལ། འདུས་མ་བྱས་ཀྱི་ནམ་མཁའ་ཡིན་
པའི་ཕྱིར། རྩ་བར་འདོད་ན། ནམ་མཁའ་ཆོས་ཅན།
རང་གི་དངོས་མིང་ལ་དགག་ཚིག་སྦྱར་བའི་ཚིགས་
ཡིན་པར་ཐལ། ཁྱེད་ཀྱི་དངོས་མིང་གི་ཐུར་དུ་
དགག་ཚིག་མེད་པའི་ཕྱིར། མ་གྲུབ་ན། ནམ་
མཁའ་ཆོས་ཅན། ཁྱེད་ཀྱི་དངོས་མིང་གི་ཐུར་དུ་
དགག་ཚིག་མེད་པར་ཐལ། ནམ་མཁའ་ཞེས་
པའི་སྒྲ་དེ་ཁྱོད་ཀྱི་དངོས་མིང་ཡིན་པ་གང་ཞིག།
ནམ་དང་མཁའ་གཉིས་གང་ཡང་དགག་ཚིག་
ཡིན་པའི་ཕྱིར། གཞན་ཡང་། ཆོས་ཉིད་ཆོས་
ཅན། རང་གི་དངོས་མིང་གི་མཐར་དགག་ཚིག་
སྦྱར་བའི་ཚིག་ཡིན་པར་ཐལ། དགག་པ་ཡིན་
པའི་ཕྱིར། ཁྱབ་པ་ཁས། རྟགས་གྲུབ་སྟེ། མེད་
དགག་ཡིན་པའི་ཕྱིར། རྩ་བར་འདོད་ན། མི་ཤུས་ཏེ།
རང་གི་དངོས་མིང་གི་མཐར་དགག་ཚིག་མ་
སྦྱར་ཀྱང་། རང་དངོས་སུ་རྟོགས་པའི་བློས་
རང་གི་དགག་བྱ་དངོས་སུ་བཅད་ནས་རྟོགས་

དགོས་པའི་ཆོས་ཡིན་པའི་ཕྱིར། ཁྱབ་སྟེ།
རང་དངོས་སུ་རྟོགས་པའི་བློས་རང་གི་དགག་
བྱ་དངོས་སུ་བཅད་ནས་རྟོགས་དགོས་པའི་
ཆོས་ཡིན་ན་དགག་པ་ཡིན་པས་ཁྱབ་པའི་
ཕྱིར། དེ་ལ་ཁ་ཅིག་ན་རེ། གཟུགས་ཆོས་ཅན།
དགག་པ་ཡིན་པར་ཐལ། རང་དངོས་སུ་རྟོགས་
པའི་བློས་རང་གི་དགག་བྱ་དངོས་སུ་བཅད་
ནས་རྟོགས་དགོས་པའི་ཆོས་ཡིན་པའི་ཕྱིར།
མ་ཁྱབ་ན། གཟུགས་ཆོས་ཅན། དེར་ཐལ།
རང་དངོས་སུ་རྟོགས་པའི་རྟོག་པས་རང་གི་
དགག་བྱ་དངོས་སུ་བཅད་ནས་རྟོགས་དགོས་
པའི་ཆོས་ཡིན་པའི་ཕྱིར། མ་གྲུབ་ན། གཟུགས་
ཆོས་ཅན། དེར་ཐལ། རང་འཛིན་པའི་རྟོག་
པས་རང་མ་ཡིན་པ་རྣམ་པར་བཅད་ནས་
རྟོགས་དགོས་པའི་ཆོས་ཡིན་པའི་ཕྱིར་ཏེ་
ན་མ་ཁྱབ། མ་གྲུབ་ན། གཟུགས་ཆོས་ཅན།
ཁྱོད་འཛིན་པའི་རྟོག་པས་ཁྱོད་མ་ཡིན་པ་
རྣམ་པར་བཅད་ནས་རྟོགས་དགོས་པའི་ཕྱིར་

ཡིན་པར་ཐལ། ཁྱོད་གཞི་གྲུབ་པའི་ཕྱིར། ཁ་
ཅིག་ན་རེ། བུམ་པ་ཆོས་ཅན། སྒྲུབ་པ་མ་
ཡིན་པར་ཐལ། དགག་པ་ཡིན་པའི་ཕྱིར།
མ་གྲུབ་ན། བུམ་པ་ཆོས་ཅན། དགག་པ་ཡིན་
པར་ཐལ། རང་དངོས་སུ་རྟོགས་པའི་རྟོག་པས་
རང་མ་ཡིན་པར་རྣམ་པར་བཅད་ནས། རྟོགས་
དགོས་པའི་ཆོས་ཡིན་པའི་ཕྱིར་ཟེར་ན་མ་
ཁྱབ། མ་གྲུབ་ན། བུམ་པ་ཆོས་ཅན། ཁྱོད་དངོས་
སུ་རྟོགས་པའི་རྟོག་པས་ཁྱོད་མ་ཡིན་པར་
རྣམ་པར་བཅད་ནས་རྟོགས་དགོས་པའི་ཆོས་
ཡིན་པར་ཐལ། ཁྱོད་གཞི་གྲུབ་པའི་ཕྱིར།
རྩ་བར་འདོད་ན། བུམ་པ་ཆོས་ཅན། དགག་
པ་མ་ཡིན་པར་ཐལ། སྒྲུབ་པ་ཡིན་པའི་
ཕྱིར། མ་གྲུབ་ན། བུམ་པ་ཆོས་ཅན། སྒྲུབ་
པ་ཡིན་པར་ཐལ། བུམ་པ་དང་གཅིག་ཡིན་
པའི་ཕྱིར། ཁ་ཅིག་ན་རེ། མ་ཡིན་དགག་ཡིན་
ན། རང་ཉིད་བརྗོད་པའི་སྒྲས་རང་གི་དགག་
བྱ་བཀག་ཤུལ་དུ་ཆོས་གཞན་མ་ཡིན་

དགག་དང་སྒྲུབ་པ་གང་རུང་དངོས་སུ་འཕེན་པའི་
ཚིག་ཡིན་པས་ཁྱབ་ཟེར་ན། ལྷས་སྦྱིན་
ཚོན་པོ་ཉིན་པར་ཟས་མི་ཟ་བ་ཆོས་ཅན། དེར་
ཐལ། དེའི་ཕྱིར། ཁྱབ་པ་ཁས། མ་གྲུབ་ན། ལྷས་
སྦྱིན་ཚོན་པོ་ཉིན་པར་ཟས་མི་ཟ་བ་ཆོས་ཅན།
མ་ཡིན། དགག་ཡིན་པར་ཐལ། རང་ཞེས་བརྗོད་
པའི་སྒྲས་རང་གི་དགག་བྱ་ཚིག་ཟིན་ལ་དངོས་
སུ་བཀག་ནས་ཆོས་གཞན་མ་ཡིན་དགག་དང་
སྒྲུབ་པ་གང་རུང་འཕེན་པར་བྱེད་པ་ཡིན་པའི་
ཕྱིར། དེར་ཐལ། རང་ཞེས་བརྗོད་པའི་སྒྲས་
ཉིན་པར་ཟས་ཟ་བ་དངོས་སུ་བཀག་ནས་
མཚན་མོ་ཟ་བ་ཤུགས་ལ་འཕང་བ་གང་ཞིག
མཚན་མོ་ཟ་བ་སྒྲུབ་པ་ཡིན་པའི་ཕྱིར། རྩ་བར་
འདོད་མི་ནུས་ཏེ། ལྷས་སྦྱིན་ཚོན་པོ་ཉིན་པར་
ཟས་མི་ཟ་བ་ཞེས་པའི་སྒྲ་འདིས་རང་གི་དགག་
བྱ་ཚིག་ཟིན་ལ་དངོས་སུ་བཀག་ནས་ཆོས་
གཞན་མ་ཡིན་དགག་དང་སྒྲུབ་པ་གང་རུང་
དངོས་སུ་མི་འཕེན་ཀྱང་ཤུགས་ལ་འཕེན་པ་

ཁྱེད་པ་དེ་ཡིན་པའི་ཕྱིར། དེར་ཐལ། ལྷས་སྦྱིན་
ཚོན་པོས་ཉིན་པར་ཟས་མི་ཟ་བ་ཞེས་པའི་སྒྲ་
འདིས་ཉིན་པར་ཟས་ཟ་བ་དངོས་སུ་བཀག་
ནས་མཚན་མོ་ཟ་བ་ཤུགས་ལ་འཕེན་པ་
ཡིན་པའི་ཕྱིར། ཁྲུས་པ་ལ་ལ་ན་རེ། ལྷས་
སྦྱིན་ཚོན་པོ་ཉིན་པར་ཟས་མི་ཟ་བ་ཞེས་པའི་
སྒྲ་འདིས་རང་གི་དགག་བྱ་ཚིག་ཟིན་ལ་དངོས་
སུ་བཀག་ནས་ཆོས་གཞན་མ་ཡིན་དགག་དང་
སྒྲུབ་པ་གང་རུང་ཤུགས་ལ་འཕེན་པར་བྱེད་པ་
མ་ཡིན་པར་ཐལ། བྲམ་ཟེ་ཆང་མི་འཐུང་བ་
ཞེས་པའི་སྒྲ་འདིས་རང་གི་དགག་བྱ་ཚིག་ཟིན་ལ་
དངོས་སུ་བཀག་ནས་ཆོས་གཞན་མ་ཡིན་
དགག་དང་སྒྲུབ་པ་གང་རུང་ཤུགས་ལ་འཕེན་
པ་མ་ཡིན་པའི་ཕྱིར་ཟེར་ན་མ་ཁྱབ། རྟགས་
གྲུབ་སྟེ། བྲམ་ཟེ་ཆང་མི་འཐུང་བ་ཞེས་པའི་
སྒྲ་འདིས་རང་གི་དགག་བྱ་ཚིག་ཟིན་ལ་དངོས་
སུ་བཀག་ནས་ཆོས་གཞན་མ་ཡིན་དགག་དང་
སྒྲུབ་པ་གང་རུང་དངོས་ཤུགས་གང་རུང་དུ་མི

འཛིན་པ་ཡིན་པའི་ཕྱིར། དེར་ཐལ། བྲམ་ཟེ་ཆང་
མི་འཐུང་བ་ཞེས་པའི་སྒྲ་འདིས་བྲམ་ཟེ་ཆང་་་
འཐུང་བ་ཚིག་ཟིན་ལ་དངོས་སུ་བཀག་ནས་་་
ཆོས་གཞན་མ་ཡིན་དགག་དང་སྒྲུབ་པ་གང་རུང་
མི་འཕེན་པར་བྱེད་པ་ཡིན་པའི་ཕྱིར། དེར་ཐལ།
བྲམ་ཟེ་ཆང་མི་འཐུང་བ་མེད་དགག་ཏུ་འཇོག་དགོས་
པའི་ཕྱིར། ཁ་ཅིག་ན་རེ། མ་ཡིན་དགག་ཡིན་ན།
པ་ཡིན་
རང་ཞེས་པ་བརྗོད་པའི་སྒྲས་རང་གི་དགག་བྱ་ཚིག
ཟིན་ལ་དངོས་སུ་བཀག་ནས་ཆོས་གཞན་མ་་
ཡིན་དགག་དང་སྒྲུབ་པ་གང་རུང་འཕེན་པར་་་
བྱེད་པ་ཡིན་པའི་ཕྱིར་ཟེར་ན། རྟག་པ་ཆོས་་
ཅན། དེར་ཐལ། དེའི་ཕྱིར། ཁྱབ་པ་ཁས། མ་
གྲུབ་ན། རྟག་པ་ཆོས་ཅན། མ་ཡིན་དགག་་་
ཡིན་པར་ཐལ། དགག་པ་གང་ཞིག །མེད་དགག
མ་ཡིན་པའི་ཕྱིར། རྟགས་དང་པོ་མ་གྲུབ་ན།
རྟག་པ་ཆོས་ཅན། དགག་པ་ཡིན་པར་ཐལ།
རྟག་པ་ཡིན་པའི་ཕྱིར། མ་ཁྱབ་ན་ཁྱབ་པ་ཡོད་
པར་ཐལ། རྟག་པར་གྱུར་པའི་སྒྲུབ་པ་་་རང་

དབང་བ་མེད་པའི་ཕྱིར། དེར་ཐལ། སྒྲུབ་པ་རང་དབང་བ་ཡིན་ན་དངོས་པོ་ཡིན་པས་ཁྱབ་པའི་ཕྱིར། གོང་དུ་འདོད་མི་ནུས་ཏེ། རང་ཞེས་བརྗོད་པའི་སྒྲ་ཆོས་གཞན་མ་ཡིན་དགག་དང་སྒྲུབ་པ་གང་རུང་འཕེན་པར་བྱེད་པ་ཡིན་ཀྱང་། རང་གི་དགག་བྱ་ཚིག་ཟིན་ལ་འགོག་པར་བྱེད་པ་མ་ཡིན་པའི་ཕྱིར། དེར་ཐལ། རྟག་པ་ཞེས་པའི་ཚིག་འདི་ལ་དགག་ཚིག་སྦྱར་བ་མེད་པའི་ཕྱིར། ཁ་ཅིག་ན་རེ། རང་ཞེས་བརྗོད་པའི་སྒྲ་ཆོས་གཞན་མ་ཡིན་དགག་དང་སྒྲུབ་པ་གང་རུང་འཕེན་པར་བྱེད་པ་ཡིན་ན། རང་ཉིད་དགག་པ་ཡིན་པས་ཁྱབ་ཟེར་ན། བུམ་པ་ཆོས་ཅན། རང་ཉིད་དགག་པ་ཡིན་པར་ཐལ། རང་ཞེས་བརྗོད་པའི་སྒྲ་ཆོས་གཞན་མ་ཡིན་དགག་དང་སྒྲུབ་པ་གང་རུང་འཕེན་པར་བྱེད་པ་ཡིན་པའི་ཕྱིར། ཁྱབ་པ་ཁས། མ་གྲུབ་ན། བུམ་པ་ཆོས་ཅན། ཁྱོད་ཞེས་བརྗོད་པའི་སྒྲ་ཆོས་གཞན་མ་ཡིན་དགག་དང་སྒྲུབ་པ་གང་རུང་

འཕེན་པར་བྱེད་པ་ཡིན་པར་ཐལ། བྱེད་ཞེས་
བརྗོད་པའི་སྒྲས་བྱེད་ཀྱི་རྒྱུ་རྐྱེན་འཕེན་པར་
བྱེད་པ་ཡིན་པའི་ཕྱིར། རྩ་བར་འདོད་ན།
བྱས་པ་ཆོས་ཅན། དགག་པ་མ་ཡིན་པར་
ཐལ། སྒྲུབ་པ་ཡིན་པའི་ཕྱིར། མ་གྲུབ་ན།
བྱས་པ་སྒྲུབ་པ་ཡིན་པར་ཐལ། དངོས་པོ་
སྒྲུབ་པ་ཡིན་པ་གང་ཞིག །དེ་གཉིས་འདྲ་
བའི་ཕྱིར། ཁ་ཅིག་ན་རེ། བྱས་པ་ཆོས་ཅན།
སྒྲུབ་པ་མ་ཡིན་པར་ཐལ། དགག་པ་ཡིན་
པའི་ཕྱིར། མ་གྲུབ་ན། བྱས་པ་དགག་པ་ཡིན་
པར་ཐལ། སྒྲ་བྱས་པ་དགག་པ་ཡིན་པའི་ཕྱིར།
མ་གྲུབ་ན། དེར་ཐལ། སྒྲ་བྱས་པ་ཡིན་ནོ་
ཞེས་པའི་སྒྲ་འདིས་སྒྲ་བྱས་པ་མ་ཡིན་པ་
རྣམ་པར་བཅད་ནས་བརྗོད་དགོས་པའི་ཆོས་
ཡིན་ཞེར་ན་མ་ཁྱབ། ཅོ་ན། བྱེད་རང་ལ་གཟུགས་
དགག་པ་ཡིན་པར་ཐལ། གཟུགས་ཞེས་
བརྗོད་པའི་སྒྲས་གཟུགས་མ་ཡིན་པ་རྣམ་
པར་བཅད་ནས་བརྗོད་དགོས་པའི་ཆོས་ཡིན་

པའི་ཕྱིར། འདོད་ན། སྒྲུབ་པ་མེད་པར་ཐལ། གཟུགས་སྒྲུབ་པ་མ་ཡིན་པའི་ཕྱིར། འདོད་ན། གཞི་གྲུབ་ན། དགག་པ་ཡིན་པས་ཁྱབ་པར་ཐལ། སྒྲུབ་པ་ཡིན་པའི་ཕྱིར། རྟགས་ཁས། འདོད་མི་ནུས། ཁ་ཅིག་ན་རེ། གཟུགས་དེ་གཟུགས་ཞེས་བརྗོད་པའི་སྒྲ་འདིས་གཟུགས་མ་ཡིན་པ་རྣམ་པར་བཅད་ནས་བརྗོད་དགོས་པའི་ཆོས་ཡིན་ཟེར་ན། དེ་ཡིན་པར་ཐལ། གཟུགས་ཞེས་བརྗོད་པའི་སྒྲས་གཟུགས་མ་ཡིན་པ་རྣམ་པར་བསལ་ནས་བརྗོད་དགོས་པའི་ཆོས་ཡིན་པའི་ཕྱིར། དེར་ཐལ། གཟུགས་ཞེས་བརྗོད་པའི་སྒྲ་གཟུགས་ལ་སེལ་འཇུག་ཡིན་པའི་ཕྱིར། ཁྱབ་སྟེ། སེལ་འཇུག་ཞེས་པའི་སེལ་བའི་དོན་ཕྱི་མོས་དེ་མ་ཡིན་པ་རྣམ་པར་སེལ་བ་ལ་སྦྱོར་དགོས་པ་ཡིན་ནོ།། ༈ །།

རང་གི་ཤུགས་ལ། དགག་པའི་མཚན་ཉིད་ཡོད་དེ། རང་དངོས་སུ་རྟོགས་པའི་བློས་རང་གི་དགག་བྱ་དངོས་སུ་བཅད་ནས་རྟོགས་

དགོས་པའི་ཆོས་དེ་ཡིན་པའི་ཕྱིར། དགག་བྱ་
དང་། སེལ་བ་དང་། གཞན་སེལ་དང་། ལྡོག
པ་བཞི་དོན་གཅིག །དགག་པ་ལ་དབྱེ་ན་
གཉིས་ཡོད་དེ། མ་ཡིན་དགག་དང་མེད་
དགག་གཉིས་ཡོད་པའི་ཕྱིར། མ་ཡིན་དགག
གི་མཚན་ཉིད་ཡོད་དེ། རང་ཞེས་བརྗོད་
པའི་སྒྲས་རང་གི་དགག་བྱ་བཀག་ཤུལ་དུ་
ཆོས་གཞན་མ་ཡིན་དགག་དང་སྒྲུབ་པ་གང་
རུང་འཕེན་པའི་དགག་པ་དེ་ཡིན་པའི་ཕྱིར།
མཚན་གཞི་ནི་ཡོད་དེ། སྒྲ་མི་རྟག་པ་དེ་
ཡིན་པའི་ཕྱིར། མེད་དགག་གི་མཚན་ཉིད་ཡོད་
དེ། རང་ཞེས་བརྗོད་པའི་སྒྲས་རང་གི་དགག
བྱ་བཀག་ཤུལ་དུ་ཆོས་གཞན་མ་ཡིན་དགག
དང་སྒྲུབ་པ་གང་རུང་མི་འཕེན་པའི་དགག
པ་དེ་ཡིན་པའི་ཕྱིར། མཚན་གཞི་ནི་ཡོད་
དེ། གང་ཟག་གི་བདག་མེད་དེ་ཡིན་པའི་
ཕྱིར། དེ་ལ་དབྱེ་ན་ལྔ་ཡོད་དེ། རང་ཞེས་
བརྗོད་པའི་སྒྲས་རང་གི་དགག་བྱ་དངོས་ཟིན་

ལ་དངོས་སུ་བཀག་ནས་ཆོས་གཞན་མ་ཡིན་དགག
དང་སྒྲུབ་པ་གང་རུང་དངོས་སུ་འཕེན་པ་དང་། ཀུ་
ལ་འཕེན་པ་དང་། དངོས་ཤུགས་གཉིས་ཀར་
འཕེན་པ་དང་། སྐབས་ཐོབ་ཀྱི་འཕེན་པ་དང་།
རང་ཞེས་བརྗོད་པའི་སྒྲས་རང་གི་དགག་བྱ་ཚིག
ཟིན་ལ་བཀག་ནས་ཆོས་གཞན་མ་ཡིན་དགག
དང་སྒྲུབ་པ་གང་རུང་མི་འཕེན་པ་དང་ལྔ་ཡོད་
པའི་ཕྱིར། དང་པོ་རང་ཞེས་བརྗོད་པའི་སྒྲས་
རང་གི་དགག་བྱ་ཚིག་ཟིན་ལ་དངོས་སུ་བཀག་
ནས་ཆོས་གཞན་མ་ཡིན་དགག་དང་སྒྲུབ་པ་
གང་རུང་དངོས་སུ་འཕེན་པའི་དགག་པ་ཡོད་
དེ། བུམ་པ་གང་ཟག་གི་བདག་མེད་ཡོད་པར་
ཡིན་པའི་ཕྱིར། མ་གྲུབ་ན། དེ་ཆོས་ཅན། རང་
ཞེས་བརྗོད་པའི་སྒྲས་རང་གི་དགག་བྱ་ཚིག་ཟིན་
ལ་དངོས་སུ་བཀག་ནས་ཆོས་གཞན་མ་ཡིན་
དགག་དང་སྒྲུབ་པ་གང་རུང་དངོས་སུ་འཕེན་
པའི་དགག་པ་ཡིན་པར་ཐལ། རང་ཞེས་བརྗོད་
པའི་སྒྲས་རང་གི་དགག་བྱ་ཚིག་ཟིན་ལ་དངོས་

སྒྲ་བཀག་པ་གང་ཞིག །ཆོས་གཞན་མ་ཡིན་
དགག་དང་སྒྲུབ་པ་གང་རུང་དངོས་སུ་འཕེན་པ་
ཡིན་པའི་ཕྱིར། རྟགས་དང་པོ་གྲུབ་སྟེ། བུམ་པ་
གང་ཟག་གི་བདག་མེད་ཡོད་པ་ཞེས་བརྗོད་པའི་
སྒྲ་འདིས་བུམ་པ་གང་ཟག་བདག་ཚིག་ཟིན་པ་
འགོག་པར་བྱེད་པ་ཡིན་པའི་ཕྱིར། རྟགས་
གཉིས་པ་གྲུབ་སྟེ། བུམ་པ་གང་ཟག་གི་བདག་
མེད་ཡོད་པ་ཞེས་བརྗོད་པའི་སྒྲ་འདིས་བུམ་
པ་གང་ཟག་གི་བདག་མེད་ཡོད་པ་དངོས་སུ་
འཕང་བ་གང་ཞིག་བུམ་པ་གང་ཟག་གི་བདག་
མེད་ཡོད་པ་མ་ཡིན་དགག་ཡིན་པའི་ཕྱིར།
རྟགས་དང་པོ་སླ། གཉིས་པ་མ་གྲུབ་ན། བུམ་
པ་གང་ཟག་གི་བདག་མེད་ཆོས་ཅན། ཁྱོད་ཡོད་
པ་མ་ཡིན་དགག་ཡིན་པར་ཐལ། ཁྱོད་གཞི་
གྲུབ་པའི་ཕྱིར། གཉིས་པ་གྲུབ་སྟེ། རང་ཞེས་
བརྗོད་པའི་སྒྲས་རང་གི་དགག་བྱ་ཚིག་ཟིན་
ལ་དངོས་སུ་བཀག་ནས་ཆོས་གཞན་མ་ཡིན་
དགག་དང་སྒྲུབ་པ་གང་རུང་ཤུགས་ལ་འཕེན་

པའི་དགག་པ་བཞག་ཏུ་ཡོད་དེ། ལྷས་སྦྱིན་ཆེན་པོ་ཉིན་པར་ཟས་མི་ཟ་བ་དེ་ཡིན་པའི་ཕྱིར། དེར་ཐལ། ལྷས་སྦྱིན་ཆེན་པོ་ཉིན་པར་ཟས་མི་ཟ་བ་ཞེས་པའི་ཚིག་འདིས་རང་གི་དགག་བྱ་ཉིན་པར་ཟས་ཟ་བ་དངོས་སུ་བཀག་ནས་མཚན་མོ་ཟ་བ་ཤུགས་ལ་འཕངས་པ་གང་ཞིག །མཚན་མོ་ཟ་བ་སྒྲུབ་པ་ཡིན་པའི་ཕྱིར། དེར་ཐལ། ཟས་ཟ་བ་སྒྲུབ་པ་ཡིན་པའི་ཕྱིར། གསུམ་པ་སྒྲུབ་སྐྱེ། ངང་ཞེས་པ་བརྗོད་པའི་སྒྲས་རང་གི་དགག་བྱ་ཚིག་ཟིན་ལ་དངོས་སུ་བཀག་ནས་ཆོས་གཞན་མ་ཡིན་དགག་དང་སྒྲུབ་པ་གང་རུང་དངོས་ཤུགས་གཉིས་ཀར་འཕེན་པའི་དགག་པ་བཞག་ཏུ་ཡོད་དེ། ལྷས་སྦྱིན་ཆེན་པོ་ཉིན་པར་ཟས་མི་ཟ་བ་ལུས་རིད་པ་མ་ཡིན་པ་ཡོད་པ་དེ་ཡིན་པའི་ཕྱིར། དེར་ཐལ། ལྷས་སྦྱིན་ཆེན་པོ་ཉིན་པར་ཟས་མི་ཟ་བ་ལུས་རིད་པ་མ་ཡིན་པ་ཡོད་པ་དེ་ཡིན་པའི་ཕྱིར། དེར་ཐལ། ལྷས་སྦྱིན་ཆེན་

པོ་ཉིན་པར་ཟས་མི་ཟ་ལུས་རིད་པ་མ་ཡིན་
པ་ཡོད་པ་ཞེས་པའི་སྒྲ་དེས་ཉིན་པར་ཟས་ཟ་བ་
དངོས་སུ་བཀག་ནས་མཚན་མོ་ཟ་བ་ཤུགས་ལ་
འཕངས། ལུས་རིད་པ་མ་ཡིན་པ་ཡོད་པ་དངོས་སུ་
འཕངས། པ་ཊར་ཉིད། མཚན་མོ་ཟ་བ་སྒྲུབ་པ་
དང་། ལུས་རིད་པ་མ་ཡིན་པ་ཡོད་པ་མ་ཡིན་
དགག་ཡིན་པའི་ཕྱིར། བཞི་པ་གྲུབ་སྟེ། རང་ཞེས་
བརྗོད་པའི་སྒྲས་རང་གི་དགག་བྱ་ཚིག་ཟིན་ལ་དངོས་
སུ་བཀག་ནས་ཆོས་གཞན་མ་ཡིན་དགག་དང་
སྒྲུབ་པ་གང་རུང་ཤུགས་ཀྱིས་འཕེན་པའི་
དགག་པ་བཞག་ཏུ་ཡོད་དེ། གང་ཟག་གཅིག་
རྒྱལ་རིགས་དང་བྲམ་ཟེའི་རིགས་གང་རུང་དུ་ངེས་
ནས་ཁྱད་པར་མ་ངེས་པའི་ཚིག་འདི་ནི་བྲམ་ཟེ་
མ་ཡིན་པ་ཞེས་པའི་སྒྲ་དེས་བྲམ་ཟེ་ཡིན་པ་
ཚིག་ཟིན་ལ་དངོས་སུ་བཀག་ནས་རྒྱལ་རིགས་
ཡིན་པ་སྐབས་ཀྱིས་འཕངས་པ་ཡིན་པའི་ཕྱིར།
ཀྱིས་བརྗོད་པའི་སྒྲས་རང་གི་དགག་བྱ་ཚིག་ཟིན་
ལ་དངོས་སུ་བཀག་ནས་ཆོས་གཞན་མ་ཡིན་

དགག་དང་སྒྲུབ་པ་གང་དུང་མི་འཕེན་པ་རེ་དགག་
པ་བཞག་ཏུ་ཡོད་དེ། བྲམ་ཟེ་ཆང་མི་འཐུང་ངོ་
དེ་ཡིན་པའི་ཕྱིར། དེར་ཐལ། བྲམ་ཟེ་ཆང་མི་
འཐུང་ང་ཞེས་པའི་སྒྲ་འདིས་བྲམ་ཟེ་ཆང་
འཐུང་བ་ཚིག་ཟིན་ལ་དངོས་སུ་བཀག་ནས་
ཆོས་གཞན་མ་ཡིན་དགག་དང་སྒྲུབ་པ་གང་
དུང་དངོས་སུ་ཡང་མི་འཕེན་ཤུགས་ལ་ཡང་
མི་འཕེན། སྐབས་ཐོབ་ཀྱི་ཡང་མི་འཕེན་པ་
ཡིན་པའི་ཕྱིར། དེ་དག་མ་ཡིན་དགག་དང་
མེད་དགག་གཉིས་སུ་འདུ་ཚུལ་ཡོད་དེ།
དང་པོ་བཞི་པོ་མ་ཡིན་དགག་དང་། ཕྱི་མ་
མེད་དགག་ཏུ་འཇོག་དགོས་པ་ཡིན་པའི་ཕྱིར།
དགག་པ་ཡིན་ནུ་རང་ཞེས་བརྗོད་པའི་སྒྲས་
རང་གི་དགག་བྱ་ཚིག་ཟིན་ལ་བཀག་པས་མ་
ཐུབ་པ་ཡིན་ཏེ། མ་ཡིན་དགག་ལ་མ་ཁྱབ་
པ་གང་ཞིག །མེད་དགག་ལ་མ་ཁྱབ་པའི་
ཕྱིར། རྟགས་དང་པོ་གྲུབ་སྟེ། རྟག་པ་དང་
ཤེས་བྱ་གཉིས་མ་ཡིན་དགག་ཡིན་ཀྱང་བ

རང་ཞེས་བརྗོད་པའི་སྒྲས་རང་གི་དགག་བྱ་
ཚིག་ཟིན་པ་འགོག་པར་བྱེད་པ་མ་ཡིན་པའི་
ཕྱིར། རྟགས་གཉིས་པ་གྲུབ་སྟེ། ནམ་མཁའ་
དང་ཆོས་ཉིད་གཉིས་མེད་དགག་ཡིན་ཀྱང་
རང་ཞེས་བརྗོད་པའི་སྒྲས་རང་གི་དགག་བྱ་ཚིག་
ཟིན་པ་འགོག་པར་བྱེད་པ་མ་ཡིན་པའི་ཕྱིར། །༔ །

གཞན་སེལ་གྱི་རྣམ་བཞག་བཤད་པ་
ལ་༔ ཁ་ཅིག་ན་རེ། བྱེད་ཀྱི་གཞན་སེལ་གསུཾ་
པོ་གང་རུང་ཡོད་ན། བྱེད་ཀྱི་གཞན་སེལ་
ཡོད་པས་ཁྱབ་ཟེར་ན། རི་བོང་རྭ་ཆོས་ཅན།
བྱེད་ཀྱི་གཞན་སེལ་ཡོད་པར་ཐལ། བྱེད་ཀྱི་
གཞན་སེལ་གསུམ་པོ་གང་རུང་ཡོད་པའི་
ཕྱིར། ཁྱབ་པ་ཁས། མ་གྲུབ་ན། རི་བོང་རྭ་
ཆོས་ཅན། བྱེད་ཀྱི་གཞན་སེལ་གསུམ་པོ་
གང་རུང་ཡོད་པར་ཐལ། བྱེད་ཀྱི་བློའི་གཞན་
སེལ་ཡོད་པའི་ཕྱིར། མ་གྲུབ་ན། རི་བོང་རྭ་
ཆོས་ཅན། བྱེད་ཀྱི་བློའི་གཞན་སེལ་ཡོད་
པར་ཐལ། བྱེད་འཛིན་རྟོག་པ་ལ་བྱེད་མ་

Edited Tibetan text

of

"The Sautrāntika Tenet System"

from Jang-gya's Presentation of Tenets

(*Grub mtha'i rnam bzhag*)

ཀ

༄། །གྲུབ་པའི་མཐའི་རྣམ་པར་བཞག་པ་གསལ་བར་
བཤད་པ་ཐུབ་བསྟན་ལྷུན་པོའི་མཛེས་རྒྱན་
ཞེས་བྱ་བ་ལས་སྡེ་ཚན་དང་པོ་
བཞུགས་སོ། །

v གཉིས་པ་མདོ་སྡེ་པའི་གྲུབ་མཐའ་འཆད་པ་ལ་གསུམ། སྒྲ་བཤད་པ། དབྱེ་བ། གྲུབ་མཐའི་འདོད་ཚུལ་ལོ། །དང་པོ་ནི་མདོ་སྡེའི་རྗེས་སུ་འབྲངས་ནས་གྲུབ་པའི་མཐའ་རྣམ་པར་འཇོག་པས་མདོ་སྡེ་པ་དང་། དཔེས་སྟོན་པ་ལ[1]་མཁས་པས་ན་དཔེ་སྟོན་པར་གྲགས་ཞེས[2]་བྱང་ཆུབ་བཟང་པོ་སོགས་ཀྱིས་བཤད་དོ། །དབྱེ་བ་ལུང[3]་གི་རྗེས་འབྲངས་དང་། རིགས་པའི་རྗེས་འབྲངས་གཉིས་དེ་སྔ་མ་ནི་མདོ་སྡེ་ལས་ཇི་ལྟར་བྱུང་བ་སྒྲ་ཇི་བཞིན་དུ་ཁས་ལེན་པ་ཙམ་ཀྱི་སྒོ་ནས་གྲུབ་པའི་མཐའ་སྨྲ་བ་དང་། ཕྱི་མ་ནི་ཚད་མ་སྡེ་བདུན་ནས་བཤད་པ་ལྟར་གྱི་རིགས་པའི་རྗེས་སུ་འབྲངས་པའི་མདོ་སྡེ་པའོ། །ཕྱི་མ་འདི་ལ། རྣམ་པའི་འདོད་ཚུལ་གྱི་སྒོ་ནས་གསུམ་དུ་ཡོད་དེ་འོག་ཏུ་འཆད་དོ། །གསུམ་པ་གྲུབ་མཐའི་འདོད་ཚུལ་ལ། གང་གི་རྗེས་སུ་འབྲངས་པའི་གཞུང་དང་། དེའི་རྗེས་སུ་འབྲངས་ཏེ་གྲུབ་མཐའི་འཇོག་ཚུལ་ལོ། །དང་པོ་ནི། མདོ་སྡེ་པའི་གྲུབ་མཐའ་རང་དགའ་བ་སྟོན་པའི་གཞུང་དངོས་བོད་དུ་མ་འགྱུར་ཞིང་འདོད་པ་ཕལ་ཆེར་ནི། མཛོད་ཀྱི་རང་འགྲེལ་དང་འགྲེལ་བཤད་རྣམས་དང་། མངོན་པ་ཀུན་བཏུས་ཀྱི་འགྲེལ་དང་། ཚད་མའི་བསྟན་བཅོས་སྡེ་བདུན་མདོ་དང་བཅས་པ་རྣམས་ལས་མང་དུ་འབྱུང་

ཁ

ཞིང་། ལེགས་ལྡན་དང་ཞི་བ་འཚོ་ཡབ་སྲས་ཀྱི་གཞུང་དབང་ཕྱོར་བྱ་ཕྱོར་བྱར་བཤད་དོ།། །མངོན་པ་སྡེ་བདུན་ནི་བཀའ་མ་ཡིན་ཞིང་དགྲ་བཅོམ་པ་རྣམས་ཀྱིས་བྱས་པར་འདོད་པ་དང་། ཡང་མདོ་སྡེ་པ་ཕལ་མོ་ཆེས་དགྲ་བཅོམ་པས་བྱས་པའང་མ་ཡིན་ཏེ། ནམ་མཁའ་རྟག་རྫས་སུ་བཤད་པ་སོགས་མི་འཐད་པ་མང་བའི་ཕྱིར། དེ་འདྲའི[4]་མིང་ཅན་གྱི་སོ་སོ་སྐྱེ་བོ་དག་གིས་བྱས་པར་འདོད་དོ། །སློབ་དཔོན་ནི་ཀུ་མ་ར་ད་དང་། ཤཱི་རི་ར་ད་དང་། བཙུན་པ་ར་ད་ལ་སོགས་པ་ཡིན་པར་སྨྲ་མ་རྣམས་ལ་གྲགས་སོ། །གཉིས་པ་ལ་གཞི་ལམ་འབྲས་བུའི་འདོད་ཚུལ་གསུམ་ལས། དང་པོ་ལ་སྤྱིར་བཤད་པ་དང་། ཞིབ་པས་ཡུལ་འཛིན་ཚུལ་གྱི་ཁྱད་པར་བྱེ་བྲག་ཏུ་བཤད་པ་གཉིས་སོ། །དང་པོ་ལ། བདེན་པ་གཉིས་ཀྱི་འདོད་ཚུལ། རྟག་མི་རྟག་དང་ཕྱི་དོན་འདོད་ཚུལ་གཉིས། དང་པོ་ལ། ལུང་གི་རྗེས་འབྲང་གི་མདོ་སྡེ་པའི་འདོད་ཚུལ་ནི། གང་ལ་བཅོམ་དང་བློ་ཡིས་གཞན། །ཞེས་སོགས་གོང་གི་བྱེ་སྨྲའི་ལུགས་དང་འདྲ་ལ། རིགས་པའི་རྗེས་འབྲང[5]་གི་འདོད་ཚུལ་ནི། རྣམ་འགྲེལ་ལས། དོན་དམ་དོན་བྱེད་ནུས་པ་གང་། །དེ་འདིར་དོན་དམ་ཡོད་པ་ཡིན།[6] །གཞན་ནི་ཀུན་རྫོབ་ཡོད་པ་སྟེ། །དེ་དག་རང་སྤྱིའི་མཚན་ཉིད་བཤད། ཅེས་གསུངས་པ་ལྟར། དངོས་པོ་དང་། རང་མཚན་དང་། དོན་བྱེད་ནུས་པ་དང་། དོན་དམ་བདེན་པ་རྣམས་དོན་གཅིག་པ་དང་། དངོས་མེད་ཀྱི་ཆོས་དང་། སྤྱི་མཚན་དང་། དོན་བྱེད་མི་ནུས་པའི་ཆོས་དང་། ཀུན་རྫོབ་བདེན་པ་རྣམས་དོན་གཅིག་པར་འདོད་པས། དོན་དམ་བདེན་པའི་ངོ་བོ་ནི། སྒྲ་དང་རྟོག་པས་བཏགས་པ་ལ་མ་ལྟོས་པར་རང་གི་སྡོད་ལུགས་ཀྱི་ངོས་ནས་རིགས་པས་དཔྱད……བཟོད་དུ་གྲུབ་པ་དང་། ཀུན་རྫོབ་བདེན་པའི་ངོ་བོ་ནི། རང་ལས་གཞན་པའི་ཡིད་བྱེད་སོགས་སྒྲ་དང་རྟོག་པས་བཞག་པ་ཙམ་དུ་གྲུབ་པའམ། རང་ལས་གཞན་པའི་སྒྲ་

དང་རྟོག་པ་ཡོད་པ་ཙམ་གྱིས་རང་ཉིད་གཞལ་ནུས་པའོ། །མཚན་ཉིད་འཇོག་ཚུལ་འདི་རྗེ་བདག་ཉིད་ཆེན་པོ་འི་སྲས་ཀྱི་ཐུ་བོ་གཉིས་ཀྱིས་གསལ་བར་གསུངས་པ་ལྟར་ཡིན་ལ། དོན་དམ་དོན་བྱེད་ནུས་པ་གང་། །ཞེས་སོགས་ན། དེ་གཉིས་ཀྱི་མཚན་གཞི་སྟོན་པ་ཡིན་གྱི། མཚན་ཉིད་སྟོན་པ་མིན་ནོ། །དེས་ན། མདོ་སྡེ་པའི་ལུགས་ལ་དོན་དམ་པར་ཡོད་པ་དང་། དོན་དམ་བདེན་པ་གཉིས་ཡིན་ཁྱབ་མཉམ་དང་། ཀུན་རྫོབ་ཙམ་དུ་ཡོད་པ་དང་ཀུན་རྫོབ་བདེན་པ་གཉིས་ཀྱང་ཡིན་ཁྱབ་མཉམ་ཡིན་ནོ། །བདེན་གཉིས་ཀྱི་མཚན་ཉིད་འདི་ནི་སེམས་ཙམ་པས་ཀྱང་འདོད་མོད་ཀྱང་མཚན་གཞི་འཇོག·····ཚུལ་མི་གཅིག་གོ །མཛོད་ནས་བཤད་པ་དང་ཡང་མི་གཅིག་སྟེ། དེས་བུམ་པ་ལ་སོགས་པ་ཀུན་རྫོབ་བདེན་པར་བཞག་ཅིང་འདིས་ནི་བུམ་པ་རང་མཚན་དང་དོན་དམ······བདེན་པར་འཇོག་པའི་ཕྱིར་རོ། །བདེན་གཉིས་ཀྱི་སྒྲ་བཤད་ནི། སྤྱི་མཚན་རྣམས་ཆོས་ཅན། ཀུན་རྫོབ་བདེན་པ་ཞེས་བྱ་སྟེ། བློ་ཀུན་རྫོབ་པའི་ངོར་བདེན་པའི་ཕྱིར་རོ། ། འདིའི་བློ་ཀུན་རྫོབ་པ་ནི་རྟོག་པ་སྟེ། རང་མཚན་དངོས་སུ་གཟུང་ཡུལ་དུ་བྱེད་པ་ལ་སྒྲིབ་པས་ན་ཀུན་རྫོབ་ཅེས་བྱའོ། །རང་མཚན་རྣམས་ཆོས་ཅན། དོན་དམ་བདེན་པ་ཞེས་བྱ་སྟེ། བློ་དོན་དམ་པའི་ངོར་བདེན་པའི་ཕྱིར་རོ། །འདིའི་བློ་དོན་དམ་པ་ནི་སྣང་ཡུལ་ལ་མ་འཁྲུལ་བའི་ཤེས་པའོ། །ལུང་གི་རྗེས་འབྲང་གི་མདོ་སྡེ་པས་བདེན་གཉིས་ཀྱི་མཚན་ཉིད་དང་མཚན་གཞིའི་འཇོག་ཚུལ་ཙམ་བྱེ་སྨྲ་དང་འདྲ་ཡང་དེ······དག་གི་རྣམ་གཞག་འཇོག་ཚུལ་ནི་ཆེས་མི་འདྲ་སྟེ། བྱེ་སྨྲས་ཡོད་པར་འདོད་ཕྱིན་ཆད་རྫས་གྲུབ་ཏུ་འདོད་ལ། མདོ་སྡེ་པ་སུས་ཀྱང་དེ་ལྟར་མི་འདོད་པའི་ཕྱིར་རོ། །འདིའི་སྤྱི་མཚན་ནི་ནམ་མཁའ་ལ་སོགས་པའི་འདུས་མ་བྱས་ཀྱི་ཆོས་རྣམས་ཡིན་ལ། སྤྱི་དང་། གཞི་མཐུན་དང་། བྱེ་བྲག་དང་། གཅིག་དང་། ཐ་དད་དང་། འབྲེལ་བ་དང་

བསྒྲུབ་བྱ[8]་སྒྲུབ་བྱེད་ལ་སོགས་པ་སྒྲོ་བཏགས་པའི་ཆོས་རྣམས་ཀྱང་སྤྱི་མཚན་ཡིན་མོད་······ཀྱང་། དེ་དག་ཡིན་ན་སྤྱི་མཚན་ཡིན་མི་དགོས་སོ། །དེའི་རྒྱུ་མཚན་ཡང་རྟོག་པའི་དངོས་ཡུལ་གྱི་རང་ལྡོག་རང་མཚན་མ་ཡིན་ཀྱང་རང་མཚན་རྟོག་པའི་དངོས་ཡུལ་དུ་འགྱུར་བ···མི་འགལ་བས། གསེར་བུམ་བུམ་པར་འཛིན་པའི་རྟོག་པ་ལ། གསེར་བུམ་ཡང་བུམ་པར་སྣང་ཞིང་རང་གི་དངོས་ཀྱི་གཟུང་བྱ་དེའང་བུམ་པར་སྣང་ལ། སྣང་བའི་དོན་དེ་གཉིས་གཅིག་ཏུ་འདྲེས་ནས་སྣང་ཞིང་སྣང་ངོར་དབྱེར་མེད་པས་སྣང་བཏགས་གཅིག་ཏུ་བསྲེས་པ་ཞེས་བྱ་སྟེ། སྣང་བ་ནི་རང་མཚན་དང་། བཏགས་པ་ནི་སྒྲ་དོན་ནོ། །སྒྲ་དོན་ཞེས་པ་གང་ལ་བྱ་སྙམ་ན། བུམ་འཛིན་རྟོག་པའི་མདུན་ན་འདུག་པ་ལྟ་བུར་སྣང་བའི་གསེར་བུམ་བུམ་པར་སྣང་བ་དེ་དང་། སྣང་བ[9]་དེ་ཉིད་བུམ་པ་མ་ཡིན་པ་ལས་ལོག་པར་སྣང་བ་གཉིས་ཀའོ། །གསེར་བུམ་བུམ་པ་མ་ཡིན་པ་ལས[10]་ལོག་པར་སྣང་བ་དང་། སྣང་བ་དེ་ཉིད་བུམ་མ་ཡིན་པ་ལས་ལོག་པར་སྣང་བ་གཉིས་འདྲེས་ནས་སྣང་ཞིང་། སྣང་ངོར་སོ་སོར་མི་ཕྱེད་ཀྱང་དེ་གཉིས་གཅིག་གོ་སྙམ་དུ་རྟོག་པས་འཛིན་པ་ནི་མ་ཡིན་ནོ། །དེས་ན་རྟོག་ངོར་གསེར་བུམ་བུམ་པར་སྣང་བ་དེ་ཉིད་བུམ་མ་ཡིན་ལས་ལོག་པ་མ་ཡིན་བཞིན་དུ་དེར་སྣང་བས་སྣང་ཡུལ་ལ་འཁྲུལ་བ་ཡིན་ཀྱང་བློ་དེ་འཛིན་སྟངས་ལ་གསེར་བུམ་བུམ་པའོ···སྙམ་དུ་འཛིན་གྱི། སྒྲ་དོན་བུམ་པའོ་སྙམ་པ་དང་གསེར་བུམ་སྣང་བ་འདི་ཉིད་བུམ་པའོ་སྙམ་དུ་ཞེན་པ་སོགས་མེད་པས་ཞེན་ཡུལ་ལ་འཁྲུལ་བ་མིན་ནོ། །སྒྲ་དོན་ཞེས་པ་སྤྱིར་བཤད་པ་ལྟར་ཡིན་གྱི་སྒྲ་སྤྱི་དང་དོན་སྤྱི་ཞེས་སོ་སོར་ཕྱེ་ནས་འཆད་རྒྱུ་མིན་པར···རྗེ་ཡབ་སྲས་རྣམས་ཀྱིས་ལན་དུ་མར་བཤད་ལ། ཕྱི་དུས་ཀྱི་རང་རེའི་མཁས་པ་ཕལ་མོ་ཆེས་སྒྲ་དོན་འཛིན་པའི་ཞེན་རིག་རྟོག་པའི་མཚན་ཉིད་དུ་སྨྲས་པ་ལ་བརྟ[11]་ལ་མ་བྱུང་བའི···བྱིས་པའི་རྒྱུད་ཀྱི་རྟོག་པས་མ་ངེས་པའི་སྐྱོན་སྨྲས་ནས་རང་ལུགས་འཛུག་སྐབས་སྒྲ་དོན······

འདྲེས་ཚུང་དུ་འཛིན་པའི་ཞེན་རིག་རྟོག་པའི་མཚན་ཉིད་དུ་འཇོག་པའི་ཞིབ་ཆ་མཛད་པ་ནི་དོན་ཆུང་བར་སེམས་ཏེ། གཞུང་ཆེན་མོ་རྣམས་ལས་མཚན་ཉིད་དང་མཚན་གཞི་སོ་སོར་ཀྱི་རྣམ་གཞག་གསུངས་པ་རྣམས་ནི་དོན་གྱི་ངོ་བོ་དང་ཁྱད་པར་སོ་སོར་ཀྱི་དོན་ལྡོག་ཤེས་པའི་ཕྱིར་དུ་གསུངས་པ་ཡིན་གྱི་གང་ཟག་གི་གསལ་བའི་དབྱེ་བ་མཐའ་དག་གི་འཛིན་ཚུལ་ཀུན་མིང་མ་ཡིན་པ་མཐའ་དག་མཚན་ཉིད་ཀྱི་ཟུར་ལ་ཚང་མི་དགོས་པའི་ཕྱིར་དང་། གཞན་དུ་ན་ཁྱེད་རང་རྣམས་ཀྱིས་བྱས་པའི་སྒྲ་དོན་འདྲེས་ཚུང་དུ་འཛིན་པའི་ཞེན་རིག་བྱས་འཛིན་རྟོག་པའི་མཚན་ཉིད་དུ་སྨྲ་བ་པའང་མི་འཐད་པར་འགྱུར་ཏེ། ལྡོ་ཕྱིར་བ་ལ་བྱས་པ་ནི་ཐ་སྙད་མ་གྲགས་ཤིང་ཐ་སྙད་ཀུན་གྱིས་འཛོད་པའི་ཡུལ་དུས་ཀྱི་དབང་དུ་བྱས་ང་ནི་གང་ཟག་གི་རྒྱུད་ཀྱི་རྟོག་པས་མ་ངེས་པའི་ཕྱིར་རོ། །གཞན་ཡང་བཟ་ལ་མ་
[12]ཕྱུང་བའི་བྲིས་པ་ལ་བྱས་པ་རང་གི་ངོ་བོ་དང་ཁྱད་པར་དུ་སྒྲོ་འདོགས་པའི་ཐ་སྙད་ཀྱི་གཞིར་སྣང་བ་དང་། དེ་འདྲའི་ཐ་སྙད་ཀྱི་གཞིར་ཞེན་པའི་འཛིན་ཚུལ་ཡོད་པར་ནི་གདོན་མི་ཟ་བར་ཁས་ལེན་དགོས་ཏེ། དེའི་རྒྱུད་ཀྱི་བུམ་པ་དེ་འདྲའི་ཐ་སྙད་ཀྱི་གཞིར་རང་གི[13]་མཚན་ཉིད་ཀྱིས་སྣང་བའི་སྣང་ཚུལ་དེ་དོན་སྤྱི་ལྟར་ན་འཐད་ལྡན་དང་། རྣམ་རིག་པ་ལྟར་ན་འཁྲུལ་བ་ཡིན་པར་དྲང་ངེས་རྣམ་འབྱེད་དང་དེའི་མཐའ་དཔྱོད་རྣམས་ཀྱིས་ལན་ཅིག་མ་ཡིན་པར་བཤད་པའི་ཕྱིར། གལ་ཏེ་དེ་ནི་བཟ་བྱུང་གི་གང་ཟག་ཁོ་ནའི་དབང་དུ་བྱས་སོ་ཟེར་ན། དེ་ལྟར་ན་བཟ་ལ་མ་བྱུང་བའི་བྲིས་པའི་དབང་དུ་བྱས་པའི་ངོ་བོ་དང་ཁྱད་པར་དུ་སྒྲོ་བཏགས་པའི་ཆོས་ཀྱི་བདག་འཛིན་གྱི་འཛིན། ཚུལ་སོར་རྣམ་རིག་པའི་ལུགས་ལ་ཇི་ལྟར་འཇོག ཅི་སྟེ་བུམ་པ་ཞེས་བརྗོད་པའི་སྐད་འཇུག་གཞིའི་འཛིན་ཚུལ་མེད་མོད་ཀྱང་བུམ་པའོ་སྙམ་པའི་རྟོག་པའི་ཞེན་གཞིའི་དབང་དུ་བྱས་སོ་ཞེ་ན། གང་ཟག་དེའི་རྒྱུད་ཀྱི་རྟོག་པ་དེ་སྐའི་ཐ་སྙད་གང་ལའང་མ་བརྟེན་པའི་རྟོག་པ་ཞིག་ཡིན

ནམ།   འོན་ཏེ་བུམ་པའོ་ཞེས་པའི་མིང་དང་བུམ་པའི་གཟུགས་སོ་སྙམ་པའི་ཁྱད་པར་གྱི་རྟོག་གེ་སྒྲའི་ཐ་སྙད་ལ་བརྟེན་པའི་རྟོག་པ་ཞིག་ཡིན་ནམ།   མིང་དང་ཚིག་གི་སྒྲའི་ཐ་སྙད་གཞན་ཞིག་ལ་བརྟེན་པའི་རྟོག་པ་ཡིན་གྲང་།   དང་པོ་ལྟར་ན་རྟོག་པ་རེས་ཡུལ་དེ་ལ་ཇི་ལྟར་ཞེན་ཅིང་ཡུལ་དེ་རྟོག་པ་དེ་ལ་ཇི་ལྟར་སྣང་བའི་ཁྱད་པར་བརྗོད་པར་བྱ……དགོས་སོ།   །གཉིས་པ་ལྟར་ན་དེ་འདྲའི་གང་ཟག་དེ་བརྡ་ལ་མ་བྱང་བར་བྱུར།   གསུམ་པ་ལྟར་ན་ངོ་བོ་དང་ཁྱད་པར་གྱི་ཐ་སྙད་གཞན་ཇི་ལྟ་བུ་ཞིག་ལ་བརྟེན་པ་བརྗོད་པར་གྱིས་ཤིག   །གལ་ཏེ་བརྡ་ལ་མ་བྱང་བའི་[illegible]ས་པ་དེའི་རྒྱུད་ལ་བུམ་ལྟོ་ལྡིར་བ་དེ་བུམ་པ་ཞེས་སོགས་ཀྱི་སྒྲ་ཁྱད་པར་ཅན་གྱི་འཇུག་གཞིར་ཞེན་པ་མེད་ཀྱང་སྤྱིར་རྟོག་ངོ་ན་ཇི་ལྟར་ཡོད་པའི་ཐ་སྙད་ཀྱི་བརྗོད་གཞིར་ཞེན་པ་ཡོད་པས་མི་འགལ་ལོ་ཞེར་ན།   དེའི་རྟོག་ངོ་ན་ཇི་ལྟར་ཡོད་ཚུལ་དེ་ཡང་མཚན་ཉིད་ཀྱི་ཟུར་ལ་བརྗོད་པར་རིགས་སོ།   །དེ་ལྟར་ན་གང་ཟག་གི་གསལ་བའི་དབྱེ་བ་མཐའ་ཡས་པས་བརྗོད་ཀྱིས་མི་ལང་ངོ་ཞེར་ན།   །དེ་ནི་ཤིན་ཏུ་བདེན་མོད།   དེ་ལྟར་ན་གཞུང་ཆེན་མོ་སྤྱི་དང་ཇོ་ཡབ་སྲས་ཀྱི་གསུང་རབ་རྣམས་ལས་གསུངས་པའི་མཚན་ཉིད་དང་།   དབྱེ་བ་དང་།   གྲངས་ངེས་སོགས་ཀྱི་རྣམ་གཞག་ལ་ཡུལ་དུས་གང་ཟག་གི་གསལ་བའི་དབྱེ་བས་མ་ངེས་པའི་སྐྱོན་བརྗོད་ནས་ཤེས་རྡའི་··གྲངས་དང་མཉམ་པའི་མཚན་ཉིད་ཀྱི་ཟུར་ཚང་དགོས་པའི་ཞིབ་ཆ་བྱེད་པ་དེར་ནས……དགོངས་འགྲེལ་ཆེན་པོ་རྣམས་ཀྱི་གཞུང་ཚིག་གོ་བ་སྟེར་ཕྱུལ་ཆེ་བ་རྣམས་སྒྲ་སོར་བཞག་··མཇེད་ན་ལེགས་སམ་སྙམ་མོ།   །རྒྱལ་ཚབ་ཐམས་ཅད་མཁྱེན་པས་ཚད་མ་ཀུན་བཏུས་ཀྱི་རྣམ་བཤད་ལས།   མིང་དང་རིགས་སོགས་སྦྱོར་བ་ཡི།   །རྟོག་པ་དང་བྲལ་མངོན་སུམ་མོ།   །ཞེས་པའི་ཐད་དུ་བརྡ་ལ་མ་བྱང་བའི་བྱིས་པའི་རྒྱུད་ཀྱི་བརྗོད་བྱ་དང་རྗོད་བྱེད[14] འདྲེས་རུང་གི་རྟོག་པ་བསྟུ་པར་གསུངས་པ་ཡང་རྟོག་པའི་དངོས་ཡུལ་གྱི་སྒྲ་དོན་ལ་

སྒྲ་སྤྱི་དང་དོན་སྤྱི་ཞེས་སོ་སོར་ཕྲལ་ནས་སྦྱོར་བའི་དོན་མིན་ནོ། །དེས་ན་རིག་པའི་དབང་ཕྱུག་གིས། ཤེས་གང་གང་ལ་སྒྲ་དོན་འཛིན། །དེ་ནི་15 དེ་ལ་རྟོག་པ་ཡིན། ཞེས་སོགས་ཀྱི་འགྲེལ་པ་འགྲེལ་བཤད་རྣམས་དང་དེ་གཞི་ཐད་ཀྱི་རྗེ་བདག་ཉིད་ཆེན་པོ་ཡབ་སྲས་ཀྱི་གསུང་རབ་ཏུ་མར་རྟོག་པའི་དངོས་ཡུལ་དང་སྒྲའི་བརྗོད་བྱའི་རང་ལྡོག་ཉིད་ལ་སྒྲ་དོན་དུ་བཤད་ཅིང་སྒྲ་སྤྱི་དང་དོན་སྤྱི་ཞེས་སོ་སོར་ཕྲལ་དེ་འཆད་རྒྱུ་མིན་པར་གསུངས་སོ། །དེ་ལ་སྒྲ་དོན་ཞེས་བརྗོད་པའི་རྒྱུ་མཚན་ཡང་འདི་ལྟར་ཡིན་ཏེ། སྤྱིར་གཞི་དཀར་ཟལ་ལྟ་བུ་བ་ལང་གི་བརྡ་སྦྱོར་བའི་གཞི་དང་། གསལ་བ་གཅིག་གཞིར་བཟུང་ནས་བརྡ་སྦྱར་བས་ཀུན་གོ་བ་དང་། བརྡ་སྦྱོར་བ་ཐ་སྙད་ཀྱི་ཆེད་དུ་ཡིན་པར་ཕྱི་ནང་གཉིས་ཀ་མཐུན་ཡང་དེ་ལྟར་གོ་བའི་རྒྱུ་མཚན་ལ་མི་མཐུན་ཏེ། གཞན་སྡེ་ནི་བརྡ་སྦྱར་བའི་སྤྱི་ཆ་མེད་གཅིག་གསལ་བ་ཀུན་ལ་ཡོད་པས་གཅིག་ལ་བརྡ་སྦྱར་བའི་རྗེས་སུ་གསལ་བ་གཞན་ཡང་སྤྱི་དེ་མཐོང་ནས་བ་ལང་དུ་གོ་བས་གསལ་བ་རེ་རེ་ནས་བརྡ་སྦྱོར་མི་དགོས་ཟེར་རོ། །རང་སྡེ་སངས་རྒྱས་པ་ནི་བ་ལང་མ་ཡིན་པ་ལས་ལོག་པའི་གཞན་སེལ་བ་ལ་བརྡ་སྦྱར་བར་འདོད་ཅིང་། དེ་ཉིད་བ་ལང་གི་གསལ་བ་ཀུན་ལ་ཁྱད་མེད་པར་རྗེས་སུ་འགྲོ་བས་རེ་རེ་ནས་བརྡ་སྦྱོར་མི་དགོས་པར་བཞེད་དོ། །དེས་ན་བརྡ་སྦྱོར་དུས་ཀྱི་དཀར་ཟལ་དང་བ་ལང་མ་ཡིན་པ་ལས་ལོག་པའི་ཚོགས་པ་ལ་བརྡ་སྦྱར་བ་མིན་ཡང་། དཀར་ཟལ་གཞིར་བཟུང་ནས་བརྡ་སྦྱར་བའི་ཚེ་ནོག་དང་ལྐོག་ཤལ་སོགས་ལྡན་པ་རྒྱུ་མཚན་དུ་བྱས་ནས་བ་ལང་མ་ཡིན་པ་ལས་ལོག་པའི་གཞན་སེལ་བ་ལ་བརྡ་སྦྱར་བ་ཡིན་པས་དེ་ལ་སྒྲ་དོན་དུ་བརྗོད་པའི་རྒྱུ་མཚན་ནི་དེའོ། །དེ་ལྟར་ཡང་སློབ་དཔོན་ཀ་མ་ལ་ཤཱི་ལས། སྒྲ་རྣམས་ཀྱིས་དངོས་སུ་བསྟན་པ་དང་དགག་པ་སྒྲས་དངོས་པོ་འདི་རང་བཞིན་དུ་སྒྲུབ་པར་བྱེད་པའི་ཕྱིར་སྒྲུབ་པ་ཉིད་སྒྲའི་དོན་ཡིན་ནོ་ཞེས་བྱ་བ་ནི་སྒྲའི་དོན་སྒྲུབ་པར་སྨྲ་བ་

[16]

ཉམས་ཀྱི་ལྟ་བའོ། །སེལ་བར་སྨྲ་བ་རྣམས་ནི་དམ་པའི་དོན་དུ་དངོས་པོའི་རང་གི་ངོ་བོ་ལ་སྒྲ་རྣམས་ཀྱིས་བརྗོད་པར་བྱ་བ་ཅུང་ཟད་ཀྱང་ཡོད་པ་མིན་ཏེ། སྒྲའི་ཤེས་པ་ཐམས་ཅད་ཉིད་ནི་འཁྲུལ་པས་ཐ་དད་པའི་དོན་རྣམས་ལ་ཐ་མི་དད་པའི་རྣམ་པས་འཇུག་པ་ཡིན་ཏེ། གང་ལ་བརྒྱུད་པས་དངོས་པོ་དང་འབྲེལ་བ་དེ་ནི་འཁྲུལ་བ་ཉིད་ཡིན་ཡང་དོན་ལ་མི་སླུ་བ་ཉིད་ཡིན་པར་ལྟ་བ་ཡིན་ཏེ། དེ་ལ་སྒྲོ་བཏགས་པ་རྣམ་པར་རྟོག་པའི་བློ[17]་གང་ཡིན་པ་དེས་དོན་དང་ཐ་མི་དད་པའི་ངོ་བོ་དེ་ལས་གཞན་པ་ལས་ལྡོག་པའི་དངོས་པོ་ཉམས་སུ་མྱོང་བའི་སྟོབས་ལས་འོངས་པའི་ཕྱིར་དང་། རང་ཉིད་ཀྱང་གཞན་ལས་ལོག་པར་སྣང་བའི་ཕྱིར་འཁྲུལ་པ་ཡིན་ཡང་གཞན་ལས་ལྡོག་པར་དོན་དང་ལྷན་ཅིག་པར་ངེས་པའི་ཕྱིར་དང་། གཞན་སེལ་བའི་དངོས་པོ་རྟོགས་པ་འདྲས་བུ་ཡིན་པའི་ཕྱིར། གཞན་སེལ་བ་ཞེས་བརྗོད་དོ། །དེས་ན་སྒྲའི་དོན་ནི་སེལ་བ[18]་ཡིན་པར་གྲུབ་པོ[19]་ཞེས་གསུངས་སོ། །དེས་ན་གཞན་སྡེ་རྣམས་ཀྱིས་བྱས་པའི་སྐྱམ་པའི་བློ་ལ་དགག་བྱ་བཅད་ལྡོག་མི་སྣང་བར་སྒྲུབ་པ་རང་དབང་བའི་ཚུལ་གྱིས་སྣང་བ་རྒྱ་མཚན་དུ་བྱས་ནས། སྒྲ་རྟོག་ཐམས་ཅད་དངོས་དབང་གིས་འཇུག་པ་ཡིན་པས་སྒྲུབ་འཇུག་ཏུ་འདོད་དོ། །དྲངས་མ་ཐག་པའི་གཞུང་འདིརས་སྒྲ་དོན་ཞེས་པ་སྒྲའི་དོན་ཟེར་རྒྱུ་ཡིན་པར་བཤད་ཅིང་སྒྲའི་དོན་ཞེས་རྣམ་དབྱེ་དྲུག་པར་བྱུང་བས་སྒྲ་སྤྱི་དང་དོན་སྤྱི་ཞེས་སོ་སོར་ཕྲལ་ནས་དེ་གཉིས་ཀ་རྟོག་པ་གཅིག་གི་ཡུལ་དུ་བྱེད་ནུས་པ་ལ་འདྲེས་པ་དང་། བརྡ་ལ་མ་བྱང་བས་དེ་གཉིས་གང་རུང་ཡུལ་དུ་བྱེད་པ་བསླུ་བའི་ཕྱིར་དུ་འདྲེར་རུང་བ་ཞེས་སོགས་ཀྱི་ངལ་བ་དེ་ཙམ་མི་དགོས་སོ། །དེ་ཡང་རྣམ་ངེས་ལས། རྟོག་པ་ནི་བརྗོད་པ་དང་འདྲེར་རུང་བར་སྣང་བའི་ཤེས་པ་སྟེ་ཞེས་གསུངས་པའི་དོན་ནི། རྟོག་པ་ལ་སྒྲ་དོན་སྣང་ཞིང་སྒྲ་དོན་དེ་ཡང་དངོས་སུ་བརྡ་སྦྱར་བའི་ཡུལ་ཡིན་པའི་ཕྱིར་བརྗོད་པ་དང་འདྲེར་རུང་བ་ཞེས་གསུངས་པ་ཡིན་གྱི།

རྟོག་ངོ་ན་སྒྲ་སྤྱི་དང་དོན་སྤྱི་གཉིས་ཀ་ཡོད་པ་ལ་དེ་གཉིས་འདྲེས་པའི་ཐ་སྙད་ཉུས་པ་མ···
ཡིན་པར་སྟེ་བཏུན་ཡོད་ཀྱི་ཐུན་སེལ་དུ་བཤད་དོ། །དེ་ལྟར་ན་འདི་བ་ལང་ངོ། །སྐྱེས་
པའི་བློ་འི་ཐ་སྙད་དང་དེ་ལྟར་བརྗོད་པའི་སྒྲའི་ཐ་སྙད་འཇུག་པའི་གཞིའི་རང་ལྡོག་ནི······
རྟོག་པས་བཏགས་པ་ཙམ་དང་སྤྱི་མཚན་ཡིན་ལ། དེ་དག་གི་གཞི་ལྡོག་ཏུ་གྱུར་པའི་བ་
ལང་སོགས་ནི་རང་མཚན་ཡིན་པས་གསལ་བ་རྣམས་ལ་རྗེས་སུ་འགྲོ་བའི་སྤྱི་ལ་ནི་དངོས་
པོང་[20]ནཱ་དངོས་པོ་མེད་པ་གཉིས་གཉིས་ཡོད་དེ། དཀར་ཟལ་དང་ནག་ཀྲུར་གཉིས་ཀ་ལ་
རྗེས་སུ་འགྲོ་བའི་བ་ལང་མ་ཡིན་པ་ལས་ལོག་པའི་དོན་གྱི་གཞན་སེལ་དང་། རྟོག་པ་ལ་
བ་ལང་མ་ཡིན་པ་ལས་ལོག་པར་སྣང་བ་སྒྲ་དོན་གྱི་མཚན་གཞིར་གྱུར་པའི་བློ་འི་སེལ······
བ་གཉིས་སོ། །དོན་འདི་ནི་མཁས་པའི་དབང་པོ་ཀ་མ་ལ་ཤཱི་ལས་ཚད་མའི་དེ་ཁོ་ན་
ཉིད་བསྡུས་པའི་སྒྲ་དོན་བརྟག་པའི་[21]འགྲེལ་པར་ཞིབ་ཏུ་གསུངས་ཤིང་། རྣམ་འགྲེལ་
ལེའུ་དང་པོ་འི་འགྲེལ་བཤད་སློབ་དཔོན་ཤཱཀྱ་བློས་མཛད་པ་དང་། རྗེ་ཐམས་ཅད་མཁྱེན་
པའི་སྲས་ཀྱི་ཐུ་བོ་གཉིས་ཀྱི་ཚད་མའི་བརྗེད་བྱང་སོགས་དང་། རྣམ་འགྲེལ་ངེས་ཀྱི་
ཊཱིཀྐ་ཆེན་མོ་རྣམས་སུ་ཞིབ་པར་མཐའ་དཔྱད་[22]པའི་སྒོ་ནས་གསལ་བར་བཀའ་དྲིན་མཛད···
མོད་ཀྱང་། དེང་དུས་ཀྱི་རྟོག་གེ་པ་གང་དག་གཞུང་ལུགས་ཆེན་མོ་རྣམས་ལ་ཀ་ཏིགས་ [23]
སུ་མི་བྱེད་པར་གཞན་དང་གཤའ་[24]འཕྱེད་པའི་ཚེ་ཚིག་འཕྲིའི་མགོ་ཡོར་ཁོ་ན་ལ་སྐྱབས···
སུ་འཛིན་པ་དང་། དོན་གྱི་གནད་འགག་པོར་བའི་ཐལ་འགྱུར་སྐམ་པོ་འི་བླུ་བའི་
འཕྲེང་བ་ལ་སྙིང་པོ་འི་མཆོག་ཏུ་འཛིན་པ་དག་ལ་ནི་ཕྱོགས་མཐོང་ཙམ་ལས་དགོངས་པ··
ཇི་བཞིན་པ་བསྐལ་དོན་དུ་སོང་བས་གསུང་རབ་དེ་དག་ཀྱང་ཇོ་ཇེའི་ཚིག་ལྟ་བུར་གྱུར་ཏོ། །
གཉིས་པ་རྟག་མི་རྟག་དང་ཕྱི་དོན་འདོད་ཚུལ་ལ་གཉིས་ལས། དང་པོ་ལ་རྟག་མི་རྟག་གི་
འདོད་ཚུལ་དངོས་དང་། ཞར་བྱུང་སེལ་བའི་རྣམ་གཞག་གཉིས། དང་པོ་ནི། གཞན་

ཕྱི་དང་རང་སྡེ་བྱེ་བྲག་སྨྲ་བས་རྟག་པའི་འདོད་ཚུལ་གོང་དུ་བཤད་པ་ལྟར་རྟག་པ་ཡིན་ཕྱིན་ཆད་དུས་སྔ་མ་ན་གང་ཡོད་དུས་ཕྱི་མ་ནའང་ཡོད་པར་འདོད་ལ། མི་རྟག་པའི་འདོད་ཚུལ་ནི་བྱེ་བྲག་སྨྲ་བས་དངོས་པོ་ལ་རྟག་མི་རྟག་གཉིས་ཡོད་པར་འདོད་པ་དང་། འདུས་བྱས་ཀྱི[25]་མཚན་ཉིད་སྐྱེ་འཇིག་གནས་པ་རྣམས་ཀྱིས་གཟུགས་སྔོན་ལྟ་བུ་གཅིག་འདུས་བྱས་སུ་མཚོན་པ་ན་རང་ཉིད་སྐྱེ་བ་སོགས་ཡིན་པས་མི་མཚོན་གྱི་རང་སྐྱེད་བྱེད་སོགས་དོན་གཞན་ཡོད་པས་འདུས་བྱས་སུ་མཚོན་པ་ཡིན་ལ། དེས་ན་མཚན་ཉིད་རྣམས་ནི་སྐྱེ་བའི་བྱ་བ་སོགས་ལ་མི་འདོད་ཀྱི་སྐྱེ་བར་བྱེད་པ་པོ་དང་གནས་པར་བྱེད་པ་པོ་དང་འཇིག་པར་བྱེད་པ་པོའི་རྫས་དོན་གཞན་ཞིག་ལ་འདོད་དོ། །གཟུགས་ལ་སོགས་པའི་མཚན་གཞིའི་དངོས་པོ་རྣམས་ལ་མཚན་ཉིད་བཞི་དུས་གཅིག་ཏུ་ཡོད་ཀྱང་དང་པོར་སྐྱེ་བའི་བྱ་བ་དང་དེ་ནས་གནས་པ་དང་དེ་ནས་རྒ་བ་དང་དེ་ནས་འཇིག་པའི་བྱ་བ་རྣམས་རིམ་པ་བཞིན་དུ་འཇུག་པར་འདོད་དོ། །དེ་ལ་མདོ་སྡེ་བས་དེ་ལྟ་ན་འདུས[26]་བྱས་རྣམས་སྐད་ཅིག་མ་མ་ཡིན་པར་འགྱུར་རོ། །ཞེས་སྐྱོན་བརྗོད་པ་ལ་བྱེ་བྲག་སྨྲ་བས། ཁོ་བོ་ཅག་གི་སྐད་ཅིག་མ་ནི་ཅི་ཙམ་གྱིས་བྱ་བ་འདི་བཞི་པོ་རྫོགས་པ་དེ་ལ་ཟེར་རོ། །ཞེས་མཛོད་རང་འགྲེལ་ལས་བཤད་པས་ན་བྱེ་སྨྲས་མི་རྟག་པ་སྐད་ཅིག་མ་མ་ཡིན་པར་མི་འདོད་མོད་ཀྱང་སྐད་ཅིག་མ་འཇོག་ཚུལ་མདོ་སྡེ་པ་ཡན་ཆད་དང་མི་འདྲའོ། །མདོ་སྡེ་པས་ནི་འདུས་བྱས་ཀྱི་མཚན་ཉིད་སྐྱེ་བ་ལ་སོགས་པ་རྣམས་གཟུགས་ལ་སོགས་པའི་ཆོས་དེ་རྣམས་ཀྱི་སྐྱེ་བའི་བྱ་བ་དང་འཇིག་པའི་བྱ་བ་དང་གནས་པའི་བྱ་བ་ལ་འདོད་ཅིང་། དེ་ཡང་ནོག་དང་ལྐོག་ཤལ་ལ་སོགས་པ་འདུས་པ་བ་ལང་གི་མཚན་ཉིད་ཡིན་ཀྱང་བ་ལང་ལས་རྫས་གཞན་མ་ཡིན་པ་ལྟར་སྐྱེ་བ་སོགས་ཀྱང་གཟུགས་སོགས་ལས་རྫས་གཞན་མིན་པས་བཏགས་ཡོད་དང་། མྱུ་གུ་ལྟ་བུ་སྔོན་མེད་གསར་དུ་བྱུང་བ་སྐྱེ་བ་དང་། སྔ་

མའི་རིགས་འདྲ་གནས་པ་གནས་པ་དང་། རང་གྲུབ་དུས་ལས་དུས་གཉིས་པར་མི་སྡོད་པ་འཇིག་པ་དང་། སྐད་ཅིག་སྔ་མ་ལས་ཕྱི་མ་མཚན་ཉིད་མི་འདྲ་བ་ནི་རྒ་བ་ཡིན་ལ་མཚན་ཉིད་དེ་དག་དུས་གཅིག་ཏུ་གྲུབ་པར་འདོད་དོ། །གཞན་ཡང་རྒྱུ་རྐྱེན་ཚོགས་ཤིང་འདུས་བྱས་པའི་དངོས་པོ་རྣམས་ནི་སྐྱེ་བའི་སྐད་ཅིག་ཙམ་ཁོ་ན་ཡིན་པ་དང་། དེའི་ཡང་སྐྱེ་བའི་ངོ་བོ་དང་འཇིག་པའི་ངོ་བོ་གཉིས་གཞན་དུ་བརྗོད་མི་ནུས་པའི་ཕྱིར་སྐད་ཅིག་མ་ཁོ་ན་ཡིན་པར་འདོད་དོ། །དེའི་ཕྱིར་དངོས་པོ་རྣམས་ནི་རང་གི་རྒྱུས་འཇིག་པའི་བདག་ཉིད་ཅན་དུ་བསྐྱེད་པ་ཡིན་གྱི་བརྟན་པར་བསྐྱེད་པ་མ་ཡིན་པས་རང་གྲུབ་དུས་ལས་སྐད་ཅིག་གཉིས་པར་མི་སྡོད་པའི་འཇིག་པ་ཁོ་ནར་ཤེས་པར་བྱ་སྟེ། འདི་ལ་སྦྱོར་བ་ནི། གང་ཞིག་གང་གི་ཚེ་འཇིག་པའི་བདག་ཉིད་ཅན་ཡིན་པ་དེ་ནི། དེའི་དེ་མ་ཐག་ཏུ་མི་གནས་པ་ཡིན་ཏེ། དཔེར་ན་མཐའི་སྐད་ཅིག་ལ་གནས་པའི་ངོ་བོ་བཞིན། གཟུང་ལ་སོགས་པ་ཡང་སྐྱེ་བའི་དུས་ན་འཇིག་པའི་ངང་ཚུལ་ཅན་ཡིན་ནོ། །ཞེས་པ་རང་བཞིན་གྱི་རྟགས་སོ། །འཇིག་པའི་བདག་ཉིད་ཅན་ཡིན་པ་སྒྲུབ་བྱེད་[27]ནི། གང་ཞིག་གང་གི་ངོ་བོར་འགྱུར་བ་ཕྱིས་འབྱུང་བའི་རྒྱུ་གཞན་ལ་ལྟོས་པ་མེད་པར་[28]དེའི་ངོ་བོར་གྲུབ་པ་དེ་ནི་དེའི་ངོ་བོར་ངེས་པས་ཁྱབ་སྟེ། དཔེར་ན་ནས་ཀྱི་སྨྱུ་གུའི་རྒྱུ་ཚོགས་ཐ་མས་ནས་ཀྱི་སྨྱུ་གུ་བསྐྱེད་པ་བཞིན། བྱས་པ་[29]ང་འཇིག་པའི་ངོ་བོར་འགྱུར་བ་ཕྱིས་འབྱུང་བའི་རྒྱུ་གཞན་ལ་ལྟོས་པ་མེད་པར་འཇིག་པའི་ངོ་བོར་གྲུབ་པ་ཡིན་ནོ་ཞེས་བྱ་བའོ། །དེའི་ཁྱབ་པ་ནི་མངོན་སུམ་གྱིས་གྲུབ་ཅིང་། ཕྱོགས་ཆོས་ནི་གནོད་པ་ཅན་གྱི་རྟགས་ལས་ཤེས་པར་བྱ་སྟེ། འདིར་མངས་ཀྱིས་དོགས་ནས་མ་བྲིས་སོ། །རང་གྲུབ་དུས་ལས་དུས་གཉིས་པར་མི་སྡོད་པའི་འཇིག་པ་ནི་དངོས་པོ་དེའི་རྒྱུ་ཉིད་ལས་སྐྱེས་པས་དངོས་པོ་ཡིན་ཀྱང་སྐད་ཅིག་གཉིས་པར་ཞིག་པ་ནི་དངོས་མེད་ཡིན་པས་རྒྱུ་མེད་པར་འདོད་དོ། །དེས་ན་རྟག་

པའི་འཇོག་ཚུལ་ཡང་། རིག་པའི་དབང་ཕྱུག་གིས། གང་གི་རང་བཞིན་འཇིག་མེད་པ། །དེ་ལ་མཁས་རྣམས་རྟག་ཅེས་བརྗོད། ཅེས་གསུངས་པ་ལྟར། རང་བཞིན་འཇིག་པ་མེད་པའི་ཆོས་ལ་འདོད་པ་ཡིན་གྱི་གཞན་སྡེ་དང་བྱེ་སྨྲའི་འདོད་པ་ལྟར་མ་ཡིན་ནོ། །དེ་ཡང་རྫ་བུམ་ཞིག་པའི་ཞིག་པ་ནི་སྔར་རྫ་བུམ་མ་ཞིག་པའི་དུས་ན་མེད་ལ་ཕྱིས་ཡོད་ཀྱང་རྟག་པར་འཇོག་དགོས་པས། དུས་ཐམས་ཅད་པ་རྟག[30]་པ་ལ་མི་དགོས་ཏེ། དཔེར་ན་མཐོང་སྤང་སྤངས[31]་པའི་སྤངས་པ་སོ་སོར་བརྟགས[32]་འགོག་ནི། སྤང་བྱ་དེ་མ་ཟད་པར་དུ་མེད་ལ་ཟད་པའི་དུས་སུ་ཡོད་ཀྱང་རྟག་པར་འཇོག་པ་བཞིན་ནོ། །ཐལ་འགྱུར་བས་ཞིག་པ་དངོས་པོར་བཞེད་མོད་ཀྱང་འདིར་ནི་མདོ་སེམས་དབུ་མ་རང་རྒྱུད་པ་རྣམས་ཀྱི་དབང་དུ་བྱས་པའོ། །དེ་བཞིན་དུ་རང་བཞིན་རྣམ་དག་གི་ཆོས་ཉིད་ཀྱང་ཆོས་ཅན་སྔ་མ་དེ་ལོག་པ་ན་ལྡོག་པས་དུས་རེས་འགའ་བ་ཡིན་ཀྱང་མི་རྟག་པར་མི་འགྱུར་ཏེ་དགག་བྱ་རྣམ་པར་བཅད་ཙམ་གྱི་མེད་དགག་ཡིན་པའི་ཕྱིར་དང་། ཁྱད་གཞི་ལོག་པ་ན་ཁྱད་ཆོས་ལྡོག་པ་ཡིན་གྱི་རང་གི་ངོ་བོ་འཇིག་པའི་བདག་ཉིད་ཅན་ཡིན་པས་ཞིག་པ་མ་ཡིན་པའི་ཕྱིར་རོ། །དུས་སྔ་ཕྱི་དང་འབྲེལ་བའི་ཆོས་ཉིད་ནི་གཅིག་གི་མཚན་གཞིར་རུང་ཡང་དེའི་ཆ་ཤས་ནི་དུ་མ་ཡོད་དོ། །བུམ་མེད་ལྟ་བུ་རང་གི་དགག་བྱ་བཀག་ཤུལ་དུ་རང་ཉིད་ཡོད་པར་འཇོག་པ་དང་། སྒྲ་ཀུ་ལྟ་བུ་རང་གི་རྒྱུས་བསྐྱེད་པའི་ཚེ་རང་ཉིད་ཡོད་པར་འཇོག་པ་གཉིས། ཡོད་པར་འཇོག་པ་ཙམ་དུ་མཚུངས་ཀྱང་ཡོད་ཚུལ་མི་མཚུངས་ཏེ། སྔ་མ་ནི་དགག་བྱ་བུམ་པ་ལྟ་བུ་འདི་འདྲ་བ་གཅིག་མེད་པས་དེ་ཡོད་དོ་ཞེས་དགག་བྱ་བཅད་ཤུལ་ནས་འཇོག་པ་མ་གཏོགས་རང་གི་ངོ་བོ་འདི་སྒོ་ནས་བཞག་ཏུ་མེད་པའི་ཕྱིར་དང་། ཕྱི་མ་ནི་གཞན་བཅད་པའི་སྒོ་ནས་འཇོག་མི་དགོས་པར་རང་གི་ངོ་བོ་འདི་སྒོ་ནས་བཞག་ཆོག་པའི་ཕྱིར་རོ། །གཞན་སྡེ་རྣམས་ཀྱིས་དངོས་

ཁ

པོ་རྣམས་ཀྱི་འཇིག་པ་ཕྱིས་འབྱུང་གི་རྒྱུ་གཞན་ལ་ལྟོས་དགོས་པར་འདོད་པ་དང་ཁྱེ······ སྨྲས་ཀྱང་སྐྱེ་བ་དང་འཇིག་པ་ལས་གཞན་དེ་གཉིས་ཀྱི་བར་ན་གནས་པའི་གནས་སྐབས··· ཁས་ལེན་པས་མི་རྟག་པའི་འདོད་ཚུལ་འདི་དང་གདན་མི་འདྲ་ལ། རྟག་པ་རྣམས་ཀྱང་ རང་གི་ངོ་བོ་དེ་སྔོ་ནས་ཡོད་པར་འཇོག་པས་འདུས་མ་བྱས་ཀྱི་ནམ་མཁའ་སོགས་དངོས་·· པོར་ཁས་ལེན་དགོས་བྱུང་བས་རྟག་པའི་འདོད་ཚུལ་འདི་དང་གདན་མི་གཅིག་གོ །

དངོས་པོ་རྣམས་འཇིག་པའི་བདག་ཉིད་ཅན་དུ་རྒྱུས་བསྐྱེད་པས་སྐད་ཅིག་མ་ཡིན་པ་དང་། དངོས་མེད་རྣམས་དེ་ལྟར་མ་ཡིན་པས་སྐད་ཅིག་མ་མ་ཡིན་པར་འཇོག་དགོས་པའི་གནད་ འདི་མ་ཤེས་པས། སྔོན་གྱི་མཁས་རློམ་འགའ་ཞིག་དང་དེང་དུས་ཀྱི་གཞུང་གི་ཚིག་ ཁ་དོན་དུ་བྱང་བ་ལ་སྙིང་པོར་རློམ་པ་དག་གིས། སྐད་ཅིག[33] མ་སྔ་མའི་དུས་ན་ཡོད་ པ་ཕྱི་མའི་དུས་ན་མེད་པ་ཙམ་ལ་སྐད་ཅིག་མའི་དོན་དུ་འཛིན་པ་མང་དུ་བྱུང་སྣང་ཞིང་། ད་ལྟ་ཡང་དབུ་ཚད་ལ་སྦྱངས་པར་རློམ་པ་ཕལ་མོ་ཆེའི་[34]ཞེ་ཕྱོགས་ན་དེ་ཁོ་ན་ལྟར་སྣང··· བས་མ་བརྟགས་ཉམས་དགའ་བ་ཚིག་ཙམ་ལ་འཁྲུལ་བ་མིན་པར་ཞིབ་ཏུ་བརྟགས་ན་རྒྱུ··· གུ་སི་རྟག་པའི་དོན་ལོག་གོ་བ་ཡང་དཀའ་བར་སྣང་ངོ་། །འོ་ན་འདིའི་ལུགས་ཀྱི་དུས་ གསུམ་གྱི་རྣམ་གཞག་ཇི་ལྟར་བྱེད་ཅེ་ན། བཤད་པར་བྱ་སྟེ། མདོ་སེམས་དབུ་མ་ རང་རྒྱུད་པ་རྣམས་ཀྱི་དུས་གསུམ་གྱི་རྣམ་གཞག་བྱེད་ཚུལ་འདྲ་ལ། དེ་ཡང་དངོས་པོ་ ཡིན་ན་ད་ལྟར་བ་ཡིན་པས་ཁྱབ་པ་དང་། འདས་མ་འོངས་ཡིན་ན་དངོས་པོ་མ་ཡིན་ པས་ཁྱབ་པར་འདོད་དེ། དེ་ཡང་མྱུ་གུ་ལྟ་བུའི་དངོས་པོ་གཅིག་ཞིག་པ་ན་མྱུ་གུའི་ ཆ་ཤས་ཀྱི་ངོ་བོ་ཐམས་ཅད་ནི་འགགས་ལ།[35] དངོས་པོ་གཞན་གང་ཡང་མ་ཐོབ་ཅིང་ འདས་མ་འོངས་གཉིས་ཀ་ལའང་དགག་བྱ་རྣམ་པར་བཅད་ཙམ་མ་ཡིན་པའི་རང་གི་ངོ་·· བོ་ཙུང་ཟད་ཀྱང་གྲུབ་པ་མེད་པས། དེའི་ཕྱིར་འདས་མ་འོངས་ཡིན་ན་དངོས་པོར་མ་

གྲུབ་པས་ཁྱབ་པོ་སྙམ་དུ་བསམས་པའོ། །དེ་ཡང་མྱུ་གུ་ལ་མཚོན་ན་རྒྱུ་རྐྱེན་ལས་སྐྱེས་ཟིན་པའི་མྱུ་གུ་རང་གི་དུས་གཉིས་པར་ཞིག་པ་ནི་མྱུ་གུའི་འདས་པའི་དུས་དང་། སྤྱིར་མྱུ་གུ་སྐྱེད་བྱེད་ཀྱི་རྒྱུ་ཡོད་ཀྱང་དགུན་དུས་ཀྱི་ཤར་ཕྱོགས་ཀྱི་ཞིང་ལྟ་བུ་ཡུལ་དུས་འགའ་ཞིག་ཏུ་རྒྱུ་རྐྱེན་མ་ཚང་བའི་དབང་གིས་ཡུལ་དུས་དེར་མྱུ་གུ་རེ་ཞིག་མ་སྐྱེས་པ་ནི་མྱུ་གུའི་མ་འོངས་པའི་དུས་དང་། མྱུ་གུ་སྐྱེས་ལ་མ་འགགས་པ་མྱུ་གུ་རང་གི་གྲུབ་པའི་དུས་ནི་མྱུ་གུའི་ད་ལྟར་བའི་དུས་སོ། །དེས་ན་ཆོས་དེའི་འདས་མ་འོངས་ཀྱི་དུས་གཉིས་ནི་ཆོས་དེའི་ད་ལྟར་གྱི་དུས་ལ་བལྟོས་ནས་[36]འཇོག་པ་ཤིང་རྟ་ཆེན་པོ་དག་གི་གཞུང་ལས་མཐུན་པར་འབྱུང་ངོ་། །དེ་ལྟར་ན་འདས་པའི་མཚན་ཉིད་ནི། ཁྱོད་དུས་གང་དུ་འཇོག་པ་དངོས་པོ་གང་གི་རང་དུས་ལ་བལྟོས་ནས་བཞག་དགོས་པའི་བལྟོས༔ [37]ར……གྱུར་པའི་དངོས་པོ་འདི་རང་དུས་དེ་ལས་ཐལ་ཟིན་པ། མ་འོངས་པའི་མཚན་ཉིད། ཁྱོད་དུས་གང་དུ་འཇོག་པ་དངོས་པོ་གང་གི་རང་དུས་ལ་བལྟོས་ནས་བཞག་དགོས་པའི……ལྟོས༔ [38]ར་གྱུར་པའི་དངོས་པོ་འདི་རང་དུས་དེར་མ་སླེབ་པའི་ཆོས། ད་ལྟར་བའི་མཚན་ཉིད། རང་དུས་ན་སྐྱེས་ལ་མ་འགགས་པའི་ཆོས་སོ། །མཚན་ཉིད་དེ་དག་ཀྱང་གཞུང་ཆེན་མོ་རྣམས་ལས་འབྱུང་བ་ལྟར་གོ་ཐོབ་ཀྱི་དབང་དུ་བྱས་པ་ཡིན་གྱི་སྐྱོན་ཅན་དང་རྗེས་སྒྲི་སོགས་ཀྱི་ཚིག་འཁྲི་གཅོད་པ་གཙོ་བོར་བྱས་པ་མ་ཡིན་དེ། རིགས་པར་སྨྲ་བ་རྣམས་ལ་གདམས་དུ་བྱས་པ་ཡིན་གྱི་ལྟག་ཆོད་ཀྱིས་ཏི་མ་འཕྲུལ་ཐབས་ལྷུར་ལེན་པའི…བྱིས་པ་བརྡོལ་ཐབས་སྨྲ་བ་རྣམས་ལ་གདམས་དུ་བྱ་བ་མ་ཡིན་པའི་ཕྱིར་རོ། །ལ་ལ་དག་འདས་པ་དང་མ་འོངས་པ་གཉིས་གཞིར་གྲུབ་པར་སྨྲས་ནས་ཡང་དེ་གཉིས་ཀྱི་མཚན……ཉིད་རྣམ་པར་འཇོག་པར་བྱེད་པ་ནི་གྲུབ་མཐའ་སྨྲ་བ་བཞི་པོ་གང་གི་ཡང་ལུགས་མ་ཡིན…གྱི་སྟོན་གྱི་བླུན་པོ་སྙིང་ཁམས་ཅན་དག་གི་ཟེར་སྒྲོས་འབའ་ཞིག་གཞིར་བཞག་པར་ཟད…

དེ༑ རི་བོང་རྭའི་མཚན་ཉིད་འཛོག་པའི་ངལ་བ་བྱེད་པའི་མཁས་པ་སུ་ཡང་མེད་པའི་ཕྱིར་རོ། །གཉིས་པ་ཞར་བྱུང་སེལ་བའི་རྣམ་གཞག་ལ། འདིར་[39] སེལ་བ་དང་དགག་པ་དོན་གཅིག་པས་དེ་ལ་དབྱེ་ན། མ་ཡིན་དགག་གི་གཞན་སེལ་དང་མེད་དགག་གི་གཞན་སེལ་གཉིས། དང་པོ་ལ་དོན་ཆོས་དང་བློ་ཆོས་གཉིས་རྣམས་སུ་ཡོད་དེ། སློབ་དཔོན་ཞི་བ་འཚོས། འདིར་ནི་སེལ་བ་རྣམ་གཉིས་ཏེ། །མ་ཡིན་པ་དང་མེད་པ་འོ། །མ་ཡིན་པ་ཡང་རྣམ་གཉིས་ཏེ། །བློ་དང་དོན་གྱི་དབྱེ་བས་སོ། །ཞེས་གང་གསུངས་པའོ། །དེ་ལ་དོན་གྱི་དབང་དུ་བྱས་པའི་མ་ཡིན་དགག་གི་གཞན་སེལ་ནི། བུམ་པ་མ་ཡིན་པ་ལས་ལོག་པ་དང་སྒྲ་མི་རྟག་པ་མ་ཡིན་པ་ལས་ལོག་པ་ལ་སོགས་པ་ལྟ་བུ་སྟེ། རྣམ་འགྲེལ་ལས། སྒྲུབ་བྱེད་སྒྲ་མ་དག་གིས་ནི། །མ་ཡིན་སྒྲུབ་[40]པར་བྱེད་ཕྱིར་རོ། །ཞེས་སོ།། བློའི་གཞན་སེལ་ནི། བུམ་འཛིན་རྟོག་པ་ལ་བུམ་མ་ཡིན་ལས་ལོག་པར་སྣང་བ་ལྟ་བུ་སྟེ། འདི་ལ་བསལ་བྱ་དངོས་སུ་བསལ་བའི་སྒོ་ནས་རྟོགས་པ་ཞིག་དགོས་སོ། །མཚན་ཉིད་ནི། སེལ་བ་ཙམ་གྱི་མཚན་ཉིད་དགག་བྱ་དངོས་སུ་བསལ་བའི་སྒོ་ནས་རྟོགས་པར་བྱ་བའོ། །མ་ཡིན་དགག་གི་སེལ་བའི་མཚན་ཉིད། སེལ་བ་གང་། སྒྲུབ་པའི་ཆོས་གཞན་འཕེན་པའོ། །མེད་དགག་གི་སེལ་བའི་མཚན་ཉིད། སེལ་བ་གང་། སྒྲུབ་པའི་ཆོས་གཞན་མི་འཕེན་པའོ། །འདིའི་ཆོས་གཞན་འཕེན་པ་དང་མི་འཕེན་པ་ཡང་རང་གི་དགག་བྱ་བཀག་ཤུལ་དུ་[41] འཕེན་མི་འཕེན་ལ་བྱའོ། །བློ་འི་གཞན་སེལ་གྱི་མཚན་ཉིད། མ་ཡིན་དགག་གི་སེལ་བ་གང་། བློས་སྒྲོ་བཏགས་པ་ཙམ་དུ་གནས་པ། དོན་གྱི་གཞན་སེལ་གྱི་མཚན་ཉིད། མ་ཡིན་དགག་གི་སེལ་བ་གང་། སྒྲོ་བཏགས་ཙམ་མིན་པར་རང་གི་མཚན་ཉིད་ཀྱིས་གྲུབ་པའོ། །ཁ་ཅིག་དེ་དེ་ལྟ་ན་བུམ་པའི་རང་མཚན་ཡང་གཞན་སེལ་དུ་འདོད་དགོས་ཏེ། བསལ་བྱ་རིགས་མི་མཐུན་སེལ་བའི་

ཁ

ཕྱི་ར་རོ་སྙམ་ན། འོ་ན་ཁྱོད་རང་ལ། དེ་དགག་པར་ཡང་ཐལ། དགག་བྱ་རིགས་མི་མཐུན་འགོག་པའི་ཕྱི་ར་རོ། །མ་ཡིན་དགག་གི་ཆོས་གཞན་འཕེན་ཚུལ་ལ་ཡང་བཞི་ཡོད་དེ། མཆོད་སྦྱིན་ཆེན་པོ་ཉིན་པར་མི་ཟ་བ་ཞེས་པ་ལྟ་བུ་སྒྲུབ་ཆོས་གཞན་དོན་གྱིས་འཕངས་པ་དང་། བདག་ལས་མ་སྐྱེས་པ་ཡོད་ཅེས་པ་ལྟ་བུ་ཚིག་གཅིག་གིས་དགག་བྱ་གཅོད་པ་དང་ཆོས་གཞན་དངོས་སུ་འཕེན་པ་གཉིས་ཀ་སྟོན་པ་དང་། མཆོད་སྦྱིན་ཆེན་པོ་ཉིད་པར་མི་ཟ་བ་རིད་པ་ཟིན་པ་ཡོད་ཅེས་པ་ལྟ་བུ་ཚིག་གཅིག་ཤ་ཊ་དངོས་ཤུགས་གཉིས་ཀར་ཆོས་གཞན་འཕེན་པ་དང་། སྐྱེས་བུ་གཅིག་རྒྱལ་རིགས་དང་བྲམ་ཟེའི་རིགས་གང་རུང་ཞིག་ཏུ་ངེས་ཤིང་ཁྱད་པར་མ་ངེས་པའི་སྐབས་སུ་འདི་བྲམ་ཟེ་མ་ཡིན་ཞེས་པ་ལྟ་བུ་སྐབས་སྟོབས་ཀྱིས་འཕངས་པ་སྟེ་བཞིའོ། །དེ་ལྟར་ཡང་། ཤེས་ 42
རབ་སྒྲོན་མེའི་འགྲེལ་བཤད་དུ་དྲངས་པ་ལས། དགག་པ་དོན་གྱིས་བསྟན་པ་དང་། །ཚིག་གཅིག་སྒྲུབ་པར་བྱེད་པ་དང་། །དེ་ལྡན་རང་ཚིག་མི་སྟོན་པ། །མ་ཡིན་ཞེས་དང་། དེ་བཞི་གང་ཡང་མ་འཕངས་པའི་དགག་པ་ནི་མེད་དགག་སྟེ། གཞན་པ་གཞན་ཡིན་ནོ་ ཞེས་སོ། །དེས་ན་དངོས་པོ་ལ་དགག་བྱ་བཅད་པས་མི་ཚིག་གི་རང་བརྗོད་པའི་སྒྲས་བཅད་པ་དང་རང་རྟོགས་པའི་བློ་ལ་དངོས་སུ་དགག་བྱ་བཅད་པའི་རྣམ་པ་ཅན་དུ······འཆར་བ་གང་རུང་ཞིག་དགོས་སོ། །ཆོས་གཞན་འཕངས་པ་ལའང་མ་ཡིན་དགག་དང་སྒྲུབ་པ་གང་རུང་ཞིག་དགོས་ཀྱི་ཆོས་གཞན་མེད་དགག་འཕངས་ཀྱང་མ་ཡིན་དགག་··ཏུ་མི་འགྱུར་རོ། །དངོས་པོ་ཐམས་ཅད་ངོ་བོ་ཉིད་ཀྱིས་རང་རང་གི་ངོ་བོ་གཞན་དང་མ་འདྲེས་པར་གནས་པ་ཡིན་པས་རིགས་མཐུན་རིགས་མི་མཐུན་ཀུན་ལས་ལོག་པར་གནས་པ་ཡིན་ལ། དེས་ན་གཞི་སྒྲ་ལྟ་བུ་གཅིག་ལ་ཡང་རིགས་མཐུན་ལས་ལོག་པ་དང་རིགས་མི་མཐུན་ལས་ལོག་པའི་ལྡོག་པ་དུ་མ་ཞིག་དབྱེར་རུང་བ་ཡིན་ནོ། རིག་པའི་དབང་

ཕྱུག་གིས། གང་ཕྱིར་དངོས་ཀུན་རང་བཞིན་གྱིས། རང་རང་ངོ་བོ་ལ་གནས་ཕྱིར། མཐུན་དངོས་གཞན་གྱི་དངོས་དག་ལས། ལྡོག་པ་ལ་ནི་བརྟེན་པ་ཅན། ཞེས་གསུངས་སོ། །ལྡོག་པ་དེ་དག་གི་སྒོ་ནས་སྒྲ་མི་རྟག་པ་ལྟ་བུའི་རང་གི་མཚན་ཉིད་དབྱེས་ཕྱིན་པར་རྟོགས་པས་དགག་སྒྲུབ་ཀྱི་དངོས་རྟེན་དོན་དམ་པར་མ་གྲུབ་ཀྱང་དེ་ལ་བརྟེན་ནས····

···ན་དམ་པའི་གནས་ལུགས་ལེགས་པར་རྟོགས་ནུས་པ་འདི་ནི་ཐ་སྙད་པའི་ཚད་མ་དོན་དམ་པའི་གནས་ལུགས་རྟོགས་པའི་རྒྱུར་འགྱུར་ཚུལ་སོགས་ལུགས་འདི་དག་གི་བདེན་གཉིས་ཀྱི་རྣམ་དབྱེ་ཤེས་པ་ལ་མེད་དུ་མི་རུང་བ་ཡིན་ནོ། །དེས་ནད་དུང་ཞིབ་ཏུ་གདན་ལ་འབེབས་དགོས་མོད་ཀྱང་མངས་པས་འཇིགས་ནས་མ་བྲིས་སོ། །གཉིས་པ་ཕྱི་དོན་འདོད་ཚུལ་ལ། དངོས་དང་། རྣམ་པར་རིག་བྱེད་མ་ཡིན་པའི་གཟུགས་ཀྱི་འདོད་ཚུལ་ལོ། །དང་པོ་ནི། ལུགས་འདིས་ཀྱང་རྡུལ་ཕྲན་ཆ་མེད་འདོད་པ་ཡིན་ཏེ། དེ་ཡང་རྡུལ་ཕྲ་བའི་མཐར་ཐུག་པ་དང་དེ་ལས་ཆུང་ངུར་གསིལ་དུ་མེད་པར་འདོད་དེ། མངོན་པ་ཀུན་ལས་བཏུས་ལས། རྡུལ་ཕྲ་རབ་བསགས་པ་ནི་གཟུགས་འདུས་པའོ་ཞེས་གང་བརྗོད་པ་དེ་ལ་རྡུལ་ཕྲ་རབ་ལུས་མེད་པར་རིག་པར་བྱའོ། །བློས་མཐར་རབ་ཏུ་ཕྱེ་ནས་རྡུལ་ཕྲ་རབ་ཏུ་རྣམ་པར་བཞག་སྟེ། ཞེས་སོ། །དེ་ལྟ་བུའི་རྡུལ་ཕྲ་རབ་དེའང་འབྱུང་བ་བཞི་དང་འབྱུང་འགྱུར་བཞིའི་བདག་ཉིད་ཅན་ཡིན་ཡང་། བྱེ་བྲག་སྨྲ་བ་ལྟར་རྫས་རྡུལ་ཡན་གར་བ་བརྒྱད་འདུས་སུ་འདི་པ་མི་འདོད་དོ། །རྡུལ་ཕྲ་རབ་དང་རྡུལ་ཕྲན་ཙམ་ལའང་ཁྱད་ཡོད་དེ། རྡུལ་ཕྲ་རབ་བདུན་འདུས་པ་ལ་རྡུལ་ཕྲན་གཅིག་ཏུ་འདོད་པའི་ཕྱིར་ཏེ། མཛོད་ལས། སྐད་ཅིག་ཕྲ་རབ་རྡུལ་དང་ནི། །རྡུལ་ཕྲན་དང་ནི་དེ་བཞིན་དུ། ཞེས་སོགས་གསུངས་པས་སོ། །རྡུལ་ཕྲ་རབ་བསགས་པས་བེམ་པོ་འགྲུབ་ཚུལ་ནི། སྔར་བྱེ་སྨྲའི་སྐབས་སུ་བཤད་པ་ལྟར་འབྱར་བ་དང་བསྐོར་བ་དང་བར་མེད་

པ་སྟེ་གསུམ་དུ་ཡོད་དེ། དབུ་མ་རྒྱན་རྩ་འགྲེལ་གྱི་བཤད་པ་དེ་བྱེ་མདོ་གཉིས་ཆར་ལ་སྦྱར་ཆོག་པའི་ཕྱིར་མཁས་པ་ཁ་ཅིག །རིགས་པའི་རྗེས་འབྲང་གི་མདོ་སྡེ་པ་ལ་རྡུལ་ཕྲ་རབ་ཆ་བཅས་སུ་འདོད་པ་ཡོད་དེ། མདོ་སེམས་གཉིས་བརྩད་པའི་ཚེ་ཆ་དང་བཅས་པའི་རྡུལ་ཕྲ་རབ་ཚོགས་ཚེ་རེ་རེས་ཀྱང་རང་འདྲའི་རྣམ་པ་གཏོད་པར་མདོ་སྡེ་པས་ཁས་བླངས་པར་དམིགས་བརྟག་རྩ་[43]འགྲེལ་ལས་བཤད་པའི་ཕྱིར། ཞེས་གསུངས་སོ། །འོན་ཀྱང་དེ་ནི་གཞུང་དེར་རྣམ་རིག་པའི་རིག་པས་[44]པའི་ཚེ་མདོ་སྡེ་པས་རྡུལ་ཕྲ་རབ་དུ་མ་ཚོགས་ནས་རགས་པར་འགྱུར་པ་ན། རགས་པ་དེ་ཕྱོགས་ཀྱི་ཆ་དང་བཅས་ལ་དེས་རང་འདྲའི་རྣམ་པ་གཏད་པ་ན་རང་གི་རྫས་གཞིར་གྱུར་པའི་རྡུལ་ཕྲ་རབ་ཀྱིས་ཀྱང་རང་གི་རྣམ་པ་གཏོད་པ་མི་འགལ་བར་སྨྲས་ན་དེ་འགོག་ལུགས་འདི་ལྟར་བྱེད་ཅེས་བཤད་པ་ཙམ་ཡིན་གྱི་མདོ་སྡེ་པ་རང་གི་རྩ་བའི་གྲུབ་མཐའ་[45]ལ་རྡུལ་ཕྲ་རབ་ཆ་བཅས་སུ་ཁས་བླངས་པར་བཤད་པ་མིན་ནམ་སྙམ་སྟེ། དེའི་རྒྱུ་མཚན་ཡང་མང་དུ་ཡོད་མོད་འདིར་མ་བྲིས་ཏེ། བློ་ལྡན་རྣམས་ཀྱིས་ཞིབ་ཏུ་བརྟག་པར་བྱའོ།[46] །གཉིས་པ་ནི། ལུགས་འདིས་རྣམ་པར་རིག་བྱེད་མ་ཡིན་པའི་གཟུགས་ཡོད་ཀྱང་དེ་གཟུགས་མཚན་ཉིད་པ་མ་ཡིན་པར་འདོད་དེ། བདེར་གཤེགས་གཞུང་གི་རབ་བྱེད་ལས། ཐོགས་པ་མེད་པའི་གཟུགས་ཡོད་མིན། ཞེས་དང་། ཊཱིཀ་ཆེན་དེ་ཉིད་སྣང་བ་ལས་ཐོགས་པ་མེད་པའི་རྣམ་པར་རིག་བྱེད་མིན་པའི་གཟུགས་གཟུགས་མཚན་ཉིད་པར་གྲུབ་པ་ཡོད་པ་མ་ཡིན་ནོ། །ཞེས་གསུངས་སོ། །རིགས་པའི་སྒྲུབ་བྱེད་ནི། འཛོད་[47]འགྲེལ་ལས། མདོ་སྡེ་པ་རྣམས་ན་རེ་དེ་ཡང་རྫས་སུ་མེད་དེ། ཁས་བླངས་ནས་མི་བྱེད་ང་ཙམ་གྱི་ཕྱིར་དང་། འདས་པའི་འབྱུང་བ་ཆེན་པོ་རྣམས་ལ་ཡང་བརྟེན་ནས་འདོགས་པའི་ཕྱིར་དང་། དེ་དག་ཀྱང་རང་གི་ངོ་བོ་མེད་པའི་ཕྱིར་དང་། གཟུགས་ཀྱི་མཚན་ཉིད་མེད་པའི་

ཀྱི་ར་རོ་ ཞེས་ཟེར་རོ། །ཞེས་གསུངས་པ་ལྟར་རོ། །འོ་ན་རྣམ་པར་རིག་བྱེད་མ་
ཡིན་པའི་གཟུགས་ཅི་ཞིག་ཏུ་འདོད་པ་ཡིན་ཞེ་ན། ཆོས་ཀྱི་སྐྱེ་མཆེད་པའི་ཀུན་བརྟགས་ 48
པའི་གཟུགས་སུ་འདོད་དེ། དེ་ཉིད་ལས། བསྟན་དུ་ཡང་མེད་ལ་ཐོགས་པ་མེད་པའི་
གཟུགས་གང་ཡིན་པ་དེ་ཉིད་ཆོས་ཀྱི་སྐྱེ་མཆེད་དུ་གཏོགས་པ་ཡིན་པའི་ཕྱིར་རོ། །ཞེས་
གསུངས་སོ། །འདི་ལ་བྱེ་མདོ་གཉིས་ཀྱིས་འདོད་ཚུལ་རྒྱས་པར་ནི་མཛོད་ལས། རྣམ་
གསུམ་དྲི་མེད་གཟུགས་གསུངས་དང་། །འཕེལ་དང་མ་བྱས་ལམ་སོགས་ཕྱིར། ཞེས་
སོགས་ཀྱི་རང་འགྲེལ་ལས་བཤད་དེ། ཤེས་པར་འདོད་ན་དེ་དག་ཏུ་བལྟ་བར་བྱའོ། །
གཉིས་པ་ཤེས་པས་ཡུལ་འཛིན་ཚུལ་བྱེ་བྲག་ཏུ་བཤད་པ་ལ་གསུམ། དངོས་དང་།
འཇལ་བྱེད་ཚད་མའི་རྣམ་གཞག །དེའི་ཡན་ལག་གདན་ཚིགས་བཤད་པའོ། །དང་
པོ་ནི། ཤེས་པ་རྣམས་ཀྱིས་ཡུལ་འཛིན་པ་ན་རྣམ་པ་མེད་པ་མ་ཡིན་གྱི་རྣམ་པ་དང་
བཅས་པ་ཡིན་ཏེ། གལ་ཏེ་རྣམ་པ་མེད་པར་ཡུལ་ཁོ་རང་གསལ་བར་རིག་ན་ཡུལ་ཉིད་
གསལ་བའི་ངོ་བོར་ཐལ་བར་འགྱུར་བའི་ཕྱིར་དང་། དེ་ལྟ་ན་ཤེས་པ་ལ་མ་ལྟོས་
པར་ཡང་འཛིན་པར་འགྱུར་བའི་ཕྱིར་རོ། །དེས་ན་ཤེས་པས་ཡུལ་རིག་པ་ནི། ཚོན་
གྱིས་ཁ་དོག་བསྒྱུར་བའི་ཤེལ་དག་པ་ལ་སྐྱེས་བུས་ ལྟས[49]་པའི་ཚེ་ཤེལ་དང་ཚོན་གཉིས་
ཀ་ཡིག་གིས་བཟུང་བ་ན། ཤེལ་ནི་མངོན་སུམ་གྱིས་བཟུང་བ་ཡིན་ལ། ཚོན་ནི་གཟུང་
བརྒྱུད་ཀྱིས་བཟུང་བ་ཡིན་པས་སྐྱེས་བུས་གཟུང་བ་གཉིས་བཟུང་བ་ལྟར། མངོན་སུམ་
གྱིས་སྣང་བ་ནི་ཤེས་པ་ཁོ་ནའི་རྣམ་པ་ཡིན་ལ། ཤེས་པ་ཁ་དོག་དང་དབྱིབས་སུ་སྣང་
བའི་གཞི་ནི་ཤེས་པ་ལས་ངོ་བོ་ཐ་དད་པར་གྱུར་པའི་རྡུལ་ཕྲ་རབ་ཚོགས་པ་ཕྱི་རོལ
ཀྱི་དོན་ཡིན་པར་འདོད་ཅེས་སློབ་དཔོན་བྱང་ཆུབ་བཟང་པོ་ དི་ཡེ་ཤེས་ཀུན་ལས་བཏུས
ཀྱི་རྣམ་བཤད་དུ་བཤད་པ་ལྟར་ཡིན་ནོ། །བྱེ་སྨྲ་ལྟར་མིག་དབང་གཟུགས་ཅན་བས་

མཐོང་བ་མ་ཡིན་གྱི་མཐོང་བ་པོ་ལ་སོགས་པ་ནི་རྣམ་པར་ཤེས་པ་ཁོ་ན་ཡིན་མོད་ཀྱང་། རྟོག་པ[50]་ལ་སོགས་པས་བར་དུ་ཆོད་པ་ལ་ནི་རྣམ་པར་ཤེས་པ་ལ་སྣང་བའི་བགེགས[51]་དང་…… བཅས་པས་མ་མཐོང་བ་ཡིན་ནོ། །ཅི་སྟེ་རྟེར་དབང་པོ་གཟུགས་ཅན་བས་མཐོང་བ་དང་། བར་དུ་ཆོད་པ་ཐམས་ཅད་མི་མཐོང་བ་ནི་མི་འཐད་དེ། མཆིང་བུ་དང་། ཤླང་ཆེར་དང་། ཤེལ་དང་། ཆུ་དག་གིས་བར་དུ་ཆོད་པ་ཡང་མཐོང་བའི་ཕྱིར་རོ། །མིག་གིས་གཟུགས་མཐོང་ཞེས་པ་ཡང་མི་འགལ་ཏེ། བརྟེན་པ་རྣམ་པར་ཤེས་པའི[53]་ལས་རྟེན་དབང་པོ་གཟུགས་ཅན་པ་ལ་ཉེ་བར་བཏགས་ནས་བསྟན་པ་ཡིན་པའི་ཕྱིར། དེས་ན་བཅོམ་ལྡན་འདས་ཀྱིས་འཇིག་རྟེན་གྱི་ཐ་སྙད་དང་མཐུན་པར་ཆོས་ཀྱི་བརྡ་གསུངས་པ…… ཡིན་པས་དོན་ལ་རྟོན་པར་བྱ་ཡི་ཚིག་ཙམ་ལ་ཞེན་པར་མི་བྱའོ། །ཞེས་ཟེར་ཏེ། མཛོད་འགྲེལ་ཀྱི་གནས་དང་པོ་ལས་རྒྱས་པར་བཤད་དོ། །ཤེས་པ་རྣམ་བཅས་སུ་འདོད་ཚུལ་ལ་གསུམ་སྟེ། ཤེས་པ་གཅིག་ལ་རྣམ་པ་དུ་མ་འཆར་བར་ཁས་ལེན་པ་སྣ་ཚོགས་གཉིས་མེད་པ་དང་། ཤེས་པ་གཅིག་ལ་རྣམ་པ་ཡང་གཅིག་ཁོ་ན་འཆར་བར་ཁས་ལེན་པ་སྒོང་ང་ཕྱེད་ཚལ་བ་དང་། རྣམ་པ་དུ་མ་ཤར་བ་ན་ཤེས་པ་ཡང་དུ་མར་ཁས་ལེན་པ་གཟུང་འཛིན་གྲངས་མཉམ་པ་གསུམ་མོ། །རྣམ་འགྲེལ་ངེས་ཀྱི་སྐབས་སུ་མདོ་སྡེ་པའི་ལུགས་ཁས་ལེན་པའི་ཚེ་སྣ་ཚོགས་གཉིས་མེད་པ་ལྟར་བྱེད་པར་རྗེ་ཡབ་སྲས་ཀྱིས…… བཞེད་དོ། །དེ་ལ་དང་པོ་ནི་སྔོན་པོ་དང་སྒྲུབ་བདེ་རྫས་གཅིག་པའི་སྔོན་པོ་འདི་བྲམ་མི་རྟག་སོགས་ཇི་སྙེད་ཡོད་པ་དེ་སྙེད་ཀྱིས་ཡུལ་གྱི་རྣམ་པ་གཏད་ཀྱང་། ཡུལ་ཅན་ཤེས་པ་དེ་སྔོན་པོ་ཙམ་ཁོ་ནའི་རྣམ་ལྡན་དུ་སྐྱེ་བ་སྟེ། དཔེར་ན་ཁྲ་འཛིན་དབང་ཤེས་ལ་ཡུལ་ཁྲ་བོ་འདི་སྔོ་སེར་སོགས་ཀྱི[54]་རྣམ་པ་དུ་མ་གཏད་ཀྱང་མིག་ཤེས་དེ་དེ་སྙེད་ཀྱི་གྲངས…… ལྡན་དུ་མི་སྐྱེ་བར་ཁྲ་ཙམ་གྱི་རྣམ་ལྡན་དུ་སྐྱེ་བ་བཞིན། གཉིས་པ་ནི། ཡུལ་རྟོན་

པོ་དང་གྲུབ་བདེ་རྫས་གཅིག་པའི་བུམ་སོགས་ཀྱི་[55]རྣམ་པ་སོ་སོར་མི་གཏོད་པར་སྤྱི་....
ཙམ་ཞིག་གི་རྣམ་པ་གཏོད་ཅིང་ཤེས་པའང་སྤྱི་ཙམ་ཞིག་གི་རྣམ་ལྡན་དུ་སྐྱེ་བ་ཡོད་དེ།
ཁྲ་འཛིན་མིག་ཤེས་ལའང་ཡུལ་གྱིས་ཀྱང་ཁྲ་ཙམ་ཞིག་གི་རྣམ་པ་གཏད་ལ། ཡུལ་ཅན་
ཡང་ཁྲ་ཙམ་ཞིག་གི་རྣམ་ལྡན་དུ་སྐྱེ་བའོ། །གསུམ་པ་ནི། སྔོན་པོ་དང་གྲུབ་
བདེ་རྫས་གཅིག་པའི་སྔོན་པོ་ནི་སྔོང་གི་བུམ་མི་རྟག་སོགས་ཇི་སྙེད་ཡོད་པ་དེ་སྙེད་ཀྱི་[56]...
རྣམ་པ་གཏད་ཅིང་ཤེས་པ་ཡང་དེ་སྙེད་ཀྱི་རྣམ་ལྡན་དུས་གཅིག་ལ་སྐྱེ་བའོ། །དེ་ལ་
དང་པོ་ནི། དབུ་མ་རྒྱན་རང་འགྲེལ་ལས། གལ་ཏེ་རྣམ་པར་ཤེས་པ་ནི་གཅིག་
པུ་ཁོ་ནའི་རང་བཞིན་ཡིན་ལ་རྣམ་པ་ནི་དུ་མ་ཡིན་ན་དེའི་ཚེ་འགལ་བའི་ཆོས་སུ་གནས་...
པས་རྣམ་པ་དང་རྣམ་པར་ཤེས་པ་ཉིད་ཐ་དད་པ་མ་ཡིན་པ་ནི་འགལ་ལོ། །ཞེས་པའི་
ཕྱོགས་སྔ་མའོ། །གཉིས་པ་ནི། ཛཻ་ཏ་རིས། ནང་དུ་སྣང་བའང་གཞན་ཉིད་
ལ། ཕྱི་རུ་སྣང་བའང་དེ་གཞན་ཉིད། །གསལ་བར་བྱ་དང་གསལ་བྱེད་འདི། །མར་
མེ་བཞིན་དུ་དེ་ཉིད་མིན། །ཞེས་དང་། གསུམ་པ་ནི། དབུ་མ་རྒྱན་ལས།
རི་མོ་བཀྲ་པ་མཐོང་བའི་ཚེ། དེ་ལ་དེ་བཞིན་སེམས་མང་པོ། །ཅི་སྟེ་གཅིག་
ཆར་ཚུལ་གྱིས་སུ། །འབྱུང་བར་འགྱུར་བར་འདོད་ན་ཀོ། །ཞེས་སོགས་ཀྱི་སྐབས་
སུ་གསུངས་པའོ། །རྣམ་པའི་འདོད་ཚུལ་འདི་གསུམ་མདོ་སེམས་གཉིས་ཀའི་ལུགས་
ལ་ཡོད་སོད་ཀྱང་སེམས་ཙམ་པ་རྣམས་ནི་[57]ཕྱི་རོལ་དོན་གྱིས་རྣམ་པ་གཏོད་པར་ཁས་མི་....
ལེན་ཞིང་འདི་པས་ཁས་ལེན་པ་ནི་ཁྱད་པར་རོ། །དབུ་མ་རྒྱན་ལས། དཀར་པོ་
དག་ལ་སོགས་པ་ལ། །ཤེས་པ་དེ་ནི་རིམ་འབྱུང་སྟེ། ཞེས་སོགས་ཀྱི་སྐབས་
ནས་བསྟན་པའི་སྣ་ཚོགས་རིམ་འབྱུང་བ་ནི་ལུང་གི་རྗེས་འབྲང་གི་མདོ་སྡེ་པ་ཁོ་ན་ཡིན་...
པར་ཕྱི་ས་ཀྱི་མཁས་པ་རྣམས་འཆད་དོ། །དབུ་མ་རྒྱན་རྩ་འགྲེལ་གྱིས་བཤད་པའི་

གོ་རིམ་དང་སྔ་ཕྱིའི་འབྲེལ་ལ་བརྟགས་ན་གཟུང་འཛིན་གྲངས་མཉམ་པ་ཉིད་ལ་ཞེས་པ་སྣ་ཚོགས་པ་དག་ཅིག་ཅར་འབྱུང་བ་དང་རིམ་གྱིས་འབྱུང་བའི་ཕྱོགས་གཉིས་ཡོད་པར་བྱས་ཀྱང་མི་འགལ་ལོ། །འདི་དག་སོ་སོའི་རྟོགས་ཚུལ་སོགས་ནི་དབུ་མ་རྒྱན་རྩ་འགྲེལ་ལས་ཤེས་པར་བྱའོ། །འོན་ཀྱང་མདོ་སྡེ་པ་ལ་སྒོང་ཕྱེད་ཚལ་བའི་རྣམ་པའི་འདོད་ཕྱོགས་ཡོད་མེད་རྗེ་ཐམས་ཅད་མཁྱེན་པ་ཡབ་སྲས་ཀྱིས་གསལ་བར་བཤད་པ་མི་སྣང་ཞིང་། སྡེ་བདུན་ཡིད་ཀྱི་མུན་སེལ་དུ་ཟུར་ཙམ་བྱུང་བ་དང་། རྗེའི་དངོས་སློབ་གུང་རུ་རྒྱལ་མཚན་བཟང་པོའི་དབུ་མའི་སྟོང་ཐུན་དུ་སྔར་ལྟར་བཤད་ལ། མཁས་ཞིང་གྲུབ་པའི་དབང་ཕྱུག་ཆེན་པོ་རྗེ་བཙུན་འཇམ་དབྱངས་བཞད་པའི་རྡོ་རྗེས་རྗེ་ཏ་རིའི་ལུང་རིས་མདོ་སེམས་ཐུན་མོང་དུ་བསྟན་ཟེར་ན་མ་གདོགས་རྣམ་པའི་འདོད་ཚུལ་གཉིས་པ་འདི་མདོ་སྡེ་པའི་ཕྱོགས་སུ་འཛོག་པ་འཐད་དཀའ་བར་སྣང་ངོ་། །ཞེས་གསུངས་པ་ནི་དེ་ཁོ་ན་ལྟར་འདུག་གོ། གཉིས་པ་འཇལ་བྱེད་ཚད་མའི་རྣམ་གཞག་ལ། གཞལ་བྱ་རང་སྤྱི་གཉིས་སམ་མངོན་ལྐོག་གཉིས་སུ་ངེས་པའི་དབང་གིས་ཚད་མ་ལ་མངོན་རྗེས་གཉིས་སུ་ངེས་པར་བསྒྲུབ་པ་དང་། དེ་ཡང་དགག་ཕྱོགས་དང་སྒྲུབ་ཕྱོགས་གཉིས་ཀས་ཕྱུང་གསུམ་སེལ་དགོས་པར་འདོད་པ་ལ་མདོ་སྡེ་པ་ནས་རང་རྒྱུད་པའི་བར་ཐམས་ཅད་མཐུན་ནོ། །ཚད་མའི་མཚན་ཉིད་ནི། གསར་དུ་མི་སླུ་བའི་རིག་པའོ། །མངོན་སུམ་ཚད་མ་ནི། ཚད་མ་གང་། རྟོག་བྲལ་མ་འཁྲུལ་བའི་ཞེས་པའོ། །དབྱེ་ན། གཞན་རིག་དང་རང་རིག་གཉིས། དང་པོ་ལ་བདག་རྐྱེན་གྱིས་ཕྱེ་ན། དབང་པོའི་མངོན་སུམ། ཡིད་ཀྱི་མངོན་སུམ། རྣལ་འབྱོར་མངོན་སུམ་ཡོད་ལ། དེའི་དང་པོ་ནི་བདག་རྐྱེན་དབང་པོ་གཟུགས་ཅན་པ་དང་། གཉིས་པ་ནི་བདག་རྐྱེན་ཡིད་ཙམ་དང་། གསུམ་པ་ནི་བདག་རྐྱེན་ཞི་ལྷག་ཟུང་འབྲེལ་ལ་བརྟེན་པའོ། །འདིའི་ཡིད་མངོན་ནི་དབང་མངོན་གྱི་རྒྱུན་

ཁ

མཐར་སྐད་ཅིག་མ་གཅིག་ཁོ་ན་ཞུ་བ་དང་། དེ་ཡང་སོ་སྐྱེ་ལ་ཤིན་ཏུ་ཉོག་གྱུར་ཡིན་པར་པཎ་ཆེན་རྒྱལ་ཛ་བདུན་པའི་རྗེས་སུ་འབྲངས་ནས་རྒྱལ་ཚབ་ཐམས་ཅད་མཁྱེན་……པ་བཞེད་པ་ལྟར་དེང་སང་གྲགས་པ་ལ།[58] མཁས་གྲུབ་ཐམས་ཅད་མཁྱེན་པས་ནི་དེ་དང་ཅུང་ཟད་མི་འདྲ་ཙམ་བཤད་དེ་འདིར་མ་སྤྲོས་སོ། །རང་རིག་ནི་ཁ་ནང་བལྟས་འཛིན་རྣམ་ཡིན་གར་བ་སྟེ། ཡུལ་ཡུལ་ཅན་གྱི་གཉིས་སྣང་ནུབ་པ་ཞིག་གོ །མངོན་སུམ་རྒྱུན་ཕྱི་མ་རྣམས་བཅད་ཤེས་སུ་པཎ་ཆེན་ཆོས་མཆོག་གིས་བཤད་ཅིང་རང་རེའི་མཁས་པ་ཕལ་ཆེར་ཡང་དེ་ལྟར་བཞེད་དོ། །འོན་ཀྱང་ལུང་གི་རྗེས་འབྲང་གི་མདོ་སྡེ་པས་རང་རིག་འདོད་པའི་རྣམ་གཞག་གསལ་བར་བཤད་པ་མི་སྣང་……ངོ་། །རྗེས་དཔག་ནི། རང་གི་རྟེན་ཚུལ་གསུམ་པའི་རྟགས་ལ་བརྟེན་ནས་བྱུང་བའི་བསྒྲུབ་བྱ་ཡོངས་སུ་དཔོག་པའི་ཤེས་པའོ། །དབྱེ་ན། དངོས་པོ་སྟོབས་ཞུགས་ཀྱི་རྗེས་དཔག་ཚད་མ། གྲགས་པའི་རྗེས་དཔག་ཚད་མ། ཡིད་ཆེས་པའི་རྗེས་དཔག་ཚད་མ་སྟེ་གསུམ་མོ། །ཤར་བྱུང་མདོ་སྡེ་པའི་ལུགས་ཀྱི་དབང་མངོན་གྱི་རྐྱེན་གསུམ་བཤད་པ་ལ། བདག་རྐྱེན་ནི་རང་འབྲས་དབང་ཤེས་ཀྱི་ཐུན་མོང་མ་ཡིན་པའི་ཁྱད་པར་ལ་དབང་བྱེད་པའི་དབང་པོ་འོ། །དམིགས་རྐྱེན་ནི་རང་འཛིན་ཤེས་པ་རང་གི་རྣམ་ལྡན་དུ་དངོས་སུ་སྐྱེད་པར་བྱེད་པའི་དོན་གང་ཡིན་པའོ། །དེ་མ་ཐག་རྐྱེན་ནི་ཤེས་པ་གཞན་གྱིས་བར་མ་ཆོད་པའི་རང་གི་སྔ་ལོགས་ཀྱི་ཤེས་པ་གང་། རང་ཉིད་མྱོང་བའི་ངོ་བོར་སྐྱེད་[59]བྱེད་དོ། །འདི་པའི་ལུགས་ལ་དམིགས་རྐྱེན་དང་གཟུང་དོན་གཉིས་ཡིན་ཁྱབ་མཉམ་ཡིན་ནོ། །གསུམ་པ་དེའི་ཡན་ལག་རྟགས་ཀྱི་རྣམ་གཞག་བཤད་པ་ལ། རྣམ་འགྲེལ་ལས། ཕྱོགས་ཆོས་དེ་ཆས་ཁྱབ་པ་ཡི། །གཏན་ཚིགས་དེ་ན་རྣམ་གསུམ་ཉིད། །ཅེས་སོགས་གསུངས་པ་ལྟར། ཚུལ་གསུམ་ཡིན་པ་རྟགས་ཡང་

དག་གི་ངོ་བོ་དང་། དབྱེ་ན་འབྲས་རང་མ་དམིགས་པའི་རྟགས་གསུམ་དང་། འབྲས་བུའི་རྟགས་ལ་ཡང་། རྒྱུ་དངོས་སྒྲུབ་པ། རྒྱུ་སྔོན་སོང་སྒྲུབ་པ། རྒྱུའི་སྤྱི་སྒྲུབ་པ། རྒྱུའི་ཁྱད་པར་སྒྲུབ་པ། རྒྱུའི་ཚོས་དཔོག་པའི་འབྲས་རྟགས་ཏེ་ལྔའོ། །རང་བཞིན་གྱི་རྟགས་ལ། ཁྱད་པར་དག་པ་པའི་རང་བཞིན་གྱི་རྟགས་དང་། ཁྱད་པར་ལྟོས་པ་པའི་རང་བཞིན་གྱི་རྟགས་གཉིས་[60]ཕྱི་མ་ལ་ཁྱད་པར་གྱི་ཆོས་རྫས་གཞན་འཕེན་པ་དང་། རྫས་གཞན་མ་ཡིན་པ་འཕེན་པ་གཉིས་རྣམས་སོ། །མ་དམིགས་པའི་རྟགས་ལ། མི་སྣང་བ་མ་དམིགས་པའི་རྟགས་དང་། སྣང་རུང་མ་དམིགས་པའི་རྟགས་གཉིས། ཕྱི་མ་ལ་འབྲེལ་ཟླ་མ་དམིགས་པ་དང་། འགལ་ཟླ་དམིགས་པ་གཉིས། དེའི་དང་པོ་ལ། རྒྱུ། ཁྱབ་བྱེད། རང་བཞིན། དངོས་འབྲས་མ་དམིགས་པ་སྟེ་བཞི། ཕྱི་མ་ལ། རང་བཞིན་འགལ་དམིགས། འགལ་འབྲས་དམིགས་པ། རྒྱུ་འགལ་དམིགས། རྒྱུ་དང་འགལ་བའི་འབྲས་བུ་དམིགས་པ། ཁྱབ་བྱེད་འགལ་དམིགས། འབྲས་བུ་འགལ་དམིགས་ཏེ་དྲུག་གོ །དེ་ལྟར་ན་དགག་རྟགས་བཅུར་གྲངས་ངེས་པ་ཡང་རྣམ་ངེས་ལས། དེ་ལྟར་ན་མ་དམིགས་པ་འདི་ནི་སྦྱོར་བའི་ཏེ་[61]བྲག་གིས་རྣམ་པ་བཅུ་ཡིན་ནོ། །ཞེས་པའི་དོན་དུ་རྒྱལ་ཚབ། མཁས་གྲུབ། རྗེ་དགེ་འདུན་གྲུབ་རྣམས་ཀྱིས་མཐའ་གཅོད་པ་དང་བཅས་ཞིབ་ཏུ་རྒྱས་པར་གསུངས་པས་དེ་ལས་གཞན་དུ་གྲངས་མང་པོར་འཆད་པ་ནི་སྙིང་པོ་མེད་པ་ཁོ་ནའོ། །གཞན་ཡང་ཕུང་ཁམས་སྐྱེ་མཆེད་དང་ཤེས་བྱ་གཞི་ལྔའི་འདོད་ཚུལ་ལས་ཆེར་སྤྲར་དང་འདྲ་ཤིང་སེམས་བྱུང་ང་གཅིག་ལྡན་མིན་ཉེར་གསུམ་སོགས་ཀྱི་འདོད་ཚུལ་དང་། འདུས་མ་བྱས་ཀྱི་དབྱེ་བ་སོགས་ཁྱད་པར་རྣམས་ནི་གཞན་དུ་བལྟ་བར་བྱའོ། །གཉིས་པ་ལམ་ལ། བྱང་ཕྱོགས་སོ་བདུན། མཐར་གནས་སྙོམས་འཇུག་དགུ །ཕར་ཕྱིན་དྲུག །ཞུགས་གནས་བརྒྱད་སོགས་ཀྱི་

རྣམ་གཞག་འདི་པས་ཀྱང་འདོད་ཅིང་ཉན་རང་བྱང་སེམས་གསུམ་གྱི་ལམ་གྱི་ཁྱད་པར་ལ། བདག་མེད་རྟོགས་པའི་རྩ་ ལ་སོ་འདྲ་བ་མེད་ཀྱང་སྙིང་རྗེ་ཆེན་པོ་སོགས་ཐབས་ཀྱི་ཆ་མི་འདྲ་བས་ཕྱེ་བར་འདོད་དོ། ལམ་གྱི་ཡུལ་བདེན་བཞིའི་ཁྱད་ཆོས་མི་རྟག་སོགས་བཅུ་དྲུག་གི་རྣམ་གཞག་གཏན་ལ་འབེབས་པ་ནི་ལམ་གྱི་སྙིང་པོར་ཆེད་དུ་མི་རུང་བས་དེའི་ཚུལ་ཅུང་ཟད་བཤད་ན། ཐོག་མར་གང་ཟག་གི་བདག་མེད་གཏན་ལ་འབེབས་ཚུལ་ནི། རང་གི་ཕུང་པོ་དང་རང་བཞིན་གཅིག་དང་ཐ་དད་པ་གང་དུའང་མེད་ན་རང་བཞིན་མེད་པས་ཁྱབ། དཔེར་ན་རི་བོང་གི་རྭ་བཞིན། ཚོགས་རྒྱུད་གང་ལའང་བཏགས་པ་ཙམ་མ་ཡིན་པའི་གང་ཟག་རང་རྐྱ་བ་དེའང་ཕུང་པོ་དང་རང་བཞིན་གཅིག་ཐ་དད་གང་དུའང་མ་གྲུབ་པོ། །ཞེས་བྱ་བ་ནི་ཁྱབ་བྱེད་མ་དམིགས་པའི་རྟགས་སོ། །གཏན་ཚིགས་འདི་དོན་དང་ཐ་སྙད་གཉིས་ཀྱི་ནང་ནས་ཐ་སྙད་བསྒྲུབ་ཡིན་པར་བཞེད་དོ། །གལ་ཏེ་གཏན་ཚིགས་འདི་ནི་གཏན་ཚིགས་ཡང་དག་ཏུ་མི་རིགས་ཏེ། རྟགས་ཀྱིས་གཞི་ཆོས་ཅན་བཀག་པའི་ཕྱིར། དེས་ན་རྟགས་དང་ཆོས་ཚོགས་པའང་ཁེགས་པས་དམ་བཅའ་ཚད་མས་བསལ་བ་དང་། རྟགས་ཕྱོགས་ཆོས་མ་གྲུབ་པར་འགྱུར་བའི་ཕྱིར་རོ་ཞེ་ན། སྐྱོན་མེད་དེ། རྟགས་ཆོས་གཉིས་རྣམ་པར་བཅད་ཙམ་ཡིན་པ་ལ་གཉིས་མ་གྲུབ་པ་དེ་ལྟ་བུ་ཆོས་ཅན་དུ་རུང་བའི་ཕྱིར་རོ། །དེའི་རྒྱུ་མཚན་ཡང་། སློབ་དཔོན་ཕྱོགས་[62] ཀྱི་གླང་པོས། མངོན་སུམ་དོན་དང་རྗེས་དཔག་དང་། །ཡིད་ཆེས་གྲགས་པས་རང་ཉིད་ལ་དོ། །ཞེས་གསུངས་པའི་དོན། དཔལ་ལྡན་ཆོས་ཀྱི་གྲགས་པས་འཆད་པའི་ཚེ། བསྒྲུབ་བྱའི་ཆོས་རང་གི་ངེར་ཀྱི་ཆོས་ཅན་དང་། དེ་གཉིས་ཚོགས་པ་བསལ་ན་གཏན་ཚིགས་ཀྱི་སྐྱོན་ཡིན་པར་བསྟན་པའི་དོན་དུ་རང་ཉིད་ཞེས་གསུངས་པ་ཡོད་ཀྱི་ཆོས་ཅན་འབའ་ཞིག་པ་དང་། བསྒྲུབ་བྱའི་ཆོས་གཉིས་ཚོགས་པའི་ཚོགས་དོན་བསལ་ཡང་

སྐྱོན་མ་ཡིན་པར་བཤད་དོ། །ཆོས་ཅན་འབའ་ཞིག་པ་ཞེས་པ་ནི་ཆོས་ཅན་དུ་སྨྲས་ཀྱང་སྐབས་དེའི་བསྒྲུབ་བྱའི་ཆོས་ཀྱི་རྟེན་མིན་པས་ཆོས་ཅན་ཡན་ག་བར་[63] སོང་བའི་དོན་ནོ། །གཏན་ཚིགས་འགོད་པའི་སྐབས་སུ་རྩོད་གཞིར་གང་བྱུང་དེ་ཉིད་ལ་ཕྱོགས་ཆོས་འགྲུབ་དགོས་ན་ཆོས་ཅན་འབའ་ཞིག་པ་དང་། རང་རྟེན་གྱི་ཆོས་ཅན་གཉིས་སུ་འབྱེད་པའི་དོན་མེད་དོ། །དེའི་ཕྱིར་བདག་དང་གཙོ་བོ་སོགས་འགོག་པའི་ཚེ་རང་ལྟོག་ནས་དགག་དགོས་པས་རང་རྒྱུད་ཀྱི་སྦྱོར་བའི་རྩོད་གཞིར་བཟུང་དགོས་པ་དང་། དེའི་ཚེ་དེ་དག་དངོས་མེད་དུ་སྒྲུབ་པའི་རྟགས་ཀྱིས་ཆོས་ཅན་བཀག་ཀྱང་སྐྱོན་དུ་མི་འགྱུར་ཏེ། བསྒྲུབ་བྱ་བདག་དང་གཙོ་བོ་སོགས་མེད་པར་རྟོགས་པའི་རྗེས་དཔག་སྐྱེ་བ་ལ་དེ་ཉིད་ཐབས་ཡང་དག་པར་འགྱུར་བའི་ཕྱིར་རོ། །དེས་ན་མཁས་གྲུབ་ཐམས་ཅད་མཁྱེན་པ་ནི། དེ་ལྟ་བུའི་རྟགས་ལ་ནི། ཆོས་ཅན་དང་མེད་ངེས་ཀྱི་ཚོགས་དོན་བསྒྲུབ་བྱ་ཡིན་པས་ཆོས་ཅན་གཞི་མ་གྲུབ་པ་ཉིད་དམ་བཅའ་ཚད་མས་གྲུབ་པའི་སྒྲུབ་བྱེད་ཡིན་པས་སྐྱོན་མེད་ལ། གཞི་མ་གྲུབ་ཀྱང་རྟགས་ངེས་པའི་ཤེས་འདོད་ཆོས་ཅན་ཡིན་པ་མི་འགལ་ཏེ། གཞི་མ་གྲུབ་ཀྱང་ཁྱབ་པ་ངེས་པའི་མཐུན་དཔེ་ཡིན་པ་མི་འགལ་བ་བཞིན་ནོ། །དེས་ན་རང་རྟེན་པའོ་ཞེས་པ་ཡང་རང་གི་རྟེན་དུ་གཞི་གྲུབ་པའི་ཆོས་ཅན་བཀག་ན་རྟགས་ཀྱི་སྐྱོན་དུ་སོང་པ་ཡིན་གྱི་ཆོས་ཅན་ཡོད་པ་བཀག་ཙམ་རྟགས་ཀྱི་སྐྱོན་དུ་སོང་པ་མིན་ནོ། །དེའི་ཕྱིར་བདག་དང་གཙོ་བོ་སོགས་ཁོ་ན་ཆོས་ཅན་དུ་འཛིན་གྱི་དེ་དག་གི་སྒྲ་དོན་ཆོས་ཅན་དུ་མི་འཛིན་པར་གསུངས་སོ། །རྒྱལ་ཚབ་ཐམས་ཅད་མཁྱེན་པས་ནི་ཕྱིར་རྒོལ་གྱིས་གང་ཟག་རང་རྐྱ་བ་དང་། དེར་སྣང་བ་གཉིས་གཅིག་ཏུ་འཁྲུལ་ནས་ཤེས་འདོད་ཞུགས་ཤིང་སྣང་བའི་སྒྲ་དོན་གྱི་སྟེང་དུ་རྟར་ཚད་མས་གྲུབ་ལ། གང་ཟག་རང་རྐྱ་བ་ཆོས་ཅན་དུ་མ་བཟུང་ན་གང་ཟག་གི་བདག་རང་ལྟོག་ནས་མི་ཁེགས་ཤིང་ཕྱིར་རྒོལ་གྱིས་དེར་སྣང་གི་སྒྲ་དོན་

དང་གཅིག་དུ་ཞེན་ནས་འཛིན་པས་སྒྲ་དོན་ཆོས་ཅན་དུ་མི་རུང་བའི་སྐྱོན་ཡང་མེད་དོ། །
དེས་ན་རྟགས་ཡང་དག་ཡིན་ན་ཤེས་འདོད་ཆོས་ཅན་གཞི་གྲུབ་པས་ཁྱབ་ཀྱང་། རྟགས་
ཡང་དག་གི་ཤེས་འདོད་ཆོས་ཅན་ཡིན་ན་གཞི་གྲུབ་པས་མ་ཁྱབ་པོ། །ཞེས་གསུངས་
སོ། །དེ་ལ་རྗེ་ཐམས་ཅད་མཁྱེན་པར་སྐུས་ཀྱི་ཕྱི་བོ་གཉིས་ཀྱི་བཞེད་པ་ནི་ཤིན་དུ་ཟབ་
པས་བདག་ལྟ་བུས་འདི་འཆད་དང་འདི་མི་འཐད་ཅེས་པའི་རྣམ་གཞག་བྱེད་ག་ལ་ནུས།
འོན་ཀྱང་རྗེ་ཐམས་ཅད་མཁྱེན་པ་རང་ཉིད་ཀྱིས། དབུ་མ་རྒྱན་གྱི་ཊིན་ཕྲིས་སུ་དོན་འདི་……
གསལ་བར་བཀའ་སྩལ་པ་རྣམས་ནི་ཕྱོགས་ཕྱི་མ་དང་མཐུན་ཤས་ཆེ་ཞིང་གོ་བ་སྟེར་……
བྱུང་ཤིན་དུ་ཆེ་བར་འདུག་པས་གསུང་རྗེ་ལྟ་བ་བཞིན་དུ་ཡི་གེ་མ་ཉམས་པར་དགོད་པར་··
བྱ་སྟེ། དེ་ཉིད་ལས། ཕྱོགས་གླང་གིས་གསུངས་པའི་དོན་རྣམ་འགྲེལ་ལས།
དཔག་བྱ་རབ་ཏུ་རྟོགས་པར་བྱེད་པ་ཡི། །དོན་གྱི་ཐ་སྙད་གནས་པ་འདི། །ཞེས་པ་ལ་གྲུབ་
ཐ་དད་ལ། །བརྟེན་ནས་རྣམ་པར་བརྟགས་པ་ཡིན། །ཞེས་གསུངས་པ་ལྟར་གཞི་དངོས་
པོ་དགོས་པ་བྱས་པས་སྒྲ་མི་རྟག་པ་དང་། དུ་བ་ལ་ལ་མེ་ཡོད་དུ་བསྒྲུབ་པ་ལ་ཡང་རྟོག་
པ་ལ་སྒྲ་དང་ལ་གཉིས། དེ་གཉིས་ཡིན་པ་ལས་ལོག་པར་སྣང་བའི་དོན་ཉིད་དགག་
སྒྲུབ་ཀྱི་དངོས་རྟེན་ཡིན་གྱི་སྒྲ་དང་ལ་ཉིད་དངོས་ཀྱི་རྟེན་མིན་ནོ། དགག་སྒྲུབ་བྱེད་པའི་
རྟོག་པ་ལ་དངོས་སུ་མི་སྣང་བའི་ཕྱིར་དང་། ཆོས་གཅིག་ཅིག་བསྒྲུབས་ན་དེའི་ཆོས་
ཐམས་ཅད་ཅིག་ཅར་དུ་བསྒྲུབས་པར་འགྱུར་བའི་ཕྱིར་རོ། །འོན་ཀྱང་དེ་ལྟར་སྣང་བའི་
སྣང་གཞི་ནི་སྒྲ་དང་ལ་ཡིན་པས་གཞི་དངོས་པོར་གྲུབ་པ་དགོས། གཞི་ཆོས་ཅན་དངོས་
པོ་ཡིན་པ་མི་དགོས་པ་གཙོ་བོ་དང་དབང་ཕྱུག་ལ་སོགས་པ་རྩོད་གཞིར་བཟུང་བ་ལ……
ཡང་རྟོག་པ་ལ་གཙོ་བོ་དང་དབང་ཕྱུག་མ་ཡིན་པ་ལས་ལོག་པར་སྣང་བ་ནི་ཡོད་ལ། དེ་
ཉིད་ལ་དམིགས་ནས་དངོས་པོར་མེད་ཅེས་བསྒྲུབ་པས་གཞི་དེ་ལ་ཕྱིར་རྒོལ་ལ་ཤེས……

ཁ

འདོད་དང་།[64] སྤྱིར་གྲོལ་ལ་དཔག་འདོད་མེད་པའི་སྐྱོན་མེད་ལ། སྣང་གཞི་དངོས་པོར་ཡོད་པ་དོན་བྱེད་ནུས་སྟོང་དང་། སྣང་གཞི་བདེན་པར་ཡོད་པ་བདེན་པའི་གཅིག་དུ་བྲལ་གྱིས་བཀག་པ་ན། རྟགས་དེ་གཉིས་གཙོ་བོ་དང་དབང་ཕྱུག་མ་ཡིན་པ་ལས་ལོག་པར་སྣང་བ་དེ་ཉིད་ལ་འགྲུབ་ལ། དེ་ཉིད་བསྒྲུབ་བྱའི་ཆོས་གང་གི་ཆོས་སུ་འདོག་པའི་ཆོས་ཅན་དང་། ཕྱོགས་ཀྱི་ཆོས་གང་གི་ཆོས་སུ་བཞག་པའི་ཕྱོགས་སུ་བརྟགས་པ་ཉིད་ཡིན་པས་ཆོས་ཅན་འབའ་ཞིག་ང་བཀག་པས་ཀྱང་ཕྱོགས་ཆོས་མི་འགྲུབ་པའི ··· སྐྱོན་མེད་དོ། །ཁྱབ་པས་སྣ་མི་རྟག་པར་བསྒྲུབ་པ་ན། རྟོག་པ་ལ་སྣ་མ་ཡིན་པ་ལས་ལོག་པར་སྣང་བའི་སྣང་ཡུལ་དངོས་པོར་མེད་པས། བྱས་པའི་རྟགས་དེ་ལ་གྲུབ་པ་མིན་གྱི། སྣང་གཞི་སྒྲ་ལ་གྲུབ་དགོས་ཏེ། དངོས་པོ་རྟགས་དང་བསྒྲུབ་བྱའི་ཆོས་སུ་བྱེད་པའི་གནད་ཀྱིས་སོ། །དོན་བྱེད་པས་སྟོང་པ་གཅིག་ཏུ[65] བྲལ་རྟགས་སུ་བྱེད་པའི་ཚེ་ན། སྣང་གཞི་དང་སྣང་ཡུལ་གཉིས་ཀ་རྟགས་དེ་ཡིན་པར་གྲུབ་ཅིང་། སྣང་གཞི་རྟགས་དེ་ཡིན་པར་གྲུབ་ན། དེ་བཀག་ཀྱང་སྣང་ཡུལ་སྒྲུབ་ཆོས་དང་ཕྱོགས་ཆོས་ཀྱི་ཆོས་གཉིས་བརྟེན་པའི་ཆོས་ཅན་དུ་འགྲུབ་པོ། །འདི་ནི་སྙིང་པོ་བསྡུས་པ་སྟེ། རྒྱས་པར་དབུ་མ་སྣང་བ་ལས་ཤེས་དགོས་སོ། །ཞེས་གསུངས་སོ། །གསུང་འདི་[66]དག་ཤིན་ཏུ་བརླིང་ཞིང་དོན་ཆེ་བར་ཡོད་པས་འབྲུ་སྣོན་ཞིབ་ཏུ་བྱ་དགོས་མོད་ཀྱང་འདིར་ནི ······ སྐབས་དོན་སྦྲིབ་པར་འགྱུར་བས་མ་སྤྲོས་ལ། དོན་དུ་འགྱུར་ན་གཞན་དུ་འཆད་པར་འདོད་དོ། །མདོར་ན་ཡབ་སྲས་གསུམ་གྱི་བཞེད་པ་གུང་བསྒྲིགས་ན་རྟགས་ཆོས་རྣམ་པར་བཅད་ཙམ་ལ་གཞི་ཆོས་ཅན་གཞི་གྲུབ་མི་དགོས་པས་བདག་དང་གཙོ་བོ་སོགས··· ཆོས་ཅན་དུ་བཞག་པས་ཆོག་ལ། ཕྱིར་རྒོལ་གྱི་རྒྱུད་ལ་རྗེས་དཔག་སྐྱེ་བའི་ཚེ་རྟགས་དངོས་སུ་སྒྲ་དོན་གྱི་སྟེང་དུ་འགྲུབ་ཅིང་ངེས་སྐྱེས་པའི་ཆོས་ཅན་ཁེགས་པར་འགྱུར་བས།

བདག་མེད་རྟོགས་པའི་རྗེས་དཔག་སྐྱེད་པ་ལ་ཡོན་ཏན་ཁོ་ན་འབྱུང་གི་སྐྱོན་མི་འབྱུང་བ··· དང་། དགག་སྒྲུབ་ཀྱི་དངོས་དེན་སྒྲ་དོན་དེ་ཉིད་ཀྱང་ཆོས་ཅན་བཏགས་པ་བར་བཞག་པས་ཆོག་པ་ཡིན་ནོ། །བྱས་པས་སྒྲ་མི་རྟག་པར་བསྒྲུབ་པ་ལ་མི་མཚུངས་ཏེ། རྟགས་ཆོས་དངོས་པོ་ཡིན་པས་སྒྲའི་སྒྲ་དོན་གྱི་སྟེང་དུ་འགྲུབ་དུ་མི་རུང་བའི་ཕྱིར་རོ། །ཞེས་པ་འདི་ཡབ་སྲས་གསུམ་གྱི་དགོངས་པ་རྨ་མེད་པའོ། །འདི་དག་ནི་མདོ་སྡེ་པ་ཡན་ཆད་ཀྱི་རང་སྡེ་མཐའ་དག་གི་འདོད་ཚུལ་ཐུན་མོང་བ་ཡིན་ལ་རྟགས་ཆོས་དོན་གསུམ་གྱི··· སྒྲུབ་ཚུལ་ཐལ་འགྱུར་བ་ལ་ཞིབ་ཆ་ཆུང་ཟད་དགོས་སོ། །དོན་འདི་དབུ་མ་སྣང་བ་ལས་བཤད་ཚུལ་སོགས་ནི་འོག་ཏུ་འཆད་དོ། །རྟགས་འདིའི་ཁྱབ་པ་སྒྲུབ་ཚུལ་ནི། རང་བཞིན་གཅིག་དང་ཐ་དད་པན་ཚུན་སྤངས་འགལ་ལ་བརྟེན་པའི་དངོས་འགལ་དུ་ངེས་པའི·· ཚད་མས་དགག་བྱའི་ཆོས་ལ་རྟགས་ལོག་གི་ཁྱབ་པ་ངེས་ཤིང་། ཕྱོགས་ཆོས་ངེས་པའི་ཚད་མ་དང་གཉིས་སྡོམ་པའི་བྱེད་པས་རྟགས་མི་མཐུན་ཕྱོགས་ལས་ལྡོག་པ་དང་། མཐུན་ཕྱོགས་ཁོ་ན་ལ་ཡོད་པར་ངེས་པའི་རྗེས་ཁྱབ་ངེས་པར་བྱེད་པ་ཡིན་ནོ། །ཕྱོགས་ཆོས་ནི་ཕུང་པོ་དང་གང་ཟག་རང་རྐྱ་བ་རང་བཞིན་ཐ་དད་དུ་མེད་པ་དབང་རྟོན་གྱིས········ མངོན་སུམ་གྱིས་འགྲུབ་ཅིང་དབང་རྟུལ་གྱིས་རང་བཞིན་མ་དམིགས་པའི་རྟགས་ལ་བརྟེན·· པའི་རྗེས་དཔག་གིས་ངེས་སོ། །རང་བཞིན་གཅིག་ཏུ་མ་གྲུབ་པར་སྒྲུབ་པ་ལ་རྟགས་དགོད་པ་ནི། རང་རྒྱུད་ཀྱི་ཕུང་པོ་འདི་གང་ཟག་རང་རྐྱ་བ་དང་རང་བཞིན་གཅིག་ཏུ་མེད་དེ།། མི་རྟག་ཅིང་གཞན་དབང་ཅན་ཡིན་པའི་ཕྱིར་རོ། །ཁྱབ་སྟེ། གང་ཟག་རང་རྐྱ་བ་ཡིན་ན་རྟག་པ་དང་རང་དབང་ཅན་ཡིན་དགོས་པའི་ཕྱིར། རྟགས་སྒྲུབ་པ་ནི། རང་རྒྱུད་ཀྱི་ཕུང་པོ་ཆོས་ཅན། གཞན་དབང་ཅན་ཡིན་ཏེ། ལས་ཉོན་གྱིས་འདུས་བྱས་པའི་ཕྱིར། དེ་ཆོས་ཅན། མི་རྟག་སྟེ། བྱས་པའི་ཕྱིར། འདིའི་ཁྱབ་པ་སྒྲུབ

པ་ནི། རྗེས་ཁྱབ་སྒྲུབ་བྱེད་ལྟོས་མེད་ཀྱི་རྟགས་དང་། ལྡོག་ཁྱབ་སྒྲུབ་བྱེད་གནོད་པ་
ཅན་གྱི་རྟགས་ལ་བརྟེན་ནས་སྒྲུབ་དགོས་ཏེ་མ་སྤྲོས་སོ། །གཅིག་དུ་བྲལ་གྱི་གཏན་ཚིགས་
འདིའི་ཕྱོགས་ཆོས་དང་ཁྱབ་པ་སྒྲུབ་ཚུལ་དང་། དོན་དང་ཐ་སྙད་བསྒྲུབ་གང་ཡིན་པ་
སོགས་ཀྱི་རྣམ་གཞག་ཞིབ་པར་ཤེས་དགོས་སོད། དེང་སང་ནི་དབུ་མར་གྱི་ཡིག་ཆ་
རྩོམ་པ་པོ་ཕལ་མོ་ཆེ་ཞིག་གིས་གཏན་ཚིགས་འདིའི་སྐོར་ལ་ཞིབ་བྲུ་གང་མང་དྲིས·····
འདུག་ཀྱང་གནད་དོན་ཇི་བཞིན་ཕེབས་པ་དཀའ་བར་བྱུང་སྣང་ན། དེ་དག་གི་རྗེས་སུ་
འབྲངས་པའི་བློ་ཆུང་གཞན་གྱི་གཡམ་ལ་རྒྱུག་པ་དག་གིས་གཅིག་དུ་བྲལ་གྱི་གཏན་ཚིགས་
67 ཞེས་བྱང་པའི་མ་ཉི་འདྲེན་པ་ལྟར་འདོན་ཀྱང་དོན་ཇི་བཞིན་གོ་བ་ལྟ་ག་ལ་ཞིག །དེ་
དག་གི་རྣམ་གཞག་ཚུང་ཟད་ཙམ་ནི་རང་རྒྱུད་པའི་སྐབས་སུ་འཆད་པར་འགྱུར་རོ། །
ད་ནི་དཀྱུས་ལ་འཇུག་པར་བྱ་སྟེ། དེ་ལྟར་ལམ་གྱི་གཙོ་བོ་ནི་བདག་མེད་རྟོགས་པའི་
ཤེས་རབ་ཉིད་ཡིན་ལ། དེ་ཡང་ལུགས་འདིས་བདག་མེད་རྟོགས་པའི་ཤེས་རབ་ཀྱིས་
བདག་གིས་དབེན་པའི་འདུ་བྱེད་དངོས་སུ་རྟོགས་ཤིང་བདག་བཀག་པའི་མེད་དགག་ནི···
ཤུགས་ལ་རྟོགས་པར་འདོད་དོ། །བདེན་པའི་རྣམ་པ་བཅུ་དྲུག་གི་རྣམ་གཞག་མདོ་
ཙམ་ནི་འདི་ལྟར་ཡིན་ཏེ། སྡུག་བསྔལ་བདེན་པ་ལ་བརྟེན་པའི་ལོག་རྟོག་གཙང་བདེ་
རྟག་བདག་ཏུ་འཛིན་པ་བཞིའི་གཉེན་པོར། མི་རྟག་པ། སྡུག་བསྔལ་བ། སྟོང་པ།
བདག་མེད་པའི་རྣམ་པ་བཞི། སྒྲུབ་བྱེད་ཀྱི་གཏན་ཚིགས་ནི། རིམ་པ་བཞིན་ཉེར་ལེན་
གྱི་ཕུང་པོ་དེ་སྐད་ཅིག་རེ་རེ་ཞིང་འཇིག་པའི་ཕྱིར་དང་། ལས་ཉོན་གྱི་གཞན་དབང་
ཅན་ཡིན་པའི་ཕྱིར་དང་། དོན་གཞན་གྱི་བདག་གིས་སྟོངས་པའི་ཕྱིར་དང་། རང་
གི་ངོ་བོར་གྲུར་བའི་བདག་མེད་པའི་ཕྱིར་ཞེས་པའོ། །ཀུན་འབྱུང་བདེན་པ་ལ་བརྟེན་
པའི་ལོག་རྟོག །སྡུག་བསྔལ་རྒྱུ་མེད་དུ་འཛིན་པ་དང་། རྒྱུ་གཅིག་པུ་འབའ་ཞིག་ལས་

སྐྱེ་བར་འཛིན་པ་དང་། སྐྲའི་ཚངས་པ་འགྱུར་བས་བྱས་པར་འཛིན་པ་དང་། དབང་ཕྱུག་སོགས་ཀྱིས་བློ་སྔོན་དུ་བཏང་ནས་བྱས་པར་འཛིན་པ་བཞིའི་གཉེན་པོར། རྒྱུ། ཀུན་འབྱུང་། རབ་སྐྱེ། རྐྱེན་གྱི་རྣམ་པ་བཞི། སྒྲུབ་བྱེད་ནི། ཟག་བཅས་ཀྱི་ལས་དང་སྲེད་པ་ནི་རང་འབྲས་སྡུག་བསྔལ་གྱི་རྩ་བ་ཡིན་པའི་ཕྱིར་དང་། སྡུག་བསྔལ་རྣམ་པ་ཐམས་ཅད་པ་ཡང་དང་ཡང་དུ་སྐྱེད་པའི་ཕྱིར་དང་། སྡུག་བསྔལ་ཤུགས་དྲག་པར་སྐྱེད་པའི་ཕྱིར་དང་། སྲིད་པའི་སྲེད་པ་ནི་སྡུག་བསྔལ་གྱི་ལྷན་ཅིག་བྱེད་རྐྱེན་ཡིན་པའི་ཕྱིར་ཞེས་པའོ། འགོག་པའི་བདེན་པ་ལ་བརྟེན་པའི་ལོག་རྟོག་ཐར་པ་ཡེ་མེད་དུ་འཛིན་པ་དང་། ཟག་བཅས་ཀྱི་ཁྱད་པར་འགའ་ཞིག་ཐར་བར་འཛིན་པ་དང་། སྡུག་བསྔལ་འགགས་པ་[68]ལས་ལྡོག་པའི་ཐར་པ་ཡོད་པར་འཛིན་པ་དང་། རེ་ཞིག་ཐར་ཡང་གནད་དུ་ཐར་པ་མི་སྲིད་པར་འཛིན་པ་བཞིའི་གཉེན་པོར་འགོག་པ། ཞི་བ། གྱ་ནོམ། [69]
ངེས་འབྱུང་གི་རྣམ་པ་བཞི། སྒྲུབ་བྱེད་ནི། རིམ་པ་བཞིན་དུ། གཉེན་པོ་འདི་སྟོབས་ཀྱིས་སྡུག་བསྔལ་གནད་ཟད་པའི་བྲལ་བ་དེ་ནི་སྡུག་བསྔལ་སྤངས་པའི་བྲལ་བ་ཡིན་པའི་ཕྱིར་དང་། ཉོན་མོངས་སྤངས་པའི་བྲལ་བ་ཡིན་པའི་ཕྱིར་དང་། དེ་ལས་མཆོག་དུ་གྱུར་པའི་ཕན་བདེའི་ངོ་བོར་གྱུར་པ་གཞན་མེད་པའི་ཐར་པ་ཡིན་པའི་ཕྱིར་དང་། ཐོབ་ནས་སླར་མ་ལྡོག་པའི་ཆོས་ཅན་གྱི་ཐར་པ་ཡིན་པའི་ཕྱིར་ཞེས་པའོ། །ལམ་གྱི་བདེན་པ་ལ་བརྟེན་པའི་ལོག་རྟོག་ཐར་ལམ་གནད་མེད་དུ་འཛིན་པ་དང་། ཐར་ལམ་ཡང་དག་པ་ཐར་ལམ་མ་ཡིན་པར་འཛིན་པ་དང་། བདག་མེད་རྟོགས་པའི་ཤེས་རབ་ཡུལ་ལ་ལོག་པར་ཞུགས་པར་འཛིན་པ་དང་། དེ་སྡུག་བསྔལ་གནད་དུ་ཟད་བྱེད་མ་ཡིན་པར་འཛིན་པ་བཞིའི་གཉེན་པོར། ལམ། རིགས་པ། སྒྲུབ་པ། ངེས་འབྱིན་གྱི་རྣམ་པ་བཞི། སྒྲུབ་བྱེད་ནི། རིམ་པ་བཞིན་དུ། བདག་མེད་མངོན་སུམ་དུ་རྟོགས་པའི་

ཞེས་རབ་དེ་ཐར་པར་བསྒྲོད་པར་བྱེད་པ་ཡིན་པའི་ཕྱིར་དང་། ཉོན་མོངས་པའི་དངོས་གཉེན་ཡིན་པའི་ཕྱིར་དང་། སེམས་ཀྱི་གནས་ལུགས་ཕྱིན་ཅི་མ་ལོག་པར་རྟོགས་པའི་ཕྱིར་དང་། དག་པའི་གནས་སུ་གདོན་མི་ཟ་བར་ཕྱིན་པར་བྱེད་པའི་ཕྱིར་ཞེས་པའོ། །གསུམ་པ་འབྲས་བུའི་རྣམ་གཞག་ནི། ཉན་ཐོས་དང་རང་རྒྱལ་དགྲ་བཅོམ་པ་རྣམས་སྤངས་རྟོགས་ལས་ཉམས་པ་མི་སྲིད་པ་དང་། བྱང་སེམས་འཕགས་པ་ལ་མཉམ་གཞག་པས་ཁྱབ་པ་དང་། ཕྲག་མེད་སྤྱང་འདས་གསུམ་གའི་[70]ཚེ་ངེས་རིག་རྒྱུན་ཆད་པར་ཐལ་མོ་[71]ཆེས་འདོད་ཀྱང་རིགས་པའི་རྗེས་འབྲང་གི་མདོ་སྡེ་པ་ལ་ཞིབ་དགོས་སམ་སྙམ། ཆོས་སྐུ་དང་གཟུགས་སྐུ་གཉིས་ཀ་སངས་རྒྱས་ཡིན་པར་འདོད་ལ། ཆོས་འཁོར་ནི་བདེན་བཞིའི་ཆོས་འཁོར་ཁོ་ནར་འདོད་ཅིང་ལུང་དང་རྟོགས་པའི་ཆོས་འཁོར་གཉིས་ཀ་འདོད་དོ། བདེན་བཞི་ལ་ལན་གསུམ་དུ་བཟླས་ཤིང་རྣམ་པ་བཅུ་གཉིས་སུ་སྐོར་ཚུལ་ནི་བྱེ་སྨྲ་དང་མི་འདྲ་སྟེ། འདི་ནི་སྡུག་བསྔལ་འཕགས་པའི་བདེན་པའོ་ཞེས་སོགས་བཞི་ནི་ངོ་བོ་ལ་བཟླས་པ་དང་། ཤེས་པར་བྱ། སྤང་བར་བྱ། མངོན་དུ་བྱ། བསྒོམ་པར་བྱ། ཞེས་པ་བྱ་[72]བ་ལ་བཟླས་པ་དང་། ཤེས་སོ། །སྤངས་སོ།། མངོན་དུ་བྱས་སོ། །བསྒོམས་སོ་ཞེས་པ་བྱེད་པ་ལ་བཟླས་པ་སྟེ་རྣམ་པ་བཅུ་གཉིས་ཀྱང་དེ་ཡིན་ནོ། །འདི་ནི་མདོ་སྡེ་པ་ཡན་ཆད་པལ་ཆེར་འདྲའོ། །དོན་སྨྲ་སྡེ་གཉིས་ཀྱིས་ཐེག་ཆེན་བཀར་ཁས་མི་ལེན་པས་བཀའ་བར་པ་མཚན་ཉིད་མེད་པའི་ཆོས་འཁོར་སོགས་ཐེག་ཆེན་གྱི་མདོ་རྣམས་ཆོས་འཁོར་གྱི་མཚན་གཞིར་མི་འདོད་པ་སྔ་རབས་པ་རྣམས་ལ་གྲགས་ཤིང་བྱེ་མདོ་སྤྱི་ཙམ་ན་དེ་ལྟར་འཐད་པར་རྗེ་ཡབ་སྲས་ཀྱང་བཞེད་མོད། འོན་ཀྱང་བློ་སློབ་ཡབ་སྲས་བྱུང་བའི་རྗེས་ཀྱི་ཉན་ཐོས་སྡེ་ང་འགའ་ཞིག་གིས་ཤེར་ཕྱིན་སོགས་མདོ་ཡིན་པར་ཁས་ལེན་ཚུལ་རྒྱལ་ཚབ་ཐམས་ཅད་མཁྱེན་པའི་སྤྱོད་

ང

འཇིག་དང་ཊཱི་ཀ་དང་རྒྱུད་བླ་དང་། ཊཱིཀ་སོགས་སུ་གསུངས་པ་ལྟར་ཁས་བླང་བར་བྱའོ། །
དེ་ལྟ་ན་ཡང་རྣམ་འགྲེལ་ལས། ཕུང་པོ་ལ་སོགས་བྱེ་བྲག་ཅན། །མཚན་ཉིད་ཐམས་
ཅད་བྱེད་པ་ཡི། །ཁྱད་པར་ཅན་དེའང་དེ་ཉིད་མིན། །དེས་ཀྱང་དེ་དག་མཚན་ཉིད་བྲལ།།
ཞེས་པ་འདི་མདོ་སྡེ་པས་ཤེར་ཕྱིན་གྱི་མདོའི་དགོངས་པ་འགྲེལ་ཚུལ་དུ་འཆད་པ་ནི་
འཐད་པར་མ་མཐོང་སྟེ། དེའི་ཐད་ཀྱི་ལྷ་དབང་བློ་དང་རྒྱན་མཁན་པོའི་འགྲེལ་པར་
དོན་སྨྲ་དང་ཐུན་མོང་དུ་གསུངས་པ་ནི་ཚིགས་བཅད་འདིས་བསྟན་པའི་དོན་ཙམ་མདོ་སྡེ་
པས་ཀྱང་ཁས་ལེན་པ་ལ་དགོངས་པ་ཡིན་པར་རྗེ་ཐམས་ཅད་མཁྱེན་པ་ཡབ་སྲས་ཀྱིས་
གསུངས་ཤིང་། [73]ལམ་རིམ་ཐེག་པ་ཐ་ཤལ་བའི་འདོད་ཚུལ་དུ་བཤད་པ་མཁས་གྲུབ་
རྗེས་བཀག་པའི་ཕྱིར་དང་། ཚིག་རྐང་ཐ་མའི་དེས་ཀྱང་ཞེས་པའི་ཚིག་གིས་སེམས་
ཙམ་པས་བཤད་པའི་རྣམ་གྲངས་གཉིས་པ་ཞིག་ཡིན་པར་བསྟན་ཞེས་རྒྱལ་ཚབ་མཁས་
གྲུབ་གཉིས་ཀས་བཤད་པའི་ཕྱིར་དང་། ཁྱད་པར་དུ་རྗེའི་གསུང་བཞིན་དུ་རྒྱལ་ཚབ་རྗེས་
བཀོད་པའི་ཚད་མའི་བརྗོད་བྱང་ཆེན་མོར་ཡང་། ཚིགས་བཅད་དེའི་དོན་འགྲེལ་བའི་
སྐབས་སུ་འདི་ལྟར་འབྱུང་སྟེ། ཚིགས་བཅད་གསུམ་པས་རང་བཞིན་མེད་པའི་དགོངས་
པ་འདི་བཞིན་དྲང་བཤད་དུ་རུང་ངོ་ཞེས་པའི་འགྲེལ་ཚུལ་གཞན་འཆད་པ་ཡིན་གྱི་དེ་
ཉིད་མདོ་སྡེ་པ་ལ་སྦྱོར་བ་མི་འཐད་དེ། ཉན་ཐོས་སྡེ་པ་ཕལ་ཆེར་ཐེག་པ་ཆེན་པོའི་
མདོ་སྡེ་བཀར་མི་འདོད་པས་དེའི་དགོངས་པ་མི་འཆད་དཀའ་[74]མེད་མིན་པའི་ཕྱིར་དང་།
དེས་ཀྱང་དེ་དག་མཚན་ཉིད་བྲལ་ཞེས་པའི་ཀྱང་གི་སྒྲས་སྔ་མ་བསྡུས་པའི་ཕྱིར་རྣམ་རིག་
པ་རང་གི་ལུགས་ཡིན་ནོ་ཞེས་གསལ་བར་གསུངས་པའི་ཕྱིར། དེས་ན་རྗེ་ཐམས་ཅད་
མཁྱེན་པས་དྲང་ངེས་རྣམ་འབྱེད་དུ་ཚིགས་བཅད་དེ་དྲངས་པའི་མཇུག་ཏུ། འདི་ནི་ཉན་
ཐོས་སྡེ་པ་དང་ཡང་ཐུན་མོང་བའོ་ཞེས་བཀའ་སྩལ་པའི་དོན་ཡང་། ཚིགས་བཅད་

དེའི་བསྟན་དོན་ཕུང་སོགས་རང་གི་མཚན་ཉིད་དང་ལྡན་ལུགས་དེ་ཉན་ཐོས་སྡེ་པས་ཁས་... 75
བླང་དུ་རུང་བའི་དོན་ཡིན་གྱི་ཤེར་ཕྱིན་གྱི་དགོངས་པ་ལེན་ལུགས་ཉན་ཐོས་སྡེ་པ་དང་ཐུན་...
མོང་བར་བཤད་པ་མ་ཡིན་པས་ཚིག་ཙམ་ལ་ཆགས་པར་མི་བྱའོ། །དབུ་མ་རྒྱན་གྱི་རང་
འགྲེལ་ལས། ཆོས་ཐམས་ཅད་དངོས་པོ་མེད་པ་དང་སྐྱེ་བ་མེད་པར་གསུངས་པའི་དོན་
ཉན་ཐོས་སྡེ་པས་ཉུང་བ་དང་སྨད་པའི་དོན་དུ་འདོད་པར་བཤད་པ་ནི། དེ་དག་གིས་ཤེར་
ཕྱིན་གྱི་མདོ་འདི་དགོངས་པ་ལེན་ཚུལ་དུ་འགྲེལ་བཤད་ལས་བཤད་སོད། དེ་ནི་ཀླུ་སྒྲུབ་
བྱུང་རྗེས་ཀྱི་ཉན་ཐོས་སྡེ་པར་མངོན་ནོ། །ཀ་མ་ལ་ཤཱི་ལས་ཆོས་ཐམས་ཅད་བདག་མེད་དོ་
ཞེས་པའི་དོན་གནས་མ་བུ་བས་ཕུང་པོ་ལས་དོན་གཞན་པའི་བདག་མེད་པ་ལ་འདོད་པར་
བཤད་པ་ནི་ཉན་ཐོས་སྡེ་གཉིས་ཀྱིས་ཤེར་ཕྱོགས་ཀྱི་མདོ་འདི་དགོངས་པ་འགྲེལ་ཚུལ་...
དེ་ལྟར་བཤད་པ་མ་ཡིན་གྱི། ཉན་ཐོས་སྡེ་པ་རང་ལ་གྲགས་པའི་ལུང་ལས་བདག་མེད་
པའི་ཚིག་བྱུང་བ་རྣམས་ཀྱི་དོན་འགྲེལ་ལུགས་བཤད་པའོ། །ལུགས་འདིས་ཆོས་ཕུང་
ལ་ཆོས་འཁོར་གྱིས་ཁྱབ་པ་ཁས་མི་ལེན་པས་ཤེར་ཕྱིན་སོགས་ཐེག་ཆེན་གྱི་མདོ་ཁས་...
ལེན་པ་རེ་གཉིས་བྱུང་ཡང་། མདོ་དེ་དག་ཆོས་འཁོར་དུ་འདོད་མི་དགོས་པར་མ་
ཟད་བདེན་བཞི་ལ་ལན་གསུམ་དུ་བཟླས་ཤིང་རྣམ་པ་བཅུ་གཉིས་སུ་བསྐོར་བའི་མདོ་...
ཚིག་དེ་དག་མ་གཏོགས་ཐེག་དམན་གྱི་མདོ་གཞན་རྣམས་ཀྱང་ཆོས་འཁོར་ཡིན་པར་མི་...
འདོད་དེ། བྱེ་མདོ་གཉིས་ཀྱིས་ཆོས་ཀྱི་འཁོར་ལོ་ཞེས་པའི་མིང་དོན་འཆད་ཚུལ་གྱིས་
ཤེས་སོ། །དེས་ན་འདི་དག་གི་ལུགས་ལ་སངས་རྒྱས་ཀྱི་བཀའ་ཡིན་ན་ཆོས་འཁོར་
ཡིན་པས་མ་ཁྱབ་བོ། །ཆོས་ཀྱི་ཕུང་པོ་འི་ཚད་ཀྱང་དུག་གསུམ་རེ་རེ་བ་དང་ཆ་མཉམ་
ལ་སྤྱོད་པ་ཉི་ཁྲི་ཆིག་སྟོང་རེ་ཡོད་པས་སྤྱོད་པ་རེའི་གཉེན་པོ་ཡོངས་སུ་རྫོགས་པ་རེ་...
གསུངས་པ་ལ་བྱ་ཞིང་། ཆོས་ཕུང་དེ་དག་ཀྱང་གཟུང་ཀྱི་ཕུང་པོས་བསྡུས་པར་འདི་པ་

ཁ

འདོད་དོ། །གོང་དུ་བཤད་པ་ལྟར་བདེན་མེད་ལ་སོགས་པ་གསུངས་པའི་དོན་སྐྲས་ཟིན་
ལས་ཚུར་ཟད་འཁྲོགས་དེ་[76]བཤད་པ་རེ་གཉིས་ཡོད་ལ། ཉན་ཐོས་སྡེ་གཉིས་ཕལ་མོ་
ཆེས་མངས་རྒྱལ་གྱི་བཀའ་ཡིན་ན་ངེས་པའི་དོན་ཅན་ཁོ་ན་ཡིན་པས་ཁྱབ་པར་འདོད་ཅིང་
དྲང་ངེས་གཉིས་ཀ་འདོད་པ་ཡང་ཡོད་པར་རྟོག་གེ་འབར་བ་ལས་བཤད་དོ།། ||